Kantian Ethics

In this book, Allen W. Wood investigates Kant's conception of ethical theory, using it to develop a viable approach to the rights and moral duties of human beings. By remaining closer to Kant's own view of the aims of ethics, Wood's understanding of Kantian ethics differs from the received "constructivist" interpretation, especially on such matters as the ground and function of ethical principles, the nature of ethical reasoning, and autonomy as the ground of ethics. Wood does not hesitate to criticize and modify Kant's conclusions when they seem inconsistent with his basic principles or fail to make the best use of the resources that Kantian principles make available. Of special interest are the book's treatment of such topics as freedom of the will, the state's role in securing economic justice, sexual morality, the justification of punishment, and the prohibition on lying.

Allen W. Wood is Ward W. and Pricilla B. Woods Professor at Stanford University. He was a John S. Guggenheim Fellow at the Free University in Berlin and a National Endowment for the Humanities Fellow at the University of Bonn. He developed parts of this book in the 2005 Isaiah Berlin Lectures at Oxford University. Along with Paul Guyer, Professor Wood is co-editor of the *Cambridge Edition of The Works of Immanuel Kant* and translator of the *Critique of Pure Reason*. He is the author or editor of numerous writings, mainly on Kant, Fichte, Hegel, and Karl Marx.

*To the memory of
Terence Moore,
My editor and friend*

Kantian Ethics

ALLEN W. WOOD

Stanford University

CAMBRIDGE UNIVERSITY PRESS

CAMBRIDGE UNIVERSITY PRESS
Cambridge, New York, Melbourne, Madrid, Cape Town,
Singapore, São Paulo, Delhi, Tokyo, Mexico City

Cambridge University Press
32 Avenue of the Americas, New York, NY 10013-2473, USA

www.cambridge.org
Information on this title: www.cambridge.org/9780521671149

First published 2008
Reprinted 2009, 2011

A catalog record for this publication is available from the British Library.

Library of Congress Cataloging in Publication Data

Wood, Allen W.
Kantian ethics / Allen W. Wood.
  p. cm.
Includes bibliographical references and index.
ISBN 978-0-521-85494-8 (hardback) – ISBN 978-0-521-67114-9 (pbk.)
1. Kant, Immanuel, 1724–1804. 2. Ethics, Modern. I. Title.
B2799.E8W58 2008
170.92 – dc22   2007004873

ISBN 978-0-521-85494-8 Hardback
ISBN 978-0-521-67114-9 Paperback

Contents

Preface

This book attempts to sketch an ethical theory based on the principles found in the writings of Immanuel Kant. It is not primarily a study of those writings but an attempt to develop out of Kant's thought the most defensible theory possible on that basis. Thus I will not refrain from criticizing Kant – at times, quite roundly – when I think his moral opinions or conclusions do not follow from or cohere well with his fundamental principles, or when I think a more defensible approach to some topic involves correcting or revising what Kant thought and wrote.

The idea of writing the present book was suggested to me by the late Terence Moore of Cambridge University Press. The basic reading of Kant represented here was presented in my 1999 book *Kant's Ethical Thought*. But Moore thought it would be a good thing if I provided a briefer, less scholarly, and more approachable version of Kantian ethics. The present book, however, is only a partial fulfillment of his request. Though shorter than my earlier book, it is probably longer (and no doubt less popular) than he had in mind. Its primary focus is on Kantian ethics rather than on Kant scholarship. This book fulfills a promise of the earlier book by developing Kant's conception of virtue and his theory of duties in greater detail than was done there. In the course of doing these things, it also discusses a number of specific topics in ethics that were not discussed in the earlier book.

In addition to that, whole chapters offer thoughts on the Kantian approach to further ethical topics that were much more briefly discussed, or not covered at all, in *Kant's Ethical Thought*, such as virtue, conscience, social justice, sex, punishment, lying, consequentialism, the personhood of persons, and the moral status of nonrational animals. In the past seven years, however, I think I have been able to sharpen parts of my interpretation as compared with the earlier book, especially regarding the aims of ethical theory and the Kantian conception of autonomy. I have even changed my mind about a few things. My reading of Kant is now even further from traditional interpretations of Kant than it was before, but I believe it is closer to the truth.

The general enterprise in which I am engaged here is one that has attracted the efforts of a number of able moral philosophers in recent years, chiefly through the influence of John Rawls and his many talented students. The study of ethics in the analytical tradition owes a great deal to Rawls and his followers. In some respects, it could even be called chiefly their product. Until well after the mid–twentieth century, the subject of ethics in the analytical tradition was preoccupied with metaethical reflections, the dominant position even encouraging the hopelessly nihilistic thought that ethics is not a fit subject for rational discourse at all, but only for the expression of attitudes, or at most for rhetorical exhortation and the nonrational manipulation of other people's emotions so as to bring them into line with your own. Theoretical reflection on ethics was further discouraged by the fact that of those who still thought it could be reasoned about, most took it for granted that utilitarianism was the only possible basis for rational discussion, thus drastically narrowing the range of philosophical options it was thought worthwhile even to consider.

John Rawls's *A Theory of Justice* (1971) changed everything. It showed not only that ethical theory could be treated with analytical sophistication and applied to issues of vital social concern but also that Kantian ideas were indispensable to doing this in the right way. Rawls's thought never stagnated, however. He continued reflecting on how the Kantian liberal tradition can best be articulated in the late twentieth century. In the 1980 Dewey Lectures at Columbia University, he developed an approach to ethical theory he called "Kantian constructivism," and then responded to later cultural and political developments in *Political Liberalism* (1993) and *The Law of Peoples* (1999). He also inspired a number of brilliant students, who became both able Kant scholars and original ethical theorists who followed out, in various ways, the "constructivist" approach to Kantian ethics. Rawls and these students are responsible both for returning Kantian ethics to its rightful place at the center of ethical reflection among philosophers and also for the way Kantian ethics has come to be understood by contemporary analytical philosophers.

My own studies in Kantian ethics would have been impossible without this tradition. My understanding of Kant's ethical thought has been decisively shaped in many respects by Rawls and some of his followers and students, among whom I should mention especially Christine Korsgaard, Onora O'Neill, Thomas Hill, Barbara Herman, Andrews Reath, and Tamar Schapiro. This book, however, will understand "Kantian ethics" in a way that differs significantly in several respects from this Rawlsian tradition.

Over the years I have come to realize (somewhat too haltingly and reluctantly, I must now admit) that I simply cannot accept the "constructivist" reading of Kant. I have especial trouble with the elements in it that are most familiar to and taken for granted by moral philosophers – I mean especially the overemphasis on, and misconstrual of, the Formula of Universal Law. But the constructivist reading also seems mistaken in the metaethical conclusions it wants to draw from Kant's conception of autonomy, and perhaps most of all its basic conception of the aims and methods of ethical theory – all of which seem to me deeply at odds both with what Kant himself actually thought about these matters and also with the best way Kant's thinking about ethics can be appropriated by us today. Though my primary focus is on developing Kantian ethics for its own sake in a manner that remains faithful to Kant, I will have occasion along the way to criticize the Rawlsian "constructivist" interpretation of Kantian ethics at several points, chiefly in Chapters 3 through 6. My version of *Kantian* ethics will be much closer to *Kant's* ethics than I think the Rawlsians' are, or were intended to be. Whether this is an advantage or a disadvantage must be left to each individual reader to decide.

My interpretation of Kant, as I have said, is also at odds with a lot of what has been traditionally thought about his moral philosophy. I reject the reading of the early pages of the *Groundwork* that takes Kant to be dividing the heart from the head and placing moral value only in actions that we do without desire. More generally, I reject the reading of Kant that understands his moral psychology as involving a sharp separation or "dualism" between "nature" and "freedom." This interpretation receives considerable support from the *Groundwork*, I admit, and no doubt that is why prevails among those whose understanding of Kant's ethics is based exclusively on that work; but it is incompatible with his later ethical writings, which in my judgment represent a superior position in moral psychology.

In discussing Kant's formulations of the moral law, I do my best to sever the nerve that, in most readers of Kant, connects the stimulus "Kantian ethics" with the reflexive reaction "Universalize your maxims." In Chapter 3, I argue that Kantian ethics conceives the aims of ethical theory in a fundamentally different way from what is now fashionable, representing an older alternative model that Kant shares with other great moral philosophers, notably John Stuart Mill. In Chapter 4, I claim that Kant's formulations of the moral law are by no means "equivalent" but constitute a developmental progression, of which the Formula of Universal Law is only the first (hence the poorest and most provisional) stage. Chapter 5 explores the other two main formulas, which I take to be more adequate and useful expressions of the principle. In Chapter 6, I offer a reading of Kant's conception of autonomy of the will that puts this doctrine at odds with much that its later reception (including the current "constructivist" interpretation) has found appealing about it. Chapter 7 attempts a sympathetic presentation of Kant's attempt to rest morality on freedom of the will – as a theoretical claim that cannot be theoretically established but must nevertheless be presupposed by us as rational agents. The second half of the book (Chapters 8–15) deals with a variety of topics in moral philosophy that were of explicit concern to Kant. In them I try to say what Kantian ethics ought to say about these topics, whether or not it agrees with what Kant himself said. On most topics, I think Kant's views, when correctly understood, are more defensible than they are often given credit for. But on some topics, such as suicide, sex, and punishment, I conclude that a consistent and defensible Kantian ethics must come to conclusions quite different from Kant's own.

Throughout the book, I emphasize the crucial importance for Kantian ethics of Kant's empirical theory of human nature. This has usually been totally ignored, through the pernicious influence of a grossly fallacious inference from the true premise that Kant thought the principle of morality is *a priori* and independent of empirical human nature to the disastrously false conclusion that Kant gave no thought to the empirical nature of human beings or human history and regarded them as of no importance to morality.

In the course of presenting my reading of Kantian ethics, I have noticed one source of opposition to it that is especially worthy of mention. Many accept my view that Kant is a more appealing moral philosopher on my reading than on the traditional one. They may even reluctantly admit that it is better supported by the texts than they thought it could be. But they still resist, because they feel their philosophical world deprived of a significant inhabitant – namely, the stiff, inhuman, moralistic Prussian ogre everyone knows by the name Immanuel Kant. They may not like him, but he plays an important role in their moral world – if not as the villain in a cautionary tale, then at least as the personification of a one-sided truth that becomes dangerous if we go that far. Without him, they feel disoriented. If this Kant did not exist, it would be necessary to invent him. They therefore think it might be better to keep the traditional interpretation of his writings even if it is wrong – and even if the position it represents is unappealing – not despite, but even precisely because of that fact.

I must declare to such people that it is indeed my intention to deprive their world of the philosopher who they thought could play that role. For I think that if that Kant's position is unhealthy, then so is their negative reaction to it, and both should die the same death (like Professor Moriarty and Sherlock Holmes at the Reichenbach Falls, and without the unpersuasive later return of either character). I am trying to get them to rethink their options in moral philosophy – to realize that the very spot on the moral map that they always thought occupied by a rigoristic monster is a place they need to consider residing themselves, or at least visiting now and then. I do not believe in conversions on the road to Damascus, and it would be quixotic of me to think I could reconfigure the landscape of anyone's moral world. But rational reflection (usually over a period of time) can sometimes significantly change someone's attitude toward a philosophical option he or she earlier dismissed.

This book was written mainly in the United States, between 2004 and 2006. The history of this period is a disgraceful one. It feels as if we have been living under a malignant alien occupation. An unelected political regime, representing everything that is worst about American culture, compiled a record of injustice, corruption, and gross incompetence at home, and of numerous and aggravated war crimes abroad. Then it was confirmed in office by another election of dubious legitimacy so that it might continue unrelentingly its monstrous wrongfulness and stupidity. Those with the power to oppose its crimes instead acquiesced in them, or else resisted too late, and too feebly. The very ideas of democracy, community, and human rights are in the process of dying in our civilization – or they are being willfully murdered by those in power and by that segment of the population which supports this regime. All they give us in place of these ideas is the empty words (and plenty of those). People have now perhaps begun to awaken to the situation, but the historical roots of what has happened are sunk deep in political trends of the previous century, and I fear these trends will not be reversed soon or easily. There are references here and there in the book to this dismal history, usually to illustrate arrogance, lying, and egregious violations of right. A few readers of my earlier work have told me they think this sort of thing is inappropriate in a scholarly book. But my worries about appearing "unscholarly" pale next to my shame, which all Americans should feel at having failed to prevent the disastrous course of events.

A draft of roughly one-third of this book was presented in the form of the Isaiah Berlin Lectures at Oxford University in 2005. Some of it was also presented as a lecture series at Chengchi University, Taipei. One chapter or another was presented at several other places. I have benefited from all these discussions, as well as from interactions with colleagues and students at Stanford University. The individuals to whom I owe such thanks are too numerous to name.

Abbreviations

Ak   *Immanuel Kants Schriften.* Ausgabe der königlich preussischen Akademie der Wissenschaften (Berlin: W. de Gruyter, 1902–). Unless otherwise footnoted, writings of Immanuel Kant will be cited by volume:page number in this edition.

Ca   *Cambridge Edition of the Writings of Immanuel Kant* (New York: Cambridge University Press, 1992–) This edition provides marginal Ak volume:page citations. Specific works will be cited using the following system of abbreviations (works not abbreviated below will be cited simply as Ak volume:page).

ANG   *Allgemeine Naturgeschichte und Theorie des Himmels,* Ak 1
Universal Natural History and Theory of the Heavens, Ca Writings on Natural Science

ED   *Das Ende Aller Dinge,* Ak 8
The End of All Things, Ca Writings on Religion and Natural Theology

EF   *Zum ewigen Frieden: Ein philosophischer Entwurf* (1795), Ak 8
Toward perpetual peace: A philosophical project, Ca Practical Philosophy

G   *Grundlegung zur Metaphysik der Sitten* (1785), Ak 4
Groundwork of the metaphysics of morals, Ca Practical Philosophy

I   *Idee zu einer allgemeinen Geschichte in weltbürgerlicher Absicht* (1784), Ak 8
Idea toward a universal history with a cosmopolitan aim, Ca Anthropology History and Education

KrV   *Kritik der reinen Vernunft* (1781, 1787). Cited by A/B pagination.
Critique of pure reason, Ca Critique of Pure Reason

KpV   *Kritik der praktischen Vernunft* (1788), Ak 5
Critique of practical reason, Ca Practical Philosophy

KU   *Kritik der Urteilskraft* (1790), Ak 5

	Critique of the power of judgment, Ca Critique of the Power of Judgment
MA	*Mutmaßlicher Anfang der Menschengeschichte* (1786), Ak 8 *Conjectural beginning of human history,* Ca Anthropology History and Education
MCP	*De medicina corporis quae philosophorum est,* Ak 15 On philosophers' medicine of the body, Ca Anthropology History and Education
MS	*Metaphysik der Sitten* (1797–8), Ak 6 *Metaphysics of morals,* Ca Practical Philosophy
O	*Was heißt: Sich im Denken orientieren?* (1786), Ak 8 *What does it mean to orient oneself in thinking?* Ca Religion and Rational Theology
P	*Prolegomena zu einer jeden künftigen Metaphysik* (1783), Ak 4 *Prolegomena to Any Future Metaphysics,* Ca Theoretical Philosophy after 1781
R	*Religion innerhalb der Grenzen der bloßen Vernunft* (1793–4), Ak 6 *Religion within the boundaries of mere reason,* Ca Religion and Rational Theology
RS	*Recension von Schulz's Versuch einer Anleitung zur Sittenlehre,* Ak 8 *Review of Schulz's Attempt at an introduction to a doctrine of morals,* Ca Practical Philosophy
SF	*Streit der Fakultäten* (1798), Ak 7 *Conflict of the faculties,* Ca Religion and Rational Theology
TP	*Über den Gemeinspruch: Das mag in der Theorie richtig sein, taugt aber nicht für die Praxis* (1793), Ak 8 *On the common saying: That may be correct in theory but it is of no use in practice,* Ca Practical philosophy
TPP	*Über den Gebrauch teleologischer Prinzipen in der Philosophie,* Ak 8 *On the Use of Teleological Principles in Philosophy,* Ca Anthropology History and Education
VA	*Anthropologie in pragmatischer Hinsicht* (1798), Ak 7 *Anthropology from a pragmatic point of view,* Ca Anthropology, History and Education *Vorlesungen über Anthropologie,* VA 25 *Lectures on Anthropology,* Ca Lectures on Anthropology
VE	*Vorlesungen über Ethik,* Ak 27, 29 *Lectures on Ethics,* Ca Lectures on Ethics
VL	*Vorlesungen über Logik,* Ak 9, 24 *Lectures on Logic,* Ca Lectures on Logic
VM	*Vorlesungen über Metaphysik,* AK 28, 29 *Lectures on Metaphysics,* Ca Lectures on Metaphysics
VP	[*Vorlesungen über*] *Pädagogik,* Ak 9 *Lectures on Pedagogy,* Ca Anthropology, History and Education

VpR   *Vorlesungen über die philosophische Religionslehre*, Ak 28
           Lectures on the Philosophical Doctrine of Religion, Ca Religion and Rational Theology

VRL   *Über ein vermeintes Recht aus Menschenliebe zu lügen*, Ak 8
           On a supposed right to lie from philanthropy, Ca Practical Philosophy

WA   *Beantwortung der Frage: Was ist Aufklärung?* (1784), Ak 8
           An answer to the question: What is enlightenment? Ca Practical Philosophy

Other works referred to more than once:

Aristotle	Aristotle, *Nicomachean Ethics*, tr. Terence Irwin. Second edition. Indianapolis: Hackett, 1999. Referred to by book, chapter, and Becker number.
Baron	Marcia Baron, *Kantian Ethics (Almost) Without Apology*. Ithaca, N.Y.: Cornell University Press, 1995.
Fichte GA	*J. G. Fichte-Gesamtausgabe*. Edited by Reinhard Lauth and Hans Gliwitzky. Stuttgart-Bad Cannstatt: Friedrich Frommann, 1962–. Cited by part/volume:page number.
Fichte SW	*Fichtes Sammtliche Werke*, ed. I. H. Fichte. Berlin: deGruyter, 1970. Cited by volume:page number Reference will also be made to two recent excellent translations of Fichte's two main works on right and ethics: Fichte, *Foundations of Natural Right*, tr. Michael Baur, ed. F. Neuhouser. Cambridge: Cambridge University Press, 2000. Fichte, *System of Ethics*, tr. D. Breazeale and G. Zöller. Cambridge: Cambridge University Press, 2006.
Hegel EL	G. W. F. Hegel, *The Encyclopedia Logic*, tr. T. F. Geraets, W. A. Suchting, and H. S. Harris. Indianapolis: Hackett, 1991. Cited by paragraph (§) number.
Hegel ETW	G. W. F. Hegel, *Early Theological Writings*, tr. T. M. Knox. Philadelphia: University of Pennsylvania Press, 1971.
Hegel PR	G. W. F. Hegel, *Elements of the Philosophy of Right*, tr. H. B. Nisbet, ed. A. Wood. Cambridge: Cambrige University Press, 1991. Cited by paragraph (§) number.
Herman	Barbara Herman, *The Practice of Moral Judgment*. Cambridge, Mass.: Harvard University Press, 1993.
Hill	Thomas Hill Jr., *Human Welfare and Moral Worth*. Oxford: Clarendon Press, 2002.
Hume D	David Hume, *Dialogues Concerning Natural Religion and the Posthumous Essays*, ed. Richard H. Popkin. Indianapolis: Hackett, 1983.

Hume E   David Hume, *Enquiry Concerning Human Understanding* and *Enquiry Concerning the Principles of Morals*, ed. Selby-Bigge and Nidditch. Oxford: Oxford University Press, 1995.

Hume T   David Hume, *A Treatise on Human Nature*, ed. Selby-Bigge. Oxford: Clarendon Press, 1967.

Korsgaard CKE   Christine Korsgaard, *Creating the Kingdom of Ends.* Cambridge: Cambridge University Press, 1996.

Korsgaard FC   Christine Korsgaard, "Fellow Creatures: Kantian Ethics ad Our Duties to Animals," in Grethe B. Peterson (ed.), *The Tanner Lectures on Human Values*, Vol. 25. Salt Lake City: University of Utah Press, 2005.

Korsgaard SN   Christine Korsgaard, *The Sources of Normativity.* Cambridge: Cambridge University Press, 1996.

Mill   John Stuart Mill, *Utilitarianism*, ed. George Sher. Second edition. Indianapolis: Hackett, 2001.

O'Neill   Onora O'Neill, *Constructions of Reason.* Cambridge: Cambridge University Press, 1989.

Rawls TCR   John Rawls, "Two Concepts of Rules," *Philosophical Review* 64 (1955), pp. 3–32.

Rawls TJ   John Rawls, *A Theory of Justice.* Cambridge, Mass.: Harvard University Press, 1971.

Rawls Lectures   John Rawls, *Lectures on the History of Moral Philosophy*, ed. Barbara Herman. Cambridge, Mass.: Harvard University Press, 2000.

Reath   Andrews Reath, *Agency and Autonomy in Kant's Moral Theory: Selected Essays.* Oxford: Oxford University Press, 2006.

Rousseau D   Jean-Jacques Rousseau, *Discourse on the Origin of Inequality*, tr. Donald Cress. Indianapolis: Hackett, 1992.

Rousseau E   Jean-Jacques Rousseau, *Émile,* or On Education, tr. B. Foxley. New York: Dutton, 1969.

Rousseau SC   Jean-Jacques Rousseau, *On the Social Contract*, tr. Victor Gourevitch. Cambridge: Cambridge University Press, 1997. Cited by book and chapter.

Scanlon   T. M. Scanlon, *What we owe to each other.* Cambridge, Mass.: Harvard University Press, 1998.

Sidgwick   Henry Sidgwick, *The Methods of Ethics.* Indianapolis: Hackett, 1981.

Williams   Bernard Williams, *Moral Luck.* Cambridge: Cambridge University Press, 1981.

1

Reason

1. What Is Kantian Ethics?

Some recent moral philosophers draw a distinction between *Kant's ethics* and *Kantian ethics*.[1] *Kant's* ethics is contained in Kant's own writings: the *Groundwork*, the *Critique of Practical Reason*, the *Metaphysics of Morals*, and the others. It is the theory Kant himself put forward, the fundamental principle of morality as he formulated it, the system of duties as he presented it, even the moral conclusions he thought followed from them. To write about *Kant's ethics* is to interpret that theory, to show how its parts are supposed to fit together, to relate it to Kant's philosophy as a whole. *Kantian ethics*, on the other hand, is an ethical theory formulated in the basic spirit of Kant, drawing on and acknowledging a debt to what the author of the theory takes to be his insights in moral philosophy. Kantian ethics is not *merely*, or even mainly, an interpretation of what Kant said. It is put forward instead as a theoretical option in thinking about ethical questions and philosophical questions about ethics. It is answerable not to textual accuracy or exegetical standards of Kant interpretation but to the right standards for thinking philosophically about ethical theory and ethical issues.

It should be clearly understood, however, what these standards are – and what they are not. Some philosophers seem to think that each proposition in a theory must be argued for entirely on its own, using arguments that are supposed to persuade anyone at all, even someone with no sympathy whatever for the project in which the theory is engaged. That is a standard that no significant philosophical theory could ever meet. In fact, the best defense of any philosophical conception is always a more or less systematic exposition of it. It is reasonable to ask for arguments on behalf of individual claims, especially fundamental ones, but these too are to be understood in the context of the theory as a whole. A philosophical theory is best defended by letting us see clearly how it conceives its task, how it performs it, and how the resulting conception of the subject matter addresses the questions

1

reasonable people have about that subject matter. No philosophical theory is going to persuade everyone. What we should look for in a philosophical theory is one that, when presented in this comprehensive way, not only looks appealing, but its rejection also can be seen to incur significant intellectual costs that we should be reluctant to pay.

This means that "Kantian ethics" as I mean the term may sometimes look something like a sympathetic interpretation of Kant's writings, even if its aim is quite different. Kantian ethics, however, certainly may depart freely from what Kant wrote and thought. It may criticize and modify the theory Kant put forward as well as sympathetically interpret or defend it. The present book is intended as an exercise in Kantian ethics in this sense. But it will also have a lot to say about Kant's ethics. This is because I do not think the most defensible version of Kantian ethics needs to depart as far from what Kant thought and wrote as most recent practitioners of Kantian ethics do. What is needed instead, in many cases, is only a better understanding of Kant's own thoughts.

One way of understanding the term 'Kantian ethics,' however, involves the at least tacit assumption that we already know what ethics is (from currently fashionable ideas about the aims and methods of ethical theory). "Kantian ethics" is simply a matter of seeing what Kant has to contribute to this project. In my view, however, the main benefit of studying an important figure in the history of philosophy, such as Kant, is that doing so helps us learn that the current philosophical fashions are not the only way to think about things. Philosophers (like other people) have a deplorable tendency to think in terms of entrenched prejudices. On many points, I will criticize standard interpretations of Kant for having interpreted Kant in terms of fashionable assumptions about ethical theory that have frequently been imposed on his writings – sometimes with charitable intent, but often with profoundly distorting effect. In Chapter 3, I argue that Kant's conception of ethical theory – its aims, methods, and conception of ethical reasoning – differs significantly from prevailing conceptions.

A much better reason for developing Kantian ethics in ways that diverge from Kant himself is indicated by the wry title of Marcia Baron's book *Kantian Ethics (Almost) Without Apology*. Those who find Kantian ideas in ethics appealing also sometimes feel that there is something about this for which they need to apologize. No doubt some of Kant's opinions on particular ethical topics are – or at least seem at first glance to be – so out of touch with enlightened opinion today as to seem either ridiculous or repugnant. But I suspect that those who think we need to apologize for Kantianism in ethics are using these opinions only to confirm a certain traditional image of Kantian moral philosophy. Kant is seen exclusively as a representative of moralistic strictness and sternness, downright hostile to human happiness, mercilessly unsympathetic to human weakness, allowing no place in the moral life for natural human feelings and desires. People may sometimes see an element of truth in this aspect of morality, but they view the Kantian version of this truth as wildly exaggerated, one-sided to the point of inhumanity. This image of Kant is colorfully presented by Simon Blackburn:

> For Kant, so the contrast goes, there is indeed the Humean crew. But standing above them, in the quarter-deck, there is another voice – a voice with ultimate authority and ultimate power. This is the Captain, the will, yourself as an embodiment of pure practical reason, detached from all desires. The Captain himself is free. But he always stands ready to stop things going wrong with the crew's handling of the boat. Sometimes, it seems, the happiest ship will have no crew at all, but only a Captain . . . Thus the Kantian Captain. He is a peculiar figure, a dream – or nightmare – of pure, authentic self-control. He certainly appeals to our wish to be, ourselves, entirely the masters of our own lives, immune in all important respects from the gifts or burdens of our internal animal natures, or of our temperaments as they are formed by contingent nature, socialization, and external surrounds. Context-free, non-natural, and a complete stickler for duty, perhaps the Kantian self is nothing but the sublimation of a patriarchal, authoritarian fantasy.[2]

Even more flamboyant is the following remark by Richard Taylor:

> I have known many admirers of Kant, and include myself with them; but if I were ever to find, as I luckily never have, a man who assured me that he really believed Kant's metaphysical morals, and that he modeled his own conduct and his relations with others after those principles, then my incredulity and distrust of him as a human being could not be greater than if he told me he regularly drowned children just to see them squirm.[3]

The starting point for a less fantastic image of Kantian ethics was well stated by John Rawls. He regarded Kantian ethics "not as a morality of austere command but an ethic of mutual respect and self-esteem" (Rawls TJ, p. 256). Kant was a philosopher of the Enlightenment – perhaps the greatest of all Enlightenment philosophers. For Kant, the principle of Enlightenment is: "Think for yourself!" (WA 8:35, O 8:146). This means: Take the responsibility for your own actions and convictions. Do not put yourself under the *tutelage* or *authority* of others or let them do your thinking for you, however much, in thinking for yourself, you may need to listen to their arguments or treat their expertise as good evidence in the formation of your own judgments. This principle is based on respect for yourself as a rational being, arising from the recognition of rational nature in your own person as an end in itself (G 4:429). The same principle, however, requires you to respect rational nature in the person of every other human being. Each human being, as rationally self-governing according to universally valid standards, has *dignity* or *absolute worth* (G 4:431–6). Because the worth of every human being is absolute, the worth of all persons is fundamentally *equal.*

Kant's moral outlook, in its fundamentals, is a characteristically Enlightenment outlook. In its time the Enlightenment was an important part of an emerging intellectual movement, a way of thinking that still exists today. In the eighteenth century this outlook was strongly opposed by antirationalistic and traditionalist ways of thinking, and it is still under attack in our time both from antirationalists and conservatives. To see Kantian ethics only through the lens of malicious or condescending caricatures is therefore not only to misread an influential historical philosopher but also to blind yourself to a lot of the ongoing cultural life of modernity. If you are on the Enlightenment side of the ongoing struggle, then to confuse Kantian ethics with your own nightmares about moral authoritarianism is to mistake one of your closest friends for one of your worst enemies.

2. Human Nature

To Rawls's felicitous formulation I want to add something else almost as important. Kant's moral outlook is also fundamentally determined by a subtle, shrewd, historically self-conscious (and characteristically Enlightenment) conception of human nature and human psychology that most treatments of Kantian ethics (even sympathetic ones) have largely overlooked. This side of Kant owes a great deal to Jean-Jacques Rousseau, and it belongs to a radical tradition in the social criticism of modernity whose later representatives include Johann Gottlieb Fichte and Karl Marx. The Kantian mistrust of our empirical desires reflects a Rousseauian picture of the way our natural desires have been influenced by the loss of innocence – the restless competitiveness – characteristic of human beings in the social condition, especially as found in the social inequalities of what Rousseau and Kant called the "civilized" stage of human society but was later renamed "modern bourgeois society" or "capitalism." Again, to miss this continuity is not only to misread Kant; it is badly to misread the history, and even the living reality, of the social order that is all around us.

Kant's famous mistrust of our empirical "inclinations" is mistrust of "nature" only insofar as our nature has been shaped by *society*. Kant asserts (as explicitly as it would be possible for him to do) that there is nothing at all in our "animality" – our animal instincts for survival, reproduction, and sociability – that could be called "evil" or held responsible for it. Our inclinations, considered in themselves, as expressions of our bodily or animal nature are entirely good and "display themselves openly" for what they are. Kant holds that they become evil only insofar as vices have been "grafted onto them" by "an invisible enemy, one who hides behind reason and is hence all the more dangerous" (R 6:26–7, 57). This enemy is competitiveness, social inequality, the passion for domination over others.

Rousseau called it *amour propre* (Rousseau D, pp. 36, 53–4, 90; Rousseau E, pp. 172–6). Kant has various names for it. Alluding to Montaigne, he calls it "unsociable sociability" (I 8:20),[4] at other times "self-conceit" (KpV 5:73), or, finally, the "radical propensity to evil" (R 6:28–32). For Kant, as for Rousseau, this propensity develops along with our reason, hence only in the social condition (R 6:27).

> It is not the instigation of nature that arouses what should properly be called the passions, which wreak such great devastation in his originally good [animal] predisposition. His needs are but limited and his state of mind in providing for them is moderate and tranquil. He is poor (or considers himself so) only to the extent that he is anxious that other human beings will consider him poor and will despise him for it. Envy, addiction to power, avarice, and the malignant inclinations associated with these, assail his nature, which on its own is undemanding, *as soon as he is among human beings*. Nor is it necessary to assume that these are sunk into evil and are examples that lead him astray: it suffices that they are there, that they surround him, and that they are human beings, and they will mutually corrupt each other's moral disposition and make one another evil. (R 6:93–4)

Against those theories that want to ground ethics on natural feelings, inclinations, or passions (such as sympathy), Kant has two main objections. One is that feelings and inclinations do not suffice to ground clear and determinate principles for action. But the deeper objection is that in human beings, no feelings, empirical desires, or passions are merely "natural" – that is, good or innocent. All are at the same time *social* (and socially corrupted), so that the most we can expect from them is a correspondence to what is morally good that is contingent and at best precarious. Ethical theories grounded on them therefore might give the right results for a different species of rational creatures, a species that was asocial or whose sociability was not, like ours, infected with self-conceited ambition and a passionate need to dominate our fellows. When applied to us, such theories are either too naïve or too complacent, especially in the context of our more developed or "civilized" societies.

In other words, Kantian ethics is fundamentally committed to a radical critique of human social life, especially of social life in its "civilized" form. This critical tendency is not a mere ancillary feature or contingent concomitant of Kantian ethics. It conditions the fundamental conception of Kantian ethical theory. For it is Kant's view that our only resource in combating the radical evil of our social condition is the faculty of reason, whose development accompanies that of our propensity to evil, and which alone enables us to recognize evil for what it is. This is why moral principles for Kant must be *a priori* rather than empirical in origin, and why we cannot trust our natural feelings, inclinations, or passions to provide us with moral distinctions, judgments, and motives.

Our use of reason itself, of course, is subject to the very same subversion as natural feelings and desires. Ordinary moral thinking, Kant says, is therefore vulnerable to a "dialectic" in which we tend to quibble with the demands of morality or adjust them to our wishes (G 4:405). Wouldn't it be nice if we had some other faculty, or some infallible (divine) source of moral wisdom that is not subject to such corruption? But even supposing we did have such a source, our use of it would still be conditioned by our own interpretation, which would necessarily be our own thinking, hence subject to the same fallibility and corruption. Some circumvent this inconvenience either by saying that they are taking the word of this source "literally," or else by attributing their interpretation to the same infallible sources. It is almost charming how naïvely they thereby assert what is now obviously only their own infallibility. Such blasphemous arrogance would be only comical if its real-world consequences were less monstrous.

Thus in the end there is no escaping the fact that human reason – feeble, fallible, imperfect, corrupted reason – is always our last resort, even our only ultimate resource, for criticizing everything, including our own misunderstandings and abuses of reason itself. Kant's "critique *of reason*" thus takes "reason" in both the objective and subjective genitive – it is a critique *carried out by* reason *upon* reason. We rely on reason to criticize feelings, desires, inspirations, revelations, and even reason itself, not because it is infallible but rather because it is only through reason that we have the capacity to criticize or correct anything at all.

Kant's ethical theory holds that every human being has equal dignity as an end in itself, but his theory of human nature and history is based on the idea that civilized human beings tend to assert their self-worth antagonistically in relation to others, seeking superiority over them. Kant is sensitive to this tendency at work in all our desires, and also to the way it leads us to deceive ourselves about our own motives, our merits, and about what morality demands of us. He therefore thinks we need to guard against our corrupt tendency to quibble with the strictness of the moral law and make exceptions to moral rules in our own favor. This is even the reason why Kant thinks we need moral *philosophy* in addition to moral common sense or "common rational moral cognition" (G 4:405).

Kant thinks that the chief benefit of our social condition, in combating the evils that come along with it, is the development of *reason* – which he understands as the capacity to regulate our conduct by universal principles of respect and concern that we are capable of sharing with other rational beings. Reason is a capacity for self-government (which Kant emphasizes that human beings exercise with only very limited success) based on mutual respect and free communication, yielding a system of principles people can all share, and aiming at what he calls a "realm of ends," a system of human ends that can be rationally shared between all people because the dignity and welfare of all rational beings are equally included in it.

3. Gender and Race

Through the intellectual and cultural movement the eighteenth century called "Enlightenment," modernity is still struggling to free itself from the chains and the pollution of traditional ideas and traditional ways of life and find a path toward a more rational and decent human future. In the writings of eighteenth-century representatives of this movement, we sometimes find a torch we may still use to light our way. At other times, however, we see them fettered by the very traditions – cultural or religious – from which, in their best thoughts, they were still trying to free themselves. Kant may be the greatest philosopher of the Enlightenment, but in this way he is also typical of it.

Kant's view of women. There are some special worries in this respect about Kant's views on race and gender. Although Kant's ethics is based on radically egalitarian principles, Kant accepted quite complacently the social and political subordination of women that prevailed in his time, and in some of his writings on anthropology he expressed views that can be described only as racist. The enterprise of interpretation, moreover, is sufficiently holistic in character that we cannot automatically dismiss the thought that these views might possibly require us to qualify in disturbing ways the seemingly egalitarian principles on which Kantian ethics appears to rest. It has been maintained, for example, that when Kant speaks of the dignity or absolute worth of humanity or rational nature, the referent of these terms must be understood as restricted only to white males.[5]

Such an extreme conclusion as that, however, is rendered indefensible by Kant's explicit statements including women and human beings of any and all races as rational beings and hence as falling within the scope of principles of right. For example, Kant's entire theory of marriage right, however repugnant parts of it may be, is motivated mainly by the need to protect the rights and human dignity of women. It is nevertheless true that he regarded women as weaker than men not only physically but also intellectually and thought it appropriate that they should be in a permanent condition of civil guardianship (*Vormundschaft*), represented in the public sphere by their fathers or husbands (VA 7:209).

Kant is a subject of lively controversy among feminist philosophers, some of whom see his entire moral philosophy as nothing but an ideology of patriarchy and male supremacy, while others regard Kantian ethics as the original articulation of principles of morality and right that are indispensable to women's liberation and equality of the sexes.[6] Some of these issues will be addressed later, in Chapter 13. It is also relevant to point out that the criticisms of the former group of feminists often tend to follow a pattern of Kant interpretation and criticism that is by no means characteristically feminist but familiar from Romantic, Hegelian, virtue ethics, and other older traditions.[7] This is precisely the misreading of Kantian ethics I have criticized above and will continue to criticize, especially in Chapters 2 and 8.

Kant on the inferiority of nonwhite races. During the 1770s and 1780s, Kant became increasingly interested in the empirical study of human nature, and one side of this was the development of a theory of race. He held that the human species was biologically one, but that differing geographical conditions, leading to different modes of life, resulted in the differentiation of the species into four different races: white, yellow Indian (Asian), black (African), and copper-red Indian (American).

Kant never says in so many words that the white race is superior to the others, but he obviously regards the greatest achievements of the "yellow" race as belonging to the past, the "black" race as capable of discipline and industry but not of further cultural development, and he thinks of American Indians as occupying the lowest level of all: They have been stunted, in his view, by the fact that their ancestors developed in a very different climate and later migrated to one unsuited to them. He even conjectures that American Indians may be in the process of dying out – though he regarded the active extermination of them by whites as "gruesome" (VA 25: 840). In print, Kant presented these views in *Of the Different Races of Human Beings* (1775) and *Determination of the Concept of Race* (1785). In an essay with the seemingly innocuous title *On the Use of Teleological Principles in Philosophy* (1788) Kant then defended the more pernicious aspects of his theory of race, as part of a controversy with Georg Forster, a much more farsighted thinker on this topic, who had lived among non-Europeans and challenged the racist preconceptions then prevailing among Europeans.[8]

Kant argues that certain races have developed under geographical conditions that make them incapable of adaptation to other climates or ways of life. This in effect pretty clearly underwrites a kind of racial hierarchy, in which only the white race has developed under conditions suitable for making contributions to the future progress of the human species. Nonwhite races, especially the Negro, are presented as fit only for manual labor directed by Europeans (TPP 8:173–5). Though Kant never directly defends the institution of black slavery, in a footnote he quotes with approval the observations of a German opponent of its abolition, who claims that freed slaves generally lose the laboring skills they formerly possessed (TPP 8:174n). Some have argued that Kant's theory of race played an influential role in the development of dominant racialist theories in the eighteenth and nineteenth centuries.[9] Though I do not pretend to know the details of the intellectual history involved, this seems to me quite plausible.

One natural response to this situation is to claim that although Kant regarded nonwhite races as inferior to whites, he also held on basic philosophical grounds an egalitarian position about all human beings regardless of gender or race, and it is this latter position that matters to Kantian ethics.[10] This has been the main response, in fact, by the leading writers on Kantian ethics who have addressed this issue.[11]

The controversy often seems to be between those who take philosophical principles seriously and those who are skeptical about the whole project of systematic philosophy, and especially the serious study of its history for the philosophical insights that may be obtained both from its achievements and from critical reflections on it. For the attacks on political grounds are never aimed at achieving philosophical insights of any kind. (Often enough, it remains wholly obscure what philosophical conclusions, if any, the attackers intend us to draw from their sensational exposés.) And Kant is far from being the only philosopher who can be attacked in this way: Locke, Rousseau, Hume, Fichte, Hegel, Marx, Mill . . . virtually every significant figure in the history of philosophy is vulnerable to attack in this manner. The critics apparently think we can learn something worthwhile from reading a past philosopher only when we examine, as artifacts of intellectual history, his (often flawed) judgments about particular social issues and situations, interpreting his philosophical claims only as a set of disingenuous ideological rationalizations for these judgments.

I suspect part of the motivation for these attacks is based on a mistaken analogy between the right way to view historical philosophers and the right way to view present-day political figures. When we hear a politician stating grand ethical principles, within which his actions and stands on particular issues stand in blatant contradiction, the natural conclusion to draw is that his moral pronouncements are hypocritical and should not be taken seriously. Thus it may be tempting to look similarly at the analogous phenomenon in the case of important figures in the history of philosophy. We show our own enlightened outlook and critical distance from these dead white men not by being taken in by their high-sounding philosophical pronouncements but by revealing with merciless accuracy the naked historical facts about their dreadful political opinions.

This seems to me a fundamentally wrong way to look at the matter. For one thing, great figures in the history of philosophy are often great precisely because their insights into highly abstract matters of principle far outrun the capacity of their own time – and often enough, also their own capacity – to understand fully what these insights mean in practice. To see this gap – either in the case of the philosopher or in the case of the entire age – as a case of simple hypocrisy is to misunderstand badly the relation of important philosophical principles to the historical conditions of their genesis. To a more judicious way of looking at things, it might even be expected that the greatest philosophical insights will be those that furthest outrun the philosopher's own ability to absorb and apply them. Kant's assertion of the equal dignity of rational nature in all persons is a striking example of this, when we come to some of his opinions about the family, political, and economic relations, and the concept of race.

The other main disanalogy between the historical philosopher and the hypocritical politician is that when we study texts in the history of philosophy in order to learn from them, we should care only marginally, if at all, about the moral character of the philosopher. Politicians are people who wield power over us, and it is important that we be able to have personal trust in their sincere adherence to the principles they advocate. This is not true of long-dead philosophers whose texts we study, or at least it should not be. What we learn from them should rest not on the author's moral authority but on the content of the doctrines and the strength of the arguments for them. Whether Kant's personal adherence to the moral principles he articulated was sincere or hypocritical might be of interest to biographers, but it should be of little or no interest to philosophers today who are attempting to construct a Kantian ethical theory.[12]

Did Kant change his views on race in the 1790s? However we decide this question, new light has recently been shed on the issue by Pauline Kleingeld. She argues, quite plausibly, that Kant's views on the topic of race underwent a dramatic change around 1792–3, probably as a consequence of his increasing interest in questions of right and justice.[13] He never openly repudiated his racial theory of the 1770s and 1780s, but the observations about race present in his lectures on anthropology throughout the 1780s are conspicuously absent from *Anthropology from a Pragmatic Standpoint* (1798). There the entire topic of race is dealt with in two brief paragraphs: The first praises a book by C. G. Girtanner that proposed to expound Kantian views on natural history but whose treatment of race was devoted mainly to the argument that racial differences are entirely matters of anatomy and physiology and provide no "moral characterization."[14] The second defends the claim that "the fusion of races" promotes vitality and fertility among the offspring, while proximity of kinship has the opposite tendency (VA 7:320–1).

In his writings on right in the 1790s, Kant adds to the traditional headings of "right of the state" and "right of nations" a new heading: "cosmopolitan right," which includes principles that are supposed to govern the commerce between people of different nations (EF 8: 357–60, MS 6:352–4). Under this heading, Kant mounts a remorseless attack on the injustices perpetrated by Europeans in their dealings with other peoples.[15] Kant's position probably comes to fullest expression in the following remarks from *Perpetual Peace*:

If one compares with [this right of hospitality] the inhospitable behavior of civilized, especially commercial, states in our part of the world, the injustice they show in *visiting* foreign lands and peoples (which with them is tantamount to *conquering* them) goes to horrifying lengths. When America, the negro countries, the Spice Islands, the Cape, and so forth were discovered, they were, to them, countries belonging to no one, since they counted the inhabitants as nothing. In the East Indies (Hindustan), they brought in foreign soldiers under the pretext of merely proposing to set up trading posts, but with them oppression of the inhabitants, incitement of the various Indian states to widespread wars, famine, rebellions, treachery, and the whole litany of troubles that oppress the human race.

China and Japan (*Nipon*), which had given such guests a try, have therefore wisely [placed restrictions on them], the former allowing them access but not entry, the latter even allowing access to only a single European people, the Dutch, but excluding them, like prisoners, from community with the natives. The worst of this (or considered from the standpoint of a moral judge, the best) is that the commercial states do not even profit from this violence; that all these trading companies are on the verge of collapse; that the Sugar Islands, that place of the cruelest and most calculated slavery, yield no true profit but serve only a mediate and indeed not very laudable purpose, namely, training sailors for warships and so, in turn, carrying on wars in Europe, and this for powers that make much ado of their piety and, while they drink wrongfulness like water, want to be known as the elect in orthodoxy. (EF 8:358–9)

Kleingeld's conclusion, both from the absence of any new statements of Kant's earlier hierarchical theory of race and his assertions about the rights of non-Europeans in the 1790s, is that they represent a significant change of mind late in his career on the subject of race.

Modern civilization, moral ideals, and hypocrisy. It is important to draw a distinction between what Kantian doctrines imply, in abstract philosophical terms – and what even Kant himself may have intended them to imply – and what social arrangements Kant himself accepted and approved – or what even Kantians today may accept and approve. As Kant himself realized (and often emphasized), there are systematic contradictions within modern civilization between the moral ideals and principles people recognize and the ways they actually live. It is entirely appropriate to inquire about the discrepancy between what Kantian principles say and what Kant thought about the treatment of women and nonwhites, just as it is important to wonder whether in the American Declaration of Independence "all men are created equal" was ever meant to include women and people of color. It is also correct and important to point out the way such conflicts show themselves within Kant's own doctrines. But all this remains true only as long as we understand the situation in the right way.

It is easier for us, with two hundred years' hindsight, to see such contradictions in Kant himself (or in other eighteenth- or nineteenth-century thinkers) than to see them in ourselves. In that sense, it is dangerous for us to focus on Kant's (now obvious) errors about issues of race or gender, as if we thought that we ourselves might be immune to similar criticisms by future philosophers reflecting on our views. On the contrary, Kant's errors should make us that much more aware of the likelihood that this will occur, and in that sense they should cause us to identify with him rather than hold him at arms' length. They should serve as a warning to us, based on the limited historical, cultural, and human perspective that we inevitably have in common with him.

Often, criticisms of Kant (or any other historical philosopher) on such grounds are really an indirect way of arguing against the contemporary use of a philosopher's ideas by others who obviously do not share Kant's errors about race or gender. It is a cheap way of resisting an important philosopher's influence. Often enough this is nothing but a strategy of "guilt by association," practiced by those who are evidently incapable of challenging the philosopher's ideas on their genuine merits. There is no plausibility at all, for example, in the suggestion that such Kantian principles as human equality, rationalism, universalism, and cosmopolitanism are in their content favorable to racism, sexism, or other forms of oppression, and such a thesis needs only to be stated explicitly to discredit itself. But this highly implausible thesis may be put forward by implication if it can be associated with the quite distinct but correct point that *even* a cosmopolitan and universalistic ethical theory, such as Kant's, can be combined with racist or male-supremacist views in its application. It is also true that egalitarianism, rationalism, universalism, and cosmopolitanism are especially liable to rhetorical abuse by those who advocate policies in direct violation of them, because subscribing to the correct principles at an abstract level is often enough a shabby ploy used to protect contrary policies from criticism.

The thought that this point has any *philosophical* significance, however, rests on an error of abysmal proportions about philosophy and its relation to human practices. If someone thinks there is a philosophical theory of morality whose uncritical adoption and mechanical application would suffice to protect us from evil, then that person is looking for something that could never exist. The correct standard for an ethical theory is whether it gets things right at the level of basic principles and values, not whether it contains some magical property that protects us, in the application of the theory, from every perversion or abuse through the influence of tradition and prejudice or the infinite human ingenuity of rationalization. All theories are about equally subject to such abuse, and no theory is immune to it. In fact, if we think that the adoption of a certain philosophical theory, or a certain set of religious dogmas, will protect us from all moral error, that way of thinking itself is extremely dangerous, quite irrespective of the content of the theory or dogma with which we associate it. That thought itself is actually responsible for a lot of the evil that people do.

4. Rationalism

It ought to be utterly uncontroversial that whatever we do, we should act for reasons, and therefore from reason. It is a virtual tautology to say that what we should do is the same as whatever there are the best (or at least good enough) reasons to do, and that we should do it for (or from) those reasons. When people profess to act apart from or against reason, and even recommend acting that way, the only sense to be made of this is that there really are good reasons for acting that way, but the agents do not know what they are, under that description, yet have practical access to them through something else – "emotions" or "faith" (Pascal's "reasons of the heart"). What is said is then sometimes correct, at least in substance. For emotions, or other sources of action that people distinguish from "reason," do sometimes provide access to what we have best reason to do. Whether or not the substance is right, however, the sources of action appealed to here can never be self-authenticating – this would have to be decided by rational reflection. And the state of mind that appeals to nonrational sources over reason, even when it is right in substance, is in form never far removed from self-deception.

"Reason" as a cover for unreason. A great deal of people's thinking about "reason" – both pro and con, both in everyday life and in philosophy – is afflicted with rationalization, denial, and self-opacity. In everyday life, there is something inherently suspicious about the rhetoric of second-order claims of the form that I am acting rationally, or that you should act rationally (which, according to me, you are not doing at present). People who are really acting rationally usually attend to the (first-order) reasons for doing what they do. Second-order claims appear necessary only in order to preempt, or dogmatically squelch (perhaps quite reasonable) doubts about whether their behavior really is rational. This means that second-order claims that something is rational (like second-order rejections of reason) are often bogus, mere rationalizations for something far less respectable than it pretends to be. People often resort to second-order judgments about what is rational precisely in order to shield their closed minds *against* the threatening intrusion of reasons. What is said, at second-order, to be "rational" is often precisely *not* that for which there are the best (first-order) reasons, and this is precisely *why* people feel it necessary to make the second-order claim.

Philosophers, however, have good grounds for making second-order claims about reason and rationality that are different from this, because philosophy is basically a reflective or second-order discipline. Philosophy looks at all thought and conduct in a second-order way, and its very business is to seek second-order principles for first-order reasons. So we must not automatically assume that a philosophical theory which focuses on second-order claims about reason is doing so only to pull the wool over our eyes. But of course it can happen in philosophy too. Second-order judgments that a course of action is rational are often invoked on behalf of what counts as rational according to some misguided prejudice, and philosophical theories can sometimes be mouthpieces for such prejudices.

Mr. Darcy proposes marriage to Miss Elizabeth Bennet, declaring in a state of great agitation that he loves her *even against his reason*. In her blunt refusal, Lizzie proves herself to be the greatest heroine in all romantic fiction simply by having the plain good sense to take any such declaration as an obvious *insult*. She also correctly takes it as good evidence that Darcy could not possibly be the kind of man any woman should want for a husband. (For who would want to be married to someone who makes the most important decisions in life in direct defiance of his reason?)

If Lizzie was mistaken, it was only in taking Darcy's declaration of love at face value. As Darcy later comes to find out, what he really meant was only this: Falling in love with Lizzie went against the conventional notions of his social class about what would be "rational" grounds for a man in his position to consider in making a marital choice. It takes Lizzie's blunt rejection (and a dozen chapters or so more of *Pride and Prejudice*) before Darcy eventually comes to see that these prejudices were mistaken, and that intelligence and character are much better reasons for loving and marrying a woman. Darcy's discovery might disappoint romantics, but what he finds out is that his love for Lizzie was rational after all.[16] The moral of the story, in other words, is (as I have already said) that emotions, and other things conventionally distinguished from "reason," are often entirely rational. They are sometimes an even better guide to what is rational than our sadly muddled reasonings, and especially our reflective appeals to "reason," which often serve only as a defense mechanism to protect prejudice and unreason.

Another charge sometimes brought against rationalists is that they overestimate the degree to which they – and people in general – are rational. There are the inevitable jocular references to the fact that human beings are not really "rational animals" at all, followed with almost equal inevitability by the lightheartedly invalid inference that human irrationality constitutes some sort of justification, or at least an acceptable excuse, for the wretched mess people so often make of things – not only of their own lives, but also of the lives of others – when they fail to act rationally. The Enlightenment tradition, however, emphasizes the importance of living according to reason precisely because it takes this way of living to be difficult for us and holds that we all too seldom act according to reason. Kant rejects the traditional characterization of the human being as *animal rationale* in favor of the formula *animal rationabilis* (VA 7:321). That is, the Kantian position is that we humans are *capable* of rationality but on the whole not very successful at being rational. This is precisely why Enlightenment thinkers insist on talking so much about reason – even at the second-order level. They are trying (admittedly, always against the odds) to make human beings and human life at least a bit more rational than they are.

The gender and color of "reason." To be taken more seriously are those criticisms of reason which take the form of claiming that the traditional notion of reason, in both philosophy and culture, is gendered (masculine) or ethnically biased (in favor of imperialist Europeans). Just as for Darcy 'reason' refers to the deliverances of his class prejudices, so it can be true for a lot of our culture, and also for even its greatest philosophers, that what is taken to be "rational" is systematically determined by social ideologies and traditions, so that "rational nature" may take on for them the characteristics of their culture, or gender or class, and related notions like 'universal law' come to express some invidious particularism. In the previous section we have even seen some solid grounds for raising questions of this kind about Kant himself.

The crucial point, however, is that notions like 'reason' and 'universal validity' could not play this ideological role if they did not *also, and more fundamentally*, refer to the human capacity that enables people (often only gradually and painfully) to criticize their false conceptions (including their false conceptions of reason itself). For it is only by appealing to the critical capacity of reason (which we ourselves presuppose even in criticizing the "gendered" or "colored" character of "reason" in philosophy or in other areas of life) that the ideologies are capable of mystifying, deceiving, and passing off one thing for another. If Kantians use standards of "reason" that are biased in such ways, then that is a legitimate issue, to be settled on the merits of each case where the charge is brought. It cannot be settled either way by the fact that Immanuel Kant was a white Prussian male. (This fact no doubt arouses legitimate suspicion on some topics, given Kant's prejudiced views about women and nonwhites; but to use it as an *argument* is only to display yet another prejudice.)

The human critical and self-directive capacity is the only legitimate referent of 'reason' in Kantian ethics, especially when it comes to the task of separating Kant's errors, or the prejudices of his time or his personality, from the philosophical principles on which we are grounding ethical theory. For Kant, what we say about (or with the pretended authority of) reason is always fallible, subject to critical scrutiny, and to be tested through free and open communication with others (KrV A xi and note, A 738–57/B766–85, O 8:144–6). It is therefore important, especially while criticizing Kant, always to recognize that we ourselves may be just as subject to errors and prejudices as Kant was. This, once again, is why feeling superior to him is an even more dangerous error than blindly following him, because it is the error to which we are more likely to succumb.

What is "reason"? Thomas Hill has argued that Kant's conception of reason is much closer to sound, everyday thinking about reason than are most philosophical alternatives, especially among the reigning formal theories of rational choice that continue to exercise influence on the social sciences (Hill, pp. 125–63). Many of these theories amount in effect to adopting a highly technical notion of reason that places a set of arbitrary and radical restrictions on the role reason can play in human life, and also on what could possibly count as a reason for thinking something, believing something, wanting something, or doing something.

Few philosophers have been as candid about this as Hume was when he boldly asserted such patent absurdities about reason as that it can never motivate the will and that it is not contrary to reason to prefer the destruction of the world to the scratching of my finger (Hume T, pp. 457–8, 414, 416). In these remarks Hume was not only relishing the gratification of shocking his audience but also signaling in how narrow, specialized, and artificial a sense he was using the term 'reason'. Other theorists typically narrow the scope of reason more arbitrarily, attempting to exclude from it anything that might give rise to the least hint of controversy concerning what is rational. Often they begin with the innocuous claim that rationality or irrationality always concerns the way of reaching some end in view. This claim is in a way quite defensible, if taken merely formally. Every action has some point or other, and what makes it rational or irrational is always related to this.[17] But then they infer fallaciously a series of less innocuous conclusions that radically limit the scope of reason. They conclude, for instance, that no reason can be given for choosing any end, that reason has to do only with selecting the means to ends; that only future facts – about possible states of affairs we seek or shun – can constitute reasons for action, but never past facts, about what people have promised or sacrificed or deserved by their conduct; and finally, that only the agent's own desires, interests, and preferences (but never directly anything else, such as the suffering or welfare of others) can ever count as reasons for an agent. By normal commonsense standards, these conclusions are not merely controversial; they are patently absurd.

For Kant, reason is a *faculty* (a *power* or *capacity* – we will have more to say about what that means later, in Chapter 6, §4). As we have seen, reason is even our highest capacity in the sense that it is the only one capable of directing and criticizing *all* our faculties, including itself. Reason is the unqualified capacity to think and act, because it is the capacity to think and act according to *norms*. A *reason*, in the widest sense of the term, is whatever counts as normative for beings with the capacity to give themselves norms and follow the valid norms they recognize. Rational thought and action are essentially what they are because the correct explanation of them always has reference to what is normative. This explanation involves either following the relevant norms or failing to follow them. A *rational* being is any being that has the capacity to think and act for reasons. This often involves also the possibility of *failing* to think and act as it has reason to do. In general, however, we speak of "failure" only where there is some capacity for success. In that sense, none but rational beings can ever behave *ir*rationally.

One essential feature of being rational is our capacity, and our responsibility – ultimately, our only responsibility, the only responsibility we can never avoid – of governing our own lives, both individually and in common with others. This means that reason also has another feature – it is closely related to our capacity to communicate with others, especially to the capacity to come to an understanding with them and to achieve a shared recognition of universally valid norms and reasons. Kant says that "the very existence of reason" is based on the opportunity of people to communicate freely with one other, to criticize both our own thoughts and those of others, and to be open to their criticisms (KrV A738/B766). This is because reasons – as distinct from impulses or inclinations – are inherently objective or universal in their validity. Every reason that applies only to me, or is valid only relative to my particular situation, must be grounded in some more basic reason that is objective and universal in scope. If it is not, then it is a deception to consider it a reason even for me.

If I correctly take some desire or impulse of mine as a reason for me to satisfy it, that can be only because there is a reason to satisfy that impulse, or desires of that kind, a reason that is in principle normatively acceptable both to those who happen to have the impulse and to those who do not. Many of the desires we take as reasons for action are desires based on such reasons. If we did not acknowledge the validity of those reasons, we would not have the desire at all. The same is true of preferences, utility assignments, and the like. Even brute or unmotivated desires, desires not based on such reasons, can be valid reasons for us to act only if we can reflectively regard them as desires we have reason to satisfy. An analysis of action with desires, preferences, or utility functions that does not ask about the reasons for them is therefore too superficial to say anything meaningful about the rationality of the action except for certain limited purposes.

Reason is the faculty through which we recognize beliefs, desires, or choices as grounded on something with normative authority. It is therefore as flexible and open ended as normative authority itself, and that is why it can never be reducible to any rules or procedure or calculus. For certain limited purposes, reason may be guided by various techniques or methods of calculation, but it is a fatal misstep to think that reason in general could ever be codified into some calculus of "rational choice." It belongs to the nature of reason that if we had such a calculus, it would always be a legitimate question to ask whether the "reasons" it generates are valid for the case in which we are to apply it. Though the answer might often be affirmative, it could never be generated by the calculus whose rational applicability is in question. Kant's conception of reason recognizes no mechanical set of rules as the way to determine what is rational.[18]

Three maxims of reason. A better way to think about reason is the set of three "maxims" Kant formulated for the use of reason beginning rather late in his career, sometime around 1788:

1. Think for yourself
2. Think from the standpoint of everyone else.
3. Think consistently with yourself.
    (KU 5:294–5, VA 7:220, 228, 25:1480, VL 9:57, cf. R 1486 Ak 15:715.)

Thinking for yourself is "enlightened" or "unprejudiced" thinking – in contrast to thinking in which you allow others to direct your use of reason, which is appropriate for a child but not for a mature, rational being. Thinking for yourself is not to be confused with thinking that is merely idiosyncratic or thinking that displays your whims, caprices, or eccentricities. The principle grounding all thinking for oneself, Kant says, is: "Whenever one is to accept something, ask oneself whether one could find it feasible to make the ground or rule on which one accepts it a universal principle for the use of reason" (O 8:148n). Thinking for yourself not only permits but even *requires* that you take account of the thoughts and information of others. The crucial difference is whether what others tell you contributes to your own use of your reason or instead replaces your own thinking with a prejudice, deferring to others and letting their thinking substitute for your own. This may sometimes be a subtle distinction that we do not attend to and may even find difficult to draw. But from a Kantian viewpoint, it is a distinction we must not ignore, because living autonomously as a rational adult depends upon it.

So understood, the first maxim leads all by itself to the second maxim: to think from the standpoint of everyone else. Kant call this the maxim of an "extended" (or "broad-minded") (*erweitert*) way of thinking, in contrast to "restricted" (or "narrow-minded") (*borniert*) way of thinking. Even a person whose intellectual capacities are quite limited, Kant says, can be broad-minded in this sense "if he sets himself apart from the subjective private conditions of the judgment, within which so many others are as if bracketed, and reflects on his own judgment from a universal standpoint (which he can determine only by putting himself into the standpoint of others)" (KU 5:295).

Because we can grasp the standpoint of others only through rationally communicating with them, this is the maxim that makes communication between rational beings a condition for the very existence of reason (KrV A738/B766). This also entails that the rational standpoint be essentially not a merely *self-interested* standpoint, and indeed, not even a so-called *first-person* standpoint. It is not even a standpoint oriented to the aims and goals that the subject has, because these are just the sorts of restrictions this maxim is telling us to look beyond. To act rationally is to act for grounds that are essentially intersubjective – not merely comprehensible by others, but also in some sense shared by and valid for others as well as for oneself. What it is rational for me to do may not necessarily be what is rational for others to do, because my situation may differ from theirs. But if I have a valid, rational ground for what I do, then that ground is also comprehensible from the standpoint of others.[19]

Kant's German word for 'reason' (*Vernunft*) is derived from the verb *vernehmen*, which means to hear, and more specifically to understand what you hear. A rational (or reasonable) person[20] is above all someone who "listens to reason," who is capable of hearing and understanding others when they offer reasons. The very opposite of a rational person is someone shut up in their own thoughts who is capable of attending only to their own aims and interests, someone who can't see anything from the standpoint of others. This is the person Kant calls the "egoist." A "logical" egoist is shut up in his own opinions, an "aesthetic" egoist in his own tastes, a "moral" egoist in his own interests. The opposite of egoism is "pluralism," which Kant also calls the "cosmopolitan" standpoint (VA 7:128–30). Egoism is the source of hypochondria and fanaticism (VA 25:1219–20). Pluralism is the standpoint of reason. Reasons, in other words, are essentially to be shared between people – they are never only the private possession of those for whom they are reasons.[21]

Perhaps, however, the rhetorical dynamic mentioned earlier influences some accounts of rationality on just this point, because it will be precisely those closed-minded, self-enclosed persons, those incapable of listening to reason, who will feel the greatest need to think of their conduct as "rational." Those under the deceptive sway of this irrational dynamic will thus naturally be led to think that thoughts, beliefs, and conduct are "rational" just to the extent that they tell the person in question how to effect whatever aims they already have. Thus for many formal theories of rational choice, the "rational" standpoint is exclusively a first-person standpoint, concerned obsessively with self-interested calculations, usually quite sophisticated ones, under conditions of uncertainty about a narrow range of contemplated outcomes. Such theories therefore often give the distinct impression that their proponents think of the ideally rational person as a sociopath with a gambling addiction. It is crucial in understanding the rationalism of Kantian ethics that we not import into it such notions of reason.[22]

None of Kant's three maxims, in his view, is easy to follow. All three represent regulative principles of reason that perhaps no agent ever follows perfectly. For Kant, the most difficult to follow is the third (KU 5:295). This difficulty may have to do with the fact that, in light of the first two maxims, rational thinking involves combining one's own standpoint with that of all others. This may also have to do with the fact that for Kant "consistency" or self-agreement may be a more demanding standard than the mere avoidance of direct self-contradiction. For we say that I am inconsistent not only when I assert contradictions but also when my actions fail to adhere consistently to any principle. My being consistent in this sense requires that my conduct flow from a common principle or coherent set of principles – coherent not merely in the sense that the principles do not contradict one another but in the deeper sense that the principles are all systematically connected and mutually supporting, like the actions of rational beings in a realm of ends. Kant regards reason as the faculty of principles in this sense (KrV A305–9/B362–6, A642–68/B670–96, A832–51/B860–79). I suggest that the third maxim is for Kant the most difficult to follow because it represents the final aim of reason as systematic unity.

To act rationally is to act for reasons (*genuine* reasons, *good* reasons). This means, to begin with, to act for something that is at least *ostensibly* a good reason, or has the *form* of being a good reason. Theories of rationality are nonstarters if they propose as reasons entities that do not even have the form of being a good reason. For example, to act from an attitude (e.g., of approval), or to satisfy a desire, is not (so far) to act from something that has the form of a good reason. This is because some attitudes and some desires are rational, and others are not. An attitude of approval may conform to a valid, rational principle, however, and then it is a good reason for doing whatever expresses the approval. A desire may be for something good – something that "reason, independently of inclination, recognizes as necessary" (G 4:412), or it may be the desire for something that constitutes part of the personal good (or the happiness) of a being that is an end in itself. In that case, it is a good reason for acting so as to satisfy it. In Kant's theory, good reasons fall under *principles*, which enable them to be recognized as having the form of a good reason.

5. Norms of Reason

We find in Kant two fundamental species of rationality: theoretical and practical. There are three species of practical reason: first, instrumental (technical, problematic) reason; second, prudential (pragmatic, assertoric) reason; and finally, categorical (moral, apodictic) reason (VM 28:257, 29:1017). Kant distinguishes these three in the *Groundwork*, asserting that there is "a certain difference" (or inequality, *Ungleichheit*) between them (G 4:416).

Theoretical reason. Some forms of assent (*Fürwahrhalten*) are grounded only on subjective feelings or impressions, which cannot be regarded as sufficient to justify it even to ourselves. Kant calls this form of assent 'opinion'. Kant recognizes two other forms of assent as having sufficient grounds – in one case ("belief") these grounds are only subjectively sufficient; in the other ("knowledge") they are objectively sufficient (KrV A822–3/B840–1).[23] The theoretical use of reason has to do with these objective grounds. It has authority over principles of understanding, both pure and empirical, and above all reason seeks systematic unity among cognitions according to principles as the final ground of justified assent (KrV A298–309/B355–66, A835–7/B863–5). Much more would need to be said on this topic if it were our theme here, but it is not.

Technical and pragmatic reason. Because for Kant all practical reason involves the setting of ends, instrumental reason is the most basic kind – the lowest common denominator, so to speak, of practical reason. But the lowest common denominator is not the whole. Thinking that it is might be what would lead someone to utter such nonsense as that there is nothing contrary to reason in preferring one's lesser good to one's greater, or the destruction of the world to the scratching of one's finger. What is true is that there is no objection to these preferences merely from the standpoint of instrumental reason. But of course there is an objection from the standpoint of prudential reason.

Pragmatic or prudential reason tells us to form the idea of a greatest attainable whole of satisfaction of our inclinations (under the name 'happiness'), to make this whole our end, and to prefer it to every more limited satisfaction that might conflict with it. Contrary to Scanlon, I think that Kant and many other philosophers are correct in regarding some holistic notion of our happiness or well-being as playing a significant role in prudential reasoning from a first-person point of view (Scanlon, pp. 126–33). Scanlon claims that from my own practical standpoint the idea of well-being or happiness is "transparent" – "When we focus on it, it largely disappears, leaving only the values that make it up" (Scanlon, p. 133). But this ignores the very point Kant most emphasizes – the holistic character of our prudentially rational aims and values, and the way in which only their relation to each other provides us with a standard for structuring them hierarchically and choosing between them when they conflict. This is why it makes sense, for example, for me sometimes to defer gratification and sometimes not, in my own interest.

Kant is not always clear about the status of prudential reason, sometimes regarding it as merely a species of instrumental reason, under the merely empirical assumption that we have a natural desire for happiness that is stronger than other inclinations. But he is sometimes aware that such an empirical claim is quite implausible, and that the true ground of prudence lies in a demand of reason for an end involving maximal completeness in the satisfaction of our empirical desires (KU 5:430–1). Owing to this confusion, Kant's account of the ground of prudential reason remains obscure. I submit that Kantian ethics is best served by regarding prudence as grounded in the rational value of humanity in our own person. Reason requires that our empirical desires have a rational claim on us only insofar as they answer to the systematically unified end we set for ourselves as rational beings and at the same time finite beings of need.

Moral reason. Under the thesis of the difference or inequality of the three kinds of practical reason, prudential reason overrides instrumental reason. The claims of happiness take priority over the instrumental rationality of adopting suitable means to some arbitrary end. Analogously, the third species of reason – categorical, apodictic, or moral reason – overrides prudential reason: The claims of duty take priority over the claims of one's own happiness. For Kantian ethics, there is no "dualism" of practical reason (to use Sidgwick's term). The claims of moral reason are categorical or unconditional. They provide a rational ground for the setting of ends, but they are not conditional on any end, neither an arbitrary or a discretionary end nor even the rationally necessary end of our own happiness. The principles of morality will limit our pursuit of happiness, but because their ground is honoring our worth as rational beings, they allow for what Kant sometimes calls a "rational self-love" (KpV 5:73, R 6:45n) – that is, a pursuit of one's own happiness that is moderated enough to accord with duty and to allow for the moral claims of others, who are our equals as ends in themselves.[24]

The overridingness of moral reason follows neither from the fact that it is moral nor from the fact that its imperatives are categorical rather than hypothetical. Its ground is the objective value of rational nature as an end in itself and considered as universally legislative to itself and to all rational beings regarded as a single ideal community or "realm of ends." These are relatively deep claims in Kantian ethics, to which we will return in Chapters 4 through 6. But there is also something highly paradoxical about claiming that morality is not grounded on good reasons, even the best reasons we have. For we hold people responsible for meeting moral requirements and blame them if they do not. How can we be justified in doing this if they have no reason to meet those requirements, or just as good reasons for not meeting them?

When it is suggested that morality is grounded on reason, the rejoinder is commonly made that the actions of a conniving villain, however reprehensible, are surely not *irrational*. It is probably true that in its ordinary usage, the word 'irrational' is not applied to cases in which someone's behavior involves a deliberate refusal to act according to the best reasons they have, or even to accept such reasons as reasons. But these are failures of rationality nonetheless, and thinking or behavior that exhibits it is open to rational criticism.[25]

Kant takes it to be a necessary truth that there could be no person (no morally responsible agent) for whom moral reasons are not an incentive to act (R 6:36). Of course people often refuse to act on these incentives, refuse to acknowledge them, even sometimes deny that (for them, or for anyone) they are rational incentives at all. We should not take such denials at face value. No one is ever an infallible authority on the question of what reasons they have, and people are often in denial about this. If there are reasons to act as morality requires, then the failure to so act is also a failure of rationality, and it is also a failure of rationality to think, assert, or exhibit expressed preferences to the effect that you do not acknowledge such reasons.[26]

It is a *philosophical* question – not a question about the empirical psychology of each of us as individuals – whether we have reason to respect people's rights and care about their welfare.[27] No doubt some are skeptics about the very existence of distinctively moral reasons for acting, or even about morality itself. Or they think that a tolerable facsimile of moral reasons can be cobbled together from some set of plausible assumptions about human psychology. Such a theory would make the rationality of moral requirements only a precarious contingency, a state of affairs the theorists then insist we must simply learn to live with (as if this were a strength of their position rather than – what it is – a consequence that makes the theory difficult for any reasonable person to accept). Kantians may in turn be skeptical about all such projects, and whether anything deserving to be called either 'morality' or moral 'reasons' could ever be got out of them. A long philosophical tradition claims that there are powerful reasons to meet the requirements of morality, reasons that are necessarily connected with being a rational agent at all, and hence that conduct which violates moral principles necessarily constitutes a significant failure of rationality (even if we don't customarily apply to it the term 'irrational'). Kantian ethics does not need to apologize for adhering to that tradition.

2

Moral Worth

Kant famously begins the First Section of the *Groundwork* by proclaiming that the only thing in the world or outside of it that is good without limitation is the good will. He then proceeds to associate the good will in some way with acting from duty and claims that only actions done from duty have true moral worth or moral content, while actions in conformity to duty that are done from self-interest, or even beneficent actions done from a natural inclination such as spontaneous sympathetic pleasure agents take in seeing those around them happy, are lacking in authentic moral worth or moral content.

Most readers of these statements immediately draw from them on Kant's behalf several conclusions that many find highly controversial, if not downright repellent. They conclude that for Kant the only actions that display a good will are those done from duty, so that even beneficent actions done from sympathy must be cases of a will that is not good. They infer that if Kant thinks only actions done from duty have moral worth, then he must regard even actions that otherwise would accord with duty, if done from some motive other than cold duty, as really immoral or at best morally indifferent. They think Kantian ethics must be positively hostile to all natural desires, feelings, and emotions, because it bestows moral approval only on people whose orientation to life is characterized by an unhealthy detachment from this side of their nature.

These conclusions, combined with similar invidious readings of other points of Kantian doctrine, rapidly congeal into a familiar if unlovely picture. The Kantian moral agent is a self-alienated person rent by an unbridgeable gulf between the supernatural noumenal self and the contemptible empirical self. The former self unrelentingly issues merciless moral commandments to the latter self (who seems, by the way, to lack any capacity to obey or even to understand them, because the commands speak only the language of pure reason, while the empirical self understands only the language of feeling and desire). Kantian ethics regards the very existence of feelings and natural desires as a ground of moral reproach. The "good will" is found only in those who take a self-denying attitude toward their healthy human desires, repress their emotions, and alienate themselves from their feelings, so that they perform the commands of duty with no intention except that of total, unquestioning obedience to the moral law. There is little wonder that those who see Kantian ethics only in these terms regard it with a kind of horror. Or at best they may see Kantian ethics as expressing a limited truth, but in a monstrously exaggerated form.

This reading of Kant, though familiar and widely accepted, is wrong on every single one of the foregoing counts. It commits serious philosophical as well as exegetical errors. In relation to the primary stretch of text from which it is drawn, it remains oblivious to what Kant is trying to do and misunderstands the claims he is making. From what he says it draws a series of inferences that not only do not follow, but the conclusions even contradict Kant's explicit statements, some of them occurring right in this same passage of the *Groundwork* itself.[1]

When Kant is read this way, what Kant trying to say is not making it past the censorship of people's philosophical prejudices. The worst errors come from the way certain ideas about morality drawn from our sick, repressive moral culture weigh on us like a traumatic nightmare. The bad dreams are set off by the things Kant says in the way that a Rorschach inkblot might suddenly bring back a terrifying experience of early childhood. These associations may not be purely arbitrary, but when they impose on us a lurid Gestalt that determines our reading of the opening pages of the *Groundwork*, then Kant's actual meaning will obviously be lost to us.

1. Acting from Duty

Few readers of this early passage in the *Groundwork* even attempt to understand the peculiar task Kant is undertaking in it. If they did, they might more often realize how uncharacteristic this discussion is, in certain respects, within Kant's ethical writings. In the First Section of the *Groundwork*, Kant is attempting to appeal to certain judgments of value that he thinks will be accepted by "common rational moral cognition" (roughly, healthy moral common sense) in order to motivate a formulation of the moral law. The attempt must be accounted a pretty spectacular failure, in view of how regularly and how badly the entire discussion has been misunderstood. But from the wreckage we can try to recover both what Kant meant to do and what he was actually asserting, because these may help us understand Kantian ethics better.

Let's begin with what Kant means in this passage by 'acting from duty'. The very concept of 'duty' itself is perilous enough (a theme to which we will return in Chapter 9, §1). For now, let us try to take Kant at his word when he tells us that "duty is the necessity of an action from respect for law"

(G 4:400) and also explains that the term 'law' refers to any practical principle of reason that is objectively or universally valid for all rational beings (G 4:421). "Necessity" (*Notwendigkeit*) here refers to what Kant elsewhere also calls practical "necessitation" (*Nötigung*) (G 4:413, 434), that is, *constraint* (*Zwang*). In this context, however, it does not refer to *external* constraint or coercion, as by chains, prison walls, or threats, but rather the *inner rational self*-constraint that you exercise over yourself from respect for correct principles. To act *from duty*, in short, is to do something because you know that an objectively valid moral principle demands it, so that this gives you a good reason for deciding to do it, and then making yourself do it.

Not all actions that are "in conformity with duty" (*pflichtmäßig*) are done "from duty" (*aus Pflicht*). Some dutiful actions, though possible occasions for self-constraint, do not need to be done with self-constraint, because they agree with some immediate inclination – that is, with some natural *empirical* desire, as distinct from the *rational* desire that arises in a rational agent from its successful appreciation of the fact that the action is required by rational principles. We must constrain ourselves to an action only when it is necessary to exercise self-constraint if the action is to be performed at all. In other words, we can (and should) act from duty only when no self-interested reason or empirical inclination is sufficient to motivate us to perform the action. An action can be done *from duty*, therefore, only where there is no such empirical inclination – often, though not always, when some inclinations pull *against* our doing the dutiful action.[2]

"Motivational overdetermination." It follows directly from this that nothing in this discussion could have anything to do with cases of what philosophers often call "motivational overdetermination" – cases where duty and inclination both speak in favor of the same action, and the question to be decided is which of these motives the agent is *really* acting on. Many meditations on the opening pages of the *Groundwork* attempt to present Kant's view of such cases. But they are looking for something that is simply not there, because in none of the examples is it ever an issue.

Kant begins with the example of a merchant who deals honestly with inexperienced customers. The merchant's action is in conformity with duty, but it is not done *from duty* because concern for his reputation gives him a self-interested reason for honest dealing. If Kant were interested in his "real motive," he would have to ask whether it is duty or self-interest that *really* moves him. But that question does not even come up. Instead, Kant concludes directly that he does not act 'from duty' (in the sense of that phrase that Kant means), simply because the motive of self-interest is present, and therefore moral self-constraint is unnecessary (hence also impossible). The only question that interests Kant is whether it was necessary for the merchant to constrain himself on moral grounds if he was to act in conformity with duty. Because it was not, he does not act *from duty* in the only sense Kant cares about here.

It is likewise in the cases of ordinary self-preservation, sympathetic benef-icence, and compliance with our indirect duty to secure our own happi-ness. Kant assumes in these cases that the agent normally has some imme-diate inclination for doing what morality requires. Again he infers directly (without any psychological exploration of the agent's "real motives") that the action was not done from duty (G 4:397–9). He draws this conclusion not because he tacitly makes the uncharitable assumption that these agents always act from the least morally creditable motive available to them, but rather because the "real motive" in cases of "overdetermination" is simply not what he is interested in. (In these examples, in fact, none of the inclinations in question are the least bit morally discreditable. There is nothing wrong with preserving your life from an instinctive inclination for self-preservation, or behaving prudently out of a natural desire for happiness, or especially in helping others because you take a spontaneous satisfaction in doing so.) What interests Kant in all these cases is only this: Did the agents in these cases have to constrain themselves through respect for moral principles in order to perform the dutiful action? If they did, and the agent did the dutiful action, then that action was done "from duty." If they did not, then the agent is not acting "from duty" in the sense intended in this discussion (whatever the "real motive" for the action may have been – in case that issue were to come up).

What is "authentic moral worth"? Now let us turn to the question of what Kant means by the claim that only actions done from duty have true, genuine, or authentic "moral worth" or "moral content." *Obviously* Kant does *not* mean that only actions done from duty are approved by morality or have any value at all from the moral point of view. If an action is in conformity with duty (*pflichtmäßig*), then it merits moral approval and hence clearly has value from the moral standpoint. Kant says that such an action, when done from an immediate inclination – a beneficent action from sympathy, for example, or a just action from love of honor – is "in conformity with duty," "amiable," "worthy of honor," and "deserves praise and encouragement, but not esteem" (G 4:398). In the context of this discussion, therefore, "moral worth" and "moral content" cannot possibly be value properties an action must have merely in order to merit moral approval, honor, praise, or encouragement. Many actions lacking in "true moral worth" are obviously to be valued by morality simply as conforming to its principles. The "moral worth" Kant means must instead pertain to a narrower class of those actions of which morality approves. It is a worth that is supposed to be more central and proper to morality than what belongs to actions merely in conformity with duty. "Moral worth," Kant says, entitles the action not merely to "praise and encouragement" but also to "esteem."

In this discussion, therefore, Kant is *never* interested in the difference between *good* and *bad* actions, or between actions worthy of moral approval and actions unworthy of it. All the examples, and all the variations within

each example, are of dutiful actions. None of these actions is ever subjected
to blame, or indeed any sort of *negative* moral evaluation. Kant is *not* criticizing the shopkeeper who is honest out of prudence, or "the friend of
humanity" who is beneficent out of sympathy, or most of us, most of the
time, when we preserve our lives or secure our happiness because we have
an immediate inclination to do so.

It is noteworthy that when Kant employs the term "moral worth" in this
passage he most often adds a modifier: "inner" (G 4:397), "true" (G 4:398),
or "authentic" (G 4:398, 399). When Kant distinguishes between actions
that have "moral content" or "[true, authentic, inner] moral worth" and
those that do not, he is not distinguishing what has moral value from what
has none. Instead, the distinction he is drawing is between what has a special,
fundamental, essentially or authentically *moral* value from what is valuable
from the moral standpoint but does not have the sort of value that lies right
at the heart of *morality*. This concern makes perfect sense here, because
Kant is trying to derive a formulation of the principle of morality. Hence he
is not equally interested in everything morality approves of but is especially
interested in what has the value that is most essential or central to morality.

Kant contrasts our *praise* and *encouragement* of the beneficence of the sympathetic friend of humanity with our *esteem* for the same man, when, after
his sympathy has been clouded over by his own grief and misfortune, he still
finds it in the goodness of his will, or in the goodness of his moral character, to "tear himself out of this deadly insensibility" and do the beneficent
action from duty. "Tearing himself out of deadly insensibility," by the way,
is obviously the opposite of remaining in that emotionless state, so in this
passage Kant is clearly not spurning "the emotions" (as he is often taken to
be doing). Kant's own description of the man who is beneficent from duty
therefore directly contradicts the reading on which Kantian ethics is hostile
to all feeling and emotion. The difference between the beneficent action
from sympathy and the one from duty is not that the first is performed with
feeling and the latter coldly; the questions is whether the benevolent feeling
with which it is performed is merely natural and instinctive or is a feeling
self-wrought in the agent through moral reason.

It is also important not to confuse the judgment Kant thinks we are making when we esteem the action done from duty with some other judgments
we are *not* making: First, in eliciting this contrast, and esteeming only the
action done from duty, Kant is *not* asking *which situation we should prefer to
be in.* Obviously no one would *prefer* to have their sympathetic feelings extin-
guished by grief. Everyone would want to *enjoy* being beneficent. More generally, people never *want* to be in a situation where they have to act from
duty. Nor, *second*, is Kant asking *which situation we should educate people to be
most likely to be in.* Kant wants us to educate people to act from duty *when they
have to,* but we should obviously try to educate people so that they spontaneously have inclinations that accord with the requirements of duty. Healthy

moral agents do their duty easily and reliably, and Kant thinks it usually takes both strength of character and a sensibility in tune with morality for this to happen. That is why he regards it as an (indirect) *duty* to cultivate certain inclinations, such as love and sympathy, since they make it easier to perform duties of beneficence (MS 6:457, ED 8:337–8).

The question Kant is asking is rather a *third* one: *For which agent do we feel the most properly **moral** esteem?* The judgment he hopes to elicit from "common rational moral cognition" is that this esteem (which is due only to actions with "true moral worth" or "moral content") is reserved only for those who find themselves in a situation of adversity, one in which their natural inclinations do not make it easy to conform to moral principles. The action with authentic moral worth is the one where the agent faced with adversity rises to the occasion and does the dutiful thing in spite of the adverse circumstances.

There may be moral theories that deliver the same answer to this last question as to the first two – for instance, theories that identify the essentially moral motive with natural sympathy and moral virtue with a propensity to act from that motive. If so, then Kant is hoping that his examples will help us to see that those theories get something importantly wrong about what is essential to morality. The problem is that they take what is essentially moral to show itself in actions where the agent finds it easiest and most natural to do the right thing. Perhaps at first blush that seems correct, or even self-evident. But Kant thinks that on reflection, our faculty of common rational moral cognition will reveal that it is an error. The truth about the role of morality in human life is more profound, complex, and disturbing than such theories can account for, or even acknowledge.

What rational reflection will show, Kant thinks, is that what is most essentially moral, and what is best about human beings, is not found where good actions are performed spontaneously and innocently. Genuine moral worth is instead a worth that people cannot obtain through the good fortune of nature or education but must *themselves* give to their actions. Moreover, it shows itself most when doing the right thing is hardest for the agent. The importance of morality in human life comes not from spontaneous or innocent good-heartedness but depends on the fact that the human will is corrupt, and in need of self-correction by reason and strength of character. Hence the human self that can give actions authentic moral worth can emerge only after innocence has been lost, when we can no longer depend on any goodness that is easy or spontaneous, arising from a happily constituted nature or a temperament naturally in tune with goodness.

Morality, in other words, is essentially the response to a human condition that has been torn away from natural goodness, where we must fight our way back toward goodness, or even forward to a higher kind of goodness than mere innocence could even so much as imagine. Moral worth involves the exercise of a new power, the power of reason and will. This is a power that arises in us only because our human nature, corrupted by the social condition, is fundamentally in need of correction, or even of a revolutionary upheaval.

At this point Kant is following Rousseau – whom from early in his career Kant regarded as standing to the moral world in the same relation that Newton did to the natural world (Ca *Notes and Fragments*, p. 9.) Rousseau sometimes distinguishes the *moral virtue* involved in a successful struggle against ourselves from the innocent *goodness* that comes from nature (Rousseau D, pp. 80–1, Rousseau E pp. 34–5, 194–7, Rousseau SC, Book I Chapter VIII). Kant thinks that if we see this difference, we will agree with him that the sublimity of a hard-won victory over ourselves is more to be esteemed than the ingenuous charm of a good nature that faces no such opposition.[3] But although people must not evade or shrink from the inevitable moral struggle, Kant never questions the obvious: that we should always prefer to do the right thing without having to struggle.

This should enable us to see how fundamentally we mistake what Kant is saying if we suppose that he regards the "moral worth" of actions as something we should try to maximize or at least treat in general as an *object* of our moral strivings. Many misreadings of Kant's discussion occur because that utterly alien and hostile assumption is gratuitously imported into them. Perhaps the assumption seems natural if we mistakenly think that "good will" is "fundamental" to Kantian ethics in the special sense (characteristic of consequentialist theories), that it is the chief good to be brought about, and if we then also think that for Kant "moral worth" is the value either of this good in general or of its highest exemplification. In that case, it is easy to suppose that the fundamental thing in Kantian ethics is to maximize this fundamental good, and hence that we ought to multiply instances of it wherever we can. Such an assumption here, however, is not only foreign to Kant's thinking but even quite absurd in itself. The point of the discussion is to note the judgments of common rational moral cognition about the kind of value displayed in the various examples, especially which ones exhibit a worth that is authentically *moral*. There is never any suggestion that "moral worth" is some sort of *end* that the agents in the examples are seeking in their actions, much less something they are trying unconditionally to maximize. It is entirely out of place to think of inclinations as "tainting" an otherwise dutiful action, either in the agent's eyes or in the eyes of us who are judging by the standards of common rational moral cognition. If, as Kant thinks, it is a necessary condition of an action's having genuine moral worth that it take place in a situation of moral adversity, where we must constrain ourselves if we are to do the right thing, then the assumption would entail the thought that we ought to try to make our duty harder to do, so as to increase the "moral worth" of doing it. But that thought would be utterly perverse; it would be like thinking you should set your house on fire so as to display your heroic courage in rescuing your family from the flames.[4]

2. Good Will

Kant is quite explicit about the relation between the good will and acting from duty: "We will put before ourselves the concept of duty, which contains that of a good will, though under certain subjective limitations and hindrances, which, however, far from concealing it and making it unrecognizable, rather elevate it by contrast and make it shine forth all the more brightly" (G 4:397). We see here that acting from duty is a *special case* of the good will. It contains the concept of a good will, but it also contains some other features – in particular, "certain subjective limitations and hindrances." These consist generally in the fact that an agent subject to duties has needs and inclinations that might tempt it not to fulfill them, but more specifically in the fact that the good will that acts from duty must constrain itself to fulfill its duties, because in that case its inclinations do not suffice to secure what the good will wills it to perform. This condition of moral adversity is what Kant means by the "subjective limitations and hindrances" that, far from concealing the good will, make it "shine more brightly" – that is, display most conspicuously to us the inner, true, or authentic moral worth that elicits our moral esteem.

Good will is obviously present also in the case where the innocently good-hearted person acts beneficently because she enjoys it. As already mentioned, certain moral psychologies even encourage us to think that this innocent good-heartedness is the only thing we could possibly mean by a "good will." Kant's claim is that it is not, and that the true value of good will "shines forth more brightly" when it is found in the contrasting case, where it must struggle to overcome adversity. This claim certainly has an air of paradox about it, because it means that what is most essentially deserving of moral esteem is found only in cases where the moral agent is faced with conflicting motivations, or at least with an absence of any natural, spontaneous motivation to do the right thing. Kant thinks that common rational moral cognition will, on reflection, recognize that this paradoxical claim is nevertheless correct. Unfortunately, readers have too often spared themselves the trouble of considering the paradox Kant would put before them simply by misunderstanding what he is claiming, and even evading the whole question.

Some cases of the good will, then – the cases of acting from duty – exhibit a more genuinely *moral* worth than those in which self-constraint from rational principles is not involved. We might think this conclusion would contradict Kant's claim that *the good will is good without limitation*. For the need for moral constraint implies (what Kant himself has said) that the case is one in which the good will must overcome "limitations and hindrances" (sources of moral adversity), and this might give rise to the thought that we are dealing with a troubled or impure moral situation, hence one in which "goodness" has been somehow afflicted with "limitation." But that thought misunderstands what is meant by Kant's claim that the good will is *good without limitation*. As Kant goes on to explain, this claim means that the goodness of the good will is neither enhanced nor diminished by its combination with any other thing, good or bad – while all other goods are good only as long as they are associated in the right way with the good will and become bad when they are similarly associated with a bad will (G 4:393–4). This is what Kant's comparisons of the goodness of the good will with other goods ("gifts of nature" and "gifts of fortune") are meant to show. Unlimited goodness in this sense belongs only to the good will as a *kind* of good and says nothing about the relative goodness of different instances of that kind. It therefore does not preclude there being some cases of the good will that have a higher and more properly moral worth than others. And because it has to do precisely with the value possessed by different goods when combined with other good or bad things, it does not rule out cases where the good will is found in conjunction with negative things. Cases of acting from duty, where the good will must show itself in struggle against "limitations and hindrances," are precisely the ones to which goodness without limitation applies.

What is the good will? Kant is strangely inexplicit about his answer to this very natural question. He prefers to leave the concept itself unexplicated and to focus attention instead on a special case of the good will – acting from duty. But the answer to the question is clear enough from what he says elsewhere. *Will* for Kant is *practical reason* – that is, it is the faculty of principles that recognizes laws, adopts maxims, and derives actions from them (G 4:412). A *good* will, then, is such a faculty when it adopts *good* principles and sets about acting on them. It may do so when it needs to constrain itself in order to do so, but also when it need not, because its good principles are in contingent harmony with inclinations (empirical and nonmoral desires). A good will is thus to be distinguished from what Kant later calls an "*absolutely* good will," whose principle is the categorical imperative or moral law itself (G 4:437–9, 444).

The divine will, therefore, or any "holy" will, a will that *necessarily* acts from good principles and need never constrain itself to act from them, is therefore also a good will, and even an absolutely good will (G 4:439). A will that adopts or acts on any good principle (e.g. "Deal honestly with all customers, inexperienced as well as experienced," "Act beneficently to those who need your beneficence," etc.) is a good will, whether it thereby acts from self-interest, immediate inclination, or duty. The divine will, which is beyond all need for self-constraint, hence beyond any thought of "duty," is therefore also beyond all properly *moral* worth, in the sense meant in this discussion. (*Morality*, to speak precisely, and hence also "authentic moral worth," is only for us human beings, not for God, whose perfect goodness is far above that of beings subject to morality.) Equally falling outside properly *moral* worth is the finite will so fortunately situated in a given case that it has no need to constrain itself to do its duty. Both the divine will and this fortunate finite will are ineligible for *authentically moral worth*, but they are still good wills and exemplify the sole thing in the world or out of it that is good without limitation.

3. The Duty to Act from Duty

In the *Groundwork* and elsewhere as well, Kant expresses other views that are related in one way or another to the common misreading of these early pages in the *Groundwork* and perhaps contribute to the misreading, especially when taken together with some of the errors that have just been exposed. This is not the place for a complete review of all such passages,[5] but it may help clarify matters if we at least discuss Kant's claim that we have a duty not only to act in conformity with duty but also to do our duty "for the sake of duty," or "for the sake of the law" or to do our duty from duty. For example: "Not all ethical duties are thereby duties of virtue [i.e., ends which are at the same time duties]. Those duties that have to do not so much with certain ends as merely with what is formal in the moral determination of the will (e.g., that an action in conformity with duty must be done from duty) are not duties of virtue" (MS 6:383; cf. G 4:390, KpV 5:71).

The claim that "an action in conformity with duty must be done from duty," like the claim that only actions done from duty have true or genuine moral worth, is easily misunderstood. We get it wrong if we take to be the claim that actions in conformity with duty but not done from duty are *wrong*, immoral or morally worthless. This misreading would, for instance, require us to ascribe to Kant the self-contradictory position that some actions that are in conformity with duty, hence not immoral or morally worthless, are not in conformity with duty after all – namely, those dutiful actions that are not done from duty and therefore lack true, inner or authentic moral worth. We will better understand Kant's parenthetical claim in the passage quoted at the end of the previous paragraph (and similar claims made elsewhere) if we take into account the fact that some duties are narrow, strict, or required duties whose omission is wrong or blameworthy, while other duties are wide or meritorious duties, so that action or striving on behalf of them is meritorious, but the omission of such action or striving is not blameworthy unless it involves a principle to refuse to strive in that direction and to omit all actions of that kind. In Kant's view, the duty to do our duty from the motive of duty is not a narrow duty but a wide duty. Regarding the rights of others, Kant says, it can be required of me that I act in accordance with them, "but not that the law be my incentive to such actions."

> The same holds true of the universal ethical command: "Act in conformity with duty *from* duty." To establish and quicken this disposition in oneself is, as in the previous case, meritorious, since it goes beyond the law of duty for actions and makes the law itself into the incentive. (MS 6:391)

Hence this duty too – the duty of assessing the worth of one's actions not by their legality alone but also by their morality (one's disposition) – is only of *wide* obligation.

The law does not prescribe this inner action in the human mind but only the maxim of the action, to strive with all one's might that the thought of duty for its own sake is the sufficient incentive of every action conforming to duty. (MS 6:393)

One of our wide duties is that of striving to make the thought of duty a sufficient incentive for all of our actions that conform to duty. This means that any striving in this direction is meritorious, but less striving is not blame-worthy except when we refuse in principle to strive at all toward making the thought of duty sufficient. We also incur no blame if our meritorious striving (however great or small it may be) is less than wholly successful – that is, if we continue to need incentives other than the motive of duty in order to get us to do our duty. (Kant supposes that morally frail human beings normally need such incentives and should not feel guilty because they need them.) Of course if the need of these nonmoral incentives causes me, in their absence, to violate my strict duties, then I am to blame for those vio-lations (my moral weakness is no excuse for my misconduct). But if some combination of nonmoral incentives and the thought of duty succeeds in getting my duty done, then no more is demanded of me, though of course I would have acquired greater moral merit if I had striven still harder to make duty alone a sufficient incentive.

4. Duty, Feeling, and Desire

Those who read the First Section of the *Groundwork* as expressing a hostility to "the emotions" are led into this error mainly by the one example in which Kant regards beneficence from sympathy as lacking the "authentic moral worth" found in those adverse cases where unfortunate circumstances have put sympathy out of action and the beneficent agent must fall back on moral strength of character, acting beneficently from duty. As we have mentioned, some moral theories treat natural sympathy as the basic and proper moral motive. Those who find such theories attractive might be expected to fall into consternation at this stage of his argument, and look for a way of evading it. Misreading a philosopher's arguments is one natural (though in the end unsuccessful) way of trying to resist them.

Four moral feelings. Kant thinks that we have authentically moral esteem for the agent who is beneficent from duty under conditions of adversity, but not for the agent who is beneficent because his sympathetic nature makes it pleasant for him to spread joy around. Whether or not he is right, nothing in this judgment suggests that there is no role for emotion or feeling in Kant's moral psychology. Kant in fact seems to have begun his reflections on moral theory as an adherent of Francis Hutcheson's moral sense theory. Even after abandoning it, he persists in maintaining the importance of "moral feeling" and tries consistently to make a place for it within his moral psychology.

In the *Groundwork*, the moral feeling Kant highlights is *respect* (G 4:401– 2 and note). Later in the *Metaphysics of Morals* he lists four moral feelings

(MS 6:399–402) – the one most relevant to beneficence is "love of human beings." Because this love is a *feeling*, it is not to be confused with what Kant calls "practical love" – a kind of *action* in conformity with duty (though not necessarily done from duty) (G 4:399). "Love of human beings" is a feeling produced directly by reason. Like other moral feelings, it cannot be a duty because if we were not susceptible to it we would not be rational moral agents and could not be put under moral obligation at all (MS 6:399). In short, Kant takes it to be obvious that a human being without feelings and emotions could not possibly be rational. He maintains that someone lacking certain kinds of feelings or emotions – respect, love of human beings, moral approval and disapproval, conscience – simply could not be a rational moral agent. We must be careful not to foist on Kant the crude error that opposes "reason" to "emotion" and assumes they must be mutually exclusive.

The feelings in which "acting from duty" consists are therefore more varied than the opening pages of the *Groundwork* might suggest. Some cases of duty involve faithful adherence to a principle for its own sake, while others involve maintaining the conditions of self-respect and still others involve respecting the rights or caring about the welfare of another person. Because Kant's aim in the First Section is to set up a derivation of the most formal version of the categorical imperative, the Formula of Universal Law, his general discussion of "acting from duty" tends to focus on the first kind of case: acting on principle, even in the face of inclinations that might tempt us to abandon a moral principle. Kant does not seem to notice (and therefore neither do his readers) that this is not a plausible way to think about the example of the sorrowful man who acts beneficently from duty. Help given to others, even on moral grounds, is not the result of sticking to a principle. Beneficence to others carried out from such a mindset is bound to strike us as grotesque. In Kant's own terms, however, "the motive of duty" in this example would be much more plausibly regarded as "love of human beings" – that is, the sorrowful man helps others because he has moral grounds to care about them and make their well-being his end. Realizing that this option is open to Kant may help us to correct many common errors about what Kantian ethics must say in such cases.

Rational desire. For Kant, it is necessarily true of all finite rational beings that their actions involve desire. Because every desire is a representation of the object of the desire accompanied by a feeling of pleasure, all actions also involve feeling. Actions done from duty are not exceptions to these propositions – on the contrary, they are conspicuous examples of them. Kant emphasizes that there is a fundamental difference between *inclination* (or *empirical* desire), where the feeling of pleasure accompanying a representation precedes the determination of the will to bring about the object of the representation, and rational desire, where the rational determination of the will comes first and produces in our sensibility a feeling of pleasure accompanying the object we rationally will as an end (KpV 5:9n, MS 6:212–13).

Either way, there can be no volition or action without the presence of both feeling and a desire for an end.

One of the most common claims about Kantian ethics is that it requires us to act contrary to, or at least in the absence of, all *desire*. This may be intended as a mere verbatim report of the fact that Kant thinks action from duty is not action from *inclination*. But in that case the report is badly garbled, because it has been filtered through the additional thought that "desire" is equivalent to "inclination" (perhaps the thought is that this is merely a more up-to-date or colloquial way of talking). But this is a *false* thought, and in this context, its effect is anything but harmless. All action for Kant requires both feeling and desire, but in an action done from duty the feelings and desires are *rational* (not empirical) feelings and desires. That is, they arise as effects of our rational awareness of principles or objective grounds for action on our sensibility or receptivity to feeling. Moral self-constraint itself, according to Kant, occurs only through rational feeling (especially the feeling of respect) (KpV 5:92). Moral action, which always sets ends, always involves a rational *desire* for them. There is a crucial difference between cases where the desire is produced by a rational choice to pursue the object and cases where the choice to pursue the object comes about through an empirical impulse or desire that provides the incentive for adopting a maxim to pursue it (MS 6:211). Both, however, are cases of action involving desire and feeling. Without desire and feeling, in Kant's view, there could be no action at all.[6]

The moral theories of Hutcheson, David Hume and Adam Smith, identify sympathy or love, perhaps combined with other psychological factors (such as disinterestedness, calm judgment, or impartial spectatorship) as the psychological foundation of all morality. Kant always had much respect for these theories. But it was a crucial turning point in Kant's thinking about morality when he decided that no such theory could give an adequate account of morality. Kant's use of the term "metaphysics of morals" in the late 1760s, signifying that moral judgments must be based on concepts and principles, not on sentiments, was the sign of this decisive change. In the context of the *Groundwork*, Kant's claim that the action of the man who is beneficent from duty has moral worth, while the same man's beneficent action out of sympathy does not, is a direct rejection of the most fundamental tenet of all moral sense theories.

Kant's rejection of sympathy as the basis of morality. There are two main reasons that Kant refuses to allow that sympathy or any other empirical sentiment or desire could constitute the foundation of morality. One is that no sentiment of this kind can yield the kinds of objective and universal principles that morality requires. They can approximate to this only by claiming a greater empirical uniformity in human nature than experience shows to be there. By comparison to them, Kantian ethics is much more hospitable to the empirical data that lead some to adopt the various positions that go by the name "cultural relativism."

Kant's moral rationalism is in part a recognition that however the psychology of human beings may vary in time, place, or culture, the fundamental standard of moral good and evil does not vary along with them. It is as independent of empirical human nature as the laws of arithmetic or Newtonian physics. To say that the fundamental principle of morality is objective, hence that it does not vary with the changeable empirical nature of human beings, is precisely *not* to assert the uniformity of human nature across cultures. It is rather to say that the rational foundations of morality are independent of any such variations. It is also by no means to hold that the ethical conclusions we reach by applying this principle to human beings and their empirical circumstances do not vary. As I understand Kantian ethics, it ought to allow for a lot of historical, cultural, and individual variation of the latter kind. These variations are merely the different ways in which the fundamental value – the dignity of rational nature – is understood, interpreted, and applied to widely different human beings in widely different circumstances. (We will return to this point in Chapters 3 and 9.)

When some criticize Kant's acknowledgment of a single supreme principle of morality as assuming a similar uniformity of human nature, they are in effect simply assuming the denial of Kant's most basic claim. They are assuming there are no objective or rational truths in the moral sphere at all, and that what Kant is calling principles of reason must really be dependent on the empirical constitution of human nature – which Kant, therefore, is assuming (along with the moral sense theorists) possesses greater uniformity than experience shows there to be. Their minds are apparently so closed in advance against the very possibility of moral truth that they cannot even seriously entertain Kant's basic thought that in order for moral principles to have the universality, necessity, and rational authority that all of us (including these moral skeptics) in practice take them to have, they must be independent of empirical human nature (G 4:389).

Kant's other main reason for rejecting sympathy or love as the basis of morality involves his view of the empirical psychology of these feelings as they arise in us in our social condition, and especially in the "civilized" condition of modern European society. Kant understands the feelings of sympathy and love to have been implanted in us by nature as part of our sociability, bringing us closer to one another by sharing one anothers' joys and sorrows, and desiring one anothers' good (KU 5:208). He thinks they serve as a provisional substitute for morality, until human reason is sufficiently developed (VA 7:253). But these feelings are unreliable guides to what is morally right, because the self-conceit that belongs to us as competitive social beings puts them in tension with the more essentially moral feeling of *respect* for others as ends in themselves (VE 27:406–7, MS 6:449).

By their very nature, therefore, sympathy and love (as empirical feelings and inclinations) exhibit our tendency to seek ascendancy over others and to give our own inclinations priority over moral principles of reason. This is why Kant brings love, along with all other inclinations, under the egoistic principle of self-love or one's own happiness (KpV 5:22). By this he does not mean to agree with those tedious psychological egoists who think that sympathy and love never truly aim at the good of another but always secretly aim at our own good. His point is rather that empirical love and sympathy exhibit a kind of second-order partiality in the selection of their objects. We feel sympathy only with difficulty for those who threaten our self-esteem – when we look upon their misfortunes, Kant thinks, we are more likely to feel the directly vicious sentiment of "gloating" (*Schadenfreude*) (R 6:28, MS 6:458). We more easily sympathize with those to whom we can condescend, so that relieving their distress enhances our self-esteem. Likewise, we love most easily those to whom we feel superior: "We love everything over which we have a decisive superiority, so that we can toy with it, while it has a pleasant cheerfulness about it: little dogs, birds, grandchildren. Men and women have a reciprocal superiority over one another" (R 1100, Ak 15:490). "Love, like water, always flows downward more easily than upward" (VE 27:670). It is therefore understandable that the moral sense theorists should insist, as they usually do, that sympathy or love counts as a moral sentiment only when combined with some sort of disinterestedness or impartiality. But in Kant's view, this theoretical device is always too little and too late. Love or sympathy is an unreliable substitute for genuine respect of others, which arises from a rational recognition of their objective worth as ends in themselves. This is why Kant insists that although some empirical inclinations, such as sympathy, can often motivate dutiful actions, their conformity to morality will never be more than "contingent and precarious" (G 4:390). To base morality on such sentiments is always to put it in danger of corruption.

It does not follow, however, that Kantian ethics tries to get along on respect alone and has no place for love or sympathy. We will see in Chapter 9 that Kant regards duties of love and duties of respect as two complementary classes of duties to others. We will also see that duties of love include not only duties to benefit others but also duties to care about them and involve ourselves emotionally in their fate (see Chapter 9, §5).

Must morality rest on an empirical motive? In the *Treatise of Human Nature*, Hume offers a famous and powerful argument that might seem to call into question the very coherence of the Kantian idea that actions of genuine moral worth must rest on the motive of duty:

No action can be requir'd of us as our duty, unless there be implanted in human nature some actuating passion or motive, capable of producing the action. This motive cannot be our sense of duty. A sense of duty supposes an antecedent obligation: And where an action is not requir'd by any natural passion, it cannot be requir'd by any natural obligation . . . In short, it may be establish'd as an undoubted maxim, *that no action can be virtuous or morally good, unless there be in human nature some motive to produce it, distinct from the sense of morality.* (Hume T, pp. 518, 479)

This argument says, in effect, that it makes no sense to suppose that someone acts from the motive of duty unless there is in human nature some "natural passion" providing another (empirical, nonmoral) motive to perform the action in question. Kant's attempt to associate authentic moral worth with actions performed solely from the motive of duty, apart from any incentive of empirical inclination, might therefore seem, according to this argument, to be entangled in an incoherence.

The basic premise of Hume's argument, however, is one with which Kant would agree. This is that we cannot act *from duty* unless there is some antecedent specification of what our duty is, independent of its description in terms of the motive of duty. For Kant, that specification is provided by the rational principle of morality, which tells us which actions exhibit conformity to duty and which do not. It is this principle of reason that satisfies the condition laid down in Hume's premise. Consequently, no "natural passion" or any "motive in human nature distinct from the sense of morality" is needed to satisfy it. In Hume's theory, however, we must determine which actions are virtuous based on the motives from which they are performed and the sentiments of the agent or others directed at those motives. That is why Hume thinks that the specification of the content of duty depends on there being "a motive in human nature to produce it, distinct from the sense of morality." In the context of a theory like Kant's, where the content is specified by rational principles rather than sentiments or motives, it does not follow that a virtuous action requires some natural sentiment other than the sense of duty.

A significant corollary of this point is that *motivation* is fundamental to a moral theory like Hume's in a way in which it is not at all fundamental to Kant's. This may come as a surprise to us if we are fixated on the early pages of the *Groundwork* and have drawn from them the invalid conclusion that for Kant everything depends on the motive with which we act ("the motive of duty"). On the contrary, however, much more depends for Kant on the supreme principle of morality, which it is the aim of the *Groundwork* to search for and establish. The discussion of action from duty in the First Section is merely Kant's attempt to prepare his readers, at the level of moral common sense or "common rational moral cognition," to be introduced to this principle.

Summary. People tend to be misled by the opening pages of the *Groundwork* into believing two basic falsehoods:

(1) The basis of all Kantian ethics is the unlimited goodness of the good will.
(2) For Kantian ethics, the good will is only the will that acts from duty.

It is important to rid ourselves once and for all of these two false beliefs if we are ever to acquire any idea of what Kantian ethics is about.

In fact, the unlimited goodness of the good will is mentioned relatively infrequently in Kant's ethical writings as a whole. Its position in Kantian ethics is derivative and its importance comparatively marginal. The value foundation of Kantian ethics is rather the worth of rational nature: in humanity as an end in itself, and in the dignity of autonomous personality as universally legislative. As we have seen, moreover, the will that acts from duty is only one special case of the good will. Its prominence in the early pages of the *Groundwork* is due to the peculiar strategy Kant adopts there in his attempt to derive from common rational moral cognition the first provisional formula of the supreme principle of morality. But this is only one approach to formulating the principle; a much more completely worked-out approach is the more philosophical one employed in the Second Section of the *Groundwork* – in which the authentic moral worth of acting from duty plays no significant part.

Kant is often misunderstood because he is read on the assumption, alien to his thinking, that the first task of ethical theory is to figure out what it is valuable to bring about, and the second task is then to prescribe the actions that will maximize that value. Early in the *Groundwork*, "moral worth" looks like something supremely valuable, especially if it is identified with the unlimited goodness of the good will. Then it will seem that Kant is saying we ought to maximize the good will, and hence the moral worth of our actions, by acting from duty as often as possible (which must mean suppressing our natural desires on every possible occasion).

But this line of thinking makes three big mistakes (in effect, it commits a new whopper with every step it takes). First, in Kant's view, action having moral worth (done from duty) is only one special case of the good will. There are cases of the good will that do not involve performing actions with moral worth. It is an error to think that the only the will that acts from duty is a good will.

Second, the good will has a certain special kind of value (goodness without limitation), but it is not the most basic value in Kantian ethics. Rational nature, as an objective end in itself and as possessing the dignity of being universally legislative, is better thought of as the fundamental value. This is why the unlimited goodness of the good will, accompanied with fanfare in the opening line of the First Section of the *Groundwork*, appears only rarely and incidentally elsewhere in his ethical writings.

Finally, and perhaps most basically, Kantian ethics does not regard the maximization of what it is valuable to bring about as a basic task of practical reason. Kantian ethics is based on a fundamental principle of action, not on a chief end to be maximized through action. Rational nature, as the fundamental value in Kantian ethics, is a value to be respected, not a value to be produced still less a value to be maximized in its production. For example, it is not the case that the fundamental injunction of Kantian ethics is either to maximize the number of rational beings that exist or to maximize the rationality of each rational being. (We will return to the distinctive kind of value that grounds Kantian ethics in Chapter 5, §1.)

Besides valuable ends to be produced, there are also constraints of principle (such as those based on principles of right) on by what ways it is permissible to pursue whatever ends we set. Kantian ethics does recognize many different valuable things as ends to be produced, such as all instances of human perfection or human happiness. (The "moral worth" of actions, however, is *never* thought of as an end to be pursued, much less a good to be unconditionally maximized.) Kantian ethics makes it a duty to set instances of human perfection and human happiness as ends, but it does not think of perfection or happiness as goods to be maximized. (We will return to this point in Chapter 15.) Kantian ethics might of course countenance maximizing principles as special instances of the rational pursuit of ends under certain limited conditions. For instance, if I make the happiness of another my end, then it seems right that, *ceteris paribus*, I should prefer the greater happiness of the other over their lesser happiness. But other things are usually not equal in such cases, and sometimes the notions of "greater" and "lesser" do not even apply when we are seeking to harmonize our ends with those of others. In short, Kantian ethics does not recognize "maximization of the good" as a fundamental principle. What Kant calls the "highest good" is heterogeneous in content, with one part or aspect of it (morality) constituting the condition for instances of the other part or aspect (happiness) to be good at all. Once we understand Kant's doctrine of the highest good and its role in Kantian ethics, we will not be tempted to think of it as the sort of thing whose maximization is in general a suitable guide for action.

5. Kant's Aims in the First Section of the *Groundwork*

Most of us who read the First Section of the *Groundwork* do not suspect (or if we do, we find it unacceptable) that at the end of the section, we still have not learned very much at all about Kant's moral philosophy. So we naturally want to draw large conclusions about Kantian ethical theory based solely on what he says there, and once our image of Kantian ethics is fixed on this basis, we try to read everything else he says as a confirmation of it. But in fact the First Section of the *Groundwork* gives us only very limited information about Kantian ethics, and the attempt to force it to tell us more than it does often leads to serious misunderstandings of Kant's ethical theory.

The first thing we should have tried to figure out is what Kant is up to in the First Section and how he proposes to accomplish his aim. Kant's avowed aim in this section is to derive from the admissions of "common rational moral cognition" a certain formula of the moral law: namely, the formula that says we should act only in such a way that we can will our maxim to be a universal law (G 4:402). His strategy is to identify *lawfulness* (that is, the constraint that our maxim be universally valid for all rational beings) as the property of actions from which they derive their most authentically moral worth. He does this first by specifying that actions done from duty are those having the truest or most authentic moral worth and then by concluding that this property of lawfulness is what is most essential to cases in which an action is performed from duty – that is, from necessitation or self-constraint through respect for law.

The argument of the First Section may or may not be successful in deriving the principle of morality. But the two chief elements of Kant's argument in these pages – the unlimited goodness of the good will and the moral worth of acting from duty – although (properly understood) they belong to Kantian ethics, are not particularly central or fundamental to it. Certainly after two centuries Kant's argument in these pages must be accounted at least a rhetorical failure, because a great many who have read the First Section have not only misunderstood it but also derived from it an enduring but false image of Kantian ethics. It is often an image they find problematic if not downright hateful. In this book I am trying to help us get past these errors, so as to make possible a more positive appropriation of Kantian ethics.

3

Ethical Theory

The aim of this chapter is to say what a *Kantian* ethical theory is, by characterizing Kant's conception of the aims and methods of what Kant calls a metaphysics of morals. I will do this by contrasting a Kantian conception of ethical theory with what I take to be the now dominant conception, a conception that too often influences even the way Kant is interpreted. My contrast will involve reference to great figures in the history of modern ethics such as Kant and Rawls, Mill and Sidgwick, but they will not be sorted in the customary way. And although I regard Kantian ethics as socially radical in its implications, my sympathies within the present narrative of the history of ethics will be decidedly reactionary. No doubt proponents of the dominant conception regard a reading of Kant that brings him into their fold as a charitable reading. As I mentioned in Chapter 1, they tend to take "Kantian ethics" to consist in using certain themes or doctrines in Kant to help out in "ethics" – where it is taken for granted that we already know (from the dominant conception) what *ethics* is. In this book, as I have said, the term has a different meaning.

1. The "Intuitional" or "Scientific" Model

The standard or dominant conception of ethical theory has two main characteristics, the first having to do with moral *epistemology*, the second with the nature of moral *principles* – the demands made on them, and the way they are to be applied.

The standard model takes the starting point for our moral knowledge to consist in a set of moral judgments, sometimes about general principles, but mainly about the moral rightness or wrongness of particular actions in actual or possible cases. These judgments are sometimes called "intuitions." The term "intuition' here is not usually meant to denote any special or arcane mode of moral knowledge. Our "intuitions" are simply a set of moral judgments we make that are regarded as relatively certain and stable under reflection.

The dominant model takes intuitions about particular cases as the primary ground of appeal for the authority of moral principles. A moral judgment is not counted as an 'intuition' in this sense unless it is generally accepted and made after careful consideration. But even the best intuitions about particular examples are not regarded as infallible. For one thing, it may turn out that the principles which best account for some intuitions come into conflict with the principles that best account for others, or with principles that themselves have some intuitive appeal. The task of ethical theory, according to this model, is to reconcile initially conflicting judgments and principles, either by qualifying or modifying them, or explaining away apparent conflicts, so as to produce the most coherent overall explanation of our intuitions. The aim is to give the most coherent and intuitively compelling account of all our moral intuitions, at all levels of generality, an account that both reconciles our intuitive judgments and also gives us the most satisfying explanation of why we consider them true.

This description fits a lot of what is done in moral philosophy at the present time, not only in explicit theorizing but also in the process of reflecting on many specific moral issues, insofar as these reflections seem to be theoretically guided. It fits the aims and procedures, for instance, of most philosophers who make use of carefully crafted if artificial examples in order to test and refine moral principles – examples such as those in which you happen to be positioned so as to throw the switch and alter the course of a runaway trolley, which will kill one group of people if you don't throw the switch and another group of people if you do. Cases of shipwrecks with lifeboat shortages and cases where unsuspecting patients are dismembered to save five other people who need organ transplants are also familiar ones in these moral theories (if, happily, not in real life).

It might seem that the use of such examples would have a consequentialist bias and therefore be alien to Kantian theories. But the point of many trolley problems is to enlist our intuitions *against* the thesis that it is always right to produce the best overall consequences, by calling our attention to cases in which these consequences have been produced by means of actions we intuitively regard as wrong. Kantian ethics itself has been influenced by this model, especially in the interpretation of Kant's famous formulas of universal law (FUL) and the law of nature (FLN). In the *Groundwork*, Kant himself famously applies the latter formula to four famous examples of maxims contrary to duty (G 4:421–5) and appears to do something similar at least in the *Critique of Practical Reason* regarding the example of the converted deposit (KpV 5:27–8). Kant's formulas are often integrated into the standard model by being treated as proposals for a procedural specification of the conception of practical reason that operates in moral decisions and moral judgments. Kant's formulas are then treated as candidates for a universal moral criterion for the permissibility of maxims, to be tested against our intuitions regarding the best cases that inventive philosophers can devise as apparent counterexamples. If one interpretation of Kant's formula yields counterintuitive results, then another interpretation is proposed. The fate of Kantian ethics itself, as a moral theory, is then seen as depending on this enterprise of interpretation, and how well our best interpretation of Kant's principle fares against our intuitions about the most challenging examples against which we can test it.

This way of understanding Kantian ethics could hardly get Kant's conception of ethical theory more wrong even if it tried. It utterly misunderstands not only Kant's aims in presenting these examples but even Kant's very conception of what a principle of morality is, how it is to be employed, and what it is supposed to accomplish. But my argument on this point must be postponed until after we understand the dominant model of ethical theory a little better.

To find a more or less explicit statement of the standard model of ethical theory, I will look back a little in the history of moral philosophy. For like all dominant views, this one did not always exist. It came into existence not so very long ago, often as the creation of a single superior mind. Further, its creator understood the theoretical project a lot better than most philosophers do now and also – perhaps for just this reason – was also more aware of at least some of its limitations. The great moral philosopher I am talking about is, of course, Henry Sidgwick.

Sidgwick's "intuitional" method. Sidgwick's *Methods of Ethics*, especially its crucial Book III, dealing with Intuitionism and the critical appropriation of the morality of Common Sense, represents this kind of ethical theory in an impressively sophisticated form. Sidgwick carefully defines "intuitions," as he means to use the term, as reflective judgments of Common Sense, regarded as immediately certain and commanding a virtual consensus among the moral community we recognize (Sidgwick, pp. 212–15). He denies that the psychological origin (or what he calls the "psychogonical" explanation) of intuitions is relevant to their value for ethics (Sidgwick, p. 211). Sidgwick also distinguishes intuitions from "blind impulses to certain kinds of action or vague sentiments of preference for them" and from judgments that are not immediate but result from deductions or inferences from general principles (Sidgwick, pp. 211–12).

Sidgwick distinguishes three distinct species, or phases or methods of intuitional ethics: the Perceptual, dealing with particular examples; the Dogmatic, involving the intuitive acceptance of general principles; and the Philosophical, which attempts to discover an ultimate basis for the other two (Sidgwick, pp. 97–102). Neither intuitions about particular cases nor intuitions about general principles are regarded as infallible or immune to error. "In calling any affirmation as to the rightness or wrongness of actions 'intuitive', I do not mean to prejudge the question as to its ultimate validity"

(Sidgwick, p. 211). But an intuition can be shown to be in error only through conflict with other intuitions that we regard, in the end, as more reliable (Sidgwick, p. 213). "The aim of Ethics," he says, is "to systematize and free from error the apparent cognitions that most men have of the rightness or reasonableness of conduct" (Sidgwick, p. 77).

The same general conception of ethical theory is easily recognizable in John Rawls's method of "reflective equilibrium" (Rawls, TJ p. 20). Rawls begins with "considered judgments," and with principles or theoretical constructs, such as the Original Position, or an account of our sense of justice, such as Justice as Fairness, that we find "intuitively appealing" (Rawls, TJ p. 48). The set of considered judgments initially may not entirely match the theory, but then we "go back and forth," adjusting the theory (as by changing our conception of the Original Position) and even sacrificing some of the considered judgments that seem less secure in light of their conflict with a coherent and compelling theory, until we reach a state of "reflective equilibrium" in which "at last our principles and judgments coincide" (Rawls, TJ pp. 20, 48–51).

The Sidgwickian model makes its appearance at some crucial points in Rawls's later "constructivist" interpretation of Kant. Rawls claims that "Kantian constructivism" *shares* with the "rational intuitionism" he finds in Sidgwick, Moore, and Ross the feature that principles and procedures are to be tested and revised "according to whether [they] fit with our convictions after full consideration" or "what we think on reflection" (Rawls, Lectures, p. 242). The only difference, he says, is in the "order of explanation": The intuitionist thinks the procedure is right because it gives the right result, whereas the constructivist thinks the result is right because it results from the correct procedure (Rawls, Lectures, pp. 242–3). The moral epistemology in both cases, however, grounds principles on the consilience of intuitions.

Rawls's interpretation of Kant himself as a "constructivist" in moral theory has been very influential in the way Kant has been interpreted by his sympathizers and categorized by his critics.[1] Dissenting from this, I regard the term "Kantian constructivism in ethics" as an oxymoron, whose interest ought to lie exclusively in its shock value.[2] Kant might be accurately described as a 'constructivist' in the philosophy of mathematics, but he is no constructivist in ethics. When understood as an interpretive claim about Kantian ethics, "Kantian constructivism" gets Kant's entire conception of ethical theory, as well as his conception of autonomy and his position in metaethics (or the metaphysics of value), basically wrong.[3]

"Scientific" ethics. From the standpoint of this moral epistemology, the standard model could be given Sidgwick's name for it: the "intuitional method." But from another point of view it might be called, again using Sidgwick's term, the "scientific" conception of ethics. For another of the distinctive characteristics of the dominant theory is the way it conceives of moral principles, the kinds of demands it places on them, and the way it thinks they apply to action. On this conception, the aim of moral theory will be to settle all moral questions and make all moral decisions, as far as possible, by a rigorous derivation from precisely stated principles. The concepts used in formulating moral principles must be precise in their application, and the practical demands made by the principles must be as clear and determinate as possible, leaving minimal room for disagreement among varying interpretations or applications of the principles to specific circumstances. Where there is unclarity or indeterminacy in our principles, or a threat of conflict between them, or any uncertainty about how they apply to particular cases, we should try to remove these deficiencies by formulating the principles more precisely, testing these formulations against overall coherence with our moral intuitions.

These ambitious demands for clarity and precision are at least as important in Sidgwick's project in ethics as his reliance on intuitions. Early in the *Methods of Ethics*, Sidgwick declares that "to eliminate or reduce the indefiniteness and confusion [in our common practical reasonings] is the sole immediate end I have proposed to myself in the present work" (Sidgwick, p. 13). "We are accustomed to expect from Morality," he says, "clear and decisive precepts or counsels" (Sidgwick, p. 199). "The formulae of Intuitive Morality" (as Sidgwick calls them) are in his view unfit to do this until they are (in his words) "raised – by an effort of reflection which ordinary persons will not make – to a higher degree of precision than attaches to them in the common thought and discourse of mankind in general" (Sidgwick, p. 215). Thus Sidgwick rejects the notion of self-realization, for example, "on account of its indefiniteness" (Sidgwick, p. 91). The results of his review of Common Sense morality are, on subject after subject, the same as what he says about Benevolence, namely, "it is difficult or impossible to extract from [the rules of Common Sense] any clear and precise principles for determining the extent of the duty in any case" (Sidgwick, p. 262, cf. pp. 293, 311, 326). Sidgwick therefore aims at making the ethics of Common Sense "scientific" (Sidgwick, pp. 360–1), by exchanging the current moral concepts, which are "deficient in clearness and precision" (Sidgwick, p. 215), for others that are clearer and more precise, thus obtaining "as explicit, exact and coherent a statement as possible of the fundamental rules" of morality (Sidgwick, p. 216).

2. Doubts about This Model

The standard model of ethical theory may seem like merely a necessary consequence of applying to normative ethics the high standards of clarity and rigor prized by all of us who like to think of ourselves as philosophers in the analytic tradition. This way of doing ethics obviously parallels the way analytical philosophers treat many other subjects – by formulating generalizations about this or that and testing them against intuitive counterexamples. But I think the Sidgwickian method of intuitional ethics, or the Rawlsian method of reflective equilibrium, is *not* the only way to think clearly about ethical theory.

Even at the most general level, this "generalization–counterexample" model of how to do philosophy can be questionable if not carried out with sufficient subtlety. It may be that on complex philosophical issues, there is no possible generalization, however fundamentally sensible in its import, that is free of exceptions (or "counterexamples") – or at least none simple enough to be intelligible and useful to us. If that is true, then philosophers ought to be less interested in locating exceptionless generalizations than in distinguishing between general principles that are basically wrong and those that are basically right though subject to exceptions ("counterexamples") in marginal cases. As practiced by analytical philosophers, the "generalization–counterexample" model of philosophical dialectic sometimes seems oblivious to this crucial distinction. This flaw is entirely remediable, of course, especially if the theorist is interested in determining when principles apply, reconciling distinct principles, or establishing priorities among them.

"Getting the right answer." We want ethics to help us decide difficult questions, to come up with clear answers to problems that trouble us. So one seemingly admirable feature of the standard model of ethical theory is that it seeks a clear and precise answer to every moral question and also has a definite method for obtaining such answers. But ethical theory should expect to obtain "right answers" to difficult moral questions only when our perplexity is of a kind that is suitable for theoretical treatment. This happens when our dilemma or uncertainty is due to the fact that we are insufficiently clear about principles, or about the proper priority to be given one competing moral consideration over another. Not all difficult moral questions, however, are difficult for these reasons. Some decisions are difficult because the agent must weigh competing principles, values, or considerations among which there simply is no clear priority – and where it would constitute a positive *moral error* to establish a clear priority. A good ethical theory ought to acknowledge that some decisions are simply difficult to make and depend on good judgment about a unique set of particular circumstances. Ethical theory should not attempt to provide a theoretical decision of questions that cannot be decided correctly on theoretical grounds.

Suppose your friend is faced with a serious moral dilemma. For instance: Her son is wanted by the police, and she must decide whether to turn him in or harbor him and lie to the authorities. You might respect whatever decision your friend makes and even be prepared to accept and support it, as long as you are sure she has taken all the relevant factors into consideration and looked at her decision in the right way. If she seems aware in the right spirit both of what she owes her child and of her duties as a citizen, you may have no reason to fault her whichever painful choice she makes. You may even be unsure yourself of what the "right answer" for her is. What she needs from you is not to be *told what to do*, but rather your sympathy with her difficult plight, and your honest assurance that she is thinking about things in the right way.

When we turn to ethical theory in the face of hard cases, we should also be less interested in *being told what to do* than in *being assisted in thinking better about what to do*. On a theoretical level, this means understanding better the reasons not only why we should do one thing rather than another but also why some moral decisions are difficult, and why there is no single, clearly right answer to some moral dilemmas. Thus an ethical theory that places first priority on "getting the right answer" is not looking at its most important tasks in the right way.

"Intuitions." In many cases, judgments about this may not be as solid as the arguments of ethical theorists pretend. On many of the standard "trolley problems," for example, the largest consensus obtainable for any answer seems to be about 90 percent; but even on relatively easy questions of ethics, it is common enough for 90 percent to be wrong.[4] Consequently it is not self-evident that the *right* answer to an ethical question, or even the best grounded answer, is always the one that would emerge from achieving maximal coherence among our preexisting ethical judgments, especially where prominence is given to judgments about bizarre examples in which you are suddenly thrust into a morally disorienting situation where you must decide between killing one person and killing five, or between killing a hundred people and blinding a thousand people.

Even if *everyone* thought the agent should do one thing rather than the other in some example, there are important residual thoughts (or "intuitions") that a normal agent would have about the case that never get registered because the only question put by the ethical theorist is *what the agent should do*. For instance, about many examples where an agent must decide on the spur of the moment whether to take one life or five lives, it is a natural thought that arrangements should have been made to prevent the terrible dilemma from arising in the first place – that some procedure should have been decided upon ahead of time that would give the agent a clear moral directive (rather than being forced to make a snap decision on the basis of a private "intuition").

There is also some reason to doubt the dependability for moral theory on what the standard model regards as "perceptual intuitions" or "considered judgments," especially when they are about examples very far from everyday life, often cartoonishly abstract, or involving science fiction in their conception. Some moral philosophers seem to think the very abstractness of such examples is itself an advantage, as if it were something like the effort of abstraction involved in geometrical thinking about the shapes of material things in terms of dimensionless points, straight lines, plane surfaces, and perfect spheres. That thought, however, would make sense only if we assumed a largely unexplicated but obviously highly controversial moral epistemology, perhaps based on an ambitious set of assumptions, to which few practitioners of the standard theory should want to be committed, about how we come by our moral knowledge and where our "perceptual intuitions" fit into its genesis and structure.

In public opinion polls, we know that a lot depends on precisely how a question is put. People often favor government provision of a new public service but are against the creation of a new bureaucracy or the imposition of a new tax. When people are asked their opinion about the permissibility of the death penalty for murderers, the percentage of those favorable to it drops sharply whenever possible alternative punishments (such as life imprisonment) are mentioned in the question. How people answer questions in polls often seems not to depend chiefly on what they really think about the issue itself – for it may be difficult, and so their opinion on it may be confused or indecisive. Rather, it depends far more on how they think the pollster will perceive them in answering. No one wants to appear "too extreme" in their opinion about an issue that perplexes them, or to be ignoring possibilities or complicating factors – which the question, in its wording, may or may not invite them to consider. Here seemingly inconsequential details, even the wording of the question, may make a big difference in their perception of how they will be perceived and hence on the answer they are likely to give. This is one reason why public opinion polls, depending on the way the questions are stated, can be used to show almost anything you want them to.[5]

There is reason to suspect that such dubious factors may also be at work in the examples used as "intuition pumps" that drive ethical theory on the standard model. Many artificial examples seem to be framed as deliberately abstracting from factors that would be present in any real situation, and our intuitive response to the example is tacitly assumed to be playing along with these abstractions. For instance, "trolley problems" often abstract artificially from the fact that it would surely be illegal for a mere bystander to touch the switches on a trolley. Or alternatively, they stipulate matters that would in any real situation be quite uncertain, such as whether farther down the track on which you see one person standing, there might be a dozen others just out of sight. In a case where most people think it would be permissible to throw the switch, would they stick with this response if told they are subject to prosecution under the law or that they might be killing more people than they first thought? Even if there is consensus about a given problem, it is seldom clear what moral beliefs the consensus response might be registering, especially where the examples involve artificial assumptions and abstract from facts about what we would and would not know in real life. If this is unclear, we should not regard responses to these examples as credible data for moral epistemology.[6]

People's intuitions or considered judgments elicited by examples are supposed to be "stable under reflection," also independent of their "dogmatic intuitions" – that is, their convictions about general principles from which these "perceptual intuitions" might be derived (or with which they might also conflict). I question whether this assumption, and with it the notion of a "considered judgment" or "perceptual intuition," is even coherent (much less whether such stable and reliable judgments are in fact empirically available to us). What would "reflection" mean here, if it did not include comparison with general principles that the subject accepts and the values on which these principles might rest? But if the subject does bring in such "dogmatic" and "philosophical" considerations, then ethical theory would surely do better to take *them* as its objects of critical examination, rather than dwell myopically on the subject's judgment about a particular case.

"Reflective equilibrium" as a criterion. Then, too, once we begin seeking reflective equilibrium between judgments of different kinds, there can be no guarantee in advance that people will agree about it. One person's reflective equilibrium may not be the same as another's. Thus the standard method would threaten us with either an indecisive result or with a plural moral truth or a form of moral relativism – different moral principles might be considered valid for different people. In this way, too, the standard model has given up on the possibility of moral truth. Perhaps surprisingly, Rawls at one point even seems to have welcomed this consequence: "Even should everyone attain wide reflective equilibrium, many contrary moral conceptions may still be held . . . The procedure of reflective equilibrium does not assume there is one correct moral conception."[7] Some may find "more than one correct moral conception" attractive, but to anyone for whom the chief aim of ethical theory is to tell us *the fundamental truth about morality,* even the possibility of such a thing looks like a *reductio ad absurdum.*[8]

Even if we grant that our intuitions or considered judgments are stable and reliable, and even if everyone were to arrive at the same reflective equilibrium between general principles and judgments about examples, the standard model of ethical theory always remains on a superficial level. It seeks only coherence among commonly held opinions. It therefore aims not at truth but only to systematize beliefs, which are left without any firm foundation.

This is even admitted by the practitioners of the method. In the preface to the sixth edition of the *Methods of Ethics,* Sidgwick remarks revealingly that he was attempting to follow Aristotle, who "gave us [in the *Nicomachean Ethics*] the Common Sense Morality of Greece, reduced to consistency by careful comparison" (Sidgwick, p. xxi). In his later protestations that "Justice as Fairness" is "political, not metaphysical," Rawls too seems to be saying that he was attempting no more than to make coherent and systematic the moral and political consensus of modern liberal Enlightenment culture. But this misses the main point of the Enlightenment, which was to subject everything – including religious beliefs, political institutions, and common moral opinions – to the judgment of reason, according to principles independent of our existing traditions and prejudices, and possess the authority to stand in judgment of them and demand their revision. This was the way Kant thought about the task of a 'critique of pure reason' in relation to metaphysics (KrV A xi–xii).[9]

Sidgwick's own doubts. Sidgwick understood the new model he was developing better than most of its practitioners do today. For this reason, he was also more aware than they are of its inherent limitations. His attitude toward perceptual intuitions is distinctly skeptical, and he makes many of the points I have made here, such as that people are often not confident of their perceptual intuitions, and the perceptual intuitions of different people often disagree (Sidgwick, p. 100). These doubts about perceptual intuitions anticipate his later worries about dogmatic intuitions, and even about the most general and generally accepted principles that can claim intuitive status (Sidgwick, pp. 379–84).[10]

Sidgwick might even be seen as calling the now dominant model as a whole into question when he comes to his third stage of intuitive ethics, the "philosophical" stage. Here he insists that Common Sense, even when made scientifically precise, supplemented by intuitive principles and rendered as coherent as possible must no longer be regarded as the ultimate authority. "For we conceive it as the aim of a philosopher, as such, to do somewhat more than define and formulate the common moral opinions of mankind. His function is to tell men what they ought to think rather than what they do think: he is expected to transcend Common Sense in his premises, and he is allowed a certain divergence from Common Sense in his conclusions" (Sidgwick, p. 373). Sidgwick takes Utilitarianism to be the fundamental moral truth.

Sidgwick's defense of Utilitarianism, in fact, seems to be an attempt at a kind of compromise between his intuitive method and something else, something more Philosophical, that would go beyond it. But the compromise is unclear and troubled. "The Utilitarian must," he says, "endeavor to show to the Intuitionist that the principles of Truth, Justice etc. have only a dependent and subordinate validity"; yet Sidgwick's method for doing this seems also to involve a fundamental appeal to Common Sense: The Utilitarian must argue "that the [non-Utilitarian] principle is really only affirmed by Common Sense as a general rule admitting of exceptions and qualifications . . . and that we require some further principle for systematizing these exceptions and qualifications" (Sidgwick, p. 421). By pressing the demands for explicitness, precision, and coherence, Sidgwick thinks he can demonstrate to Common Sense that it must advance to the Utilitarian principle as the only viable way of meeting the demands of a scientific ethics. "If systematic reflection upon the morality of Common Sense thus exhibits the Utilitarian principle as that to which Common Sense naturally appeals for that further development of the system which this same reflection shows to be necessary, the proof of Utilitarianism seems as complete as can be made" (Sidgwick, p. 422).

In Sidgwick's account of the development of his views, appended after his death to the preface to the sixth edition, he says that he began as an adherent of Mill's utilitarianism but became dissatisfied with its account of the relation between interest and duty. This led him to Kant, Whewell, and Aristotle, and then finally, by the reasoning just described, back to the utilitarianism from which he began. "I was then a Utilitarian again," he says, "but on an Intuitional basis" (Sidgwick, pp. xvii–xxii). It is therefore not entirely clear how far Sidgwick's utilitarianism is a properly Philosophical view, one that "tells mankind not what they do think but what they ought to think."

Does Kant appeal to our "intutions"? It is sometimes thought that in the First Section of the *Groundwork*, Kant's appeal to "common rational moral cognition" on behalf of his judgments about the "moral worth" of actions amounts to an appeal of the standard kind to "our moral intuitions." This thought seems to me to show only how tenacious a grip the dominant conception of ethical theory has on people's minds and how flexibly they are willing to use the term 'intuition' in order to force whatever presents itself to them into the procrustean bed of that conception. Kant's appeal to common rational moral cognition is not an attempt to establish a set of data about moral rightness and wrongness by which candidate moral principles might be tested. As we saw in the previous chapter, to read his discussion that way is fundamentally to misunderstand what he is claiming. Kant appeals to common rational moral cognition regarding a series of actions that conform to duty, solely for the purpose of eliciting judgments about which actions exhibit true or authentic moral worth, in contrast to a moral value that is less central or essential to morality. He argues from the fact that duty – self-constraint from respect for law – is essential to morality to a formulation of the moral principle. Nowhere in his discussion are there any discriminating "perceptual" intuitions about which actions are "right" and which "wrong." There is no appeal to "dogmatic" intuitions to settle questions about which rules or principles are binding. (The duties of self-preservation, beneficence, etc. involved in these examples are simply assumed to be uncontroversial; common rational moral cognition is not used to validate *them*.) Nor is the argument for the formula of the moral law based on any "philosophical" intuition about basic moral values or principles.

The dominant model employs the appeal to intuitions of common sense as a source of data for moral theory. Kant's account of the relation of common rational moral cognition to moral philosophy is quite different, and it is motivated by quite different considerations. Kant's appeal to common rational moral cognition is a rejection of the intellectual elitism of the Wolffians in favor of Rousseau's more egalitarian conviction that fundamental moral truth is just as accessible to the common human being as to the philosopher. But even this is not his main point in this passage, which is that common human reason does need philosophy, as the Wolffians claimed, but not for the reason the Wolffians thought. Rather, Kant thinks that all of us need protection from our corrupt human tendency (grounded in the social, and especially the civilized, condition) to twist the laws of duty to suit our inclinations, or to quibble with them and raise skeptical doubts about their validity, or at least their strictness (G 4:405). This is precisely why in the Second Section Kant thinks he must begin anew, undertaking a systematic derivation of the principle of morality from the philosophical concept of the rational will – rejecting precisely the approach of the popular Enlightenment, which would rest everything on the common understanding and rejecting any independent claims of "metaphysics" (G 4:406–12).[11]

Kant's definitive search for the supreme principle of morality occurs not in the First Section of the *Groundwork*, based on appeals to "common rational moral cognition," but rather in the Second Section, where it is derived from a philosophical account of volition that is wholly independent of any appeal to moral common sense and rests not at all on intuitive judgments either about particular acts or moral principles or on any "reflective equilibrium" between such judgments. Let's therefore be open minded enough to consider the possibility that Kant's model of ethical theory is simply *different in conception* from the standard one invented by Sidgwick, adapted by Rawls, and now taken for granted, in one form or another, by most moral philosophers.

3. The "Foundational" or "Philosophical" Model

The alternative I want to contrast with the Sidgwickian (or "intuitional" or "scientific") model is an older one that I imagine might be found, in some form, in quite a lot of ethical theory prior to the twentieth century. I will call this the "philosophical" model (in contrast to the "scientific"), but also the "foundational" model (in contrast to the "intuitional") because it attempts to rest ethics on an objective foundation rather than on people's "intuitions."[12] I find this kind of ethical theory not only in Kant but also in another major moral philosopher who is usually seen as having little in common with him – John Stuart Mill. Kant and Mill disagree about many things – even *basic* things – not only about the substantive foundations of ethics but also about moral psychology and about how such basic moral notions as duty and conscience are to be conceived. But these differences seem to me only to make all the clearer the close parallels in their conception of the structure and aims of ethical theory.

The fundamental principle and the fundamental value. To act rationally is to act for good reasons. Something has the form of a good reason if it falls under a rational principle, and the basic principle of ethical theory is the fundamental principle of rational action. But a rational principle also expresses, or is correlative to, a fundamental value. Kant's and Mill's theories are both grounded on a single fundamental principle. In Kant's case, this is the "categorical imperative" or "fundamental principle of morality" (G 4:420–36); in Mill's case, the "principle of utility" or "utilitarian theory of morality" (Mill, p. 7). The fundamental principle expresses, or in turn rests on, a fundamental value. In Kant's case, this value is rational nature, presented first as the objective worth of humanity (or the capacity to set ends according to reason) as an end in itself (G 4:429), then developed into the *dignity* of personality as the capacity to give and obey universal moral laws (G 4:431–5). In Mill's case, the fundamental value is the general happiness, pleasure, and the absence of pain, or what Mill also calls the 'theory of life' on which the "utilitarian theory of morality" rests (Mill, p. 7).

The basic value, in both cases, is not defended by anything like an appeal to our intuitions (in Sidgwick's sense). No doubt both philosophers do think that people are initially disposed to accept the fundamental value, and both might perhaps agree that is in the end the best (or the only) reason that can be given for it. All moral theorists make some appeal, at some stage or other, in one way or another, to what people ordinarily think. But not all these appeals follow the standard model or have the same methodological function as they do in Sidgwick or Rawls or other proponents of the now dominant conception. The appeals in Kant and Mill to "common rational moral cognition" or "the received code of morality" are not used to justify the fundamental principle of the theory, and they play at most a secondary role in arguing for its basic value. Kant and Mill attempt to ground the fundamental value not on considered judgments but on a more philosophical appeal to the basic structure of rational desire or volition. They attempt, as I would put it, to provide a *philosophical interpretation of what we are committed to* simply in rationally desiring ends and willing actions toward them.

In Kant's account, the fundamental value is uncovered by asking what could motivate us to obey a categorical imperative. The answer is the concept of an objective end in itself, which is not an end to be produced but something existing that has a value giving us an unconditional ground for acting in accordance with it. The argument that rational nature has this value is based on an argument that in acting according to reason, each of us necessarily regards his own existence as an end in itself resting on a rational ground and is also committed to regarding this same rational ground as residing in the person of every other rational being (G 4:428–9). In Mill's account, the corresponding argument is the famous (or infamous) inference that the best reason for thinking that something is desirable is that it is desired, that happiness is therefore the sole rational object of desire for each person, and hence the general happiness is the sole ultimate object of desire for the aggregate of persons (Mill, pp. 35–41). I think the strengths of both Kant's and Mill's arguments are badly underestimated by most philosophers who have considered them. The Kantian argument for the Kantian conclusion will be discussed further in Chapter 5.

In both Kant and Mill, the fundamental principle rests on the ultimate value. In both cases, however, the principle, when properly understood, may not seem to live up to the demands of a moral principle at all, as the dominant kind of theory conceives it. For this principle does not even aspire to the scientific precision, definiteness, and completeness that Sidgwick requires. Kant's principle is formulated in several different ways – basically, three – in a complex developmental argument beginning at G 4:420 of the Second Section of the *Groundwork* and ending with a systematic presentation of all three at G 4:436. Kant's way of formulating the supreme principle of morality will be the focus of Chapter 4. But even as we approach that task, we should keep in mind that Kant does not think it is the function of a fundamental principle of morality directly to tell us what to do in particular cases. As he says right at the beginning of the *Groundwork*, the fundamental principle of morality needs to be applied through a separate part of moral philosophy that he calls "practical anthropology," which considers this principle in relation to empirical human nature and the circumstances of human life (G 4:388).

An even more gross misinterpretation of Kant's illustrations of these formulas is one that simply fits them into the program of the dominant kind of theory, by seeing whether the results of their application in these four cases – or in still others that philosophers may dream up – correspond to our "intuitions" and then deciding on this basis that if the formulas cannot pass this test there is nothing worth salvaging in Kantian ethics as a whole. We find such misreadings already in the very first criticism of the *Groundwork* by G. A. Tittel, as well as in more famous philosophers such as Hegel, Mill, Sidgwick, and countless others.

Unlike many self-appointed Kantians, Kant never bothered to reply to such objections. I take this to be because Kant never saw his four illustrations as any sort of confirmation of these formulas. His argument for all the formulas is solely that they follow from the very concept of a categorical imperative, where the actual validity of such imperatives is being assumed in the Second Section and then argued for in the Third Section of the *Groundwork*. Intuitions about the correctness or incorrectness of conclusions derived from these formulas have no role whatever to play in Kant's arguments for the formulas.

The formula to which Kant himself most often appeals in justifying moral conclusions is not FUL or FLN, but FH – the requirement that we treat humanity in our own person and the person of others as an end in itself. It is a very common complaint that this formula is too vague or murky to provide practical guidance in particular situations. I think that is why philosophers who are under the influence of Sidgwickian expectations have more often favored FUL or FLN, only to be disappointed to learn that it does not do successfully everything that they expected of it. My view is that this is because they brought with them a set of unreasonable expectations that force on them unreasonable interpretations both of these formulas and of what Kant must accomplish by means of them.

The most obvious reason we do not fully understand the practical implications of the Kantian value of human dignity is that our social institutions and practices are almost infinitely far from providing for its proper recognition. Even where what this fundamental value requires is clear enough, its flagrant violation is extremely common, even built systematically into the basic familial, economic, criminal justice, military, political, and other institutions of many societies. Under these circumstances, the charge of unclarity against Kant's Formula of Humanity, or against notions like human dignity, becomes something far more problematic than an honest demand for philosophical clarity. For example, in the course of the debates over his policies of torturing detainees who are held indefinitely without charge or trial, George W. Bush referred, with evident impatience, to the Geneva Convention prohibition on "outrages upon human dignity,"[13] exclaiming: "That's very vague! What does that mean?" Philosophers who charge the Formula of Humanity with vagueness must beware lest their quibbling too should begin to sound like a fatuous confession of limitless depravity.

The structural similarity of Mill's utilitarianism. The basic value and basic principle in Mill's ethical theory are different from those in Kant's theory, but the same structural features can be seen in them. Mill's Principle of Utility reads: "Actions are right in proportion as they tend to promote happiness, wrong as they tend to produce the reverse of happiness" (Mill, p. 7). As has often been noted, this principle does not make it obligatory to maximize the general happiness. It does not choose clearly between "act-utilitarianism," "rule-utilitarianism," or any other attempt to make the utilitarian principle more precise. In fact, there is something deliberately vague (and even conspicuously weird) about Mill's principle of utility. For "right" and "wrong," as properties of actions, do not seem to come in degrees or proportions at all. Instead, they are a matter of Yes and No – hence of the "clear and decisive precepts" Sidgwick says we expect from morality. Thus Mill, in his polite Victorian way, is rather ostentatiously thumbing his nose at any such expectation. On the conception of ethical theory we find exemplified in both Kant and Mill, the function of a fundamental principle of morality is not to tell us what to do, but instead to provide a basic framework, or value-oriented background, for justifying, modifying, and applying the more particular rules or precepts of morality that do tell us this – in the way they think moral principles or precepts can do this – which, as we shall see presently, they can do only to a limited extent. All this will no doubt leave our Sidgwickian theorists shaking their heads and muttering under their breath.

Kant's fundamental principle is more complex in its formulation than Mill's, because Mill understands all practical reasoning as focused on the production of an end, in the restricted sense of a future object or state of affairs to be brought about. Kant, by contrast, begins with the concept of a rational principle to which we constrain ourselves to adhere. This concept makes its appearance in the First Section of the *Groundwork* as *duty*, or a law of reason to which we constrain ourselves out of respect for it. In the Second Section, it is presented more philosophically as the concept of a categorical imperative. Kant considers this imperative first from the side of its "form," then from the side of its "matter" – that is, the end or basic value for the sake of which we can be motivated to obey it, which for Kantian theory is not an object to be produced but an existing value to be respected. Then, finally, Kant considers the fundamental principle in relation to the source of its rational authority over the will. These three sides of the fundamental principle result in a system of three formulations, which will occupy us in Chapter 4.

Kant and Mill agree, however, in regarding the fundamental principle as grounded on a basic value. And in both cases, this is a single value, however different among themselves may be the valuable things that are based on it. For Mill, this value is happiness (pleasure and the absence of pain), and especially the general happiness (of all humanity, or even all sentient creation). For Kant it is rational nature, as an end in itself in the person of rational beings, and in its dignity as considering itself the author of universal laws.

The apriority of Kant's principle. One eye-catching difference between Kant and Mill is that Kant takes the fundamental principle of morality to be *a priori*, while Mill, as a thoroughgoing empiricist, altogether denies the *a priori*. For Kant, to say that the principle of morality is *a priori* means chiefly that it depends only on the nature of our rational faculty itself rather than on the empirical data to which this faculty is applied. Applications of the principle to specific duties or particular moral decisions are clearly not *a priori* for Kant but depend on "principles of application," drawn from "the particular nature of human beings, which is cognized only through experience" (MS 6:217). Someone might argue, however, that because our faculty of reason is part of our constitution as natural beings, the determination of its nature and the principles arising from it must also be empirical. Others might argue that because the function of reason is precisely to give objective normative principles, its constitution cannot be merely a matter of empirical facts but must go beyond them in some way and hence involve at least an *a priori* element. They might even claim that the basic function of reason, as the fundamental objective normative faculty, is to yield *a priori* knowledge.

For the present I leave these questions undecided. They depend on the concept of the *a priori* and its employment, which are matters of great confusion and controversy but not part of Kantian *ethics*. If someone is willing to agree with Kant that the principle of morality is grounded solely in the nature of the *faculty of reason*, rather in the empirical data to which it is applied, but wants to argue that this faculty is known through experience and so the moral law must be empirical rather than *a priori*, then *Kantian ethics* has no need to dispute with them. It may leave to Kantian *epistemologists* the task of pursuing the question of whether the principle in question is *a priori* or empirical.[14]

Objective value monism. Kant regards the concept of the good (as an object of pure practical reason) as consequent to rather than the foundation of the principle of morality (KpV 5:62–3). All ends to be produced that are set by morality are set on the basis of the principle of morality. If it were grounded on any of them, then that would contradict the claim that it is a categorical imperative. So Kant regards the moral principle as prior in the order of value to the good ends the moral agent ought to set in obedience to it. The principle of morality itself, however, is grounded on an objective end – humanity as an end in itself. He describes humanity as having "absolute and objective worth" as an end in itself, and the dignity of rational nature as an "inner worth" that is "beyond all price" (G 4:428–9, 434–5).

In light of these explicit statements, it seems to me highly questionable to ascribe to Kant, as many Kantians today do, a metaethical position that positively *rejects* the idea that there are objective values, and *denies* that it is true (or a fact) that humanity is an end in itself having absolute and objective worth. We will see in Chapter 4 that Kant derives the Formula of Autonomy by combining the Formula of Universal Law and the Formula of Humanity (G 4:431), so Kant regards the value basis of the law in any case as the objective worth of rational nature.

For Kant, as for Mill, it is important not only that ethics should rest on objective value but also that it should rest on a *single* basic value. 'Value monism' (as I will call it) naturally recommends itself as the only way of providing a single coherent framework for ethical theorizing, at least on the model of ethical theory represented by Kant and Mill. An ultimate plurality of values leaves us not only with incommensurable values but also with a plurality of values between which there is in principle no way of establishing any priorities – or even determining that we face dilemmas based on the absence of any clear priority. Value monism is necessary to provide even a context for making comparisons between different values, however the comparisons may come out.

This last point is important, because it means that value monism does not necessarily require us to deny the kinds of dilemmas and conflicts that value pluralists often rightly insist on. On the contrary, it is only in the context of value monism that such conflicts can become intelligible at all, as cases distinct from those in which value priorities can be clearly determined. Value pluralism, taken literally, can make no sense of such dilemmas, because it recognizes no common standard according to which the plural values could be seen even to conflict, so that the conflicts might appear either as resolvable or irresolvable. In effect, value pluralists are also assuming a single ultimate value (though they refuse to acknowledge this, because they shrink from giving it a name). For they see different values as making claims on us with something so intimately in common that the conflicts between them can be experienced as painful and anguishing. The pluralists confuse two different points: first, that we experience dilemmas or conflicts of value that they experience as irresolvable, and second, that their view acknowledges no common standard according to which these conflicts might be either resolved or judged to be irresolvable. The first point is correct, but the second does not follow: It is simply a fatal defect in their shallow conception of the first point.

Even a single value can make different kinds of demands on us and hence come into conflicts which may or not be resolvable. For example, it can be something we ought to promote, yet also something we ought to instantiate or not violate. And it is only as different claims on us of a single fundamental value, or as different interpretations of this value, that we can make any sense at all of different values as making competing claims on us – whether commensurable and decidable claims or incommensurable ones leading to perplexities and dilemmas. To borrow an example from Marcia Baron,[15] suppose a speaker comes to campus advocating religious intolerance. A desire to promote tolerance might lead us to deny him the opportunity to speak, because his speaking will foreseeably lead to more people becoming intolerant. But we might decide even so that we must let him speak, because that is the only way we ourselves can instantiate and show respect for the value of tolerance. So even with this one value, we may face a serious dilemma. Ultimate value monism permits us, however, to view all such conflicts in a single coherent context, and in principle to sort out our priorities – or to decide when they cannot be sorted out. Above all, it is only by basing ethics on a value that is defended independently of our intuitions that we can truly satisfy Sidgwick's own demand, which I think he himself never fully met, that it is the office of philosophy to "tell men not what they do think but what they ought to think."

4. The First Principle – Moral Rules or Duties – Moral Judgment

The kind of ethical theory we find in Kant and Mill could be described as having three stages or levels. In addition to the fundamental level, where we find the basic value and the fundamental principle, there is a second, quite distinct stage of moral theory, grounded on this fundamental level but nevertheless connected only loosely to it, which is charged with directly guiding our actions, and in particular with specifying our moral duties or obligations. Moral rules or duties can be *derived* from the first principle, but not if our only concept of "derivation" is a rigorous deductive procedure. Instead, we should think of the relation between the two more as interpretive or hermeneutical in character. Rules or duties result when the basic value and fundamental principle are *interpreted* in light of a set of general empirical facts about the human condition and human nature, perhaps also as modified by cultural or historical conditions. Finally, there is the application of these rules or duties to a set of particular circumstances in which a given agent must act. This too is not a deductive procedure; it involves an act of judgment that cannot be spelled out in terms of general rules and formally valid inferences.

Moral rules or duties. This means that there is a certain distance in both Kant's and Mill's theories between the fundamental principle and the more specific moral rules or obligations. In Kant, this gap is filled partly by a theory of the rights of person, partly by a set of judgments about what kinds of actions express due respect (or morally forbidden disrespect) for the person of another, but chiefly by the two objective ends of morality or "duties of virtue" – our own perfection and the happiness of others. In Mill, a similar gap is filled by a certain analysis of some crucial moral concepts, such as duty, wrongfulness, conscience, and justice, viewed as devices by which law, or public opinion, or moral education, imposes sanctions on certain kinds of conduct with the aim of promoting the general happiness or parts of it. Neither philosopher thinks determinate moral rules can be directly deduced from the fundamental principle (in any formulation), even together with complete factual information. Both think it must go through a set of intermediate rules, involving the application of the fundamental principle in light of the empirical facts.

In the preface to the *Groundwork*, Kant distinguishes two parts of moral philosophy: the "metaphysics of morals," which grounds moral philosophy on *a priori* laws, and "practical anthropology," in which these laws are applied to empirical human nature (G 4:388). In the *Metaphysics of Morals*, some twelve years later, Kant appears to include empirical "principles of application" based on "the particular nature of human beings" within the scope of the "metaphysics of morals" as necessary to the derivation of a system of duties, though he still insists that the principle of such duties must be *a priori*. "Practical anthropology" is now restricted to that study of empirical human nature which "deals only with the subjective conditions in human nature that hinder people or help them in fulfilling the laws of a metaphysics of morals" – where these laws involve applying the *a priori* principle of morality to human nature as empirically known (MS 6:217).

Despite the shift in terminology, the picture is very much the same, and it seems to be this: *Moral philosophy is grounded on a single supreme principle, which is a priori, but all our moral duties result from the application of this principle to what we know empirically about human nature and the circumstances of human life.*

As I have already mentioned, Kant appeals most often to the dignity of humanity as end in itself in justifying the particular duties that belong to the taxonomy he presents in the Doctrine of Virtue. These duties amount to moral rules determining prohibitions, permissions, requirements, and kinds of meritorious conduct. They are best understood as interpretations of what kind of conduct best expresses due respect for the dignity of rational nature. Because the transition from the first principle (in the Formula of Humanity) is not deductive but looser and more hermeneutical in character, it would be inappropriate to expect duties to be derived by some sort of rigorous deductive process. It would also be quite impossible that the actions declared to be required, forbidden, or meritorious under this system of duties should be specifiable with the kind of precision and determinacy demanded by a Sidgwickian "scientific" ethics. When philosophers complain of the "vagueness" of the Formula of Humanity, they are making these Sidgwickian demands but addressing them to a theory that takes those demands to be unreasonable.

The situation is similar in Mill's theory. Mill argues that the principle of utility is to be applied only through secondary principles and that there is no case of obligation, properly speaking, in which some such secondary principle is not involved (Mill, p. 26). Perhaps the principle of utility is in some sense the ground of these secondary principles, but they cannot be deduced from it. The source of secondary principles is instead "the received code of morality." This code – as Mill "admits, or rather earnestly maintains" – "is by no means of divine right" (Mill, pp. 23–4). As human affairs change, and as we learn more about the tendency of actions and policies for the general happiness, Mill thinks the rules of morality will be open to continual modification and correction, but by pragmatic decisions, not mechanical calculations.

Mill's extremely perceptive metaphor here is that the secondary principles are landmarks and direction posts on a road that has been laid down (Mill, p. 24). Roads are a way groups of people make it easier to travel toward a goal – in this case, promoting the general happiness. The direction posts on a road make publicly known a route toward that goal that serves to solve coordination problems in moving people toward it. Sometimes the route that has been chosen for a road is not the best one, or it was the best route for a time but is no longer satisfactory, so that a new road needs to be built. Clearly there is no precise way to determine when this new construction should be undertaken. No sane person could think that planners might come up with a precise scientific calculus for deciding precisely which day new roads need to be built, exactly where to build them, and how to arrange all the landmarks and direction posts.

The same is true regarding moral rules, through which people collectively pursue the general happiness or (in the case of Kantian ethics) act in ways required by the dignity of rational nature as an end in itself. Here the first principle may provide some guidance and constitute the ultimate ground of appeal. But it cannot specify precisely, as by some rigorous deductive procedure, what the moral rules should be or how moral rules should change in response to new circumstances or improved knowledge and understanding of our situation.

Moral judgment. Mill also insists that secondary principles require a non-trivial act of judgment in their application, and they admit of exceptions, which also cannot be subject to precise rules. "It is not the fault of any creed, but of the complicated nature of human affairs, that rules of conduct cannot be so framed as not to require exceptions, and hardly any kind of action can safely be laid down as either always obligatory or always condemnable" (Mill, p. 25). It might come as a surprise to hear that Kant agrees with this, but his practices in the *Metaphysics of Morals* strongly suggest exactly that.

The notion that Kantian ethics is committed to strict exceptionless rules because it regards moral principles as categorical imperatives is based on the crudest possible misunderstanding. A categorical imperative is unconditional in the sense that its rational validity does not presuppose any end, given independently of that imperative, that is to be reached by following it. But this is far from implying that the obligatoriness of particular moral rules or duties is unconditional. For instance, respect for rational nature might normally require compliance with a certain rule, but there could well be conditions under which it does not, and under those conditions the rule would simply not be a categorical imperative at all. Kant is also charged with excessive rigorism because his applications of FUL involve cases where people try to make exceptions for themselves to moral rules when they should not. People with a tin ear for what Kant is saying often read these arguments as claiming that moral rules should never have exceptions. Perhaps on certain topics, Kant seems (at least at first glance) to allow for fewer exceptions than we think he should. Neither feature of his theory just mentioned has any role in the explanation of this.

Once we get these common misunderstandings out of the way, it is not hard to see that Kantian theory allows considerable room for judgment and exceptions in the application of duties. Kant emphasizes that ethical duties in general are wide or imperfect, allowing for latitude or "play-room" (*Spielraum*) in their application (MS 6:388–94). In the second Critique "*exceptivae*" is one of the twelve practical categories – corresponding to the category of "limitation" in the first Critique (KpV 5:66, KrV A80/B106). The twenty-odd "casuistical questions" in the Doctrine of Virtue are devoted mostly to discussing possible exceptions to the duties in question. Sometimes Kant seems to accept the alleged exception, and sometimes not. But the point of all these discussions, as Kant says explicitly, is to help us "seek truth" (MS 6:411). The point is that when it comes to applying moral rules or duties, what moral agents need is not to be *told what to do*, but rather they need guidance in *thinking for themselves* about what they choose to do.

The exceptions we make to rules should always be made for good reasons, and these reasons necessarily relate in some pertinent way to the basic value and the fundamental principle. Kant glosses *exceptivae* as "Rules of exceptions" (KpV 5:66), and no doubt sometimes exceptions to moral rules fall under general headings. But that does not mean these reasons can always be formulated in precise rules, telling us in general terms precisely when to make exceptions. Judgment in Kant's view is a talent that may be developed through experience but cannot be formulated in any set of rules. The theorists most hopelessly addicted to rules are those who cannot imagine making an exception to a rule unless there is some other *rule* telling them when to do so.

For Kant, judgment – the act of relating a general concept or rule to particular instances – is a capacity necessarily distinct from the capacity to formulate or criticize the rules themselves (KrV A132–4/B171–4, VA 7:197–201). Judgment is a talent that may be developed and sharpened by experience but can never be formulated or taught through general rules. One of the principal tasks of "practical anthropology" for Kant is to help us exercise "the power of judgment sharpened by experience" in "distinguishing in what cases the moral laws are applicable" (G 4:389). And the general purpose of these casuistical questions is to form a "practice in how to seek truth" in the course of this task of application (MS 6:411).

There will always be questions about how far the requirements of morality can be brought under statable rules and how far they must be left to individual judgments about particular circumstances. It is simply part of the meaning of terms like "rule" and "principle" that moral rules and principles must be applied through judgment. They cannot precisely determine what we are to do in every detail.[16] Beyond this simple conceptual point, Kant and Mill have little sympathy for Sidgwick's fanatical desire to reduce all imprecision and indefiniteness to an absolute minimum. They agree with Aristotle's wise advice that we should seek no more precision in any subject matter than its nature allows (Aristotle, I 3 1094b12–15), and that in wise deliberation, it much depends on the virtue of *phronesis* (or what Kant calls "judgment"). Perhaps when they realize this, some virtue-oriented antitheorists might open their minds to the ethical theories of Kant and Mill, realizing that their only valid objections are to Sidgwickian "scientific" theories – and that these objections succeed against only the more unreasonable versions of those.

There are cases in which it is implausible to think that morality can in fact deliver anything like the "clear and decisive precepts or counsels" that Sidgwick insists upon from a "scientific" ethics. Sartre's famous example, in which his student must choose between staying with his mother and joining the Resistance, is only one of many actual ones.[17] In such cases it should even be one of the "considered judgments" of a reasonable person that no moral theory could deliver a "right answer" to the student based on a rigorous deduction from "clear and precise principles." It should even be a decisive objection to any theory that it pretended to do so.

Some have used such examples to question the whole project of ethical theory, or even (as Sartre seems to be doing) the very idea of objective ethical standards. Perhaps such arguments have some purchase against ethical theories that follow the dominant model, especially if they require too much in the way of "clarity, precision, and definiteness" in the answers to ethical questions. But such cases pose no objection at all to ethical theories that follow the Kantian–Millian model. For these theories hold that neither the first principle of ethical theory nor the secondary principles or duties grounded on it must always yield a determinate answer to every ethical problem.

The service of ethical theory in the case of an ethical dilemma, such as that of Sartre's student, is rather to provide a framework of principles and values within which to understand the problem – which means, in this instance, understanding why, in this particular case, the decision is agonizingly difficult and why ethical theory can deliver no clear and decisive answer to it. Of course such a theory will also help us to see why such cases are exceptional and not at all like Kant's example of the false promise, where there is a single clear and decisive answer.

The dominant Sidgwickian "intuitional" and "scientific" model of ethical theory is useful for reflecting on particular problems in light of our preexisting moral beliefs and also for bringing to our attention possible conflicts among these beliefs and suggesting possible ways of resolving them. Nothing I have said here is meant to deny these advantages or to suggest that this way of thinking about ethics should be abandoned. But the dominant model, if regarded as the only way of thinking about ethics, tends to encourage a certain superficiality and complacency in moral philosophy, as well as some other bad habits I have mentioned in §2 of this chapter. It is important for ethical theory what actions, states of affairs, traits, and so on we think are right and wrong, or good and bad. But it is even more important for a philosophical theory of morality to understand *why* we think they are, and why we *should* think they are. The strategy of the dominant theory is too often to answer these questions only superficially, in terms of generalizations that capture our intuitions about what is right and wrong or good and bad, using only the concepts that make for the tidiest generalizations about this. But the real theoretical reasons for any right answer must lie elsewhere, in fundamental values and principles whose validity is independent of anyone's "intuitions." They are to be obtained only by a kind of inquiry not pursued by the dominant kind of ethical theory. The dominant model is not a good one for understanding the ultimate basis of moral value, for grounding our present moral beliefs or for pointing the way to radical revisions in them. For these tasks, the older, more philosophical model found in Kant and Mill is far better. For this reason, it seems to me important not to permit this conception of ethics to be ignored or effaced. The version of Kantian ethics I am developing in this book is meant to bring Kant's thoughts to bear on the more foundational, radical, and properly philosophical aims in devising an ethical theory.

4

The Moral Law

Kant's project in the *Groundwork* is "the search for and establishment *of the supreme principle of morality*" (G 4:392). The *establishment* of the moral principle apparently relates to only one of its formulations, the third main formula, the formula of autonomy. The *search* results in formulating the principle in three ways. Two of them have significant variants that are supposed to bring the moral principle "closer to intuition, and thus to feeling" and thereby to "provide entry and durability for its precepts" (G 4:405, 436). The First Section, beginning from "common rational moral cognition," arrives only at the first and most provisional formulation of the law, while the Second Section (proceeding more philosophically from an account of the will and carrying the search to completion) arrives at all three. The argument of this section follows a progressive development proceeding from the concept of a categorical imperative. Here are the different formulations of the moral law as Kant presents them:

First formula:
FUL   *Formula of Universal Law*: "*Act only in accordance with that maxim through which you at the same time can will that it become a universal law*" (G 4:421; cf. G 4:402); with its variant,
FLN   *Formula of the Law of Nature*: "So act, as if the maxim of your action were to become through your will a **universal law of nature**" (G 4:421; cf. 4:436).

Second formula:
FH   *Formula of Humanity as End in Itself*: "*So act that you use humanity, as much in your own person as in the person of every other, always at the same time as an end and never merely as a means*" (G 4:429; cf. 4:436).

Third formula:
FA   *Formula of Autonomy*: " . . . the idea *of the will of every rational being as a will giving universal law*" (G 4:431; cf. G 4:432), or "Not to choose

otherwise than so that the maxims of one's choice are at the same time comprehended with it in the same volition as universal law" (G 4:440; cf. 4:432, 434, 438), with its variant,

FRE   *Formula of the Realm of Ends:* "Act in accordance with maxims of a universally legislative member for a merely possible realm of ends" (G 4:439; cf. 4:433, 437, 438).

1. The Concept of a Categorical Imperative

Kant proposes to derive FUL, FH, and FA (as well as their "intuitive" variants, FLN and FRE) from the concept of a categorical imperative, which (he argues) is the form all properly moral principles must take. It is with this concept, therefore, that it makes sense to begin. Kant's theory of the will takes us to be agents who are self-directing in the sense that we have the capacity to step back from our natural desires, reflect on them, consider whether and how we should satisfy them, and to be moved by them only on the basis of such reflections. An inclination (that is, a habitual empirical desire, such as hunger) moves us to act only when we choose to set its object as an end for ourselves. This choice then sets us the task of selecting or devising a means to that end. If I see an apple in a tree and a desire to eat it occurs to me, then I will eat it only if I first decide to make eating it my *end*, and then devise a *means* (such as climbing the tree, or reaching for the apple with a stick) to achieve the end. Setting an end is the most basic normative act, because (Kant holds) there is no action without an end to be produced by it. This act involves the concept of an object (or state of affairs) to be produced and also the concept of some means needed to produce it. That is why instrumental reason is the lowest common denominator, so to speak, of all practical reason.

Setting an end thus subjects me to a normative principle commanding me to perform the action required as a means to the end. Kant calls this principle a "hypothetical imperative." It is called an 'imperative' because it is a command of reason requiring the agent to do something; it is "hypothetical" because the command governs our action only on the condition that we will the end in question. By contrast, an imperative that has no such condition would be called a 'categorical imperative.' Categorical imperatives are categorical because their validity is not conditional on some *prior* end. "If you make a promise, keep it" may be a "hypothetical imperative" in the grammatical sense, but it is not one in Kant's sense, because the "if"-clause does not refer to an end that conditions the validity of the imperative.

A moral imperative is *categorical* because its function is not to advise us how to reach some prior end of ours that is based on what we happen to want but instead to command us how to act irrespective of our wants or our contingent ends. Its rational bindingness is therefore not conditional on our setting any prior end. A moral rule or principle may very well be conditional in other ways without affecting its categorical status. The supreme principle of morality admits of no conditions or exceptions, of course, because there is nothing higher by reference to which conditions or exceptions could be justified. But a secondary moral rule or principle, whose bindingness on us, when it applies, is categorical, may admit of conditions. For instance, in the principle that we should keep our promises, there may be implied conditions that would release us from a promise, and under those conditions there is no categorical imperative to keep the promise. It is therefore an elementary misunderstanding to think that Kantian ethics is committed to a system of inflexible moral rules just because it regards moral imperatives as categorical imperatives.

Because every action aims at some end to be produced, actions that follow categorical imperatives do so too. Hence, the fact that categorical imperatives are not conditional on a prior end does not mean that the actions obeying them have no end. In fact, Kant thinks that categorical imperatives would be impossible if there were not some ends that are in their concept duties. According to Kant's Doctrine of Virtue, these ends fall under two general concepts: our own perfection and the happiness of others (MS6:385–8, cf. G 4:422–3). So it is also an elementary misunderstanding of the concept of a categorical imperative to think that because Kantian ethics grounds obligation on such imperatives, it has no concern for ends or (therefore) for the consequences of actions.

2. Kant's Systematic Presentation of the Principle of Morality

After developing his various formulations of the moral law, Kant informs us (G 4:436) that these formulas consider the concept of a categorical imperative from three different points of view: "form," "matter," and "complete determination." This triad is drawn from Kant's theory of concept formation. Every concept has a "form," provided by the understanding and by the role of the concept in judgments and rational inferences. It also has a "matter" or condition of cognitive application, consisting in a possible intuition through which an instance of the concept might be given in experience. Every concept also "determines" the subject to which it is applied as a predicate in a judgment. Following Leibniz, Wolff, and Baumgarten, Kant thinks that universal concepts (such as 'human') are universal because they are not "completely determined" – the concept 'human' is undetermined relative to such pairs of opposites as "male–female," "young–old," and many others. By contrast, a fully individual concept would have to be "completely determined" with respect to every pair of contradictories.

It is far from self-evident why Kant chooses this triad as his vehicle for systematizing the formulas of the moral principle. Clearly the elements of the triad themselves are being used in extended (or even metaphorical) senses. My conjecture is that Kant's choice is based on the idea that every concept is something universal that serves as a rule (KrV A81), because this property is shared by the moral law. Kant also compares the three formulas to the three categories of quantity: unity, plurality, and totality, claiming that there is a "development" between these formulas that parallels the generation of plurality out of unity and arrives at the concept of totality by combining the categories of unity and plurality: "*A progression happens here, as through the categories of the* unity of the form of the will (its universality), the *plurality* of the matter (the objects, i.e. the ends), and the *allness* or totality of the system of them" (*Groundwork* 4:436, cf. KrV A80/B106).[1] Thus when we read Kant's various formulations of the moral law in the *Groundwork*, we must not think that these are merely casual restatements of basically the same idea (which most readers tend to regard as having been definitively stated in FUL). We cannot understand Kant's formulation of the moral law until we see why he moves from one formula to the next, and we cannot make judgments about which formula to regard as primary (or primary for which purpose) until we understand the systematic development of the formulas presented in the Second Section. Kant says that all three are formulations of "precisely the same law," but they present the moral law from different sides, hence differ both "objectively," in what they command, and even more "subjectively," in the aspect of the law they present to the moral agent.

Kant claims that the three formulas also constitute a developmental progression. This strongly suggests, first, that we need *all* the formulas in order to have a complete account of the content of the supreme principle, and, second, that the later formulas FH and above all FA and FRE should be considered more complete and adequate statements of the law than FUL and FLN. As will appear below, I think these suggestions are correct.

(a) The First Formula: FUL and FLN

It is deplorably common to regard FUL and FLN (usually not clearly distinguished from each other) as the chief, if not the only, formulation of the moral law. Even some of Kant's most faithful defenders speak of them as 'The Categorical Imperative' (with capital letters) – as if there were no other, and no more adequate, formulations of the moral principle. That seems to me almost as misleading as giving the name "Newtonian Physics" to the law of inertia – as if there were nothing else to Newtonian mechanics besides the First Law of Motion. FUL represents only the first stage of a complex argument that takes about fifteen pages to develop and culminates in Kant's systematic presentation of the three main formulas of the moral law. It is the most provisional formula, the merely *formal* one, hence the least adequate to expressing the content of the principle.

"All maxims have, namely,

(1) a *form*, which consists in universality, and then the formula of the moral imperative is expressed thus: 'That the maxims must be chosen as if they are supposed to be valid as universal laws of nature';

(2) a *matter*, namely, an end, and then the formula says: 'that the rational being, as an end in accordance with its nature, hence as an end in itself, must serve for every maxim as a limiting condition of all merely relative and arbitrary ends';

(3) a *complete determination* of all maxims through that formula, namely: 'that all maxims ought to harmonize from one's own legislation into a possible realm of ends as a realm of nature'" (*G* 4:436)

FUL corresponds to the category of unity by bringing to expression the unity of form that maxims must have in order to be compatible with the moral law. By the 'form' of a categorical imperative, Kant appears to mean a formal property of maxims such that a maxim's having this property makes it consistent with all categorical imperatives (i.e., makes acting on it morally permissible). This formal property, according to FUL, is that the agent could, without contradiction or conflicting volitions, will the maxim to be a universal law; according to FLN, it is that the agent could, without contradiction or conflicting volitions, will the maxim to be a universal law of nature.

Testing maxims for universalizability. In FUL, therefore, the term "universal law" appears to be meant *normatively*. That is, the test is whether you could will it to be *permissible* (under the moral law) for everyone to act on the maxim. In FLN, the test is whether you could will that everyone actually follow the maxim with the regularity of a law of nature. Thus in the First Section, where Kant derives only FUL, he asks: "Would I be able to say that anyone may make an untruthful promise when he finds himself in embarrassment which he cannot get out of in any other way" (*Groundwork* 4:403). In the Second Section, where FLN is applied to the same maxim, the question is whether you could will that, as a law of nature, all rational beings actually make false promises when they find themselves in financial difficulty (G 4:422). The arguments in the First and Second Sections differ correspondingly. Readers have sometimes noted this difference but have more often seen it as an inconsistency on Kant's part than as a difference in argument that is required by the objective difference between FUL and FLN.

There are two universalizability tests: whether your maxim can be thought without contradiction as a universal law (or law of nature) and whether your maxim can without conflicting volitions be willed as a universal law (or law of nature).[2] There has been much dispute in the literature about how these tests are supposed to work. Too much of this dispute is due to fundamental misunderstandings of what is going on in the *Groundwork*, and in Kantian ethical theory, which prevail almost as often among Kant's defenders as among his critics. The universalizability tests, namely, are supposed to constitute a universal moral criterion, a so-called "CI-Procedure," that is applicable to any conceivable maxim that might be proposed. It is supposed to be a method for grounding all moral duties, or even for "constructing" the content of all morality. FUL and FLN are often thought to constitute

Kant's chief (or perhaps his only significant) contribution to moral philosophy.

On the basis of these thoughts, and with the dominant (Sidgwickian) model of moral theory as the implicit background, FUL and FLN, or various (ever more creative and epicyclical) interpretations of them, are treated as candidate principles within the now fashionable agenda in moral philosophy that seeks to justify moral principles by showing that they square with our moral intuitions about real or imaginary cases. The interpretation has to make the test "come out right" even when applied to the most ravishingly ingenious maxims devised as counterexamples. The fate of Kantian ethics is even seen as turning on the success or failure of this enterprise.

In the previous chapter, we saw how that enterprise is alien to Kant's whole project, and therefore how utterly irrelevant to it would be the "success" or "failure" of Kantian ethics (as Kant conceives it) to provide an interpretation of FUL or FLN that might fit our intuitions about all cases. Kant does not propose these formulas as ways of systematizing moral intuitions. They are not grounded on any consilience of our moral intuitions but derived from the concept of a categorical imperative, and the argument that there is such an imperative, which also involves no appeal to moral intuitions, is presented in the Third Section of the *Groundwork*.

Kant's use of the universalizability tests. The four famous examples are intended not as confirmations of FLN but only as heuristic aids to the reader, illustrating how the more intuitive variant of the first, most abstract formula of the moral law might yield results that correspond to some moral duties we already recognize. Kant's universalizability tests are only tests of the permissibility or impermissibility of particular maxims. They therefore cannot possibly be ways of *deducing* the positive duties chosen to illustrate them. Because they rule out only one maxim at a time, they can never show that a *kind* of action that is contrary to duty (such as committing suicide, or making a promise you don't intend to keep) could not be permissible if performed on some other maxim.[3]

After presenting his four examples, Kant says "one must be able to will that a maxim of our action should become a universal law: this is the canon of the moral judgment of this action in general" (G 4:424). It might be natural to take this as saying that FUL (or FLN) is to be used on every possible occasion to tell us what we ought to do, or at least to decide whether the maxims we propose to ourselves are permissible. But I think it is not clear that this is Kant's intention. First, because he has yet to introduce any other formulas, it seems premature to decide that he is picking out FUL or FLN as the "canon of moral judgment" as opposed to them. Second, a "canon" for Kant is not necessarily a strict criterion. Canons are "universal rules that serve as foundations of sciences" (VL 9:77), but they often take the form of "proverbs, mottoes, or aphorisms" (VL 24:738), "the most commonly used expressions in popular judgments of the understanding and reason" (VL 24:868). *There is no basis to take Kant as saying that any formula of the moral law is be used as a strict criterion in some rigorous deductive procedure for deciding, in all cases, what we should do or even what it is permissible to do.*

The universalizability tests are in any case quite ill suited to serve as permissibility tests for any and every conceivable maxim. The tests they propose, so employed (or rather, so misemployed), are notoriously subject to both false negatives and false positives. The false negatives are morally permissible maxims that do not violate moral laws but also could not themselves serve as universal laws. (Example: "I will give a larger percentage of my income to charity than the average person does.") An infallible recipe for producing a false positive is to formulate a maxim involving a kind of action that we know is contrary to duty but is presented in the maxim in such specific terms that even if the maxim were a universal law (or a law of nature), that law would foreseeably have no instances except the present (intuitively immoral) action. In that case, it could be no more difficult for the agent to will the maxim as a universal law than to will this action itself, and so any argument from the universalizability test would either be circular or its result inconclusive. Confronted with these cases, self-appointed Kantians desperately seek ever more creative interpretations of Kant's test in a passionate effort (as they see it) to save Kantian ethics from oblivion.[4]

If we look at Kant's own use of FLN in his four famous examples (G 4:421–3), we see that whatever shortcomings there may be in his discussion, his approach is carefully limited in a way that avoids both problems just mentioned. Kant begins: "Now we will enumerate some duties, in accordance with their usual division into duties toward ourselves and toward other human beings, and into perfect and imperfect duties." Two things here are crucial: First, Kant chooses these examples because he takes them to be unproblematic illustrations of duties his audience would already recognize (some of them, especially the suicide example, may not seem so unproblematic to us, but that should not distort our understanding of what he is trying to do). Second, the maxims he goes on to formulate are chosen because they are supposed to be clear or even typical examples of maxims on which someone might violate (or be tempted to violate) these duties. From this it follows, first, that because we are considering only maxims that are assumed *already recognized to violate determinate duties*, there can be no occasion for us to consider any of the maxims that generate the problem of false negatives. Second, because the maxims he considers represent *typical* examples of maxims on which someone might be tempted to violate the recognized duty in question, this more or less guarantees that the problem of false positives will also be avoided, because the maxim is specifically formulated as to represent a determinate contrary of the moral principle behind the duty in question, a principle we already accept. Although some of the now familiar worries about the general applicability of FLN had already been expressed in his own day, Kant never bothered to reply to them.[5] I suggest that a correct understanding of his aims shows why he regarded them as beneath his notice.

If we read Kant with the assumption that FUL and FLN are candidate principles to be tested against our moral intuitions about any conceivable maxim, then these restrictions will look like mere evasions: Kant will be accused of taking up only examples where the principle "works" and excluding all the cases where it may not. But suppose we look for a moment at Kant's illustrations of FLN in light of his real intention – namely, to show how some of what we already recognize as duties can be seen to conform to the spirit of the first, poorest, and most abstract formulation he has derived from the concept of a categorical imperative, on the way to other and more adequate formulations. Then we can see that these examples are quite reasonable ways of fulfilling his aims (which do not include providing us with a general test for the permissibility of maxims, much less a universal decision procedure for morality). The chief aim is to show us that when we violate a duty, we are typically trying to make for ourselves an exception to some moral principle that we will to hold universally for all rational agents. Kant even says this explicitly right after his discussion of the examples:

> Now if we attend to ourselves in every transgression of a duty, then we find that we do not actually will that our maxim should become a universal law, for that is impossible for us, but rather will that its opposite should remain a law generally; yet we take the liberty of making an exception for ourselves, or (even only for this once) for the advantage of our inclination. (G 4:424)

If readers of the *Groundwork* tend to overlook this passage and what it says about Kant's principal motivation for presenting the examples, they often fasten tenaciously on two other promissory notes he issues, treating them as definitive of the ethical theory for which he is laying the ground: *First*, Kant says it "clearly meets the eye" that the four duties enumerated here, and others besides (note that he *never* makes the claim for *all* duties), "are derived" from the Formula of the Law of Nature (G 4:423–4).[6] *Second*, he declares that "one easily sees" that all maxims violating perfect duties fail the contradiction in conception test (G 4:424). In these remarks, Kant is often taken at his word, without one's asking whether what he says is true or whether it corresponds at all to his actual attempts to develop a moral theory in the *Metaphysics of Morals*, and a conception of Kantian ethics congeals according to which FUL or FLN (again, usually not distinguished from each other) is treated as "*The* Categorical Imperative" from which everything else is to be deduced (or as presenting us with a "CI-Procedure" from which all ethical truth is to be "constructed").

But let's face it: Neither of these claims is the least bit *obvious*. The first claim might conceivably be *true*, but only if we employ an extremely loose conception of what it is for a duty to "be derived from" the formula of a principle. We should beware here of importing conceptions of "derivation" – involving strict deductions of precise practical conclusions – drawn from now standard models of ethical theory. Perhaps by identifying a tempting policy of action we know we should avoid, Kant's illustrations do provide insight into some ways our actions are subject to constraints we recognize as the duties in question. If I am right in conjecturing that the relation of the moral law to the duties falling under it is not a rigorous deductive procedure but rather something like an act of interpretation, then Kant's claim becomes more plausible. Perhaps this is all the "derivation" from FUL or FLN that these duties admit. In any case, Kant later derives the same duties – more successfully, I think – from FH as well.

We have already seen that the universalizability tests actually give us at most permissibility tests for certain individual maxims that violate determinate duties we already recognize. Therefore no positive duties at all (to do or to omit any general kinds of actions) could ever be directly deduced from them. Note too that Kant never claims *to have derived* these four duties from FLN, only to have made it obvious *that* they "are derived" from it (in some as yet unspecified sense of that phrase, with the "derivation" itself apparently having occurred elsewhere, or being deferred to some other occasion). The contents of the *Metaphysics of Morals* belie the claim that Kant provides any sort of derivation from FLN of even these four duties, much less of his entire system of duties.

If the first of the two claims seems extremely doubtful, the second, contrary to what Kant says, seems plainly *false*. As Barbara Herman has pointed out, the maxim of "convenience killing" – "I will kill other human beings whenever that is a safe and effective way of promoting my own self-interest" – is quite thinkable as a universal law of nature, even if we could not will it to be one.[7] But the duty not to kill another is surely a perfect duty if any is. Even if Kant's claim were true, a set of generalizations about the maxims that violate various kinds of duty would not directly provide any principle for deriving (or even taxonomizing) the duties themselves. In short, neither of these statements is as obvious as Kant takes it to be, and because at the time Kant wrote the *Groundwork* he had yet to attempt anything like a derivation of duties from any formulation of the supreme principle, he was in no position to make either of them. I think too many people allow these two overconfident and unsupported remarks to determine their reading of Kant's entire ethical theory.

(b) The Second Formula: FH
One of the most common objections to Kantian ethics is that it is too "formalistic," that its moral principle misguidedly attempts to dispense with all substantive values. A corresponding objection is made to the very concept of a categorical imperative – such a concept, some argue, is unintelligible

because it is the notion of a principle that we ought to obey just because we ought, a principle we could in principle have no reason or motive to obey. Those who bring this objection almost never notice that Kant's second formula is specifically motivated by the question to which they think he can have no answer and that it provides a very direct (and I think more than satisfactory) answer to that question. Kant begins his exposition of the moral principle by considering it from the side of "form," but then he proceeds to consider the principle from the side of its "matter" – by which Kant means the objective *end* that motivates obedience to it (G 4:436). Traditionally, the end of an action is taken to be some object or state of affairs that is to be brought about by the action. Kant follows tradition in holding that every action must have an end of that kind. But if this were the end that motivated obedience to a categorical imperative, then the bindingness of the imperative would be conditional on our having set that end – and that would render the imperative only hypothetical. Therefore, he concludes that the end that grounds a categorical imperative must be a different kind of end, an objective end, for which Kant uses the term "end in itself." It will be the business of the next chapter to examine what kind of end that is, and of Chapter 9 to look at the system of duties Kant derives largely by appeal to FH.

(c) The Third Formula: FA and FRE

Kant has now derived two distinct formulas of the supreme principle of morality, both from the concept of a categorical imperative. The first was derived from the concept of the general form of a maxim that is compatible with this kind of imperative. The second was derived from the concept of the kind of substantive value (or end) that could provide a rational ground or motive for a rational agent to follow a categorical imperative. Kant's next step is to combine the two ideas behind these two distinct lines of argument in order to derive a third formula:

The ground of all practical legislation, namely, lies *objectively in the rule* and the form of universality, which makes it capable of being a law (at least a law of nature) (in accordance with the first principle), but *subjectively* it lies in the *end*; but the subject of all ends is every rational being as an end in itself (in accordance with the second principle): from this now follows the third practical principle of the will, as the supreme condition of its harmony with universal practical reason, the idea of the *will of every rational being as a will giving universal law.* (G 4:431)

The third formula combines the conception of a law valid universally for all rational beings (in FUL) with the conception of every rational nature as having absolute worth as an end in itself (FH), to get the idea of the will of every rational being as the source of a universally valid legislation (FA). FA does not "follow" *deductively* from FUL and FH but results when we combine the conception of a universally valid law (from FUL) with that of the objective worth of the rational will (from FH), which can therefore consider itself not only as subject to such a law but also, at least ideally, when it adopts the maxims it should adopt in accordance with the law, as giving the law to itself. Kant provides us with another version of this same argument a little later, when he says:

The practical necessity of acting in accordance with this principle, i.e. duty, does not rest at all on feelings, impulses, or inclinations, but merely on the relation of rational beings to one another, in which the will of one rational being must always at the same time be considered as *universally legislative*, because otherwise the rational being could not think of the other rational beings as ends in themselves. Reason thus refers every maxim of the will as universally legislative to every other will and also to every action toward itself, and this not for the sake of any other practical motive or future advantage, but from the idea of the dignity of a rational being that obeys no law except that which at the same time it gives itself. (G 4:434)

Here it is clear that we regard every rational will (not merely our own) as universally legislative – legislative for all rational beings – and for this we must also consider other wills as legislative for us because otherwise we could not think of them as ends in themselves. At the same time, however, we do not regard the law as grounded in ends or interests originating outside it, or our obedience to it as grounded in something else besides it that we will (which would render the law heteronomous). Instead, we assert the absolute worth or *dignity* of every rational will, equally our own and that of other rational beings, because in obeying the objectively valid moral law, that will regards itself as at the same time giving that law (G 4:434, 435).

The term "idea" used in Kant's formulation of FA is especially important (and is used several times in this passage: twice initially at G 4:431, twice again at G 4:432, and once more at G 4:434, perhaps again at G 4:439 cf. also G 4:409). An "idea" is a concept of reason to which no empirical object can ever correspond but which we use regulatively in arranging our cognitions in a system (KrV A312–20/B368–77, A642–704/B670–732). To regard the legislator of the moral law as the *idea* of the will of every rational being is precisely *not* to say that the law is given by your arbitrary, fallible, and corruptible will or mine.

Therefore, it is *not* any subjective "act of legislation" on *anyone's* part that grounds the validity of the moral law. Rather, the law is a practically necessary command of practical reason, grounded not in any being's volitions but absolutely, in the nature of things, independently of how any being should choose to look at the matter. It binds us not because we have willed it, but through the objective value or absolute worth of rational nature that grounds it. (We will further explore this point – which gives the lie to currently fashionable readings of Kantian ethics – in the next two chapters, especially in Chapter 6.) We may consider the law as having been legislated by each of us, however, but only insofar as our will corresponds to a pure rational concept (or idea) of what it ought to be (but always falls short of being in our actions and maxims that do not conform to law).

From this we may also infer that for a Kantian, any conception we have of our duties or principles of duty, including the moral law itself, must always be merely provisional, unless it too is supposed to represent an idea whose application to our actions is never more than a fallible approximation. This rules out the possibility that we might ever have in our possession any formula or procedure from which we could derive what we ought to do. In other words, it rules out even the possibility of what FUL and FLN are often thought to be.

I suggest that a Kantian should think of any formulation of the supreme principle of morality (including all of Kant's own formulations) as provisional expressions of a principle to the conception of which we limited and fallible rational beings must always aspire. We may treat these formulations as placeholders, so to speak, for something we will always be on the way to comprehending more perfectly. We *can* treat the moral law this way because, as I argued in the previous chapter, no formulation of it is ever to be used directly to specify what we are to do, or even directly to formulate the rules or duties through which, by moral judgment, we decide what to do. Any expression of the supreme principle of morality is merely our best attempt so far to articulate the ultimate ground of all these rules or duties.

Different ways of stating FA. Perhaps just because it is the formula in which the other two are combined or summed up, FA is stated in a variety of different ways: "Do not choose otherwise than so that the maxims of one's choice are at the same time comprehended with it in the same volition as universal law" (*G* 4:440). Or again: "Act in accordance with maxims that can at the same time have themselves as universal laws of nature for their object" (*G* 4:437).

In many of its formulations, FA sounds superficially like FUL (or FLN), but in fact it makes a much stronger demand on maxims and yields much stronger conclusions about what we ought to do. Whereas FUL and FLN provide only a permissibility test for maxims taken one by one – consisting in its being *possible* (without contradiction or conflicting volitions) for you to will some maxim as a universal law – FA tells you *positively to follow* just those maxims (that is, that collective *system* of maxims) which *actually contain in themselves the rational volition* that they should be universal laws – and therefore, under the idea of every rational being as universally legislative, *actually are universal laws*. A maxim might pass the purely negative test that there is no contradiction in thinking, or conflicting volition in willing it to be a universal law, without belonging to the system of moral laws or containing in itself the volition that it should *be* a universal law. The criterion for legislative maxims proposed in FA is significantly stronger than that for merely permissible maxims given in FUL or FLN.

Yet in fact FA does not pretend to offer us any *test at all* to discriminate
between maxims that have this rationally legislative property and maxims
that do not. Hence Kant's moral principle, in its most definitive form, simply
isn't about having nifty little tests or procedures ready to hand for telling
ourselves what to do under any imaginable circumstances. My best attempt
to say what FA is about is that it tells us to think of ourselves as members of
an ideal community of rational beings, in which each of us should strive to
obey the moral principles by which we would choose that members of the
community should ideally govern their conduct. What it gives us is a spirit in
which to think about how to act and not a procedure for deducing actions
or principles to act on. As I have already said, Kantian ethics denies there
could ever be such a procedure.

   The realm of ends. Just as Kant earlier provided a more "intuitive" version
of FUL in the form of FLN, so here he also provides a more intuitive variant
of FA, FRE. FRE provides a new characterization of the system of legislation
referred to in FA by describing the nature of the community of rational
beings that is to result from it. It calls this community a "realm of ends" (*Reich
der Zwecke*). By a 'realm' Kant means "a systematic combination of various
rational beings through communal laws," or again, "a whole of all ends in
systematic connection" (*G* 4:433). The term 'realm of ends' is therefore
used in two senses: It is either a community made up of rational beings or a
certain relationship between all the ends set by the beings that are members
of such a community.

   The terms Kant uses most often to express the relationship between the
rational beings that are members of a realm of ends are "system" (*System*) and
"combination" (*Verbindung*). At the end of the *Anthropology*, Kant describes
historical progress as "the progressive organization of citizens of the earth in
and to the species as one system, cosmopolitically combined" (VA 7:333) –
in other words, true human progress is progress toward a realm of ends. A
collection of *ends* constitutes a "realm" if these ends are not in conflict or
competition with one another but are combined into a mutually supporting
system. The *laws* of a realm of ends are those that, if followed, would combine
the ends of rational beings (both the rational beings themselves as existent
ends, according to FH, and the ends set in the maxims chosen by those
rational beings) into a mutually supporting harmony. FRE commands us to
follow maxims involving ends that belong to this system, and it forbids us to
adopt ends that would stand in the way of it. Ends that are neither required
for nor incompatible with the system are permissible.

   Kant thinks there are two main modes of human conduct that illustrate
what it is to act according to the idea of a realm of ends. One is the idea
of friendship, in which the happiness of both friends is "swallowed up" in
a common end that includes the good of both (MS 6:469–73, cf. VE
27:426–9). The other is the idea of the religious community (or free ethical
commonwealth), which for Kant should be bound together not by creeds
or scriptural traditions but by the shared pursuit of the highest good as

a common end (R 6:98–109). The all too prevalent characterization of Kantian ethics as "individualistic" usually involves overlooking FRE or failing to understand its implications.

FRE commands us to avoid all patterns of end setting that involve fundamentally competitive relations between ourselves and other rational beings. It forbids us to relate to others in any way that involves the frustration of any person's deepest ends. Conflict or competition between human ends is compatible with FRE only if it is in service of a deeper systematic unity among all human ends – a system, combination, or community in which no member of the realm of ends is left out. (A later formulation of the same idea was: "An association in which the free development of each is the condition for the free development of all."[8])

The moral law commands us, in other words, to seek the welfare of ourselves and others only on the condition that it can be united with the common welfare of all. If this means obtaining less total welfare than could be gotten by permitting fundamental conflicts between the ends of different rational beings, then less than maximal welfare belongs to the end that the moral law commands us to seek. If, as seems obvious, too much inequality between people – in power, wealth, or social status – is incompatible with their pursuit of common ends, then Kantian ethics implies that that limiting human inequality should always take priority over maximizing human welfare.

John Rawls is well known for contrasting Kantian with utilitarian ethics by claiming that utilitarianism does not take seriously enough the differences between persons (Rawls, TJ 27). This way of looking at the contrast makes Kantian ethics appear "individualistic" by comparison with utilitarianism, though this is highly misleading. A better way to look at the contrast is to point out that Kantian ethics places a higher priority on human community – it values the conditions of rational cooperation among persons, and their sharing of common ends, more than it does the aggregate welfare of individuals considered in isolation. Hence, the point that Kantian ethics really has in mind in taking seriously the differences between persons is that this is necessary in order to develop a conception of ethical norms based on a true idea of human community (instead of reducing the common deliberation of different people to the deliberation of a single individual agent). In this way, it is utilitarianism that is "individualistic" and only Kantian ethics that truly places human community at the foundation of ethics. It is not often appreciated that Rawls sees the contrast this way too (see Rawls, TJ 564–5).[9]

3. Relations among the Formulas

FA is arrived at by combining FUL with FH – that is, combining the idea of universal law with the value of the rational will, representing the latter as suitable for giving the law. Immediately after deriving FH in this way, Kant then writes: "The three ways mentioned of representing the principle of morality are, however, fundamentally only so many formulas of precisely the same law, one of which from itself unites the other two in itself (*deren die eine die anderen zwei von selbst in sich vereinigt*)" (G 4:436). This is often mistranslated as saying that *each* of the formulas unites the other two in itself. But it is only about FA that Kant ever explicitly claims that it unites the other two in itself. No such claim is ever made on behalf of FUL or FH. The idea that FA alone combines the other two formulas is also suggested by Kant's analogy with the categories of quantity, where he thinks of the concept of totality as combining the concepts of unity and plurality.[10] Consequently, FA has a privileged status among the three formulas: It is the one formula that sums up the two others. It is also, appropriately enough, the formula Kant uses to *establish* the moral law in the Third Section of the *Groundwork*.

The issue of "equivalence." How do the three (or five) formulas relate to one another in achieving Kant's aim of seeking and establishing the supreme principle of morality? As we observed earlier, in *Groundwork* 4:436 Kant presents the three formulas as a "system," organized by the triad "form," "matter," and "complete determination." A system is a whole composed of heterogeneous parts that complement one another. A whole whose parts are essentially homogeneous or interchangeable could not constitute a system. Hence if the three main formulas of the moral law constitute a system, that implies that they complement one another and hence, although they are mutually consistent, that they also differ significantly in content. Contrary to this implication, however, it is deplorably common in the literature to find ascribed to Kant the claim that the three formulas of the moral law are "equivalent." When we look at the text, however, we find him saying nothing of the kind. We find instead the following:

The three ways mentioned of representing the principle of morality are, however, fundamentally only so many formulas of precisely the same law, one of which from itself unites the other two in itself [*deren die eine die anderen zwei von selbst in sich vereinigt*]. Nonetheless, there is a variety among them, which is to be sure more subjectively than objectively practical, namely, that of bringing an idea of reason nearer to intuition (in accordance with a certain analogy) and, through this, nearer to feeling. (*G* 4:436)

Three claims are made here:

1. The three formulas are only so many formulas of "precisely the same law."
2. One of them unites the other two in itself.
3. There is a variety among them, which, however, is more subjectively than objectively practical. (G 4:436)

(1), taken all by itself, might be compatible with the claim that the formulas are equivalent, but it certainly does not assert it. The three formulas of the moral law represent three different approaches to precisely the same law. That implies that they are not inconsistent with one another, but it does not preclude differences in content between them. Two or more nonequivalent assertions might be taken as statements of the very same proposition, especially if it is also claimed that one of them combines two others and that they represent different approaches to that common proposition. For example, two signs posted in an Oxford college courtyard, one saying "Keep off the grass," the other "Walk on the path," would normally be considered two formulations of the very same injunction, even though the posted commands are not equivalent.

(2) appears to support the claim that the three formulas are equivalent only if it is mistranslated. Correctly translated, it draws a distinction in content between the single formula that unites the others in itself and the two provisional (one-sided but mutually complementary) formulas that are united in that formula.

(3) is a flat denial of the equivalence of the formulas. It asserts that there is a *difference* among them in *objective practical content*, though it also implies that this difference is not great and it emphasizes that the subjective difference between the formulas is greater than the objective difference. I submit that the chief objective difference between the formulas is that the first formula (FUL and FLN) is more abstract and poorer in content than the others, because it provides only formal tests of permissibility, provides no ground for determinate duties, and says nothing about the end of moral legislation or the ground of its authority.

However, I think even the *question* of whether the formulas are "equivalent" may already be based on a serious misunderstanding. This question suggests – what is false – that each of the formulas has, all by itself, a set of practical consequences that is determinate enough that we can compare them and decide whether they are the same or different. The question conjures up the picture that if you put one of the formulas together with all the truths holding in every possible world, then that formula divides all possible actions for each world into neat sets of the obligatory, the forbidden, and the permissible. To say that the three formulas are "equivalent" would then mean that the extension of the three sets is exactly the same for each of the three formulas. The same conclusion follows given the common mistranslation of (2), because you could deduce each formula from any other (or maybe from each of the other two taken jointly).

The entire question of "equivalence," however, seems to presuppose the conception of moral theory on which the moral status of any act is supposed to be deducible directly from a moral principle (together with the relevant facts). If, however, moral theory is conceived as Kant and Mill conceive it, then the application of the supreme principle of morality is not a deductive procedure (from a principle and a set of facts) but results instead in a set of moral rules or duties (which are not deduced from the principle). These rules require determinate actions or omissions only when applied to empirical situations through acts of judgment whose decisions are not deductively derivable from them. For instance, the maxim of making a deceitful promise to avoid financial embarrassment is wrong because it does not treat the rational nature of the person deceived as an end in itself (G 4:429–30). It seems plain enough that such a policy has that meaning, but it is not deducible from the principle together with a set of factual claims about acts of deceit. Nor does the duty in question involve a specification of the conditions under which it applies (as Kant says explicitly in the case of the duty not to commit suicide, G 4:429).

Thus even if the three formulas are all the best possible statements of the fundamental principle of morality, there is no determinate fact, prior to such an interpretive application to specific duties and the application of these through judgment, about how any of the formulas partitions possible actions into obligatory, forbidden, and permissible. *A fortiori*, in Kantian ethics there is no sense to the question of whether the formulas are "equivalent" in the sense of entailing the same extensions of forbidden, permitted, and obligatory actions. The closest you could come to claiming their "equivalence" would be to say that they do not contradict one another and that in applying them, one should interpret each in light of the others.

4. The "Universal Formula"

In presenting the formulas systematically, Kant chooses the more "intuitive" variants of the first and third formulas (FLN and FRE) over the more abstract ones. He does this, he says, because "if one wants to obtain access for the moral law, then it is very useful to take one and the same action through the three named concepts and, as far as may be done, to bring the action nearer to intuition" (G 4:436–7). "However, one does better in moral judging always to proceed in accordance with the strict method and take as a ground the universal formula of the categorical imperative: '*Act in accordance with that maxim which can at the same time make itself into universal law*'" (G 4:436–7).

The main point Kant is making here is that the way of thinking (closer to "intuition") that does best at animating human hearts and actions on behalf of morality is not the same as the way of thinking that does best when it comes time to pass critical judgment either on the actions we have performed or on the maxims we are proposing to adopt. For this latter task, a more austere and abstract principle is better because, corrupt human nature being what it is, the same feelings and intuitions that make us enthusiastic friends of virtue also make us more susceptible to self-deception and more likely to pass off corrupt actions and maxims to ourselves as morally commendable ones. In short, Kant is saying that moral sentimentalists get things exactly wrong when they suppose that moral purity is to be found in what satisfies the heart but not the head.

But what are we to make of Kant's identification of a "universal formula"? How is *this* formula supposed to relate to the three formulas he has already arrived at? A closer look reveals that the formula he uses here is very close in its wording to the supposedly definitive formulations of the law that Kant provides in the *Critique of Practical Reason* and the *Metaphysics of Morals*.

FU   "*Universal Formula*": *Act in accordance with that maxim which can at the same time make itself into a universal law* (G 4:436–7).

Compare:

FK   "So act that the maxim of your action could always at the same time hold as a principle of universal legislation" (KpV 5:30) and

FM   "Act upon a maxim that can also hold as a universal law" (MS 6:225).

In an article in *Mind* written more than sixty years ago, Klaus Reich made the interesting suggestion that this universal formula is none of the three (or five) "particular" formulas derived so far but is a distinct sixth formula.[11] Above I have followed Reich provisionally by stating this formula separately as "FU." But this only raises the question of where this new formula is supposed to have come from, and in what way it is more "universal" than the formulas that have already been derived and explained. Surely it is most natural to suppose, as the most common interpretation does, that FU is one of the formulas already derived. The question is: Which one?

Most scholars have concluded – almost without thinking, often as though it were just something Kant had explicitly said – that the "universal formula" is FUL.[12] This conclusion admittedly consorts well with the equally common view that FUL (and the associated universalizability tests) constitutes "the Categorical Imperative" – or even "the CI-procedure" for "constructing" the content of morality.[13] The thoughtless identification of FU with FUL may further be prompted by a failure to perceive the significant differences there are between Kant's different formulas, and also the failure to notice that there is even a question about how they fit together systematically. FUL is simply the only Kantian formula people pay much attention to; it sounds similar enough to FLN and to FA that it might seem to stand for them as well. How FU relates to FH and FRE, which admittedly don't sound much like FUL, may remain vague in their minds, but any worries on this score are quickly put to sleep by incanting the assertion, almost universal in the literature, that the formulas are all "equivalent" anyway. So obviously FUL seems the only possible candidate for FU. But once we look more closely at the text in light of a clearer understanding of the differences among the formulas, this obvious thought is seen to have little or no plausibility. It is supported neither by the presentation of the formula in the text, nor by the overall argument of the Second Section, nor even by what FU itself says. All three considerations point to the identification of FU with FA.

First, the "universal formula" occurs in the same paragraph devoted to FRE, which is the more "intuitive" version of FA, while FA is the more austere version of the same formula, hence the one Kant is saying we should use for moral judgment. Second, FA is the formula that combines the other two in itself, and in that sense it is already the universal formula in which the search for the supreme principle of morality has culminated. Third, there is simply what the "universal formula" *says*: It tells us to act on that maxim which can *make itself* into a universal law. If a maxim "can make itself into a universal law" by "containing in itself the volition that it should be a universal law," then this yields the equivalence of the "universal formula" to FA in several of its verbal formulations. A similar look at the wording of FK and FM shows that they are also best understood as versions of FA. For if "being able to hold" as universal law is the same as being able to "make itself into a universal law," then FK and FM say the same thing as FU, and all three say the same thing as FA. Finally, and for good measure, FK in the *Critique of Practical Reason* is said reciprocally to imply freedom of the will (KpV 5:28–30); FA is the only formula in the *Groundwork* about which this claim is made (*G* 4:446–9). That is yet another reason to think that FU must be FA and cannot be any other formula.

5

Humanity

In Kantian ethics, the fundamental value is humanity or rational nature as an end in itself. This value grounds the supreme principle of morality from the side of its matter and results in the moral law's second formulation (FH). In the most complete or universal formula of the moral law, FA, this value is developed into the ground of moral legislation itself, in the form of the dignity of rational nature as universally legislative. This chapter tries to explain the nature of this fundamental value and look at Kant's defense of the claim that rational nature has such a value. It concludes with a discussion of the possibly controversial moral status of some human beings or forms of human life, and of nonhuman animals.

1. What Is an End in Itself?

An existent or "self-standing" end. Rational nature is described as an end – an end in itself. Kant calls it a "self-sufficient," "independent," or "self-standing" (*selbständig*) end, in contrast to an "end to be produced" (G 4:437). It is an end in the sense of something *for the sake of which* we act. This is not a technical or "funny" sense of 'end'. It is simply the most basic and encompassing sense of the word. Rational nature is *not* an end, however, in another (more derivative) sense in which Kant also thinks that every action must have an end. In the claim that rational nature is an end in itself, rational nature is not being thought of a state of affairs to be produced by action. Instead, an "end in itself" is something already existing whose value grounds even our pursuit of the ends produced by our actions. The notion that the word "end" may refer only to such a producible state of affairs is simply a philosophical error about the concept "end."

Every moral action must have an end to be produced, but such actions must be grounded on a "self-standing" end. This is a direct consequence of the fact that this value is to motivate obedience to a categorical imperative – a principle that rationally constrains us without presupposing any end to be produced. The value for whose sake we follow a categorical imperative cannot be the value of any end to be produced. From this Kant infers that it must be the value of something already existing whose value is fundamental and unconditional.

As was mentioned in Chapter 4, critics of Kantian ethics sometimes complain that the concept of a categorical imperative makes no sense because there could be no reason for obeying such an imperative. This is usually because they think that the only reason for obeying an imperative must be an end in the sense of an end to be produced. They do not notice that Kant's concept of an objective end in itself is precisely his answer to their question. The conceptual features of an end in itself that we have noted follow simply from the fact that it must provide the rational motive for obedience to a categorical imperative. If there are categorical imperatives, Kant reasons, then there must be a reason for obeying them, and such a reason can consist only in something that is an end in itself.

An objective end. In order to ground a categorical imperative, the end in itself must have another distinctive property: It must be *objective* – that is, valid for all rational beings irrespective of their inclinations. Acting for its sake must constrain rational volition without presupposing or depending on any contingent empirical desire of the willing being. This does not mean that action on it must be action from which desire is absent. Rather, in accordance with the end in itself, pure reason of itself produces desires – desires for the ends to be produced that are set in accordance with the objective value of the end in itself.

'Respect' is the name for the proper attitude toward any objective value.[1] Depending on the nature of such a value, it may call for widely varied kinds of conduct. Some objective values are to be promoted, while others are to be exemplified, appreciated, or honored, or simply not violated. Sometimes the maximal promotion of a value involves its violation, so priorities among these different kinds of conduct sometimes matter. We saw in Chapter 3 that cases can arise where the promotion of a value might come into conflict with the exemplification of the same value (as when being tolerant might require us to permit someone to preach intolerance). An ethical theory that considers only the consequences of actions for the promotion of values will sometimes go far wrong if it countenances the violation of the very value promoted.

To say that we act for the sake of something already existing does not mean that we act for the sake of *bringing about* its existence or *preserving* its existence. For that existence is merely another *state of affairs*, another possible end to be produced (which would mean that the moral imperative is hypothetical after all). If it is normally a requirement of morality that we should seek to preserve rational beings in their existence, then this is a *consequence* of the fact that if an existent being has basic and unconditional value, then the state of affairs of its continued existence also has great value, at least most of the time. But from the fact that humanity or rational nature has dignity, or fundamental and unconditional value, it by no means follows that the value of human *life* is basic or unconditional. At times people are in terrible situations where living up to the dignity of their rational nature even requires them to sacrifice their continued existence. There may also be situations in which moral rules grounded on the worth of rational nature as end in itself require that human beings be killed, or even entail that the continuation of a human life should no longer be set as an end at all. FH, as a formula of the supreme principle of morality, is consistent with all these possibilities and cannot all by itself determine how often or how seldom they will occur. For better or worse, Kantian principles (rightly understood) justify attaching great importance to preserving human life, at least most of the time, but they provide no support for the idea that, as some people like to put it, "all human life is sacred."[2]

Treating a being as an end in itself means respecting the value of what makes it such an end. After we see that this value resides in rational nature, we see it implies that, at least in general, rational beings should not be subjected to deception or coercion. Instead, we should seek to harmonize our strivings with those of other rational beings toward their ends. FH thus naturally leads toward the ideal of FRE, in which the ends of all rational beings would ideally constitute a systematic combination or "realm."

"Not merely as a means." Much is sometimes made of Kant's claim that we must treat humanity as an end, *never merely as a means. Far too much*, in fact. One fallacious pattern of reasoning begins with the proposition that a person is being treated as a means and concludes merely from this that they are not being treated as an end in itself. But it is possible to treat persons as ends in themselves and also as means, as long as you respect their rights and dignity. This is not only possible, but Kantian ethics positively enjoins it. FRE tells us to obey the laws of a realm of ends. A *realm* is a combination of rational beings whose ends harmonize and all of whose actions serve as means to a systematic combination of ends. In a realm of ends, every rational being would therefore be treated as an end in itself and at the same time as a means to this system of shared ends.

It is also fallacious to infer solely from the fact that someone is not being treated merely as a means to the conclusion that they are being treated as they ought to be under FH. In sympathetic depictions of the abominable American institution of slavery, some white masters (such as the genteel Ashley Wilkes in *Gone with the Wind*) are shown caring about the welfare of their black slaves, which shows that they did not treat them *merely* as means. These supposedly exemplary masters, for all their evangelical Christian benevolence, nevertheless fail monstrously to treat their slaves as ends in themselves. Kant himself makes a similar observation about the lame excuses offered by a feudal landlord who treats his serfs with paternalistic benignity (MS 6:454).

2. Humanity Is an End in Itself

If there is to be a categorical imperative, then something must be an existent, objective end in itself. The question is: What? Kant's claim is that the sole end in itself is "humanity" or rational nature in persons. What is meant here by 'humanity'?

Humanity as a predisposition. According to Kant, our nature has three fundamental "predispositions" (*Anlagen*): animality, humanity, and personality (R 6:26). Animality contains our instinctual capacities for the survival of the individual and the species: "mechanical" (prerational) self-love (self-preservation), sexuality (preservation of the species), and the social drive – our instinctual need to be in community with other human beings. Humanity contains our rational capacity to set ends and devise means to them, and our rational self-love, giving us grounds for forming a conception of our happiness and pursuing it. Personality is our rational capacity to legislate for ourselves the moral law and obey it.

Sometimes Kant distinguishes within "humanity" between two different predispositions: the *technical* predisposition to devise means to arbitrarily selected ends, and the *pragmatic* predisposition to rational self-love, which specifically involves our sociability as rational beings (VA 7:322–4). It includes the ability to use *other human beings* as means to our ends (placing this means–ends relationship in a different category from the technical one involving the use of things) and also our capacity for culture or self-perfection, the development of new ways of thinking and modes of life, which again Kant treats as different from a merely technical relationship to skills or instrumental mechanisms). The technical and pragmatic predispositions, of course, correspond to technical (instrumental) and pragmatic (prudential) rationality, and personality corresponds to moral rationality, as we distinguished the three norms of reason in Chapter 1, §4.

It is noteworthy that what Kant claims to be an end in itself, possessing the absolute objective worth that grounds our obedience to moral laws, is *humanity* – especially in this last (pragmatic) sense. It is not animality or even the technical (instrumental) rationality that has this value. Nor (perhaps more surprisingly) is it our *moral* predisposition (though Kant holds that it is that predisposition which gives us *dignity*). The absolute worth that grounds morality is the predisposition toward prudence (rational self-love and the end of our own happiness), rational social interaction, and the cultivation of ourselves and all our faculties through society in the course of human history.

Arguments for an ultimate value. Kant's arguments for the bold thesis that humanity is an end in itself are terse and obscure. The claim that rational nature in persons has this status, however, exercises a powerful influence on modern moral thinking not only in philosophy but even in ordinary life and in moral common sense. We may have to face the fact that the mere *claim* that human beings have absolute worth as ends in themselves may in the end be more compelling all by itself than any argument that Kant or anyone else could ever offer for it. But for a proponent of the kind of ethical theory sought by Kant or Mill, this fact can never be satisfactory all by itself to justify a basic value.

As I mentioned in Chapter 3, Kant's task at this point is similar to (though obviously not the same as) the task J. S. Mill sets himself in *Utilitarianism*, where he proposes to show that happiness is desirable and even the only thing desirable for its own sake. I have always thought that Mill's argumentative strategy, and at least crucial parts of his argument, is defensible against the common criticisms. Kant's conclusion goes deeper than Mill's, enabling us to explain, in a way that Mill cannot, *why* happiness is rationally desirable. But I think both philosophers do about as well as it is possible to do in arguing for an ultimate value.

According to Mill, the only argument to which claims about ultimate value are susceptible is one that shows this value to be one we already acknowledge both in theory and in practice (Mill p. 35). The strategy of such an argument is to cite what we do, and what we must represent ourselves as thinking and doing, when we form preferences, set ends, and make decisions, and then to argue that these actions, thoughts, and representations are best understood as recognizing something as an ultimate value. The phrase "best understood" should not be taken as claiming there are no logically possible alternative understandings – to claim that would be to set an impossibly high standard for this kind of argument – but only as the claim that ascribing to ourselves this judgment of ultimate value is the most reasonable way of understanding what we are doing and thinking.

Perhaps, therefore, no argument about ultimate value can be expected to convince everyone – there are simply too many possible views about what is ultimately valuable, and too many clever philosophers too firmly attached to their own peculiar notions to expect that even a clearly more reasonable interpretation of their conduct will be able to convince them. (It should also be admitted, however, for pretty much the same reason, that no philosophical argument about *anything* can be expected to convince *everyone*.) But it helps when that claim of ultimate value is one that many people, perhaps even most people, are prepared to accept even without argument. If, in addition to this, the argument shows that this claim about ultimate value is a reasonable interpretation of what we are committed to in our thinking and doing, then it has done everything we should ever expect of it.

Kant has begun his argument already in the same spirit, by presenting moral obligation as grounded on categorical imperatives, and then showing that we can be motivated to obey a categorical imperative only if there is something that is an objective end in itself. He proceeds by eliminating some candidates for what the end in itself might be. He first argues that the objects of our inclinations cannot be objective ends in themselves because their value is subjective and conditional on our having these inclinations.

About our inclinations ourselves Kant makes a claim that shocks many people: He says that inclinations are so far from being ends in themselves that we rightly regard them as a burden, and it would be rational to wish ourselves entirely free of them (G 4:428). This is a position he often associates with the ancient Cynic school in ethics (VE 27:248, 29:604), which he regards as the least plausible of the ancient schools. We capture Kant's real views here if we expand what he says a little: "Our inclinations themselves are so little of absolute worth, to be wished for in themselves, that there was even an influential school of ancient ethics that taught that the best means to happiness was to be entirely rid of them." This does not mean that Kant actually agrees with the Cynic view: In later writings he says it would be not only irrational but even immoral to wish to be rid of our natural inclinations (R 6:57–8). What Kant needs to show here does not require his coming anywhere near agreement with the Cynics. He needs only to claim that we do not regard any of our inclinations as objects of respect or as objectively and unconditionally valuable independently of the possible rational value of their objects. And this much seems obvious. Finally, Kant invokes the distinction between things and persons, claiming that only the latter, not the former, are ends in themselves (G 4:428). This supports Kant's claim only by suggesting – quite reasonably, I think – that it might be the best explanation for this distinction and the practical use we make of it.

The worth of humanity as a necessary presupposition of rational volition. Kant then presents his principal argument that rational nature is the end in itself:

The human being necessarily represents his own existence [as an end in itself]; thus to that extent [FH] is a *subjective* principle of human actions. But every other rational being also represents his existence in this way consequent on just the same rational ground as is valid also for me; thus it is at the same time an objective principle from which, as supreme practical ground, all laws of the will must be able to be derived. (G 4:429)

What does Kant mean in claiming that *every* human being *necessarily* represents his own existence as an end in itself? He cannot possibly mean that, as a matter of contingent empirical fact, all people actually assent to the proposition that their own existence is an end in itself, in the abstract and somewhat technical sense in which Kant has just introduced the notion of an "end in itself." Most people probably never even entertain that proposition. Nor could that contingent empirical claim possibly be one he is making, because his assertion is that human beings *necessarily* represent their existence in this way. When he says that FH is to that extent "a subjective principle of human *actions*," it is more reasonable to interpret him as meaning that there is something in the way that people act, and think about their action, which *necessitates* (or commits them to) representing their own existence as an end in itself. The question is: What could that be?

Kant holds that the most basic act through which people exercise their practical rationality is that of setting an end (G 4:437). To set an end is, analytically, to subject yourself to the hypothetical imperative that you should take the necessary means to the end you have set (G 4:417). This is the claim that you rationally ought to do something whether or not you are at the moment inclined to do it. It represents the action of applying that means as *good* (G 4:414) – in the sense of "good" that Kant explicates as: what is required by reason independently of inclination (G 4:413). Kant correctly infers that any being which sets itself ends is committed to regarding its end as good in this sense, and also to regarding the goodness of its end as what also makes application of the means good – that is, rationally required independently of any inclination to apply it. The act of setting an end, therefore, must be taken as committing you to represent some other act (the act of applying the means) as good.

In doing all this, however, the rational being must also necessarily regard its own rational capacities as authoritative for what is good in general. For it treats these capacities as capable of determining which ends are good, and at the same time as grounding the goodness of the means taken toward those good ends. But to regard one's capacities in this way is also to take a certain attitude toward *oneself* as the being that has and exercises those capacities. It is to *esteem* oneself – and also to esteem the correct exercise of one's rational capacities in determining what is good both as an end and as a means to it. One's other capacities, such as those needed to perform the action that is good as a means, are also regarded as good as means. But that capacity through which we can represent the very idea of something as good both as end and as means is not represented merely as the object of a contingent inclination, nor is it represented as good only as a means. It must be esteemed as unconditionally good, as an end in itself.

To find this value in oneself is not at all the same as thinking of oneself as *a good person*. Even those who misuse their rational capacities are committed to esteeming themselves as possessing rational nature. It also does not imply that a more intelligent person (in that sense, more "rational") is "better" than a less intelligent one. The self-esteem involved in setting an end applies to any being capable of setting an end at all, irrespective of the cleverness or even the morality of the end setting. Kant's argument supports the conclusion, to which he adheres with admirable consistency throughout his writings, that all rational beings, clever or stupid, even good or evil, have equal (absolute) worth as ends in themselves. For Kantian ethics the rational nature in every person is an end in itself whether the person is morally good or bad.

Kant's argument also does not involve saying (as Korsgaard wants to) that setting an end *confers* value on the end.[3] On the contrary, setting an end is an exercise of *practical reason* only to the extent that we think there is already *some good reason* for us to set that end. The value of the end is to be located in that reason, which must have existed already prior to our rational choice. Of course, if it is true that the sole fundamental and unconditional value is the value of rational nature as an end in itself, then the goodness of any other end must somehow be grounded in this value. Ends to be produced will usually have value, for instance, because they fulfill the needs, or enrich the lives, or contribute to the flourishing and the happiness of rational beings, and so setting and achieving these ends shows respect and concern for the value of those rational beings. But to hold that the worth of other goods is derivative from or dependent on the worth of rational nature in this way is not at all the same as saying that they have their goodness *conferred* on them by the choices of rational beings. On the contrary, we choose these other goods because they fulfill our needs or contribute to our happiness. It is not the case that our choosing them *brings it about* that they fulfill our needs or make us happy. Still less should we say, as Korsgaard also has, that rational beings *confer on themselves* the value of being ends in themselves.[4] Kant's claim, as I understand it, is that we necessarily regard rational nature as an end in itself *objectively* and *unconditionally*. Its being an end in itself could therefore not be contingent on any act of ours through which that value might be conferred. Rather, the argument is that it is our basic act as rational beings, the act of setting ends and regarding them as good, that necessitates our representing ourselves as *already* ends in themselves.

Generalizing to all rational beings. The next step in Kant's argument is to claim that every other rational being represents its existence as an end in itself through the same rational ground that is valid for me. Hence FH is not merely a subjective principle but also an objective principle. Not only my rational nature, but the rational nature in every person, is an end in itself. This inference seems correct if the rational ground for regarding myself as an end in itself is the capacity to set ends. For that capacity does belong to every rational being as such, to others as well, and, once again, to stupid and wicked people exactly as much as to clever and virtuous ones.

To this claim, however, Kant appends a curious footnote, saying that it is set forth here as a "postulate," the grounds for which will be given in the next section. It is not immediately clear, however, what grounds in the Third Section Kant has in mind, or even what claim Kant is saying is being presented for now as a postulate. My best guess is that Kant's provisional "postulate" is that my representation of myself as an end in itself is based on a *rational ground* – that is, that it is not merely a contingent fancy or cobweb of my brain. For in the Third Section grounds for this are presented, in the form of the freedom of the will, which (Kant argues) is presupposed by practical reason and even by theoretical reason (G 4:447–8).[5] If that conjecture is right, then the argument here in the Second Section is that if there is such a ground (which turns out later to be freedom of the will and is for the moment merely postulated), then it must hold equally for all rational agents, who are therefore all equally ends in themselves.

It also makes sense to consider this claim a "postulate" in something like the Euclidean sense, where the Greek word for 'postulate' (*aitema*) means request. A postulate involves a request to perform an action (e.g., drawing a straight line between two points) and then also a request to grant some proposition on the basis of that action (e.g., that between any two points such a line can be drawn). At this point in the *Groundwork*, the requested action is that of setting an end, where this involves treating the end and the necessary means as good; and the proposition to be granted is that this action presupposes that there is a rational ground for regarding yourself, as a being having a capacity to do all this, as having unconditional and objective value as an end in itself.

Limits of the argument. Kant's argument does not work by showing that rational beings *are* ends in themselves but only by showing that in setting ends according to reason, *we must presuppose* that they are. But the argument also does not show that there is *no conceivable alternative* to representing one-self – and therefore every other rational being as well – as an end in itself. The setting of ends and the use of means to them might be understood, for example, not as a rational process but as a merely mechanical causal one, as Kant thinks it actually is in the instinctive teleology found in the behavior of nonrational animals. Or the representation of something as an end might be taken as a merely theoretical act of perceiving the goodness of an object, a passive state that would move us of itself, rather than an act of rational judgment carrying with it a practical authority for us that is worthy of esteem as an end in itself. No doubt there are still other alternative conceptions of our agency that philosophers might devise that do not support the commitment to represent one's rational nature as an end in itself.

Kant's argument, therefore, cannot and need not rest on the claim that all these alternatives to his interpretation of rational action can be conclusively refuted. It involves only the claim that his interpretation is more natural and reasonable than they are. I also think that so understood, Kant's argument does as much as can possibly be required of any argument purporting to establish a claim about what has ultimate value. In philosophy, as Aristotle wisely tells us, we must not apply the wrong standards to a subject matter (Aristotle 1094b25). This also means we must not expect more of a claim, or an argument for it, than is reasonable. When we ask the impossible, ignoring an argument's real but necessarily limited accomplishments, we will find the argument unsatisfactory, but that is our fault, and not a defect in the argument.

3. The Dignity of Humanity

In combining FUL with FH and advancing to FA, Kant makes a further claim
about the moral status of rational nature in persons: He claims that it has
"dignity" (*Würde*). The traditional meaning of this term involved identifying
certain classes of people possessing a determinate social status that makes
them superior to others. We have now perhaps become accustomed to Kant's
extension of the term to all human beings, but we should not fail to hear
in the phrase Kant's defiant and paradoxically egalitarian assertion that the
highest possible worth any human being can have consists in a value that all
human beings have equally – whether well born or ill born, rich or poor, intelligent or stupid, even good or evil. This radical egalitarianism, grounded in
the conception of every human being as a rationally self-governing agent, is
the most fundamental idea in Kantian ethics. The potential of this Kantian
idea to transform our relations with one another is still pitifully far from
being realized, or its implications even properly thought out consistently.

Dignity and price. That which has a "price" may be rationally sacrificed or
traded away for something else whose price is equal or greater. That which
has *dignity*, however, has a value that may not be rationally traded away or
sacrificed, not even for something else that has dignity (G 4:434). In that
sense, its value is *absolute*.[6] One conclusion that immediately follows from this
is that respecting the dignity of one person cannot ultimately conflict with
respecting the dignity of another. Thus the ends involved cannot ultimately
conflict but must constitute a systematic combination or realm. This leads
us from FA to its more intuitive variant FRE.

If being an *end in itself* constitutes the worth of *humanity* – in the technical
Kantian sense, which is the capacity to set ends according to reason – then
having *dignity* constitutes the worth of *personality* – which is the capacity to
give oneself moral laws and obey them. Kant nevertheless frequently speaks
of the "dignity of humanity" as well as the dignity of personality. Kant usually writes as if humanity and personality are necessarily coextensive.[7] I think
they *are* necessarily coextensive. For setting ends according to reason is an
act of freedom – involving at least freedom in the negative sense, because
no impulse or inclination can necessitate my setting its object as an end
(MS 6:381). But Kant holds that the concept of positive freedom, the capacity of giving oneself laws and having a reason that is of itself practical, flows
from that of negative freedom, as constituting the essence of negative freedom (G 4:446, KpV 5:33); conversely, the capacity of positive freedom clearly
entails the capacity to set ends according to reason.

Kantian ethics rests on a single fundamental value – the dignity or absolute worth of rational nature, as giving moral laws and as setting rational
ends. The fundamentally valuable thing in the universe is a rational being,
a person – or, more precisely, rational nature in a person. The demands
made on us by this value depend on the kinds of conduct required to show

respect for this value. Other things having objective value have it, in one way or another, on the ground of this basic value. For example, it grounds the value of human happiness, and also of the perfection of talents people choose to develop. Some things that people rationally choose to make their ends acquire greater objective value because they rationally choose them. If you choose to develop one talent rather than another, then others have a reason to help you develop the chosen talent that would not exist but for your choice. Yet this example represents only a special case, and even here you could *rationally* choose to develop your talent only if you recognized it as already having some objective value (as the perfection of a rational being), which your choice could not possibly have been conferred on it. The idea that any objective value could be simply *conferred* by human choice is nonsense – it contradicts the very concept of objective value.

4. The Personhood of Human Beings

Who are persons? I have claimed that in holding rational nature to be an end in itself, and to have dignity, Kantian ethics articulates an idea that is widely appealing and fundamental to modern moral consciousness. But in the precise form I have just expressed it, this idea might also be seen as having certain consequences that are paradoxical, if not objectionable. The idea seems to grant fundamental moral status solely to *persons* – that is, to rational beings who are capable of instrumental, of prudential, and above all of moral reason, and who are morally responsible for what they do. (Let's call such beings persons *in the strict sense.*) It might be thought that other beings, such as children who are not yet persons in the strict sense, or even nonrational animals, also have moral status, a claim on moral concern, even certain rights. Don't children have the same rights to life and equal concern as adults? Don't we have moral reasons to concern ourselves with the welfare of nonrational beings, such as animals? Mustn't that status rest on some value independent of the rational nature in persons?

Kantian ethics must answer the last question in the negative, but it answers the other two in the affirmative. I think the right account of the moral status of nonrational living things and of human beings who lack personality in the strict sense can best be derived from Kantian principles, even though Kant himself did not worry about these questions as much as he should have, and some of the things he said about them do not seem to me entirely cogent, or to be the best account available to him.

Let us begin with the moral status of children or other human beings who at least temporarily lack the rational capacities constituting personality in the strict sense. In discussing family right, Kant declares that children are persons and treats them as having pretty much the same status as adults (though he would not grant them the right to direct their own understanding unaided by an adult guardian until they reach the stage of life at which they are capable of this). Kant does not grant them the capacity to set ends according to reason or regard them as morally responsible for their actions, yet he never explains why for most purposes they should be treated as persons.

"Unity of the person." One approach to this topic relies on what its proponents like to call the "unity of the person."[8] They claim in effect that a human being is the same being at all stages of its existence, including those in which it is not yet (or no longer, or temporarily not) a person in the strict sense, and the Kantian view should be that such a being has the same moral status (the same rights, etc.) at all stages of its existence. The idea that every human being has the same moral status at all stages of its existence is an intuitively appealing one. The question is, Can it be defended? Of course this approach would seem to imply that not only children but also fetuses and embryos should count as persons in the strict sense, because an embryo is, on many accounts at least of the metaphysics of the situation, numerically identical with the mature human being it might become. Some proponents of this approach welcome that consequence, while others resist it.

But the entire "unity of the person" view, at least in the context of Kantian ethics, faces a fundamental difficulty: On Kantian grounds, no being can be considered a person in the strict sense at all unless it is at some stage of its existence a fully rational and morally responsible being (because rational and responsible agency are what its personality consists in). Yet not all children (much less all embryos and fetuses) ever reach that stage, and so it follows that they never do in fact become persons. Therefore on the "unity of the person" view, there seems no justification, on Kantian grounds, for saying that they are *ever* persons (at any stage of their history). This view seems committed to saying that a child who dies before it reaches maturity *never was a person.* We are required to say in retrospect that such a child *never had the status or rights of a person.*

Worse yet, it follows that we can never know about a newborn infant (not to mention a fetus or an embryo) whether it ever will be a person; its moral status seems, on this view, to be shrouded in uncertainty, or at best only presumptive rather than actual. Still worse than that, it follows on the "unity of the person" view that one could prevent an embryo, fetus, or even an immature child from ever becoming a person at all simply by killing it before it ever achieves personhood in the strict sense. And there would seem to be no possible moral objection to doing that, because the being in question never was and never will be a person. No proponent of the "unity of the person" view would welcome *that* conclusion.

Persons in the strict and the extended sense. I think Kantian ethics must therefore reject the "unity of the person" account. A more consistent Kantian approach is based on the idea that we can treat, or fail to treat, rational nature as an end in itself not only in the person of a rational being in the strict sense but also in the way we treat other beings who are not persons in the strict sense. For instance, it would surely show disrespect for rational nature not to further its development to maturity in a child in whom it has already begun to develop. The same is true if we did not care about the recovery of rational nature by an adult who has temporarily ceased to be a person in the strict sense because of injury, disease, or some other incapacitation.

Thus in order properly to respect rational nature, we are required to treat some beings who are not persons in the strict sense in certain respects just exactly as if they were persons in the strict sense. Or, to put it another way, we are required to accord, at least for certain purposes, a status equivalent to personhood to some beings that simply are not persons in the strict sense. For instance, we should treat small children as having a right not to be killed, to have their well-being looked after, and their development toward maturity cared for. I propose that we apply the term *persons in the extended sense* to beings that are not persons in the strict sense but that should be granted a moral status (in the relevant respects) exactly like that of beings that are persons in the strict sense.

Persons in the extended sense do not have precisely the same moral status as persons in the strict sense. But they do not have a *lesser* status. If they lack the rational capacities to direct their own lives without guidance from others, then they cannot have the same right to direct their lives that persons in the strict sense have. We are permitted (even required) to behave paternalistically toward them, as we are not toward persons in the strict sense (MS 6:454). For the same reason, they are not held responsible for their actions in the ways that persons in the strict sense are.

Here we must also face up to the fact that who counts as a person in the extended sense is something that must be determined by those of us who are persons in the strict sense. For it is only persons in the strict sense who have the capacity to decide such questions, and they also bear the full responsibility for deciding them. Of course, that determination must be made for good and objective reasons. Persons in the strict sense may not simply satisfy their own desires or promote their own interests when there are good grounds for doing otherwise. Thus persons in the extended sense – once we have determined how far this status should extend – have just the same right not to be killed as persons in the strict sense, and we have the same obligations to consider their interests and treat them as ends in themselves that we have toward persons in the strict sense. In fact, precisely because they are *not* fully rational and self-governing beings that are competent to look after their own welfare, that welfare arguably has claims on our concern that should sometimes take priority over the welfare of beings that are persons in the strict sense – though not a claim that could encroach on the right of persons in the strict sense freely to direct their own lives.

The limits of personhood. The obvious question at this point is: Exactly at what stages of human life should beings be regarded as persons in the extended sense? The answer to this question, as I have framed it, depends on how far our conduct in treating the human beings in question expresses due respect for the dignity of rational nature and how far it falls short of this or violates the dignity of humanity. It is relevant to the right answer to such questions not only how we are acting toward rational nature in our treatment of human beings who are not persons in the strict sense, but also whether in our conduct we duly respect this value in those who are persons in the strict sense.

For example, consider the question of whether a fetus, like an infant, is to be regarded as a person in the extended sense. That question should turn not only on whether our conduct duly respects the value of the (still merely potential) personhood (in the strict sense) of the fetus, but also on whether it duly respects the dignity of actual persons in the strict sense – in particular, the dignity of the person in whose body the fetus is developing. If that person is forced to bear a child she does not want, or if her right to control the life processes going on in her body is coercively restricted by others (as by either forcing her to have an abortion or by denying her one), then their conduct expresses extreme disrespect for the right of rational nature in her person. Regarding the question of whether an embryo *in vitro* is a person in the extended sense, that should turn on whether, in order to treat it as a person, some woman would have to be coerced into having the embryo implanted in her uterus and then compelled to carry it to term. Clearly if she would, then the embryo should not be judged a person in the extended sense.

I conclude that if granting to embryos or fetuses the same "right to life" that is thought to belong to persons in the extended sense would involve such coercive or invasive conduct, then it would constitute gross disrespect to rational nature to grant them that status. (Part of my reason for giving this answer is social and historical, having to do with the way human cultures have traditionally treated women, and how we should be trying to treat them now. I will return to this issue in Chapter 13, §2.)

The Kantian position, as I interpret it, should be that there is certainly some value in the potential personhood of an embryo or a fetus – or, I would equally say, of an unfertilized ovum, though not necessarily exactly the same value as that of an embryo or fetus. None of these entities has the sort of value that pertains to persons in the extended sense (carrying with it, for example, a coercively enforceable right not to be killed or destroyed). Generally speaking, and subject to modification in borderline or problem cases – the dividing line between a person in the extended sense and a nonperson whose life still has some value should be drawn at birth. The reason is this: Prior to birth there is no way of granting the status of personhood in the extended sense to the being without violating the right of persons in the strict sense, whereas after birth there is at least in principle the possibility of doing this.[9]

Kant's own statements. We might wonder what Kant's own position is on the personhood of a fetus or embryo. Of course he never distinguishes, as I have, between persons in the strict sense and persons in the extended sense. In fact he has all too little to say about such issues at all. Kant asserts, without any explicit argument, that even small children are persons, even that "the offspring is a person," and the parental duty to care for the offspring "follows from conception [or procreation] (*aus der Zeugung*)" (MS 6:280).[10] Kant declares in the same passage that it is "impossible to form a concept of the production of a being endowed with freedom through a physical operation" (MS 6:280). It appears he does not think the issue of when personhood begins can be settled directly by empirical inquiry. He even denies that the question of when personhood begins is properly conceptualizable empirically in biological terms.[11] But Kant does claim that "it is a necessary idea to regard the act of conception [or procreation] as one by which we have brought a person into the world without his consent and on our own initiative, for which deed the parents incur an obligation to make their child content with his condition as far as they can" (MS 6:280).

Of course it is one thing to say that parents should be thought of as bringing a person into being, and even that they have duties of care to their offspring from conception. It is quite a different thing to say that the offspring is a *person* from conception onward. The first two things Kant does appear to say; the third is something he never quite says.

There are passages in which Kant might be thought to be addressing issues about the personhood of fetuses or embryos at least indirectly. In the course of his condemnation of suicide as violation of a duty to oneself, he asserts that when a pregnant woman commits suicide, she is guilty of murdering her unborn child as well as of murdering herself (MS 6:422). On the other hand, in the course of discussing whether an unmarried mother who kills her infant to avoid dishonor is guilty of murder, Kant offers the argument (it is not clear how far he endorses it) that because an illegitimate child has come into being under conditions other than those recognized by the state, the state is not required to acknowledge its existence, or, therefore, to regard the causing of its death as the violation of anyone's rights (MS 6:336). The first passage seems to treat a fetus as a person, and by implication, abortion as murder; the second seems to claim that infanticide (much less abortion) is not murder when committed by an unwed mother to preserve her honor.

In both passages, however, the argument is being driven by quite another agenda than the question of the personhood of a fetus. In the first passage, Kant is concerned to press a controversial point that is part of his general theory of the imputability of consequences, namely that someone who does wrong is responsible for all the bad consequences of his wrongdoing, whether foreseeable or not. So he wants to heap up bad consequences as much as he can. In the second passage, he is trying to diagnose a conundrum that arises when unenlightened social attitudes – here, attitudes toward unwed motherhood – force an individual to choose between taking a life and totally sacrificing honor; he wants to explain why we are reluctant to treat such homicides simply as cases of murder. In both cases, the local agenda probably drives him to assume for the moment certain views about the personhood of the unborn that he may or may not actually embrace. For this reason, I do not think that any determinate view on this issue can be reliably ascribed to Kant, even on the basis of the passages in which he seems to be discussing it at least indirectly. Even if Kant had stated an unambiguous position on the personhood of embryos or fetuses, the task of Kantian ethics would not be to follow his errors blindly but rather to consider what Kantian principles really imply and to interpret them correctly.

Some who advocate the "unity of the person" approach, as well as some non-Kantians, have expressed discomfort with the distinction between persons in the strict sense and persons in the extended sense. If they fear that the distinction involves granting a lower moral status to persons in the extended sense than to persons in the strict sense, then the response is that the whole point of the approach is precisely *not* to do that. Persons in the extended sense have the same *dignity* as persons in the strict sense.

What often really bothers them, however, is the whole thought that moral status or personhood is tied to some property other than membership in the human species, some property that not all members of this species possess. As I see it, however, that thought is simply the inevitable result of requiring a *reason* for granting human beings the status of persons. For it is self-evident that membership in some biological species can never by itself constitute such a reason. (Peter Singer's objections to "speciesism" are obviously correct, at least to that extent.) To hold that we should regard all humans as persons because they are members of *our* species seems no better than regarding as persons only those who share our nationality or religion or skin color. To argue that certain entities are persons because they are members of a rational species, when they are not in fact rational beings, makes no more sense than arguing that children are already human adults because they belong to a species whose mature members are human adults. The right reply to such an argument is: You simply can't get there from here, at least not using that road.

If, however, we have a good reason for holding that human beings should have the moral status of persons, then that reason will have to consist in some property other than their simply being a member of our species, and whatever property it is (whether rational nature or something else), some members of the human species will possibly not have it. Thus those who do have it will be persons in the strict sense, and questions will inevitably arise about whether, why, and in what respects we should grant a like status to humans who do not have that property (thus invoking some concept like personhood in the extended sense). I conclude that discomfort with the distinction between persons in the strict sense and persons in the extended sense must display either a stubborn refusal even to ask for a reason why human beings should have the moral status of persons or else the unthinking acceptance of a patently unsatisfactory reason.

5. The Moral Status of Nonrational Animals

Kant supposed (as most of us still do) that human beings are the only creatures on earth that have the capacity to set ends according to reason, devise means to them, form a conception of their own general well-being or happiness, and regard themselves as legislators as well as subjects of moral laws. But he thought there were probably finite rational beings on other planets (ANG 1:349–68, VA 7:331), and it is still possible that we may find such beings (though the likelihood now seems far lower than it pleased people to think it was even a generation ago). Some people now think that the mental capacities of the higher primates or other mammals essentially qualify them as rational beings. If empirical research were to support such claims, then Kantian ethics should be the first to accept them and modify accordingly the system of moral rules and duties. There would still be the same questions, however, about how to treat other living beings who clearly do not share in rational nature, but do share in life, sentience, purposiveness, caring, or other substructures, fragments, and analogues of rational nature.

The approach taken here to the way Kantian ethics should regard the treatment of nonrational living things is along the same lines as above: We should ask whether our conduct toward them shows due respect for the dignity of rational nature. Yet it might seem *prima facie* as though our conduct toward beings that are not and never could be persons in the strict sense could show neither respect nor disrespect for the dignity of the rational nature – and therefore that this Kantian approach could say exactly nothing about how we would treat nonrational living things. But I claim this is not so. For the life of many nonrational living things actually shares many features with that of persons in the strict sense; and the way we treat that life, regarding these features, can and must be interpreted as expressing either respect or contempt for rational nature. I do not think that any nonrational living thing should ever be accorded the status of a person in the extended sense. Yet Kantian morality does, it seems to me, forbid certain kinds of conduct toward such beings and justifies, or even requires, some positive concern for their welfare.

"Can they suffer?" Jeremy Bentham famously said, regarding nonhuman animals: "The question is not, Can they reason? Nor Can they talk? But, Can they suffer?"[12] This is usually understood as a rejection of the Kantian position on such questions. For as a hedonist, Bentham apparently bases moral status not on the dignity of rational nature but rather solely on the capacity to feel pleasure and pain. And this is clearly different from the Kantian position. Yet I claim that Bentham's idea here is in general terms not inconsistent with Kantian ethics but is instead a corollary of the Kantian position. I would even claim that Kantian ethics provides a better justification for it than Bentham's hedonism – a shallow empiricist doctrine that cannot account properly even for the values it assigns to pleasure and pain in human beings.[13]

The happiness of human beings is an end of morality because setting this end shows respect for rational nature. Nonhuman animals, like human persons both in the strict and the extended sense, have desires, preferences, and a capacity for pleasure and pain. In these respects, they are like human beings, and their desires, preferences, and sensibilities are even analogous to the rational capacities of humans in the way they direct the behavior of the animals. Therefore, all other things being equal, when we frustrate the desires or preferences of persons (both in the strict and extended sense) or when we cause them suffering or fail to promote their welfare, we show disrespect for their rational nature (actual or potential). Likewise, when we wantonly or maliciously frustrate the desires and preferences of nonrational animals, or cause them pain, we act in a manner analogous to the way we act when we show disrespect for the rational nature of persons. The capacities of animals can be said to belong to rational nature as parts, or necessary conditions, or as its infrastructure, so to speak. Our conduct toward these animals can therefore be approved or condemned by Kantian ethics based on what it expresses toward the value of rational nature, even though non-human animals never actually possess in themselves the full capacities of rational nature that make a being into a person in the strict sense.

Nonhuman animals do not have the capacity to reason or to talk. Therefore, beyond making the obvious point that they are not persons in the strict sense, whether they have or lack these capacities is irrelevant to how we should treat them. Bentham is therefore correct in telling us not to ask about these matters when we are deciding how to treat animals. What is relevant, because it relates their capacities to those of rational nature, is the fact that they can suffer, and desire, and sometimes also care – about members of their own species, or even occasionally about members of other species, such as humans. Bentham is therefore also correct in telling us what we should ask about these capacities, for they are the relevant ones. Bentham is correct, however, not because Kant is wrong, but because Kant is right.

It would be a gross misunderstanding to take what I have been saying as the endorsement of some principle to the effect that we must place value (or equal value) on anything and everything that could be regarded as a part, or necessary condition, infrastructural element, or analogue of rational nature.[14] There are surely many such things – some physical or chemical prerequisites of life, for example – that we can obviously treat as having little or no value without showing any disrespect for rational nature. Some animals possess the capacity to care (about their young, about other members of their species, or even about human beings). This capacity is clearly a larger and much more immediate component of rational nature than the mere capacity to show a preference for moving in one direction rather than in another (as an insect does) or even the capacity to feel pleasure and pain. Hence, from a Kantian standpoint there is reason to be concerned more about animals that are capable of caring about others than about animals that are not. The relevant judgments here are hermeneutical or interpretive in nature. Such judgments are notoriously not derivable by strict deductions from general principles. Rather, the right way to look at the matter is that for Kantian ethics the way we arrive at conclusions about determinate moral rules, for the treatment of persons or anything else, is that these are the results of interpreting the supreme principle of morality – here, in the form of FH. The capacity to care about others is also a *human* capacity that belongs to human beings (such as small children, or Alzheimer's patients) who do not have the full capacities of rational action that make normal human adults persons in the strict sense.[15]

There are important factual questions that seem also to involve questions of interpretation, concerning to what degree some of the higher mammals – chimpanzees, for example, or dolphins – share in fragments of the capacity we conceptualize as human rationality. It is controversial, for instance, whether chimpanzees have a sense of "self," and to what extent the sense of themselves that they may have involves participation in the capacities for which we should value human beings. It is an interpretive judgment that we should protect the external freedom of a person in the strict sense to govern his or her life; that we should treat children, but not fetuses or embryos, as persons in the extended sense – that is, beings with the same right to life and concern for their welfare as persons in the strict sense; and that we should treat nonhuman living things – the higher mammals, for instance – as beings whose health, desires, and contentment matter to us, even though they are not persons in either the strict or the extended sense.

Kant on the treatment of animals. What I have just said about the treatment of nonhuman animals appears to differ significantly from what Kant himself says in the *Metaphysics of Morals* and elsewhere. Kant thinks the notion that we have duties to nonhuman animals results from an "amphiboly in moral concepts of reflection," where a duty to ourselves appears to us as a duty to beings other than ourselves (MS 6:442). Kant thinks that we have a duty to ourselves to display the moral perfection of kindness toward the suffering of sentient beings and avoid the moral imperfection of callousness or cruelty to them. Not fulfilling these duties, he argues, will corrupt our dispositions toward other people and their happiness or suffering. This doesn't look like the account I have just given. But the differences between my account and Kant's are not as great as they may at first appear.

It is important that Kant does *not* treat our duty regarding animals as a duty to others – as though he thought we should develop habits of kindness rather than cruelty toward animals merely for the benefit of the humans toward which we can be expected subsequently to display these traits. Rather, he regards the virtues of kindness and gratitude toward animals as in themselves perfections of our character and the vices of callousness and cruelty toward them as in themselves failings or imperfections. As I understand Kantian principles, this means that kindness toward animals itself complies with duties whose principle is treating rational nature as an end in itself, and callousness and cruelty violate duties based on the same principle. For this reason, the arguments he uses presuppose something like the account I have derived from Kantian principles.

There are also remarks in Kant's lectures that suggest something like this account. Animals, he says, are "analogues of humanity," and this is why we have duties that are also "analogues" to our duties to human beings. "If a dog, for example, has served his master long and faithfully, that is an analogue of merit, hence I must reward it, and once the dog can serve no longer, I must look after him to the end" (VE 27:459; cf. VE 27:710).

If the acts of animals arise out of the same *principium* from which human actions spring, and the animal actions are analogues of this, we have duties to animals in that we thereby promote the cause of humanity... The more we devote ourselves to observing animals and their behavior, the more we love them, on seeing how greatly they care for their young; in such a context, we cannot even contemplate cruelty to a wolf. (VE 27:459)

Kant's use of the term "analogy" here also suggests his theory of analogical or symbolic language, in which words are used that do not signify something directly but indicate it indirectly by employing a procedure of the understanding that is like that through which it might be directly signified (P 4:356–60; VpR 28:1023; KU 5:351–4). We have duties in regard to animals because their behavior and their needs have, in relation to the worth of rational nature, a significance that is similar in certain respects to the behavior and needs of rational beings. Consequently, we have duties of a comparable significance, based not directly on their animal nature but on the worth of humanity, to which the animals, their life processes, and behavior are "analogues."

Kant's own more specific views about how animals are to be treated seem to me generally sensible and decent (if not particularly remarkable). Kant thinks it is permissible to kill animals for human ends (such as for food); but he insists that this should be done as quickly and painlessly as possible (MS 6:443; VE 27:459–60). He regards killing animals for mere sport as morally wrong (VE 27:460). He insists that domestic or work animals should not be overworked, and that an animal, such as a horse or dog, that has served us well should not be cast aside like a worn-out tool when it is too old to perform its task but should be treated with gratitude and affection, like a (human) member of the household, and be allowed to live out its days in comfort. Kant regards as morally abominable "agonizing physical experiments [on animals, carried out] for the sake of mere speculation, or whose end can be achieved in other ways" (MS 6:443). He praises Leibniz for taking the trouble to place a worm back on its leaf after examining it under a microscope (KpV 5:160; cf. VE 27:459).

These seem to me generally the right kinds of conclusions to draw, based on Kantian principles. Yet some Kantians I know are vegetarians – on what they regard as Kantian grounds. Other Kantians I know think Kantian principles require even that embryos and fetuses be regarded as persons with a coercively enforceable right to life. The moral I draw from all this is that fundamental Kantian principles do not, all by themselves, necessarily determine in advance the answers to these moral questions. It is, as I have already argued, a profound misconception of moral philosophy – of its proper structure and the role of a fundamental principle of morality in it, that the fundamental principle all by itself should attempt to do anything of the kind. What is important is that the fundamental principle of morality should correctly orient our values in thinking about moral questions. The task of reaching, or even advocating, determinate answers to them belongs to a separate stage of moral philosophy, the stage that interprets the fundamental principle and derives from it moral rules and duties. What I have been arguing in the last two sections in fact more properly belongs to that stage of moral philosophy, which I will take up for itself only later, in Chapter 9.

6

Autonomy

1. Tensions within the Idea of Autonomy

Every rational being, as an end in itself, would have to be able to regard itself at the same time as universally legislative in regard to all laws to which it may be subject. (G 4:438)

Autonomy of the will is the property of the will through which it is a law to itself (independently of all properties of the objects of volition). (G 4:440)

Those of us who are sympathetic to Kantian ethics usually are so because we regard it as an ethics of *autonomy*, based on respect for the human capacity to govern our own lives according to rational principles. Kantian ethical theory is grounded on the idea that the moral law is binding on me only because it is regarded as proceeding from my own will. The idea of autonomy identifies the authority of the law with the objective value constituting the content of the law. It bases the law on our esteem for the dignity of rational nature, which makes every rational being the moral legislator.

Yet between these last two sentences (which might even be taken as saying the same thing) there in fact emerges a serious tension in the Kantian idea of autonomy. This tension threatens to pull the doctrine of autonomy apart, depending upon whether we emphasize the '*autos*' or the '*nomos*'– the rational being's will as author or legislator of the moral law, or the law itself as objectively binding on that same will. The very term 'autonomy' itself, once it has been picked up on its own – as philosophical terminology frequently is – and is separated from the Kantian doctrines that were its original home, may be understood in widely different ways. Any of these interpretations might pretend to a Kantian pedigree or, alternatively, might represent itself as the basis for an immanent critique of Kantian ethical doctrine. In fact, the last two sentences are a succinct summary of the history of the Kantian conception of autonomy from its first reception down to the present day.

Among those who stressed the '*autos*' were Kant's early Romantic followers and critics (usually both followers and critics at once) who thought that each of us should be the author of our own morality. My morality, therefore, is valid only for me, as an expression of my unique individuality.[1] After all, a moral law proceeding from *my* will seems by that fact alone to be a law valid only for me, perhaps even a law whose content is subject to my whims and arbitrariness. But that leads to a natural question: How can a law bind me at all if I am its author, because that apparently puts me in a position to change or invalidate it at my own discretion? The same thoughts, once we try to answer this question, might also lead in the direction of associating the concept of moral authority with some notion of individual "authenticity," "choosing oneself," or "becoming who one is," sometimes taking those who travel this road beyond morality entirely.

For just that reason, however, the self-esteem which appears to ground Kantian morality can begin to seem (as it does to some of Kant's critics) like a kind of arrogance or even a perverse self-deification, in which each person blasphemously usurps the traditional place of the Deity as the giver of moral laws.[2] The tradition that went in this direction therefore included some, such as the later Schelling and Kierkegaard, whose encounter with Kantian ethics ended (paradoxically) in some form of "theonomy" or theological voluntarism that either preserved the notion of autonomy only by a speculative pantheist merging of the self and the Deity or else rejected outright (as a demonic or satanic principle) the whole idea that the rational creature might tear itself away from its creator and claim authority over itself.[3]

Alternatively, even where the moral law's claim to universal validity is not given up, stress on the '*autos*' has led to the thought that the moral law's validity must arise out of acts of my own will. The doctrine of autonomy is then seen as the proclamation of a "human-made morality," and this is regarded as incompatible with granting moral claims any objectivity or reality in their own right. So Kantian ethics entails a form of metaethical antirealism. It is the very essence of Kantian autonomy that our will could never be subject to a set of truths or facts or realities "out there." Every law or value we recognize must be constituted by our volitional act in legislating it. Such acts replace the "emotive attitudes" that were thought to constitute valuation in the more empiricist versions of metaethical antirealism. The universal validity of moral principles, or "moral truth" (if it should still please us to use such a term), has to be "constructed" by us, using certain "procedures" supplied by the Kantian formulas (especially FUL). What is left of the *nomos* side of Kantian autonomy is the fact that we have followed these procedures in constructing the principles, for this is what is seen as entitling us to *think of them as objectively valid* – just as if they rested on a value lying in the nature of things; but of course any such value would be out of the question because it would infringe on our *autonomy*.

These may be historically the most popular interpretations of the Kantian doctrine of autonomy, but Kant himself does not look at autonomy in any such way. For him, content of the moral law could not be subject to my whims or an expression of my individuality, because the law is given universally, by every rational will, and not only to itself but to all other rational beings as well. I cannot loose myself from the moral law, because it is not up to me to make or unmake the idea of a rational will. The content of the law is not a creation of my will, or the outcome of any constructive procedures on my part. The law of autonomy is objectively valid for rational volition because it is based on an objective end – the dignity of rational nature as an end in itself.

Kant distinguishes between principles of the will that result from subjective acts and principles that are objectively binding on the will whatever its subjective acts might be. The former are called 'maxims'; they have only subjective validity for the will that enacts them. The latter alone are called 'laws', and Kant gives them this name because they are universally binding on all rational wills (G 4:401n, 421n; KpV 5:19; MS 6:225). The Romantic individualist interpretation of Kant in effect simply denies that there are any laws at all and turns all principles of the will into maxims. The "constructivist" version appears to permit a distinction between maxims and laws, but only because it thinks of the will as adopting a certain "legislative" stance on some of its maxims, backed up by a "CI-procedure" or "procedural conception of practical reason" based on a consilience of intuitions. From a properly Kantian point of view, however, *objectivity* can never be the outcome of any subjective volitions, stances, or procedures. Any principle that gets its validity from a subjective act of ours – no matter what "procedure" is followed in performing this act – is still only *subjectively* valid. It is only in a *maxim*, never a practical law.

2. Positive and Natural Law

There is a definite philosophical conception of "law" and "legislation" built in to Kant's idea that the moral law is a law of autonomy. It is a different conception from the one articulated by Elizabeth Anscombe in her well-known criticism of Kant, when she asserts that "the concept of legislation requires superior power in the legislator."[4] Kant is perfectly aware of the latter conception and gives it its traditional names: "positive," "arbitrary," or "statutory" legislation. Such laws rest on the arbitrary will of anyone in a position to issue commands with threats to back them up. Positive or statutory legislation, Kant says, is to be distinguished from "natural" legislation, which rests not on external coercion by a superior power but on reason (VE 27:273, 528–9; cf. R 6:103–4).[5] In Kant's view, all moral laws, even all legitimate laws of the state, must be conceived as (or as falling under) natural laws. In fact, Kant says that merely statutory or positive legislation does not, properly speaking, give "laws" at all, but only "commands" (VE 27:273).

If we understand Kantian autonomy using only the statutory or positive concept of legislation, then Anscombe is correct that the whole idea of "legislating for oneself" is absurd. No one has the superior power to issue arbitrary commands to herself. It is not absurd, however, to call certain principles "laws" because they are grounded on objective reasons valid for all rational beings (which is Kant's principal meaning of "law" in practical philosophy). Laws in this sense depend for their authority on no one's arbitrary will or coercive power (not yours or mine, not the king's or queen's or the parliament's, not even God's). It is no doubt controversial whether any such laws exist, but in the earlier chapters of this book we have seen why a Kantian would think they do.

We have also seen in the previous two chapters why Kant thinks morality requires *laws* and not merely rational grounds yielding subjective maxims. First, Kant thinks that morality involves representing rational beings as a single ideal community (or "realm of ends"), for whose members some principles are universally valid or objectively binding. Second, Kant holds that human beings, precisely in virtue of the empirical nature of the sociability that might be thought to make them resemble such an ideal community, often require self-constraint in order to overcome the unsociable propensity with which their sociability has infected their natural desires or inclinations. Finally, only principles whose rational validity is independent of any subjective will can command human beings categorically, irrespective of any ends they might set for themselves or have set for them by some coercive power that would subject their actions to its ends. Therefore, the principles resting on objective grounds must take the form of *imperatives*, constraining them to certain actions, maxims, and ends, rather than consisting merely of principles they might follow for objectively good reasons, but always at their subjective discretion.

With this explication of the meaning of '*nomos*', however, the Kantian conception of autonomy may begin to look like a mere euphemism. If the will that gives the moral law is not *my* will but an ideal rational will present as much in others as it is in me, then there seems nothing left of the assertion that the legislative will is *mine*. If the moral law is a law whose validity rests on objective values that are independent of what anyone wills, then it seems we should just stop talking about "autonomy" and "self-legislation" and simply say that when we obey the moral law we are forcing ourselves to do what is *morally right* (or "rational") and not at all doing what *we will* to do.

We seem to be faced with the following dilemma: If we emphasize the '*autos*' and mean self-legislation proceeding from subjective voluntary acts of our will as the whole point of the doctrine, we will either reject altogether the (natural) lawfulness of the moral law, its objectivity, and universal validity, or else we will treat the law's objectivity as merely a way of considering (or a "legislative" stance on) what results from our volitional acts (based perhaps on some "procedural conception of the norms of practical reason" through which we "construct" the norms to which we subject ourselves). The volitional act of legislation is then the literal content of the doctrine of autonomy, and the objectivity of the law is merely a way of *considering or regarding* the content that we subjectively will. If, however, we emphasize the '*nomos*' (the objective validity of the law, its groundedness in the objective worth of rational nature as an end in itself), then we have to treat "self-legislation" as just a certain way of *considering or regarding* a law whose rational content is truly objective and whose authority is therefore independent of any possible volitional act we might perform. In either case, half of the doctrine of autonomy turns out to be meant literally, while the other half is treated as an illuminating way of considering or regarding the half we really mean. The only question left is: Which half do we really mean? What wins out: *autos* or *nomos*?

Some might hope to avoid the dilemma by finding an interpretation of the doctrine that makes both halves of the doctrine literally meant. It might seem that this is the only possible way to be a "real Kantian" about autonomy. But this "balanced" view of the matter is wrong. The enterprise it proposes is bound to end either in a frank confession of failure or in confusion and obfuscation. And it is not even genuinely Kantian, because Kant himself sees the alternatives quite clearly and is not hesitant or indecisive in his own choice.

The issue is unavoidable, because it is nothing but a reappearance of the age-old quarrel between voluntarism and rationalism that has been with us at least since Plato's *Euthyphro*. Which comes first, desires or reasons? Is the good considered good because we will it, or do we will it because it is good? Or in its most majestic (theological) form: Does God will the good because it is good, or is the good good because God wills it? To each question, the answer is either the one or the other. Those are the only options, and there is no third alternative. You can, of course, put off the decision for a while, pretending there is some way around it, hemming and hawing the way philosophers often do, raising dust (or fog) by drawing distinctions and constructing theories that enable you to say one thing while meaning the opposite. But in the end you always have to face the music, take your pick, and come clean about it. Fortunately, in this case the choice is easy. Rationalism is the correct view and, incidentally, Kant's view. Voluntarism is a false view, though often the view of Kant's interpreters. Volition is inherently normative. But that does not mean that it creates norms; it means that it contains them, or recognizes them, or is subject to them. Volition always represents itself as grounded on reasons that, unless we are to move in a vicious circle, must be distinct from the acts of volition to which they apply. In its theological form, voluntarism is an unenlightened, authoritarian, slavish view.

(As Leibniz pointed out, theological voluntarism is so eagerly sycophantic that it even leaves divine praise empty of meaning, because whatever God wills, he would have been equally praiseworthy for willing just the opposite.) If we bring voluntarism up to date by putting ourselves in the place of the Deity, we are merely adding self-conceit to this same moral vacuousness. Or if we place idealizing constraints on our self-will, in order to rein in our arrogance (and, incidentally, to give morality some content), then we find that these constraints will not do what we need done unless we recognize them as imposing on us some objective constraints (hence as not proceeding from our own will after all).

3. The Author and Legislator of the Moral Law

If we keep in mind the issues that have just been raised, we will find that Kant's texts are not the least bit ambiguous about them. When we read the seven or so pages of the *Groundwork* in which the concept of autonomy is introduced (G 4:431–8), we should be struck by the frequency with which Kant uses expressions conveying the thought that autonomy of the will is only a way of *considering* or *regarding* the objectively valid moral law. Look at his language in the first full paragraph where he introduces this conception:

All maxims are repudiated in accordance with this principle which cannot subsist together with the will's own universal legislation. The will is thus not only subject to the law, but is subject in such a way that it must be regarded also as *legislating to itself*, and precisely for this reason as subject to the law (of which it can consider itself the author). (G 4:431)

Here and in the next few pages, Kant uses the verb "consider" (*betrachten*) no fewer than five times (G 4:431, 433, and three times on 434), the verb "regard" (*ansehen*) is used twice (G 4:431, 438), and "as" or "as if" (*als, als ob*) constructions are used four times more (G 4:431, twice on 432, and once again on 438). The presentation of the legislator of the moral law as the "*idea* of every rational being" (G 4:431 [twice], 434), which was mentioned in an earlier chapter, fits here too. For it means that we are not to think of the law as legislated by our fallible, corrupt actual wills but by the pure concept of our rational will, by our will as it would be if its volitions always accorded with the rational principles it recognizes as objectively binding. Such ways of presenting the idea of autonomy actually far outnumber the direct indicative assertions that the will legislates, gives the law to itself, or is a law to itself. When placed in that context, even those direct assertions are most plausibly read as reporting only *how the law may be considered or regarded*. They are justified ways of talking about the will's relation to the law, not literal assertions that moral laws are legislated by the will as if they were positive statutes.

By contrast, Kant never presents the dignity of rational nature as an end in itself, or the categorical nature of moral obligation, or the objective validity of the moral law, as ways in which rational nature or the law can be considered or thought about. They are simply statements of how these things *are*.[6] Read this forthright statement:

The essence of things does not alter through their external relations, and it is in accordance with that which alone constitutes the absolute worth of the human being, without thinking of such relations, that he must be judged by whoever it may be, even by the highest being. (G 4:439)

Human beings have absolute worth, which belongs to them essentially. This worth is not something conferred on them by themselves, or by God, or by anybody else. No being's stances, attitudes, judgments, or "legislative acts of will" are required for rational beings to have that worth, because they have it *essentially* – and that is the sole and sufficient reason why everyone, even God, should judge them to have it. The point is underlined by Kant's use of the word 'absolute'. For what has a property *absolutely* has it irrespective of relations to other things – in particular, independently of the way it is regarded or considered by anyone – and that is why the properties a being has "absolutely" it has also in *every* relation (KrV A324–5/B380–1). This is as unequivocal an assertion of metaethical realism as you could ask for. In light of it, you simply cannot read Kant himself as a metaethical antirealist, however you may choose, with charitable intent, to subvert his ethical theory in your appropriation of it.

Kant has two technical terms to describe the relation of a law to the will from which, in some sense, it issues: "lawgiver" (*Gesetzgeber, legislator*) and "author" (*Urheber, autor*). His clearest published explanation of this terminology is in the following passage:

A (morally practical) law is a proposition that contains a categorical imperative (a command). One who commands (*imperans*) through the law is the lawgiver (*legislator*). He is the author (*autor*) of the obligation in accordance with the law, but not always author of the law. In the latter case, the law would be a positive (contingent) and arbitrary law. A law that binds us *a priori* and unconditionally by our own reason can also be expressed as proceeding from the will of a supreme lawgiver, that is, one who has only rights and no duties (hence from the divine will); but this signifies only the idea of a moral being whose will is a law for everyone, without his being thought as the author of the law. (MS 6:227)

With this passage in mind, let us now ask: In which of these relations (legislator, author) does our own will actually stand to the moral law? The self-evident answer is: *neither one*. Strictly speaking, *our own will is neither the legislator nor the author of the moral law*. (To speak of it in either of these ways is at most merely an appropriate way of *considering* or *regarding* the matter.)

A legislator is the one who commands through the law by attaching sanctions to it, and this is also the author of those sanctions. The human will, however, attaches no sanctions – it neither rewards nor punishes itself for compliance or noncompliance with the moral law. (Kant regards the very concept of self-punishment as contradictory, MS 6:335.) Kant says the moral law "can be expressed" as proceeding from God's will as legislator – when we think of God as apportioning happiness according to worthiness, and of these as sanctions attaching to the law. Kant says explicitly that a law may have a legislator in this sense without there being any author of it. Although our will can be *regarded as* the legislator of the law, it is *not* (in the proper and literal sense) the legislator of the law.

The author of a law is the one whose will determines its content. Who, then, is the author of the moral law? The plain answer given here is: *no one*. The only laws that have an author at all are positive (contingent), arbitrary (or "statutory") laws. Moral laws, however, are *natural* laws. They have no author. So although we can *consider* our will as the author of the law, it is *not* (properly speaking) the author of the law. In his lectures, Kant is even more explicit:

> The legislator is not simultaneously an author of the law, except when the law is contingent. When the laws are necessarily practical and he only declares that they are in accord with his will, he is the legislator. Thus no one, including God, is the author of moral laws, since they do not spring from the will, but are practically necessary... Thus [God] is a legislator, but not an author. Precisely as God is not the author of the fact that triangles have three angles. (VE 27:282–3)

> All laws are natural or arbitrary. If the obligation springs from the *lex naturalis*, and has this as the ground of the action, it is *obligatio naturalis*, but if it has arisen from *lex arbitraria*, and has its ground in the will of another, it is *obligatio positiva*... But *obligatio naturalis* is *directa*: I must not lie, [not] because God has forbidden it, but because it is [bad] in itself. (VE 27:261–2)

> The legislator is not the author of the law, rather he is the author of the obligation of the law. The two can be different. God is to be regarded as the moral legislator; but he is not author of the laws, since these lie in the nature of things... God is not the author of morality, since otherwise it would come through his will and we would not come to know it through nature as well. It lies in the essence of things. (VE 29:633–4)[7]

The moral law has no author because it is a natural law, so its content is determined by no will at all. Instead of having an author, it is "practically necessary" – it commands regarding what is "[good or] bad in itself." The content of the moral law is no more dependent on anyone's will (yours, mine, or God's) than the fact that a triangle has three angles. The content of the moral law is laid down by no will but rather "lies in the nature of things... in the essence of things." Once again we see clearly that Kant is a *metaethical realist*.[8]

Moral laws "lie in the nature (or essence) of things." The nature of *what* things? Kant's doctrine of autonomy seems to make this question harder to answer: "Autonomy of the will is the property of the will through which it is a law to itself (independently of all properties of the objects of volition)" (G 4:440). The moral law, that is, must get its content independently of all "properties of its objects of volition." Here the phrase "properties of the objects of volition" might bear two distinct meanings: It might mean "the properties of all ends to be produced that are set by volition," but also "the properties of those things in the world toward which volition might be directed, including the properties of the things the will might use as means to its ends." If the moral law's commands depended on the properties of objects in the first sense, then their rational bindingness would be conditional on those objects' having those (desirable) properties. If they depended on the properties of objects in the second sense, then they would be conditional on facts about the way those objects might serve as means. In either case, the moral law would be a hypothetical rather than a categorical imperative.

Kantian autonomy has sometimes been understood as involving the thought that all "things" (of whatever nature) have been excluded, which leaves only the "acts of the will" itself to serve as the grounds of moral law (though perhaps these acts had to be certified for their legislative authority by some "CI-Procedure" fit for "constructing" the content of morality). We have seen, however, that this fashionable answer cannot be right. For it is only positive or statutory legislation that could be authored by a will, no matter what procedures it might have followed. These procedures would merely provide a way of *regarding* or *considering* the content of the law as objective, despite the fact that it is understood (voluntaristically) as proceeding from subjective acts of some will. But for Kant the moral law is a natural law, whose objectivity is the literal truth, and whose content admits of no author because it lies in the nature of things. So we must persist in our question: *The nature of what things?*

4. The Nature of the Will

Once we have excluded both kinds of "objects of the will," what "things" are left in whose "nature" the content of the moral law might lie? The thing we may have overlooked is right there in the middle of rational choice – namely, *the will itself*, or *practical reason*, with which Kant identifies the will (G 4:412). The content of the moral law lies in the nature (or essence) of the rational will or practical reason.[9] "Morals is precisely the science of all the ends that are *established through the nature of the will* and that prescribe the objective laws of the will, and according to which we direct and exert our faculties" (VA 25:438).

What is the will (or practical reason)? It is, like understanding, imagination, judgment, and theoretical reason, a power (*Kraft*), or *faculty* (*Vermögen*), or, as we might also say, a capacity. What is a power, faculty, or capacity? Here is a rough and ready answer that I think will do for present purposes: A faculty is the way that a living being achieves something through processes or actions that are normatively conceived and normatively guided.

In Kantian language, every faculty has its "natural end" (G 4:432) and also its "principles" (KpV 5:12). We conceptualize the processes of a being in terms of faculties when we think of the being in this way. For example, we think of an animal as having the faculty of vision. Through the exercise of this faculty it achieves certain determinate aims vital to its survival and reproduction: Through the presence of light rays, it becomes aware of a wide range of objects or states of affairs in its immediate environment. These include predators that threaten it, prey items it needs to catch, potential mates, places to graze or rest, and so on. The norms that guide the faculty of vision are determined by the natural teleology involved in the proper functioning of its visual organs, optic nerves, and so on. The animal has the faculty of vision when (to the extent that) these organs are in proper working order, and it exercises the faculty when (to the extent that) they function as they are supposed to. To say that a faculty is normatively guided of course does not mean that its operation involves consciousness of the norms or conscious choices to follow them. But it does mean that there is a distinction between the faculty's operating correctly, in the way it does when it is functioning properly, and its operating in some errant, flawed, diseased, or dysfunctional manner. The pertinent norms mark off its correct from its incorrect functioning.

We conceptualize in a similar way many human abilities that do not even rise to the level of being "natural faculties," such as a tennis player's capacity to hit a backhand stroke. Having the capacity to hit a backhand involves having mastered a determinate sequence of bodily motions. Exercising the capacity means executing these motions in the right way and in the proper sequence. The successful result of this exercise will get the ball over the net close to the spot where the tennis player intends it to go. A lucky but unskilled tennis player might manage to get the ball over the net in the same spot using an awkward backhand stroke that causes the tennis coach to wince because the stroke conspicuously violates the norms pertaining to the capacity. This clumsy player might win the point, but the shot would not constitute a successful exercise of the capacity to hit a backhand stroke.[10]

Practical reason or will is a faculty whose successful exercise results in *rational action*. The whole basis of Kant's argument in the Second Section of the *Groundwork* is his philosophical account of the faculty of will or practical reason, and especially of the norms (technical, pragmatic, and moral) that are constitutive of it (G 4:412–20). Kant's main business in the Second Section of the *Groundwork* is a philosophical exposition of the nature of rational will or practical reason that begins with the norms of instrumental and prudential reason but is then used to formulate systematically the highest norm of this faculty, the moral law (G 4:421–36). "We must follow and distinctly exhibit the practical faculty of reason from its universal rules of determination up to where the concept of duty arises from it" (G 4:412). We saw in Chapter 4 how Kant pursues the concept of a categorical imperative, from its *form* as of universal law (G 4:421–5), through its *matter* as humanity or rational nature as an end in itself (G 4:426–31), to the unity of both in the idea of autonomy, which brings the first two aspects of the law into unity (G 431–6).

Because a faculty is conceptualized in terms of the norms that apply to it, the very nature of every faculty is normative – its very concept, in fact, provides us with a recipe, even a standing invitation, for inferring "oughts" from "ises." In the case of most faculties, these "oughts" will be of sharply limited scope, relative to the limited aims of the faculty (and perhaps to its employment under a set of highly constrained conditions). So their normative import may look insignificant or dubious. But the scope of these "oughts" will be broader when we are dealing with the faculty of *reason* – the highest human faculty, whose function is precisely to regulate all the other faculties. And that scope will be *absolutely unlimited* when we are dealing with the highest norm of that faculty, the moral norm that commands actions categorically.

If the content of the moral law "lies in the nature" of something, therefore, the faculty of will or practical reason is precisely the sort of thing in whose nature you might have expected it to lie. The supreme principle of reason, lying in the nature of that faculty, is precisely where we should expect to find the sole source of all normativity. That the *nature of rational will* turns out to be the location helps to make intelligible, from a rationalist point of view, the appeal of voluntarist interpretations of the Kantian idea of autonomy, and even of voluntarism itself. At the same time, it also explains why voluntarism is a fundamentally erroneous representation of where rational norms come from (and then also of why all voluntarist interpretations of Kantian autonomy, whether Romantic, theonomous, or constructivist, get the doctrine so far wrong).

5. How the Will Legislates to Itself

Kant introduces FA, and the doctrine of autonomy of the will, for several distinct purposes. It helps us to understand why, and in what sense, he thinks we can regard our will as legislative of the moral law, if we get clear about them.

First, as we saw in Chapter 4, FA is a way of bringing together the form and matter of the moral law, represented respectively by FUL and FH, into a single comprehensive or "universal" formula of the moral law. We *regard* moral laws, which proceed from no will but lie in the nature of will or practical reason, *as if* the will of every rational being were their author and legislator. We are justified in considering them this way because that way of thinking about them brings together the formal conception of universal law with the material conception of the absolute value of humanity or rational nature. This way of considering things makes no alteration in either the content or the ground of the moral law, which still lies in the nature of things. But it puts the moral law in a new light that enables us to unify its formal and material aspects (G 4:431).

Second, the idea of autonomy solves a problem about how the nature of categorical obligation is possible. When we obey a moral law, how should we represent to ourselves the ground or reason on which we are acting? If we regard our obedience to the law as satisfying some independent end or interest, whatever it might be (seeking happiness or perfection, expressing love or fear of God, satisfying the demands of society, or anything else), then this way of looking at our motive transforms the categorical imperative into a hypothetical one, which contradicts the nature of moral volition and (as Kant sees it) threatens to corrupt morality at its very foundation. Kant proposes to solve this problem by regarding the law as legislated by our own will. We are justified in regarding it this way because the ground of its laws lies in the nature of that will, which is the nature of practical reason itself. Nothing beyond our will itself needs to be assumed as an end or interest that is being satisfied by our obedience to the moral law. To regard the moral law as a principle of autonomy thus solves this problem, which is left unsolved by every previous way philosophers have thought about the moral law. All their theories have falsified the character of the law by considering it as a principle of *heteronomy* (G 4:431–3, 440–4).

Third, out of the corner of his eye Kant spies another advantage of this way of regarding the law that will enable him to establish or justify it in the Third Section of the *Groundwork*. As Kant reminds us in the first two sections of the *Groundwork* with almost obsessive regularity, everything he has been saying about morality has been only provisional or conditional – morality as he has been conceiving it might turn out to be a mere illusion, a "high flown fantasy," or "figment of the mind overreaching itself through self-conceit" (G 4:392, 394, 403, 407, 408, 420, 423, 425, 426–7, 429n, 440, 444–5). Kant's attempt to confirm his account of morality, even to confirm the reality of the faculty of reason itself on whose nature his account rests, will later be seen to depend on the claim that the principle of morality, as a principle of self-legislation, stands or falls with freedom of the will (G 4:446–7). Although we can never prove theoretically that the will is free, Kant thinks we can show the inevitability of regarding it as free from a practical standpoint (G 4:448–9) and also show that this way of regarding the will can be made at least consistent with theoretical reason (G 4:450–5). (We will look at this argument in the next chapter.)

Regarding the first aim, many of Kant's statements of FA have what Andrews Reath has called a "self-referential character."[11] That is, they specify the content of the moral law (or the system of such laws) in terms of what any rational being, merely as such and without any further aim, would lay down as moral legislation. What the law *is* gets expressed in terms of what a rational being, considered simply as such, would will it to be:

Act in accordance with a maxim that at the same time contains its own universal validity for every rational being. (G 4:437);

Act always in accordance with a maxim whose universality as law you can at the same time will. (G 4:437);

Not to choose otherwise than so that the maxims of the choice can be comprehended with it in the same volition as universal law. (G 4:440);

[Act] so that [your] will could consider itself at the same time as universally legislative. (G 4:434, cf. two very similar formulations at G 4:432).

We saw in Chapter 4, §2 (c) how all these formulations differ from FUL or FLN. We also saw why they provide no "test" of moral rightness, no "procedure" for "constructing" the moral laws regarded from this standpoint as self-legislated. That was never their purpose. Their purpose was instead to link the comprehensive or definitive form of the moral law to its metaphysical ground in the nature of the rational will, while at the same time providing a transition from this thought to Kant's solution to the problem of categorical obligation, which is his second aim. Kant makes this link explicit when he claims that it never occurred to earlier moral philosophers, who grounded morality on principles of heteronomy, that the human being "was subject only *to his own* and yet *universal legislation*, and that he was obligated only to act in accord with his own will, which, however, in accordance with its natural end, is a universally legislative will" (G 4:432).

Here it is clear that "acting according to one's own will" is equated with acting "in accordance with the natural end" of the will – in other words, acting in accordance with the *nature* of the will. The will is regarded as a faculty with a nature, constituted by its function and by the norms governing its proper exercise. This "natural end" of the will, being internal to its nature, is distinct from all external ends or interests, which would undermine the categorical character of moral obligation if made the ground of actions fulfilling it. In order to regard our will as self-legislative, or to consider it as the author of the moral law, we *never* think of the will as a source of particular "legislative acts" determining the content of the law (as the will of a despot might serve as the author of arbitrary positive laws).

If we think of the self-legislative will as "acting legislatively," we think only of its actions that conform to the moral principles lying in its nature. In fact, Kant thinks of the will as self-legislative chiefly in those cases where it *obeys* the moral law, especially in those cases where its obedience has a certain principled or necessary character. This is why he says we can notice autonomy of the will most of all in a "sublime" will that lays claim to its own dignity by following the moral law solely from immediate respect for it (G 4:435, 439–40). It is also why he identifies the self-legislative will with the "*absolutely* good will," the will that "cannot be evil" because it not only acts on a maxim in conformity with the moral law but also does so from the principle "Act in accordance with maxims that can at the same time have themselves as universal laws of nature for their object" (G 4:437). Kant's formulations of FA are thus typically "self-referential" in a second way: They state the moral law in such a way that the agent, in obeying it, is explicitly regarding the moral law as precisely what that agent is willing in performing that action. In other words, the will's obedience to the moral law involves regarding the law as something it has given itself.

These texts strongly suggest that we consider ourselves as legislating the moral law only insofar as we obey it, or at least judge ourselves according to it (G 4:434–5, 433). Seen in this light, only those who obey the moral law, out of respect for its objective authority, are truly autonomous. The authority of the law over those whose maxims do not conform to it, or even over the good will whose conformity to the law is only contingent, does not reside in autonomy or self-legislation at all. It lies only in the "practical necessity" of the law that "lies in the nature of things." In other words, we don't deserve to think of ourselves as autonomous as long as we refuse to acknowledge that the law is grounded in the nature of things – that is, as long as we try (self-conceitedly) to represent our own will as the source of its normativity. We rise to the dignity of self-legislation only when we *obey* a law whose practical necessity is recognized by us as absolute and independent of our arbitrary choices. The real, absolute practical necessity of the law in the nature of things comes first and is the unvarnished literal truth of the matter. Our coming to regard the moral law as the law of our will follows from this, in light of the fact that the normativity of our own rational will is that real thing in whose nature lies the practical necessity of the law. The moral law is not a law of autonomy because we stand in some relation of sovereign authority to the law, as we would if we were the author of merely positive or statutory laws. It is a law of autonomy only insofar as we succeed in aligning our will with what the law objectively commands, thus actualizing the nature of our will as a faculty of practical reason.

If we want to consider not only the absolutely good will but also the merely good will or even the bad will *as self-legislating*, then we might regard the relation of the giver of the law to its subject in another way. Kant sometimes suggests that self-governing rational agents can be looked at from two different standpoints, as being (or containing within themselves) two distinct agencies or playing two distinct roles in regard to their rational agency (G 4:450). For example, as we will see in Chapter 9, in order to make sense of the concept of a duty to oneself, Kant thinks that a rational being must "view itself under two attributes" – as the one imposing the duty, and as the one subject to it (MS 6:418). In this connection he also employs the distinction between the *homo noumenon* and the *homo phaenomenon*, the intelligible and the empirical self – the former as the one imposing the duty, the latter as the one who owes it. In this connection, however, it is gratuitous to read into this talk any extravagant "two worlds" metaphysics[12]: The point is that when I think of myself as owing the duty, I think of myself as I act empirically, whereas when I think of myself as the one who imposes the duty, I bring myself under a concept of understanding derived from the moral law, which is *a priori* and only in that sense "noumenal" or "intelligible."

Or again, in discussing conscience (a topic we will take up in Chapter 10), Kant holds that I stand before an inner court, in which I play simultaneously the roles of accused, accuser, defender, and judge (MS 6:437–40). We should regard moral self-legislation in a similar way: In my role as *legislator* I will the moral law (as the highest normative principle of practical reason), while in my role as *subject* of the law I choose whether to obey or disobey it whenever an issue of duty arises. This would have the advantage that we would not be tempted to think of the moral law as legislated by my contingent, empirical volitions – or, therefore, according to the Romantic corruption of Kantian autonomy – as a principle whose content might vary from individual to individual, according to each one's inner "authenticity" (or arbitrary whim).

Here we must be clear that the legislator is not a separate homunculus claiming a monopoly on rationality. (The moral legislator must not be depicted as some deranged Wolf Larsen descending upon the ship from out of the noumenal world, shouting his incomprehensible commands at a confused horde of pitiful Humean inclinations as they cower on the lower deck.) The legislator is simply the rational will in its role as norm giving, while the subject of the law is the same rational being in the role of the one to whom the command of duty is addressed. This subject is a free person, for whom obedience to the law is a rational incentive – even in those cases where the subject fails to exercise practical reason successfully and prefers some other incentive to it. The point of the representation is that the idea of rational self-government requires us to distinguish the legislator of the law from its subject and to see the self-governing rational being as someone who is capable of playing both roles at once.

We should also not think of the rational legislator, our faculty of reason, as a merely "natural" faculty, if that means: not a *social* or *cultural* faculty. For Kant conceives of its law as something legislated by all rational beings to all, constituting them as a single community or "realm of ends" under "common laws" (G 4:433–4). And his conception of each individual's faculty of reason is essentially a social conception, in the sense that Kant regards reason as developed only through culture and education. Kant holds that free rational communication between people – especially the activity of "critique" that questions and demands the legitimation of laws and norms of all kinds – is a necessary condition for "the very existence of reason" (KrV A738–9/B766–7, WA 8:35–42, O 8:145–6, VA 7:321–5, VP 9:441–3, 486–93). We should not think of will or practical reason, therefore, as a faculty hidden somewhere deep inside each individual human being (for instance, tucked away in the folds of the cerebral cortex). Though it is no doubt a faculty we could not have without the possession of a human brain, each of us has it only through our communicative relations to others and exercises it only in cooperation with others.[13]

We might see this as a way of presenting the distinction Kant sometimes makes between two possible senses of the word "will" (*Wille*) – a distinction familiar already in the scholastic tradition) – between *Wille* (*voluntas*) ("will" in a narrower sense) and *Willkür* (*arbitrium*, for which the conventional English translation is "choice"):

Laws proceed from will, maxims from choice. In the human being, the latter is free choice; will, which is directed to nothing beyond the law itself, cannot be called either free or unfree, since it is not directed to actions but immediately to giving laws for the maxims of actions (and is, therefore, practical reason itself). Hence will directs with absolute necessity and is itself *subject to* no necessitation. Only choice can therefore be called free. (MS 6:226)

As "will" (in this narrow sense), the rational being is the legislator of the law. It is, Kant says, "the faculty of desire considered not so much in relation to action (as choice is) but in relation to the ground determining choice to action" (MS 6:213). "Will," in this narrower sense, is therefore what makes it the case that "will" (in the broader sense, encompassing both *Wille* and *Willkür*) can be identified with the faculty of practical reason itself.

"Will" in the narrow sense is neither free nor unfree, because it does not choose one thing or another. It simply presents to choice the reason or ground for choosing this over that (whose highest norm is the moral law). As "choice," the rational being is subject to the law. "Choice" is free because it is able to, and this also means motivated to, follow the law even when it is tempted not to and fails to do so. What "choice" chooses are maxims, or subjective principles, that may or may not conform to the laws given by "will." When "choice" is tempted not to obey the law but is inwardly constrained to do so, it is constrained by (its own) *will*, and that is what makes it *autonomous* in obeying the moral law.

Many, no doubt, when they come to understand what Kant's doctrine of autonomy of the will amounts to, will be bitterly disappointed by it, or even reject it indignantly as a sham. But in a way this is only to be expected. The doctrine of autonomy is the point at which many controversial Kantian doctrines converge – his rationalism (i.e., his rejection of voluntarism), his acceptance of the idea of a natural law lying "in the nature of things," his faculty psychology, and in particular his conception of the will as the faculty of practical reason, all of which result in the thought (no doubt repellent to some) that we are truly ourselves, and act *freely* (or even truly *act* at all), only when we act *rationally*, according to principles valid for all rational beings (involving the equal moral status of all). Anyone who rejects one or more of these doctrines either will find the whole idea of autonomy unacceptable or else (as has often happened in the tradition subsequent to Kant) will try to reinterpret it in terms of some alternative view more to his preference (and then will, as often as not, eventually present the resulting incoherence as an "immanent critique" of Kant or an "insoluble problem" for him).

Thus Kantian autonomy, once it is understood, will (and ought to) disappoint those shallow minds and immature souls who are attracted to the doctrine of autonomy for the wrong reasons. They were hoping for some radical individualist revolution in morality, in which paroxysms of human self-will overthrow the divine will's numinous majesty (thereby replacing, as many such revolutions sadly do, one arbitrary and unjust tyranny with another and bringing to power merely a different mob of unprincipled scoundrels). The sober rationalism of Kantian ethics is equally incompatible with voluntarism in its theological and its Promethean forms. Nor should we cherish the illusion that the fire of the gods will be vouchsafed us merely because we have observed "the CI-procedure" in promulgating our sovereign decrees.

7

Freedom

Kant's aim in the *Groundwork* was to search for and establish the supreme principle of morality (G 4:392). At the end of the Second Section, the search (which was "analytical") is complete, but the "synthetic" stage of the argument has not yet begun (G 4:445). It is only in the Third Section of the *Groundwork* that Kant proposes to justify morality against the skeptical worry that it might be no more than a "cobweb of the brain." He intends to do this by arguing that if we have free will, then morality is real and the moral law is valid for us (G 4:445–7). Kant's view about freedom of the will, however, is one of the most unstable areas in his philosophy. It is a topic he frequently revisited, never saying quite the same thing he ever said before. Kant's theory of freedom, and especially the idea that we are free only in the intelligible world beyond nature, has also been the chief stumbling block to the acceptance of his moral philosophy. The scandal has only increased with the passage of time, as fewer and fewer moral philosophers find it tolerable to burden morality with an extravagant supernaturalist metaphysics.

The changes in Kant's own pronouncements on the topic of freedom are so fundamental that it is not possible to offer a single theory that can be squared with all the texts in even a minimal way. In the *Groundwork*, it looks as if the transcendentally free self, the rational self that gives the law, is a noumenal being unaffected by inclinations, while the self that must obey it is a merely empirical self.[1] But then the acting self would seem subject to natural necessitation and hence should (in all consistency) be altogether exempt from moral responsibility, inviting the famous criticism Sidgwick mounted in his Appendix to the *Methods of Ethics* (Sidgwick, pp. 511–16).[2] By the time of the *Religion*, however, Kant is clear that the moral agent (located in whatever world) acts from an inclination only by incorporating it into a freely adopted maxim (R 6:24–5).[3] In many of Kant's treatments of freedom, it remains unclear whether the free will is to be found only in the noumenal world or whether freedom is also to be attributed to the empirical self; or if the latter, whether it is attributed to the empirical self only on account of the fact that this self also has an existence in the intelligible world (KpV 5:94–5). If Kant chooses this last option, then he seems to face a formidable difficulty no matter how you look at it: Either he must argue for the identity of a self that is free with one that is admittedly unfree or else justify the attribution of freedom to a phenomenal being solely on the ground that it is supposed to reside in an altogether different (noumenal) being.

Regarding Kant's use of freedom to establish (or provide a "deduction" of) the moral law, it is unclear from the second Critique onward whether Kant intends to provide such a thing – though clearly he still regards freedom of the will as necessary for the moral law to be valid.[4] According to a widely accepted reading, in the *Critique of Practical Reason* Kant abandoned that idea in favor of the claim that the moral law is a "fact of reason" needing no confirmation beyond itself (KpV 5:28–33).[5] As for the theory of noumenal freedom itself, it is not clear whether it should be regarded merely as a way of showing the bare logical possibility (freedom from contradiction) of the claims that we are free and that we are natural beings (KrV A557–8/B585–6) or whether it represents some positive doctrine about free agency. Perhaps it is offered as a "proof" of transcendental idealism (KpV 5:101–3) or even some kind of "assertoric *cognition*" (albeit "only from a practical standpoint") of the noumenal world itself (KpV 5:105).

In all these ways Kant's theory of freedom presents us with a moving target throughout his writings, as he is evicted by insuperable difficulties from each successive position he comes to occupy. Perhaps none of Kant's forced peregrinations on the subject of free will ever takes him to a dwelling place that is even minimally inhabitable. I say these things, however, not to condemn Kant but rather because they may mark him as the philosopher who understood the problem of freedom better than any other. In the end, Kant's greatest insight regarding the problem of freedom may be that it is insoluble and a source of permanent torment to philosophy – all the more so because a commitment to freedom of the will is basic to ethics, so that the anguish cannot for even an instant be dismissed, dissolved, evaded, or ignored.

A work on *Kant's* ethics should probably content itself with expounding the doctrines of particular texts, making no attempt to find any single self-consistent doctrine in them. *Kantian* ethics, by contrast, should try to take the most defensible (or, if that is too optimistic, then the least indefensible) position it can, somewhere in the neighborhood occupied restlessly by Kantian doctrines concerning freedom of the will. It should try to borrow from Kant's best insights, but it should make no pretense that it can be brought into agreement with what all his texts say.

1. Practical Freedom

Kant distinguishes between "transcendental freedom" and "practical freedom." The former is a special kind of causality, conceived metaphysically as the capacity to begin a causal series "from itself" independently of any prior causes (KrV A533/B561). "Practical freedom," on the other hand, is the freedom we ascribe to ourselves when we think of ourselves as acting, especially when we think of ourselves as moral agents. It involves, as Kant says, "a will that is a causality inasmuch as reason contains its determining ground" (KpV 5:89), or, as I will often put it, the capacity to "act for reasons." Kant distinguishes two different concepts of practical freedom, a "negative" one and a "positive" one. We have practical freedom in the negative sense if it is a "power of choice" (*Willkür*) that is "independent of necessitation through impulses of sensibility" (KrV A534/B562), "independent of alien causes determining it" (G 4:446), "independent of the matter of the law (namely, from a desired object)" (KpV 5:33), or "independent of being determined by sensuous impulses" (MS 6:213–14).

Human choice and animal choice. I take freedom in the negative sense to involve not only the capacity to act independently of (or even contrary to) some empirical desire (even the strongest one) but also the capacity to decide for ourselves how we will satisfy such desires (to devise our own means to them, rather than being hard-wired by instinct, or programmed by conditioning, in what we do to satisfy them). Even instrumental reason – action on hypothetical (technical) imperatives – involves the ability to envision more than one way of reaching our end, and also the capacity to suspend action toward some end we have already set, while we work out some new (perhaps hitherto unimagined) means of achieving it.

Kant sometimes thinks that practical freedom can be cognized empirically, or at least recognized through certain empirical signs. Experience, he thinks, shows human beings to have it, while brute animals do not.

Practical freedom can be proved through experience. For it is not merely that which stimulates the senses, i.e. immediately affects them, that determines human choice, but we have a capacity to overcome impressions on our sensory faculty of desire by representations of that which is useful or injurious even in a more remote way; but these considerations . . . depend on reason. (KrV A802/B830)

It seems right to say that humans have capacities to consider their overall welfare, and how to take care of it, that nonhuman animals lack. But Kant's view about the difference between humans and other animals goes further than this. He thinks of the "animal power of choice" (*tierische Willkür, arbitrium brutum*), once it is affected by an impulse sufficiently stronger than any contrary impulses, as incapable of suspending action on that impulse. Kant regards animal choice as always determined with mechanical necessity by instinct (though perhaps trained or modified through experiential conditioning). Thus the brute is capable of taking only a single course of action toward reaching the object of the impulse, just as a metal ball rolling down an inclined plane is capable of following only a single, mechanically determined path (KrV 534/B562, KpV 5:61, KU 5:172, SF 7:70, 88,

VA 7:212, VM 29:1015). Along with many other early moderns, in fact, Kant seems to regard nonhuman animals in certain respects as no more than machines, operating through the same kind of mechanical necessity found in watches, turnspits, robots, billiard balls careening about on a felt table, or planets revolving about the sun. "We can explain all phenomena of animals from outer sensibility and from mechanical grounds of their bodies, without assuming consciousness or inner sense" (VM 28:277).

If we are to go by a commonsense interpretation of everyday experience, however, this seems quite wrong. Animals do sometimes apparently hesitate between real possibilities and then make choices between them. However much they may be influenced by immediate impulses, they are not necessitated by them in the way that the motion of a watch is necessitated by the way it has been constructed and by the release of the potential energy that has been stored in its spring, or the way the precise motion of a billiard ball is necessitated by the momentum of the cue ball that strikes it. Unless we are willing to swallow a large chunk of now antiquated mechanistic metaphysics, there seems to be no reason to think that the futures of animals are laid out for them, like the motions of planets, watches, or billiard balls, by the causal mechanism of nature. On the contrary, the course of their lives remains open to their agency in important respects. Some animals obviously do have something like practical freedom, at least in the negative sense.

Just look out your window: A bird is sitting on a bush, pecking at a succulent berry. A cat steals silently toward the bush, stalking the bird, who notices the cat but continues eating. The bird hesitates between getting more nourishment and fleeing the danger. The cat hesitates between pouncing too soon, before it is close enough, and waiting too long, giving the bird a chance to escape. There is nothing going on in this scenario except the operation of instinctual and learned behavior through the nervous systems of the two animals. Yet *prima facie* it is obviously up to each animal how it will choose among its options concerning how and when to make a move. Will the bird fly away, and if so, precisely when? Will the cat pounce before this happens? If so, will the cat catch the bird? Or will the cat have pounced too soon, giving the bird the chance to get away, or too late, after the bird has just taken off? Or will the cat simply give up and decide it is not worth the effort this time?

As judged by common sense, the course of events here does not seem to be determined, split second by split second, merely by the same laws of mechanics that would enable us to determine precisely, to the split second, the motion of watches, clocks, or carefully programmed robots. Unless our commonsense empirical judgments have been undermined by the influence of metaphysical dogmas about how all natural causality must operate, we won't think that even La Place's demon could predict at precisely what moment the bird will fly, or the cat will pounce, or how this little story will end.[6]

This is what plain, everyday observation tells us. We could second guess it if we believed certain mechanistic dogmas about causal necessitation that prevailed during the early modern period. Today we know that at the microscopic level of quantum physics, what happens is not determined in the sense that its causes determine it and render it necessary. To be sure, quantum physics is no proof that causal determinism and necessity do not apply on a macroscopic level (it does apply to the motions of clocks, billiard balls, planets, and the like). Quantum physics certainly provides us with no model for the way in which predetermined necessity seems to be absent from either animal or human choices. But once we consider the fact of quantum indeterminacy, this should at least serve to break the grip on us that the mechanistic model of explanation still had on people in Kant's age, and the dogmas of universal causal determinism that went with it.[7]

It is certainly true that the nervous systems of both human and nonhuman animals conform to the laws of physics and chemistry. But we now understand that complex systems (such as weather patterns and ecosystems) that also consist entirely of entities conforming to these same laws can be understood only probabilistically, as the consequences of interactions we consider "chaotic" as compared with the precise determinism that seemed in Kant's day to subject the natural world to an iron mechanical necessity.[8] Not only the human brain, but even the nervous systems of birds and cats are enormously complex and possess a kind of flexibility in their operation that shows they cannot possibly work through the same kinds of mechanisms as clocks or even the most sophisticated computers we know of. Even nonrational animals, therefore – to which it would not have occurred to Kant to say that they had noumenal selves in the intelligible world – seem to have something very much like practical freedom in the negative sense.[9]

2. Acting for Reasons

Practical freedom in the *positive* sense is possession of "a causality of a particular kind" – namely, a capacity to follow determinate laws given by the faculty of reason, or "the ability of reason to be of itself practical" (MS 6:214, KpV 5:33, G 4:446). It amounts to the capacity to recognize rational nature as an end in itself as a reason for acting in certain ways, and to act in those ways on the basis of that reason. More generally, it involves the capacity to act *for reasons*, rather than only on the basis of feelings, impulses, or desires that might occur independently of reasons.

Are reasons causes? Clearly reasons are not causes when they are not heeded, as all too often they are not. When they are heeded, and we act as we have reason to act, then we might consider reasons as causing us to act that way. But if we use the word "cause" in this context, we must understand it as a more flexible and capacious term than was consistent with some eighteenth-century dogmas. For philosophers such as Hume and Kant, a cause always implies a necessary connection with its effect, so that if the cause is present nothing else but its determinate effect could possibly occur. To cause something to happen is to render any other outcome impossible.

Reasons can never be causes in that sense. Reasons have a most peculiar property: They sometimes *explain what we do*, and – if we think them good enough reasons, and if we have the strength of mind and strength of will not to be seduced away from acting on what we take to be such good reasons – they may even make it *certain* that we will do that, and *certain* that we will do nothing else. But even in those cases, reasons never deprive us of the *possibility* of doing otherwise. We can always act contrary to them. In that sense, every being that acts for reasons is a free being. Reasons, as Leibniz put it, "incline without necessitating," or as Locke put it, they act on a power that has "indifferency," so that we may "suspend action on our desires,"[10] or in Kant's language, they operate only on a will that has practical freedom in the negative sense.

This, I suggest, together with his eighteenth-century mechanistic conception of causality, explains why Kant thought that actions based on reasons could not have a natural cause but must be caused by us spontaneously or entirely from ourselves (*von selbst*) (KrV A534/B562). Of course an action done for a reason obviously does not occur just by chance, and Kant denies that free actions occur at random or through blind chance (KpV 5:95). But actions done for reasons cannot be causally necessitated by anything. If the same state of affairs that might constitute a reason for doing something truly makes it *impossible* for us to do otherwise, then that state of affairs is no longer functioning as a reason but instead as some kind of constraint on our rational agency coming from outside our rational will. For example, early in Sartre's *Nausea*, Antoine Roquentin leans down to pick up that piece of paper out of a mud puddle (a discarded school child's composition, "*Le hibou blanc*"). The filthiness of the mud clinging to the paper might have been a reason for him not to pick it up. But instead he finds, to his surprise, that he is *unable* to pick up the piece of paper ("I was unable . . . I can no longer do what I will"). Here the muddiness of the paper is no longer functioning as a reason. It has turned into an inner barrier of some kind – perhaps into some kind of psychological inhibition.[11] Strong reasons sometimes make it certain that we will do something, but never by acting as such barriers to doing otherwise.

Here is a conceptual truth about reasons: If it is *impossible* for us to do otherwise, that can *never* be because there is a *reason* to act as we do.[12] It must be either because some external obstacle prevents us from doing it, or because something inside us (such as a compulsion or an inhibition) deprives us (at least temporarily) of the power to do otherwise.[13] That means that any being whose actions are always causally necessitated is a being that utterly lacks the capacity to act for reasons. Or contrapositively, any being that is capable of acting for reasons (a being with practical freedom in the positive sense) also necessarily has practical freedom in the negative sense.[14] Its behavior cannot be causally necessitated, at least in the cases where it acts for reasons.

Freedom and imputability. Practical freedom is the capacity to act for reasons. Kant therefore regards it as the fundamental condition of being a *person* – in the sense of a being that can be held morally and legally responsible for its actions, "a subject whose actions can be imputed to him" (MS 6:223). But Kant does not *equate* practical freedom with imputability, and it is false that we need the concept of freedom only to account for our practices of holding people responsible, punishing and blaming them. There are many theories of imputability that offer us some sort of plausible rationalization for our practices of blaming and punishing. If we regard them as unsatisfactory, it is only because they provide no satisfying account of the practical freedom we must ascribe to ourselves in order to think of ourselves as acting for reasons.

The chief condition of personhood, in the sense of imputability, is that one should have the capacity to resist impulses and act for reasons, especially the capacity to obey self-legislated rational laws. Without saying so explicitly, Kant sometimes writes as if the presence or absence of this capacity were always an all-or-nothing affair. He may be reluctant to admit such cases because he is aware of the endless variety of ways in which people offer lame excuses for their bad conduct, including all sorts of sophistries they use to deflect responsibility from themselves for their actions. But in general, capacities can be possessed to greater or lesser degrees, and there is no reason not to say this about practical freedom. Kant says that we possess practical freedom except "in tenderest childhood, or insanity, or in great sadness that is only a species of insanity" (VM 28:182). But children too acquire gradually the capacity to resist impulses and to act for reasons. And various circumstances, including mental illness, addiction, brain damage, or psychic malfunction, can partially deprive adults of these capacities. Kantian ethics has no reason not to recognize these facts and admit that imputability is sometimes a matter of degree.[15]

3. Autonomy and Freedom

Kant's claim, both in the *Groundwork* and the *Critique of Practical Reason*, is that morality is not an illusion, and the moral law is valid for us if and only if we are practically free in the positive sense (G 4:446–7, KpV 5:28–30).[16] This proposition follows validly from his account of practical freedom in the positive sense, together with what Kant takes himself to have established in the Second Section of the *Groundwork*. For practical freedom in the positive sense is the capacity of a being to be a law to itself, to act for reasons on a principle lying in the nature of its own will. The Second Section has established that the supreme principle of morality (if there is to be such) must be precisely such a principle, to which we are subject because it is self-legislated. So if there is such a principle, and we have the capacity to legislate and obey it, then we are practically free in the positive sense. If we are practically free in the positive sense, then the highest capacity included in that freedom must be to give the moral law to ourselves and be able to obey it, on the basis of reasons lying in our faculty of reason itself (chiefly, the recognition that humanity is an objective end in itself).

Freedom as a necessary presupposition. For Kant, then, whether morality is real or an illusion (only a "cobweb of the brain") comes down to the question of whether we are practically free in the positive sense. Kant denies that we can prove theoretically that we are free or even comprehend how freedom is possible, consistent with natural laws determining our actions as events in the world of appearance. However, he thinks it is a sufficient justification of both freedom and morality if we can show two things:

(1) We must presuppose that rational beings are free even in order to regard them as making theoretical judgments; and

(2) There is no contradiction between the proposition that rational beings are free and the proposition that their actions in the world of sense are determined according to laws of nature.

In his argument for the first point, Kant's crucial claim is: "Every being that cannot act otherwise than under the idea of freedom is precisely for this reason free in a practical respect, i.e. all laws inseparably combined with freedom are valid for it, just as if its will had been declared free in itself and in a way that is valid in theoretical philosophy" (G 4:448). To understand this claim, we need to understand what he means by "acting under the idea of freedom" and "free in a practical respect."

Kant holds that the basic affirmative propositional attitude we can take toward any proposition or judgment is "assent" or "holding for true" (*Fürwahrhalten*). We may assent to a proposition, however, for different reasons, and even in different respects. Our assent is based on theoretical grounds, but it may also be based on practical grounds (KrV A820–5/B848–53, cf. KpV 5:142–6). That is, we may assent to a proposition not because theoretical grounds show it to be true but because it is required for a rational course of action to make sense; then we say that our assent is for practical purposes or "in a practical respect." To say that we are "free in a practical respect" means that there is justified assent to the proposition that we are free on practical grounds. An "idea" is a concept of pure reason that may serve us as a norm or goal for imitation (KrV A312–20/B368–77). To "act under an idea" is to recognize such a norm and attempt to conform to it.

The "idea of freedom," therefore, is equivalent to any norm that is self-given by reason. The *moral law* is such a norm (and the highest rational norm). Thus, attempting to conform to the moral law would be a case of "acting under the idea of freedom." Yet unless Kant's argument is to be viciously circular, this cannot be the norm he has in mind here. This is because he is trying to address the worry that the moral law is only an illusion or a figment of the mind. So he must argue that there is some *other* norm of reason that we cannot as easily dismiss as a figment of the mind, such that regarding it we "cannot act otherwise than under the idea of freedom."

The norm he cites is a *theoretical* norm (or norms of theoretical judgment generally). Kant holds that the fundamental norms of theoretical reason, which ground all the theoretical norms we recognize, are, like the moral law, given by reason to itself *a priori* (KrV A795–7/B823–5). The practical use of reason is that through which reason seeks not to conform its representations to objects but to produce objects corresponding to its representations (KrV A800/B828, KrV 5:9–10n). The use even of theoretical reason is practical in the sense that it seeks to produce well-grounded judgment or assent. Hence even in using theoretical reason to make judgments, we act under the idea of freedom. Kant's argument for freedom in the *Groundwork* is that we cannot avoid doing this:

We must necessarily lend to every rational being that has a will also the idea of freedom, under which alone it would act. For in such a being we think a reason that is practical, i.e. has causality in regard to its objects. Now one cannot possibly think a reason that, in its own consciousness, would receive steering from elsewhere in regard to its judgments; for then it would ascribe the determination of its power of judgment not to its reason but to an impulse. (G 4:448)

Is fatalism self-refuting? This argument closely parallels one Kant had used against the "fatalist" J. H. Schulz in a book review only two years earlier:

Although [Schulz] would not himself admit it, he has assumed in the depths of his soul that understanding is able to determine his judgment in accordance with objective grounds that are always valid and is not subject to the mechanism of merely subjective determining causes . . . ; hence he always admits freedom to think, without which there is no reason. (RS 8:14)

Kant's argument could be put this way: *Fatalism* is the position that our actions are necessitated by the mechanism of nature and that this precludes practical freedom. There is nothing self-refuting or incoherent about fatalism regarded merely as the content of an assertion. Considered in itself, it is a way that things might be, even a way that certain philosophical considerations might lead us to think that things *must* be. But representing fatalism, or even asserting it, is not enough. Fatalism would have no philosophical interest if fatalists could not also represent themselves as denying freedom *for good reasons*. If they hope to convince others of fatalism, they must also represent these others as capable of denying freedom for good reasons. But that means they must already presuppose both in themselves and in others the capacity to act according to rational norms in settling theoretical questions. That capacity, however – the capacity to act according to norms of reason – presupposes freedom. It follows that fatalists must presuppose the contradictory of what they are trying to prove even in undertaking to prove it. Their proofs of fatalism, however strong, not only always come too late, but fatalists must represent themselves as acting under the idea of freedom before they can even think of themselves as considering their proofs as reasons for asserting what is supposedly proved. Kant therefore thinks of fatalists as arguing theoretically for a position they show in practice that they can never accept: "One may prove or also refute freedom in the theoretical sense, as one wants, nevertheless one will always act according to ideas of freedom. There are many people who do not concede certain propositions in speculation, but still act according to them" (VM 29:898).

To say that we must represent ourselves as able to act for reasons (hence as free) is not at all the same as saying that we must represent ourselves as always acting rationally, or for the reasons we may think are moving us to act. We saw in Chapter 1 that Kant regards human beings as *capable* of acting rationally but not particularly successful at exercising this capacity.[17] Probably much of the time people in fact do not understand why they think and act as they do.[18] From the fact that we often do not act for the reasons we think we do, however, it does not follow that we might *never* be able to act for reasons at all. It would make no sense to judge that something is true, and to offer some argument or evidence as your reasons for thinking it is true, while also maintaining that you are *never capable* of judging anything for reasons, because your judgments are always necessitated by causes that – because they *necessitate* – could not be reasons at all. That would preclude you even from representing yourself as having reasons for judging that you have this incapacity. That is the point being made by Kant's practical argument for freedom in the *Groundwork*.[19]

Extension of the argument to other rational beings. An important feature of this argument is that it is supposed to not only establish that I must regard myself as acting under the idea of freedom, and hence as free in a practical respect, but also that it should justify the same conclusion regarding other rational beings. This was needed if it is to complete the argument just mentioned that humanity is an end in itself (G 4:429), because Kant regarded the applicability to others of my thinking of my existence as an end in itself as merely a "postulate" until the grounds for it have been given here in the Third Section. He therefore completes the argument as follows:

[Every rational being] must regard itself as the author of its principles independently of alien influences; consequently, it must as practical reason or as the will of a rational being, be regarded as free, i.e. the will of a rational being can be a will of its own only under the idea of freedom and therefore with a practical aim must be attributed to all rational beings. (G 4:448)

It is not immediately clear what has been added here that justifies the extension of what is true of me – viz. that I am unable to act except under the idea of freedom – to all other rational beings as well. I suggest that Kant's thought may have been this: If I am going to reason with others, even about any theoretical matter, I must presuppose in them the same capacity to govern their judgments by rational norms that I must presuppose in myself. And if I am to discuss with you what some third person has rational grounds for judging, I must presuppose in that person the same capacity I presuppose in myself, and in you, as a condition of our being able to reason together about this (or anything else). Thus the standpoint from which I declare that every rational being can act only under the idea of freedom cannot be thought of only as a "first person" standpoint (or as the "standpoint of the agent" in contrast with the "standpoint of the observer," who according to some philosophers might always look upon others – though never herself – as mere machines). Kant's point is that if we are to interact with others as rational beings – and such interaction, in Kant's view, is a necessary condition for the very existence of reason (KrV A738/B766) – then whether we are talking to them, or even talking about them, we must attribute freedom to them.

This argument shares a peculiarity with Kant's argument that humanity is an end in itself, which we examined in Chapter 5, §2. Neither is a deductively valid argument for its conclusion. All the premises of each argument, and even the proposition consisting in their conjunction, are quite consistent with the falsity of the conclusion. It may be impossible for you to do what you must represent yourself as doing when you act, judge, or even think, except by presupposing that you are free. But that is consistent with your not being able to do these things, and therefore with your not being free. In the same way, it may be impossible for you to set ends according to reason without presupposing that rational nature is an end in itself, but that is also entirely consistent with rational nature's not having this value, and even with nothing's having such a value.

These arguments, in short, do not work by excluding the possibility that their conclusion is false. Instead, they work by putting it out of reach for anyone rationally to deny the conclusion, or even to decline to assent to it. Both arguments admit the possibility that, considering the matter in itself, and apart from the rational attitudes toward ourselves that we must adopt if we are to make sense of ourselves as thinking and acting, our whole view of ourselves and of the conditions of our action might all be a hopeless illusion. Both arguments concede that a world is possible in which humanity is not an end in itself, and we are not free. What they show us is only that we could never be rationally connected to belief in such a world by reasons that we could coherently accept. In fact, we could never so much as entertain the possibility that the world is like that, because then we would have to represent ourselves as possibly being justified by reasons in assenting to the proposition that the world is like that. But this we could never do without undermining our own presuppositions and falling into incoherence.

Some may find in this state of affairs a reason for doubting or rejecting the arguments. I think they would be wrong. These arguments are *ad hominem* in one way, but not in another: They work only by involving *you* – your rational commitments in thinking of yourself as rationally valuing or rationally assenting to something. But they do not appeal to anything *peculiar* about you, or to your particular beliefs or commitments. They are not *ad hominem* arguments at all, in the sense that there is no *hominus* who could possibly exempt herself or himself from them. Both arguments hold only "in a practical respect," in the sense that the assent they motivate holds because it is the only way of making sense of what we are doing in a case where there is also no option of not doing it.[20]

4. The Fact of Reason

As was mentioned earlier, many regard Kant as having abandoned the argument we have just examined only three years after offering it. Instead of this argument, he is supposed to have rested the validity of the moral law on the repeated assertion that it is a "fact of reason" needing no deduction, and incapable of being derived from freedom of the will (KpV 5:3–6, 28–33).

Did Kant change his mind? We do not necessarily have to see Kant as changing his mind. In the preface to the second Critique, he describes its relation to the *Groundwork* as follows: "[The present work] presupposes, indeed, the *Groundwork for the Metaphysics of Morals*, but only insofar as this constitutes a preliminary acquaintance with the principle of duty and provides and justifies a determinate formula of it; otherwise, it stands on its own" (KpV 5:8). Kant described his aim in the *Groundwork* as "the search for and establishment of" the supreme principle of morality (G 4:392). It is quite possible here to read "providing and justifying" a formulation of the moral law as exactly parallel to the "search for and establishment of" it. If so, then Kant is saying that the second Critique is not giving us a new justification of the moral law (as a "fact of reason"). Rather, references to the "fact of reason" might even be seen as a summary of the argument of the *Groundwork*, not a rejection of it.

Most who see Kant as making a change in doctrine between the *Groundwork* and the second Critique seem to think the change is an improvement. Yet it is hard to see how anyone could possibly be crazy enough to think this. The reason most often given is that Kant has abandoned a deduction of the law based on a *theoretical* demonstration of freedom, which he recognized as impossible.[21] But Kant thought already in the first Critique that no such demonstration is possible, and he repeats this in the *Groundwork*, saying explicitly (and, as we have just seen, correctly) that the argument for freedom we have just examined is a *practical* argument only (G 4:448 and note). In the second Critique he even continues to assert that freedom of the will grounds speculative as well as practical reason (KpV 5:3–4). Besides, to declare the moral law a "fact of reason" seems also a practical argument, but this time based only on the moral law itself, but now with nothing to answer the charge that the moral law might be a self-conceited illusion of the human mind overreaching itself. There is (to use the wording of the *Groundwork*) a rational norm of reason (the moral law) requiring us "to act under the idea of freedom." And Kant still holds that if we were not free, the moral law would not be valid for us (KpV 5:28–9).

The issue of freedom, therefore, would seem to be essentially the same in the second Critique as in the *Groundwork*. We are not committed to freedom any less in the later work than we were in the earlier one. The only difference seems to be that in the *Groundwork*, Kant has some argument for someone who might accept the norms of theoretical reason but refuse to recognize the norm of practical reason (the moral law). In the second Critique, he has none. When confronted with someone who wonders whether the moral law is a "high flown fantasy" or "figment of the mind," his only resource now is moralistic bluster (the bare assertion that the moral law is a "fact of reason"). If we assume that Kant changed his mind, then his position in the second Critique is essentially the same, except that it is significantly weaker argumentatively.[22]

5. Noumenal Freedom

The second crucial part of Kant's defense of freedom is (2), the claim that there is no contradiction between freedom and natural causality. Kant's thinking on this point is famously characterized by his claim that we can be practically free only if we are transcendentally free, and by his notorious theory that we can be transcendentally free only as members of the noumenal world.

The intelligible world. The story goes something like this: Our actions in the world of appearance are necessitated by antecedent events according to necessary causal laws and hence appear not to be free. But this is only how things *seem*. In fact, the causal laws connecting antecedent events necessarily with our actions in part reflect our empirical character – and this has our intelligible character, chosen with transcendental freedom in the noumenal world, as its determinant. So the same actions that we regard as naturally necessitated in the world of appearance can be regarded as transcendentally free in reference to their noumenal cause. When we think of ourselves as appearances, we are determined, but when we think of ourselves as moral agents, we transport ourselves into the intelligible world, where we are transcendentally free (KrV A532–58/B560–86, G 4:451–8, KpV 5:93–106).

However extravagant this metaphysical story may be, it is, as I have argued elsewhere, self-consistent.[23] Even that is not beyond controversy, however, and beyond bare consistency the theory of noumenal freedom has little appeal (except to the most die-hard devotees of whatever Kant wrote, whether or not it is even good Kantian doctrine). Because space and even time, according to Kant, are forms of appearance, it seems that our free choices in the noumenal world must be *timeless* – and Kant sometimes says things that suggest this. So the theory seems to allow for nothing like literally choosing freely between alternatives at a time, or freely striving through time to bring about ends, or to improve one's moral character.

Others have drawn yet further conclusions on Kant's behalf from his doctrine of noumenal freedom: Schopenhauer, for example, insists that following Kantian doctrine, our moral character is unchangeable through time: No reform of a bad character is possible.[24] This, all by itself, would do away with a lot of Kantian ethics (a consequence Schopenhauer is of course eager to accept). Even more commonly it has been inferred that a Kantian moral agent, as a timeless and supernatural being, must also be totally beyond nature and history, and truly free action can have no social or historical context.

Such inferences seem so solid that they have become bedrock components of Kantian ethics in the eyes of many, even when they contradict Kant's own explicit assertions. Kant of course thinks of free actions as constituting human history (I 8:17–18, VA 7:321–33) and regards our radical propensity to evil as resulting from our social condition (R 6:27, 93–4). Kant's entire anthropology, in fact, is conceived *pragmatically*, as an account of what human beings have freely made of themselves through culture and history (VA 7:119–20, 285–6, 293–5). For those who take the theory of noumenal freedom seriously as a metaphysical dogma to which Kant is committed, we must ignore all of this, because it contradicts noumenal freedom. (Thus in one of the earliest reviews of *Anthropology from a Pragmatic Point of View*, Schleiermacher claimed that Kant's theory of freedom precludes his entire project of "pragmatic" anthropology.[25])

The compatibility of nature and freedom. So noumenal freedom, if taken literally as a piece of positive metaphysics to which a Kantian must be committed, brings with it many philosophical disadvantages. We should ask a prior question, however: What is the *status* of this noumenal story in Kant's philosophy? How far is he committed to asserting its truth? Consider what Kant says at the conclusion of his longest presentation of the story in the first Critique:

We can know (*erkennen*) that actions could be free, i.e. that they could be determined independently of sensibility, and in that way they could be the sensibly unconditioned condition of appearances. [But to understand this further] surpasses every faculty of our reason, indeed surpasses the authority of our reason even to ask for it . . . Yet the problem we had to solve does not obligate us to answer these questions, for it was only this: Do freedom and natural necessity in one and the same action contradict each other? And this we have answered sufficiently. (KrV A557/B585)

Freedom is treated here only as a transcendental idea, through which reason thinks of the series of conditions in appearance starting absolutely through what is sensibly unconditioned, but thereby involves itself in an antinomy following its own laws, which it prescribes for the empirical use of the understanding. [To show] that this antinomy rests on a mere illusion, and that nature at least **does not conflict** with causality through freedom – that was the one single thing we could accomplish, and it alone was our sole concern. (KrV A558/B586)

Consider the following comparison: There are two propositions, p and q, which stated directly one after the other look like they might contradict each other. In order to dispel this impression, I tell a little story:

Once upon a time, there was a beautiful princess from a far off land of noumenal selves ... p ... And then the fairies and witches appeared ... q ... And then she and Prince Charming entered her noumenal castle, and they all lived happily ever after.

Suppose that the dots stand for a set of assertions none of which is self-contradictory, and that contradict neither one another nor p nor q nor anything else in the story, so that the fairy tale, however fanciful, is as a whole free of contradiction. In the context of their occurrence in this narrative, then, we are able to see that p and q are consistent with each other, so that the initial impression that they contradict each other has been successfully dispelled. Now I argue: "Because this fairy tale involves no self-contradiction, it follows that p and q do not contradict each other after all."

This argument would be sound. It would show that p and q do not contradict each other. It would not matter in the least to its soundness that the narrative as a whole is false, a pure fiction, talking about fairies, witches, noble-minded handsome princes, and a lot of other things found nowhere in reality and believed in only by contemptibly superstitious people. It makes no difference that the princess, the prince, the far-off land, what is reported in the dots (which may involve more about the fairies and witches), correspond to nothing whatever in the real world. The fact that noumena (and noumenal selves) are mentioned in the story also makes no difference. We are no more committed to their existence than to that of fairies or witches or (most absurd of all) to a possible future in which some people live happily ever after (for most of our lives encounter bitter disappointment, and all end in death).[26]

If Kantian ethics is to remain consistent with Kant's own views about the uncognizability of the intelligible world, then it ought to read Kant's story about noumenal freedom in exactly the same way as this fairy tale. If the story shows that natural causality and freedom do not contradict each other, then – together with his practical argument that we must presuppose practical freedom as a condition of theoretical judgment – it has achieved everything we needed to establish the moral law in its definitive formulation as FA. No doubt this fiction leaves us – as Kant himself says – with no positive comprehension whatever of how freedom and natural causality in fact coexist in the real world. In fact, it provides no positive demonstration at all that they do coexist in reality, for that is a possibility we can never exclude on theoretical grounds. According to Kant, however, such a demonstration and such comprehension are beyond our power to obtain, even beyond the authority of reason to expect (though we cannot help asking for it). So suppose we persist in asking: "Just how do freedom and natural causality *really* relate to each other? What is the metaphysical truth about how they fit together without contradiction? Is the noumenal realm involved in that in any way?" The only permissible Kantian reply to these questions is: "I do not know, and neither do you, and neither can anyone ever know anything about this." If we are asked what we ought to *believe*, the correct critical answer is: We should believe we are practically free – but we are not justified in holding any beliefs about the noumenal world in connection with this. In short, once the idea of noumenal freedom has played its role in the fictional narrative that shows freedom to be logically consistent with natural law, it should thereafter be quarantined from Kantian ethics just as strictly as if it carried the plague.

6. How to Think about Freedom

Kant's lapses into supernaturalism. In my view, this last figure of speech is in some respects a most apt comparison, and by no means an exaggeration. That is because, unfortunately, in some places it appears that Kant himself wants to make positive use of noumenal freedom – as yet another indirect proof of transcendental idealism (KpV 5:100–3), or as some sort of intimation (or even *cognition*) of our membership in a supernatural world beyond the natural world of sense (G 4:451–3, KpV 5:105).[27] Apparently Kant also found it morally fitting that as often as we think of human beings as ends in themselves having absolute worth or dignity, we must also think of them as having some supernatural (or noumenal) destiny, setting them apart from all those lesser beings whose fate is to be merely a part of nature. Such a notion still appeals to some people today. But no rationalist – and rationalism is the very heart of Kantian ethics – should have the least patience with it. The only moral emotion it excites in me is *outrage* – that anyone could think supernaturalist superstition a necessary condition for moral decency. I completely agree with those who, thinking that the notion of noumenal freedom is indispensable to Kantian ethics, find this an insuperable obstacle to its acceptance. I add only that no positive doctrine about noumenal freedom has any place in Kantian ethics either. Whatever Kant himself said on the subject, his flirtations with supernaturalism regarding freedom are flights of transcendent metaphysics, inconsistent with the basic epistemological strictures of the critical philosophy.

The incomprehensibility of freedom. In order to make judgments about when people's actions are free, and when not, Kant does need an *empirical* account of the signs (not proofs) of freedom in the empirical world. This is a need he acknowledges in the *Critique of Pure Reason* and that he attempts to satisfy in some of his writings – too often ignored – on anthropology and the philosophy of history (KrV A802–4/B830–2; I 8:17–22, MA 8:109, 112–15, SF 7:83–4, VA 7:119, 321–5). Kant seems to have thought that the empirical criteria for rationality and responsibility could be kept apart from the transcendental problem of free will. Here he seems to me correct, at least to this extent: Empirical issues about responsibility and agency are extremely complex, and it is misguided to expect that the answers to them will be inferrable from any general position on the metaphysical problem of free will.

Regarding the metaphysical problem of free will and determinism, I think Kant was also entirely correct in regarding it as insoluble – at least in the terms it had to be posed in his time. And in our time it is still a philosophical open wound, a disease for which we have no cure.

The only view a sensible person should want to take regarding the problem of freedom – the only view that could possibly represent an acceptable *solution* to it – is some form of compatibilism or so-called "soft determinism." That is because any incompatibilist indeterminism that forces us into supernaturalism is a capitulation to superstition, while incompatibilist or "hard" determinism (what Kant called 'fatalism') is a position no rational being could coherently adopt, for reasons given in §3. Unfortunately, however, it does not follow from this that anyone has yet found an acceptable form of compatibilism or soft determinism, or even that such a thing would be possible to find. The basic objection to compatibilism is that if we are nothing but a product of our physiology plus external causal influences, then we cannot possibly be the sort of beings who could be the cause of our own actions entirely from ourselves – that is, freely. This leaves us with the equally unpalatable alternatives of denying that we are free and denying that we are parts of nature. The impulse behind this way of looking at the problem is strongly supported by the early modern mechanistic conception of nature, but clearly it is alive and well in many minds despite the demise of that conception. [28]

The basic problem with standard compatibilism. Many self-advertised compatibilist positions, for all intents and purposes, swallow whole (without even a belch) the basic incompatibilist argument just presented. As a result, they accept "hard" determinism's denial that we can cause our own actions by choosing them from a range of real possibilities that are open to us. This makes it impossible for them to reconcile freedom of the will, in any genuine sense, with natural causality. In order to maintain the pretense of doing so, their first task must always be to get us to accept under the name of 'freedom' some pitiful facsimile of the real thing. Once they have done this, they then can easily provide their comfortable naturalistic account of what freedom consists in. But it is not acceptable to pretend that judgment and choice are different from what they are, or that we may represent them to ourselves in a manner in which we cannot coherently represent them, just so that we can have a "naturalistic" account of them.

Whenever compatibilist philosopher tell you that their theory can give you "enough" freedom, or "all the freedom we really need," and that it denies freedom of the will but "only in some extravagantly metaphysical sense," that is invariably a preamble to such a pretense.

Compatibilists usually make things too easy for themselves in a couple of ways. They caricature free will as involving random or inexplicable events or unmotivated actions – whereas the whole point is that freedom is required to make sense of actions that are explained by the fact that they are done for reasons. They also cheapen their own naturalistic account by equating an adequate account of our agency with a description of "our practices" of blaming and punishing people and holding them responsible, or any specious rationalization that might be given for these practices, without asking any of the hard philosophical questions they raise. Kant was quite right when he labeled any account of this kind a mere "evasion" (*Ausflucht*) (KpV 5:93). Our practices in blaming people are never the true locus of the problem of freedom. The locus rather is the way we have to think about ourselves (and others) as agents. It is only because the standard compatibilist accounts fail as accounts of agency that there are *also* problems about them as accounts of responsibility.[29] If you have the nerve to point this out to them, they quickly descend into name calling – "libertarian" and "metaphysician" are at the polite end of the spectrum. If you make them so angry that they lose their composure, they will go further, accusing you of not being bright enough to have a "naturalistic world view,"[30] or maybe even of being a closeted *religious* person. (Given the way religious people tend to vote in the United States, that last insult is the one that really hurts your feelings.)

Perhaps someday we will understand how our brains and bodies, and our natural environment's social interactions, together furnish us with multiple future possibilities and enable us to choose between them for reasons.[31] It seems to me that our best prospect here is that the metaphysics of causality should come to accept the concept of a cause operating in material nature that does not necessitate its effect, and that our empirical sciences of neurophysiology and human communicative interaction should come to understand how reasons function as natural, material causes of that kind. We would have not only an account of responsibility but an account of how people have "indifferent powers" – the same power that they are capable of exercising either by doing this or by doing that according as their reasons for action incline them without necessitating. That would be a form of compatibilism, in the general spirit of Locke and Leibniz, that might actually solve the problem of free will. Anyone who claims to have done this already, however, should expect to be derided as a mountebank. And we cannot exclude the possibility that Kant was entirely correct in saying that "freedom can never be comprehended, nor even can insight into it be gained" (G 4:459).

We may define a *philosophical question* as one on which any position you take is open to insuperable objections. (This *of course* includes the desperate ploy of saying that the question can be ignored, dissolved, or dismissed as meaningless, which in relation to philosophical questions is the most rationally indefensible position of all.) Some may wish to deny that there could really be such questions, but they show only that they have never honestly studied philosophy. Philosophical questions are those that endlessly torment us and won't let go, because we cannot, while retaining our self-respect as rational beings, ever let go of them. Living rationally means, as Kant tells us in the opening pages of the first Critique, that we cannot dismiss any of these questions, even though our faculties are unable to resolve them (KrV Avii).

Free will is as *philosophical* a question, in that sense, as there is. Kantian ethics should not represent itself as having a solution to it. If the problem of freedom is a philosophical open wound, then the right way to think about Kant's utterly unacceptable theory of noumenal freedom is that it is the salt that philosophers have a professional obligation to rub in the wound so that they can't forget about it.

8

Virtue

1. Actions and Agents

In Anglophone moral philosophy, Kant is often pigeonholed as a "deontologist," in contrast to "consequentialism," on the one hand, and to "virtue ethics" on the other. This is supposed to mean that he places the *rightness of actions* at the center of his theory, as distinct from *consequences*, or the traits of *agents*. The main problem with this is that Kant is being too hastily assimilated to with the rationalist-intuitionist school in British ethics, which is where people get their idea of what a deontological ethical theory must be like.

This categorization does get Kant right on some things. Despite the recently fashionable Rawlsian reading, Kant agrees with the British rationalists' endorsement of the idea that values lie in the nature of things rather than being conferred on things by someone's will. Like the British rationalists, and contrary to utilitarianism, Kant thinks that some actions are intrinsically right or obligatory, while others are intrinsically wrong or forbidden, irrespective of their consequences. He also holds, contrary to the Scottish moral sense school, that reason, not sentiment, is the foundation of morality. But on other issues this categorization is wrong or misleading. It is incorrect to think of Kant as focusing, like the British rationalists, on the rightness or wrongness of particular actions. As we saw in Chapter 3, Kant's theory instead places *principles* at the center, grounded on the objective worth of humanity as an end in itself. Like Mill's utilitarian theory, Kantian ethics distinguishes between a fundamental principle, based on a fundamental value, and particular moral rules. These theorists also think that even moral rules do not always specify precisely what we must do, because they must be applied to particular cases through judgment.

We will take up what Kantian ethics has to say about consequences in Chapter 15. But if we divide moral theories into those that take *actions* as basic and those that take *agents* as basic, then Kantian ethics is hard to categorize.

What Kantian ethics takes as basic is *volition*, the self-regulated action of rational beings under laws of reason. Volition is expressed in *maxims* – an agent's *general* intentions or policies. Kantian ethics asks about maxims such questions as whether they are consistent with the idea of universal law, treat all rational beings as ends, or include in themselves the volition that they be universal laws. But is a maxim a characteristic of the *actions* that conform to it, or is it a characteristic of the *agent* who adopts it? Obviously it is both. Neither has clear priority in Kantian ethics.

Central to Kantian ethics are several concepts that designate something about agents, even in contrast to the properties of right actions – such as goodness of will and a good moral disposition. Kant's systematic ethical theory, which we will explore in the next chapter, is a taxonomy of ethical *duties*, but it is conceived as a "doctrine of virtue" – a theory about the virtue, and the virtues, of agents. No doubt Kant thinks of virtue in a different way from the way virtue ethics thinks of it. But it is false to say that the difference is that virtue ethics focuses on the qualities of agents while Kantian ethics focuses exclusively on the rightness or wrongness of actions.

"The good will" does not properly refer to a kind of person, or even to a stable characteristic of a person. A good will is volition on good maxims. Volition is the exercise of a faculty, hence sooner categorized as a kind of moral doing than as a kind of ethical being. A maxim may be acted on by an agent only once, perhaps in an action that is entirely out of character for the agent, and so the fact that an agent displays a good will, in this or that respect, on this or that occasion, tells us nothing about the enduring characteristics of the agent. The good will is an abstraction, instantiated in agents and actions in different ways at different times and in different respects. Even the most vicious people sometimes act on the right principles, and then the person's volition is just as good ("good without limitation") as the virtuous person's (more frequent) volition conforming to moral laws. Kant says explicitly that goodness of will sometimes coexists with a lack of virtue, as in a person who is childish and weak, and sincerely adopts good principles but does not have the strength of character to act on them (MS 6:408). So good will is not at all the same thing as virtue, even if the principles of the good will are presupposed by virtue.

2. Virtue as Strength

Kant treats the moral qualities of agents under three basic headings: (1) *virtue*, (2) *practical judgment*, and (3) *wisdom*. The good will, the moral disposition, and agents' maxims are not on this list, but that does not mean they are irrelevant to the moral qualities of agents. It is rather because they pervade the list, as necessary presuppositions, in one way or another, of the items on it. This fact points to one notable way in which Kant's conception of moral qualities differs from that of a lot of virtue ethics. Volition is central to Kantian ethics, while virtue ethics often includes in its conception of the virtues or good human qualities some that do not involve goodness of will, and, as Hume observed, some that may not be voluntary at all (Hume T, pp. 608–14, cf. Hume E pp. 261–7).

Early in the *Groundwork*, Kant flaunts his defiance of the traditional list of virtues by saying of courage, moderation, and self-control that they are good at all only when put in the service of a good will and become positively bad whenever they keep company with a bad will (G 4:393–4). No doubt by 'courage' and the other traditional virtue words Kant means something different from what traditional virtue ethics means by them. Further, the centrality of volition in Kant's views about the moral qualities of agents should also not lead us hastily to exaggerate his differences with virtue ethics. As we shall see presently, however, Kant too allows for nonvoluntary factors in the morally good qualities of agents.

Kant appears not to have known Aristotle's ethics very well, but as I read the two philosophers, their similarities – especially across the centuries – are at least as striking as their differences. For Kant, as for Aristotle, "virtue" (*Tugend*) is by far the most complex moral quality of an agent that he discusses. Any serviceable treatment of virtue in Kantian ethics will require some investigation of the details not only of Kant's moral psychology but also his larger empirical theory of human nature. Kant defines "virtue" as "moral strength of will," or "the moral strength of a *human being*'s will in fulfilling his duty, a moral constraint through his own lawgiving reason insofar as this constitutes itself an authority executing the law" (MS 6:405). He also describes it as "the moral disposition in the struggle (*im Kampfe*)" (KpV 5:84). Virtue in this sense is "a naturally acquired faculty of a non-holy will" (KpV 5:33). It is not a duty to have virtue in general, because only by having some degree of virtue is it possible to be placed under the self-constraint of duty at all (MS 6:405). But greater virtue is a perfection of our will, so we have a wide or meritorious duty to strive to improve ourselves in that respect, as well as in others (MS 6:446). There is no strict or narrow duty, however, to attain any specific degree of virtue. There is certainly nothing blameable in Kantian ethics about not being as virtuous as we can possibly be.

In its idea (or pure concept), Kant says, virtue is one, because the principle of duty is one (MS 6:447). Yet because we are morally imperfect beings, the strength of our will with respect to different morally prescribed ends may differ (MS 6:395). The strength of our commitment to one end may be greater than to another, or the strength of our promotion of one person's happiness may be greater than the strength of our promotion of another's. So there can be many virtues. Virtues may be discriminated as finely as ends, and also discriminated regarding other qualities that may contribute to moral strength of will (MS 6:447).

In Kantian ethics, there is no list of "the virtues" (like the eight in Confucian ethics or the four – or five – in Greek ethics, or the three – or seven – in Christian ethics).[1] This is because Kant thinks the virtues needed by a person differ with their ends and plans of life, which vary too much from person to person to make any generalized list pertinent to all of us. It is also related to the fact that Kant sees his ethical theory *historically* – his theory is *modern* ethics, an ethics of *principles*, rather than an *ancient* ethics, an ethics of *ideals*. We will return to this way of looking at the matter toward the end of the present chapter.

Virtue, habit, feeling, and rational desire. Virtue is strength. Strength is measured by its capacity to overcome resistance. A person is more virtuous the greater the inner strength of that person's will in resisting temptations to transgress duties. Moral strength, Kant says, is an "aptitude" (*Fertigkeit, habitus*) and a subjective perfection of the power of choice (*Willkür, arbitrium*) (MS 6:407). In other words, virtue is a state that makes easy something that would be difficult without it. If virtue is a habit, as Aristotle says (Aristotle Book II 1–3), then Kant insists that it is a "free habit," not merely "a uniformity of action that has become a necessity through repetition" (MS 6:407). It would be a serious misreading of Aristotle to think there is any disagreement between the two philosophers on this point, because for both virtue is exhibited in actions that are desired and done for their own sake on rational grounds. Another point of convergence is that Kant regards virtue as acquired through practicing virtuous action (not through mere contemplation) (MS 6:397). This is an important part of what Aristotle means by saying that virtue is a "habit" and a "state" (*ethos, hexis*) (Aristotle, 1103a31–1103b2, 1106a10).

Virtues involve the setting and pursuing of ends. Promoting an end involves desire for it, and desire is the representation of an object accompanied by a feeling of pleasure (or in the case of aversion, displeasure). Therefore, Kant also agrees with Aristotle that virtue involves desire for the right things, and also pleasure and pain (NE 1104b3–1105a17). Related to this is Kant's insistence – in reply to Schiller – that the typical temperament of virtue is joyous, not fearful, dejected, and ascetical (or "Carthusian") (R 6:23–4). This is why Kant regularly praises Epicurus, whose entire ethics (Kant thinks) is grounded on the correct thought that a cheerful heart is a mark of virtue (R 6:60, KpV 5:111–13, 116, MS 6:485, VE 27:249–50, 483, 29:603).

Alasdair MacIntyre writes: "To act virtuously is not, as Kant [held], to act against inclination; it is to act from inclination formed by cultivation of the virtues."[2] It is correct to say that for Kant, virtue is a strength to act against inclinations (against *habitual empirical* desires) *when they oppose duty*. But it would be quite false to say that virtue for Kant *never* involves acting from inclination. For some inclinations increase our capacity to fulfill our duty and therefore belong to virtue, or at least assist it. This is the reason why Kant thinks we have a duty to cultivate certain inclinations, such as love and sympathy, insofar as these assist us in the fulfillment of duty (MS 6:456–7, ED

8:337–8). For Kant, however (as for Aristotle), the principal desires from which we act in being virtuous are *rational* desires. They are *not* inclinations – that is, *empirical* desires arising from sensuous impulses rather than from rational principles. The incentives to duty for Kant are not inclinations but, as we have already seen, the array of nonempirical feelings that arise directly from reason – moral feeling, conscience, love of human beings, and respect (MS 6:399–402). Again, virtuous action, even when it opposes inclination, is something we *desire* to do – even something we must desire to do – for its own sake. On this point especially there is no disagreement at all between Kant and Aristotle.

Aristotle would surely reject MacIntyre's characterization of virtue as action "from inclination," if that means (what it *must* mean, because 'inclination' is Kant's term) that virtue consists simply in having one's empirical desires happily constituted so that they always incline you to do what you should. Such a piece of good fortune does not make you virtuous; it only makes virtue less necessary for you. Happily arranged inclinations are not virtue even though they make doing your duty easier, because they do not constitute a facility that makes it easier to do what is hard. But perhaps when he speaks of "inclination formed by cultivation of the virtues" MacIntyre is simply misusing the Kantian term "inclination" (equating it with "desire"), and what he means by it is *rational* desire arising from the strength to do the right thing (even against contrary inclinations). In that case, his account is perfectly faithful to Aristotle, but he is wholly mistaken in thinking there is anything in it with which Kant would disagree.

3. Virtue and Temperament

Denkungsart and Sinnesart. We have seen that for Kant if virtue is a habit, then it is a "*free* habit," not merely a pattern of conditioned behavior. Kant also calls virtue "inner freedom" (MS 6:396, 405–6). *Freedom* is the capacity to obey a law of reason that can be regarded as self-legislated. *Inner* freedom is the capacity to do this over the resistance of obstacles found in oneself. It corresponds to inner (ethical) constraint, in contrast to the external coercion that may be found in duties of right. Kant distinguishes between what we are owing to nature (or external influences) and what we are due to our own freedom – in his terminology, between our "temperament" or "natural constitution" (*Naturell*), and our "character." He sometimes draws the same distinction by differentiating between our "way of thinking" (*Denkungsart*) and our "way of sensing" (*Sinnesart*) (VA 7:285). Clearly Kant wants to think of virtue as chiefly a matter of character (or *Denkungsart*), not of temperament (natural constitution or *Sinnesart*).[3]

Kant's views are misunderstood at this point by those who think he believes in a free agency that is totally independent of any natural context. It is one thing to say there is a fundamental difference in principle between what is due to nature (or circumstances) and what is due to our own freedom, and quite another to hold that these two factors can be easily told apart in our experience of human action, or even that they are separable in our psychology. This point has important implications for his conception of moral virtue, because it means that virtue can include factors of temperament or *Sinnesart* even if it is primarily a matter of character or *Denkungsart*. It is clear from many things Kant says that he thinks what belongs to our sensible nature is too much intertwined with the exercise of our freedom for us clearly to tell them apart in practice. For this reason, Kant allows that it contributes to virtue when we cultivate the right inclinations – by, for instance, doing good to others, which makes us come to love them (MS 6:402). Further, we are also to some extent responsible for our inclinations, because an "inclination" refers not to just any desire, but only to "habitual sensible desire" (VA 7:251). This means that to the extent that our inclinations are the result of habits formed by voluntary actions, we are responsible for them (cf. Aristotle 1114a3–b25). In particular, we are responsible for our "passions" (inclinations that exclude the dominion of reason) because passions involve the adoption of maxims, and the adoption of a maxim is an act of free choice (VA 7:266).

Passions and affects. A passion is an inclination that prevents reason from comparing it with the totality of our inclinations (VA 7:251, 265). Passions are therefore frequently opposed to prudential as well as moral reason. In Kant's view, our character is decisively influenced, for good or ill, both by our natural constitution and by the society in which we are entangled, but it is nevertheless a quality of our will, for which we are therefore to blame if it is bad. Passions are always the result of our competitive social relations with other human beings; except for the presence of others, and our unsociably sociable relations with them, we would have no passions (R 6:93–4). This means that the propensity to evil in human nature, which is responsible for the passions, is to be regarded as our own work and our responsibility but is at the same time to be thought of as a product of our natural-social predicament, and it is also manifested in our inclinations. Thus despite the sharp distinction Kant draws between the voluntary and the involuntary, between the "way of thinking" and the "way of sensing," for him it is quite impossible to disentangle them in practice.

Virtue involves not only the avoidance of *passions* but also the control of what Kant calls "affects." An *affect* is a sudden access of feeling, as of fear, anger, or joy, that takes away our capacity to govern ourselves rationally. It is this absence of uncontrollable affects (and not the absence of feeling generally – which for sensible beings like ourselves would be not merely repugnant but even impossible) that Kant means by "moral apathy" – a quality he regards as necessary for virtue (MS 6:408–9). Some temperaments are more disposed to affects or to quick emotional reactions than others. Thus some natural constitutions, he says, are favorable to the formation of strong character, and others are not (VA 7:293). Kant appears to accept this as part of our human predicament. It is under this condition that we have to distinguish between what is voluntary, and our own work, and what is given in us by nature or good and bad fortune.

When is temperament a part of virtue? For Kantian ethics, this is not an easy question. ("Never" and "always" are equally unacceptable answers.) Drawing on, but significantly modifying, the traditional theory of the four humors, Kant identifies the quickly reactive (in regard to feelings and activities, respectively) with the "sanguine" and "choleric" temperaments, and the more slowly reactive (respectively) with the "melancholic" and "phlegmatic" temperaments (VA 7:287–90).[4] The latter temperaments, though belonging to the "way of sensing" and not to the "way of thinking," are in Kant's view more disposed to the kind of "apathy" and the strong character that pertain to virtue. Kant also recognizes that our degree of susceptibility to affects depends on the condition of our body. He acknowledges that diet and medication can be quite effective in controlling affects (VA 25:599–612, 1155, 1527, MCP 15:946). Such remedies, therefore, must be seen as contributing (at least indirectly) to moral virtue.[5] Traits of temperament, including empirical desires or other features of our "way of sense," that make duty easier for us to do are clearly only fortunate circumstances that make virtue less necessary. But such features could also count as part of virtue if we regard them as belonging to *the same quality of the agent* that we regard as the agent's volitional strength. Kant seems uninterested in settling this issue, perhaps because he thinks that in practice, because of the inner opacity of human psychology, it will be difficult or impossible to draw such a distinction, however important theoretically it may be.

When Kant distinguishes between character and temperament in the opening pages of the *Groundwork*, he is interested only in eliciting assent from common rational moral cognition to the proposition that it regards character and temperament very differently as regards the kind of *moral value* they possess (whether authentic moral worth or a value less central to morality) (G 4:398–9). It does not follow that they can be clearly distinguished as they occur in us, and we misread Kant if we commit this non sequitur and then ascribe it to him too.

4. Virtue, Duty, and Continence

Kant holds that we have a duty to strive to make the motive of duty a sufficient incentive in all our actions, and that only those actions done from duty have genuine or authentic moral worth (MS 6:393, G 4:397–9). From this some might infer that for Kant virtuous action requires the motive of duty alone, and that no action motivated by inclination could be virtuous. As we saw in Chapter 2, however, this inference would also be invalid, and it too would represent a very serious (if sadly common) misunderstanding of Kantian ethics.

Acting solely from moral motives constitutes what Kant calls "purity of disposition" (KpV 5:116, 128). Kant describes an agent's "disposition" as "the inner" (or "subjective") "principle of maxims" (R 6:23, 37). A pure disposition displays virtue (KpV 5:114,116, R 6:23), but Kant explicitly distinguishes the moral disposition from virtue (VE 27:300). 'Disposition', like 'the good will', refers not to abiding characteristics of an agent but to the principles or maxims on which the agent acts, or, more specifically, to the incentive on which an agent may act upon a maxim on a given occasion – which might be something momentary and might, like goodness of will, be either entirely characteristic or totally uncharacteristic of that agent (cf. KpV 5:116, 128). Like any sensible person, Kant will see no plausibility at all in Hume's weird notion that people cannot be held responsible for actions that are atypical of them (Hume E, p. 98).[6]

A disposition for Kant can be virtuous or the contrary (KpV 5:84), but that is only because virtue presupposes a certain kind of volition or disposition. Conversely, virtue can be regarded as "a firmly grounded disposition to fulfill duty precisely" (R 6:23). But that means only that *virtue* is an enduring property of an agent which manifests itself in actions having a certain disposition.[7] In short, a "disposition" for Kant is *not* what philosophers now call a "dispositional property" (such as an enduring tendency, belonging to a person's character, to feel or will or act in determinate ways). It is rather a feature of the principle (the maxim) on which an agent is acting (or of the agent's incentive in acting on it), even when the agent is acting this way only momentarily and highly uncharacteristically.

We can also act virtuously (with the moral strength to do our duty) even when we do not have a pure disposition. We have a duty to *strive* for a pure disposition, so that the motive of duty alone is *sufficient*. We have this duty because it is "hazardous" to rely on motives besides duty, because the performance of duty on such motives is always only "contingent and precarious" (G 4:390, KpV 5:73). We have no duty at all, however, to *exclude* other motives we might have for doing our duty (MS 6:393). (No text I know of in Kant says that the mere presence of such motives would "taint" a dutiful action or make it blameworthy.) The duty to strive for a pure disposition is only a wide or imperfect duty. It is meritorious to come closer to making the motive of duty sufficient, but we are not in the least to blame if we require incentives other than duty in order to do our duty, so long as we in fact do it.[8]

Kant distinguishes acting from duty from acting in conformity to duty from empirical incentives. We saw in Chapter 2 that he ascribes "true moral worth" only to the former actions not in order to assert that other performances of duty are devoid of moral value but only to distinguish what is central to morality from what is comparatively peripheral. Virtue, as the strength of our will in fulfilling duty, can also include (as part of what gives good maxims their strength) these incentives of inclination: "Virtue has the abiding maxim of lawful actions, no matter whence one draws the incentives that the power of choice needs for such actions" (R 6:47). In this respect, Kantian ethics differs significantly from the (Humean) school of virtue ethics – and *a fortiori* with James Martineau's or Michael Slote's even more extreme version of it – in that this school makes the rightness of an action consist entirely in its being done from the right motive.[9] Confusing Kant's position with this one is a common but serious misreading of the opening pages of the *Groundwork*.

Kantian and Aristotelian moral psychology. It might be thought that Kant's conception of virtue identifies virtue not with what Aristotle would call "virtue" (*arētē*) but rather with what he would call "continence" (*enkrateia*) – the capacity of a person with base desires to resist them and act according to right reason in spite of them (Aristotle Book VII, 9). This thought, however, is seriously mistaken. Continence for Aristotle is one kind of strength to resist bad desires, but so is virtue, and virtue is stronger (Aristotle 1146a5). Thus Aristotelian continence could be at most one species of Kantian virtue – an inferior species of it.[10]

An Aristotelian virtue – for instance, temperance – makes the agent *enjoy* abstaining from what is bad, whereas the person without virtue who abstains (presumably, including the continent person) is grieved by it (Aristotle 1104b7–9).[11] On this point, Kantian virtue is again more like Aristotelian virtue than Aristotelian continence, because Kant insists that the "aesthetic constitution, the temperament, as it were, of virtue" is "courageous and hence joyous" (R 6:24n). To identify Kantian virtue with Aristotelian continence is thus to underestimate (by Kant's own standards) what Kant thinks the virtuous agent will be like. In that sense, it simply provides us with an unflattering caricature of virtue itself, as Kant conceives it.[12]

Kant's concept of virtue may all too easily be misunderstood because we do not understand some important but subtle differences in the moral psychology of the two philosophers. For Aristotle, the soul is divided into rational and nonrational parts. When an agent acts virtuously, the nonrational part "listens to reason" – which is obviously different from simply having the agent's appetites so conditioned that they blindly urge the same actions that right reason would urge (if it were listened to – which it obviously isn't, if we act from mere appetite rather than from right reason) (Aristotle 1102b30–32). For Kant, however, practical reason is the will, and it directly produces desires, both good and bad, depending on which prevails – its predisposition to good or its propensity to evil. Evil is not mechanical determination of the will by empirical desires but the free adoption of a maxim that irrationally gives preference to inclination over reason (R 6:33–7). When the will chooses according to reason, inclination may (or may not) contingently agree with rational desire, but there is no question in Kantian moral psychology of inclinations "listening (or not listening) to reason" – in the sense in which in Aristotle's moral psychology the nonrational part of the soul can be guided by reason. It follows that for Kant the agreement of inclination with reason is not a condition of virtuous action in the same way that for Aristotle it is a condition for virtue that nonrational appetite should be guided by reason. For Kant, the only question is whether inclinations happen to point in the same direction as this rational desire or in the opposite direction (as Kant thinks there is an inevitable tendency for them to do, owing to the innate propensity to evil in the human power of choice). The agreement between rational desire and inclination is not essential to virtue, which is primarily strength of *character*, not a matter of fortunately constituted (or carefully cultivated) empirical temperament. For Kant, even if rational desire must overcome recalcitrant inclinations, the virtuous person, in acting virtuously, will be doing what he most truly wills to do and will therefore do it joyfully and cheerfully. For Aristotle, however, it is an essential feature of virtue that the nonrational part of the soul should be guided by reason (as a son by a wise father). If that does not happen, the best the agent can be is continent, not virtuous.

The moral of the story is that if we equate Kant's distinction between rational and empirical desire with Aristotle's talk about rational and irrational parts of the soul, then we distort the claims Kant is making about virtue. Aristotelian virtue will even seem impossible in a Kantian framework. Of course if, contrariwise, we translate Aristotelian virtue as nonrational appetite listening to right reason into Kantian terms, so that it becomes merely the fortunate coincidence of inclination urging us to do the action that happens to be our duty, then our misunderstanding of Aristotle is even more gross, because that would effectively abolish the crucial role of *right reason* in his moral psychology.

The differences between Kant and Aristotle go still deeper, however, when it comes to Kant's conception of the abysmal evil in the human faculty of desire, which attaches to it owing to the corruption of our social condition. For Kant, human beings are so constituted by nature, and by the influence of society, that what they have most reason to do, what most deeply affirms their most authentic volition – hence in that sense what they most properly desire to do – must often present itself to them as something they must inwardly constrain themselves to do, contrary to their natural inclinations (as these have been corrupted by their social condition). It is only against the background of a human nature corrupted by society – and especially by the modern bourgeois society that Rousseau and Kant call "civilization" – that true freedom for us can never consist in "the slavery of mere appetite, but only in obedience to a law we give ourselves."[13]

When Kant speaks of this moral self-constraint, we all too easily understand it (even in the face of his explicit statements to the contrary) as a kind of *external* constraint, to which a person would submit only unwillingly or grudgingly. This makes it difficult for us to accept at face value Kant's assertions that the virtuous frame of mind is cheerful and joyous.

Or perhaps the problem is that we too readily identify with those same corrupt inclinations that are fostered in us by a society based on inequality and mutual antagonism. In that case, we would misunderstand Kant only because we conspicuously lack the virtue he is talking about. We are then the morally inferior kind of person of whom Aristotle says that following right reason and denying their base desires is painful. In that case, our rejection of Kant is a symptom of vice; Aristotle would see through it, just as Kant does, and likewise regard it with contempt.

5. Practical Judgment and Wisdom

Practical judgment. Virtue, as the strength of morally good maxims, presupposes good will, because the good will is simply volition according to good principles. We have seen that there can also be good will accompanied not by virtue but by moral weakness, in which case the right thing will often not be done (MS 6:408). But there is another capacity whose lack may lead to doing the wrong thing even where both good will and virtue are present. This is a lack of *practical judgment* – the capacity to descend correctly from a universal principle to particular instances that conform to it. As we saw in Chapter 3, §4, Kant insists that judgment is a special capacity, for which we cannot substitute by supplying further instructions as to how to apply our principles, because these would only be more principles, whose correct application would once again require judgment (KrV A133/B172; VA 7:199). Judgment cannot be taught by instruction, therefore, but is either an inborn talent or else a capacity acquired (and sharpened) by experience and practice (VA 7:227–8). This is true of all forms of judgment, which Kant distinguishes into theoretical, practical, and aesthetic. Within practical judgment, he distinguishes practical judgment proper, which involves the application of moral principles, from "technical" judgment, and in some places in his lectures also from prudential judgment, which chooses the means to happiness (VA 7:199, 25:204, 403–13).

As we also saw in Chapter 3, in the *Groundwork* Kant regards practical judgment as the basic task involved in applying the moral law to human nature. "Practical anthropology" is described as the exercise of "the power of judgment sharpened by experience" in "distinguishing in what cases the moral laws are applicable" (G 4:389). In the *Metaphysics of Morals*, Kant devotes his "casuistical questions" to raising issues that concern the application to difficult or problematic cases of the principles of duty he is discussing. They are not a part of the "science" he is presenting (or of its "dogmatics") but instead belong to a "practice in how to *seek* truth" (MS 6:411). Apparently the closest Kant thinks we can come to giving instruction to judgment is to encourage reflection on examples whose difficulty gives us practice in exercising our faculty of practical judgment. It is the aim of his "casuistical questions" to offer us a few such examples. Good practical judgment presupposes a good will (both good maxims and good ends), though it *consists* in the capacity to apply the right principles to particular cases. Thus it resembles, at least in these respects, Aristotelian *phronesis* (Aristotle, Book 6, Chapters 7–8, 1141a10–1142a30).

Proponents of virtue ethics, especially so-called moral "particularists," are fond of arguing that morally correct action cannot be action on general rules, because (they say) the application of general rules to particular cases is something that cannot itself be codified according to rules. This is a point sometimes associated with the later Wittgenstein, but long before that it was a Kantian point. But, as we saw in Chapter 3, §4, the point has been hopelessly garbled when it is interpreted as an argument that there are no moral rules.

Wisdom. If there is yet another good quality of the moral agent that Kant regards as comprehensive or complete. This is *wisdom*. Wisdom is "the idea of a practical use of reason that conforms perfectly with the law" (VA 7:200). It consists more in conduct than in knowledge (G 4:405),[14] yet it also leads in the direction of a comprehensive science of the good (KpV 5:131) and involves being able to teach as well as to do (KpV 5:163). Wisdom thus involves a comprehensive knowledge of which ends to pursue, how to combine them, and how to pursue them under contingent conditions. It would seem to be enough to deny the quality of wisdom to anyone if they lacked either the good will to act from the right maxims and set the right ends or the practical judgment to select the right actions in promotion of these ends, or the virtue necessary to constrain themselves to perform those actions.

Wisdom, as far as we have it, also demands a science of moral philosophy and leads us in the direction of one. But according to Kant, this is not because the good person needs scientific instruction in order to know how to act. It is rather that without the reflection and systematization that comes with philosophical inquiry, we would be too vulnerable to the "natural dialectic" of human reason in the moral sphere – that is, to the "propensity to rationalize against the strict laws of duty and cast doubt upon their validity, or at least upon their purity and strictness, and where possible, to make them better suited to our wishes and inclinations" (G 4:405).

In other words, the closest we can ever come to wisdom are the aspiration to it and the search for it – yet not in order to find it, but rather in order to compensate in the best way we can for our corrupt tendency to deceive ourselves, for the advantage of our self-conceit and indolence, about what our duties are. The attempt to think abstractly and systematically about morality is the best way to do this because – contrary to the false doctrine later proclaimed by Nietzsche – the will to system is the highest will to integrity of which creatures like us are capable.[15] Someone who had true wisdom would deserve to be called a "practical philosopher" (MS 6:163). Kant emphasizes, however, that wisdom – an idea invented by the ancients – is more than can be asked of any human being (VA 7:200). If we entertain this idea when we think of ourselves as philosophers, Kant thinks, "it would do no harm to discourage the self-conceit of someone who ventures to claim the title of philosopher if one holds before him, in the very definition, a standard of self-estimation that would very much lower his pretension" (KpV 5:108).

Wisdom is the best concept we can form of how we ought to be. But for Kant, our main purpose in forming it is only to teach ourselves that no one is wise, hence that there are no actual human beings we should try to imitate and that the only real guide to conduct is the moral law we give ourselves. What we accomplish in comparing ourselves with the ideal of wisdom is not to become wiser but only to strike down the self-conceit that misleads us into thinking we might become wise. The closest we can ever actually come to the ideal of wisdom is to acquire that humbling item of Socratic self-knowledge.

6. Ideals and Principles

The advocates of virtue ethics usually overestimate the differences between Aristotle and Kant. This is partly because, under the influence of too many common caricatures, they underestimate Kant, lumping his ethical theory together with others to which they think they have decisive objections. Sometimes, however, it is because they underestimate Aristotle even more, by mistakenly supposing him to be more like themselves than he is like Kant.

Kant distinguishes his own ethical theory as an ethics of *principles*, along with that of all the moderns, from all ancient ethical theory, which he regards as an ethics of *ideals*. An ethics of principles is one grounded on maxims, laws, or other normative principles to which we should try to make our actions conform. An ethics of ideals is one grounded on a conception of a certain kind of person whom we should strive to be like. Kant distinguishes five different ethical ideals in antiquity, the first three focusing on our natural powers and the last two involving our relation to the supernatural:

I. The *Cynic* ideal (of Diogenes and Antisthenes), which is *natural simplicity*, and happiness as the product of nature rather than of art.

II. The *Epicurean* ideal, which is that of the *man of the world*, and happiness as a product of art, not of nature.

III. The *Stoic* ideal (of Zeno), which is that of the *sage*, and happiness as identical with moral perfection or virtue.

IV. The *mystical* ideal (of Plato) of the visionary character, in which the highest good consists in the human being's seeing himself in communion with the highest being.

V. The *Christian* ideal of holiness, whose pattern is Jesus Christ. (VE 27:100–6, 247–50, 483–5; 29:602–4).[16]

By contrast, ethical theories like Kant's, Mill's, or Sidgwick's represent an ethics of principles. What people call "virtue ethics" represents an ethics of ideals.

Kant is not opposed to the use of ideals in ethics. On the contrary, we have seen already that *wisdom* functions for him as a kind of ideal, and so does the "ideal of humanity well-pleasing to God," the Christ ideal, which (as we see from the above) he regards as the latest (and highest) of the ancient ideals. Kant's endorsement of the Christian ideal presents clearly his view about the relation of ideals to principles, for he calls it "the personified idea of the good principle" (R 6:60).

An *ideal* is the concept of an individual being (here, an individual human being) that corresponds to (or personifies) an *a priori* concept of reason, or an *idea*. But an idea, in turn, rests on a principle of reason (here, the *good principle*, which struggles against the radical evil in human nature). Ideals have their place, but they are grounded on ideas, which in turn are grounded on principles. Kant argues for this ordering in theoretical as well as practical philosophy (see KrV A298–332/B355–90, KpV 5:57–63). Recognition of the priority of principles over ideals, Kant thinks, was the basic advance of modern ethics over ancient ethics. In Kant's history of ethics, the Christian ideal, the latest and most perfect of the ancient ideals, was pivotal, because it conveyed the truth that all ideals based on human examples are imperfect and corrupt, and no human being can hope to reach the pure ideal except through supernatural divine aid. In Kant's view, this pointed the way beyond an ethics of ideals toward an ethics of principles (VE 27:251–2, 29:605).

It is not only our limitations as moral agents, however, and the absence from real life of actual individuals excellent enough to imitate that justify moderns in taking a different approach. Another problem with the ideal is that it can be actualized in too many ways by individuals whose vocation is to think for themselves and shape their own ways of life.

Kant seeks to ground goodness of will in a single fundamental principle, grounded on a single objective value. He recognizes that there are many good ends which may be set by a person acting on this principle – many diverse instances, that is, of "one's own perfection" and "the happiness of others," and endlessly many priorities among those instances that different people may choose in shaping their lives. It therefore makes more sense to think in terms of abstractions – good will, the good disposition, good practical judgment – that can be exemplified in endlessly many ways, depending on the individual circumstances and choices of self-governing agents. Kant knows that modern civilized life offers us no single kind of life, not even any finite set of lives, in which these abstractions can be combined in a manner suited to imitation. Our ethical reflections must take an altogether different form if they are to correspond to reality and give us reasonable direction.

Kant's reservations about ideal ethics are also connected to the details of his moral psychology, especially his idea of unsociable sociability (IAG 8:20) and self-conceit (KpV 5:73), born of the social (especially the modern European or "civilized") condition (VA 7:321–33; R 6:27, 93). Given these propensities, an ethics of ideals has certain features that are even likely to corrupt us and lead us astray. All rational beings have equal (absolute) worth. But an ethics of ideals, or a virtue ethics, celebrates the qualities of agents that distinguish one from another and make some objects of admiration, others of contempt. Kantian empirical anthropology tells us that an ethics which does this will feed human self-conceit, envy, and the self-deceptive wish to be superior to other human beings, which is necessarily irrational and contrary to morality because our reason tells us that all rational beings necessarily have dignity and worth as ends in themselves and as members of the realm of ends. Examples of good conduct are useful only in showing us that it is *possible* to do what we should (MS 6:480).

Kant repeatedly insists that in estimating our own morality, we must never compare ourselves with others but only with the moral law (KpV 5:76–7, MS 6:435–6, VE 27:349–50). Given our human nature, an ethics of ideals, one that encourages comparisons of moral worth between people, is likely to make us worse rather than better. If others are represented to us as better than we are, then this is not likely to cause us to imitate their virtues but only encourage our tendency to envy and hate them, which is directly contrary to duty:

People are very much inclined to take others as the measure of their moral worth, and if they then believe themselves to be superior to some, this feeds their self-conceit ... I can always think that I am better than others, although if, for example, I am better only than the worst, I am still by no means very much better ... If moral humility, then, is the curbing of self-conceit in regard to the moral law, it never implies any comparison with others, but only with that law. (VE 27:349)

Accordingly, a teacher will not tell his naughty pupil: Take an example from that good (orderly, diligent) boy! For this would only cause him to hate that boy, who puts him in an unfavorable light ... So it is not comparison with any other human being whatsoever (as he is) but with the idea (of humanity), as it ought to be, and so comparison with the law, that must serve as the standard. (MS 6:480)

When the human being measures his worth by comparison to others, he seeks either to raise himself above the other or to diminish the worth of the other. The latter is envy. (VP 9:491)

Morality, as the disposition to obey the moral law one gives oneself, is critical even of virtue, which is at most the strength of will in following this disposition. Morality must be even more critical of mere social customs, which substitute social decorum for the moral disposition and substitute for true moral virtue the mere conformity to custom. The morality of autonomy has arisen historically out of the mere conformity to custom, but we are still at such an early stage in that historical progression that we have as yet no proper word even for "morality," still using the word for it that signifies mere slavish adherence to social custom that is the direct opposite of the truly free moral disposition:

> The word *Sittlichkeit* has been adopted to express morality, although *Sitte* [custom] is really the concept of social decorum; for virtue, however, we require more than customary goodness, a certain self-constraint and self-command. Peoples can have customs and no virtue, or virtue and no customs (*conduite* is the propriety of customs). A science of customs is not yet virtue, and virtue is not yet morality ... For virtue means strength in mastering and overcoming oneself, in regard to the moral disposition. But morality is the original source of that disposition ... But because we still have no other word for morality, we take *Sittlichkeit* to signify morality, since we cannot take virtue to do so. (VE 27:300)

Human customs are generally corrupt, so that what they consider to be virtues are often not virtues at all but the reverse of what is authentically admirable or truly deserving of praise or encouragement. Virtue requires self-constraint and self-command on rational principles, not merely customary goodness. But even genuine virtues are comparatively superficial in relation to the authentic sources of morality. Virtue is not yet morality. Virtue is the strength of good maxims to overcome the bad inclinations that resist them, but we are entitled to praise them as virtues only for as long as the maxims they strengthen are truly good ones, rationally justifiable maxims that arise in us from a disposition to do what is morally right.

"Cultivation of the virtues" always means the reproduction of a certain kind of human personality that was well adjusted to a society based on unenlightened traditions, inequalities, forms of oppression – in short, on the radical propensity to evil that belongs to our nature as social beings (R 6:94–5). For Kant, as for Rousseau, this corruption has thus far only been made worse by the advance of civilization (VA 7:326–9). "We live in an age of discipline, culture and civilization, but we are still a long way off from an age in which we might make people moral (*Moralisirung*)" (VP 9:451).

An ideal ethics is suited to a more innocent, premodern age, to a society in which customs are relatively simple and uniform and the customary standards they presuppose are generally taken for granted unreflectively, so that it is even with a kind of innocence that people inflict on themselves the pernicious self-deception that there is such a thing as a "fine and good man" – that the rest of us should admire them, defer to them, and put their interests ahead of our own. This is necessarily a society that tolerates social inequalities too much and respects human individuals too little. Every ideal ethics is too deferential to "culture" itself – to unenlightened and unfree ways of thinking, or unjust inequalities of status, power, or wealth. The first principle of morality in relation to culture is that no human customs should ever be venerated or deferred to uncritically.[17] In the course of the historical development of our faculty of practical reason, an ideal ethics, or an ethics of virtue, must necessarily give way to an ethics of principles.

9

Duties

1. Kant's Concept of Duty

Why 'duty' is an odious word. 'Duty' is not only a crucial concept in Kant's ethics but also in effect a technical term in Kantian vocabulary. Whatever affinity the Kantian sense of 'duty' may have with the ordinary meaning of the word in English (or of *Pflicht* in German), any hope we might have of gaining a sympathetic hearing for Kantian ethics must depend on our putting some distance between the technical Kantian meaning of this word and the sense, and even more some of the pragmatics, of the term as it is commonly used.

Duties are often what we have in consequence of some role we play in a social institution, arrangement, or relationship. This includes many social arrangements that involve us in behavior that is morally questionable or worse. As a result, appeals to duty are commonly used not only to override our temptations to avoid playing our part in some arrangement but also to put out of action any reservations or moral scruples we might have about playing that part. People therefore appeal to duty when they want to put a stop to critical reflection about what we are doing. Soldiers are supposed to think of their duty – to their buddies, to their unit, to their commanders, to their "mission," to their country – and of nothing else. This is what makes them the fearless and efficient killing machines (and cannon fodder) the politicians and commanders want them to be. These same politicians appeal to our sense of patriotic duty to get us to accept their curtailment of our liberty and to enlist our support for their wars and other unjust or misguided enterprises. Duty is always the first deterrent used against whistleblowers: When the appeal to duty ceases, then come the threats and intimidation.[1]

Even when we are not dealing with abuses, there are connotations of "duty" that seriously mislead us about the Kantian concept. Duties are often enforced by external coercion. Some philosophers, such as Mill, think it is even part of the concept of duty that duty may be exacted from someone (like a debt) by some kind of external pressure (Mill, p. 49). This thought, especially when applied to the phrase 'acting from duty', makes 'duty' the very last word anyone would associate with autonomy or the free self-direction of one's life. If I say that I am visiting Aunt Maude in the Alzheimer's ward "solely from duty," that means I am doing it grudgingly, probably cowed into it by the thought of the dirty looks and nagging phone calls I will otherwise get from my overbearing parents and disapproving siblings. This is the main reason why, when Kant says "an action has moral worth only if it is done from duty," our first reaction is a burst of that mirthless laughter we reserve for sick jokes.

Kantian duty. In the face of all this, it may be rhetorically ineffective simply to repeat the plain truth that for Kant 'duty' refers solely to the respect we owe to humanity in ourselves and others and to the various forms of moral self-constraint that we must exercise, when necessary, in order to be rationally self-governing beings. But let's give it one last try just the same.

Kant holds that the performance of *juridical* duties may be externally coerced, but Kant's basic conception of ethical duty is *inner or self-constraint*. 'Duty' refers to the act of freely making yourself desire something and do it because you appreciate the objective moral reasons there are for doing it. "To do something from duty means: to obey reason" (VP 9:483). 'Obedience' here signifies neither external authority nor coercion but only that the reasons are *moral* reasons, as distinct from merely instrumental or prudential reasons. In Kantian ethics, 'duty' refers to *self*-constraint not only in opposition to inclinations that oppose reason but also to the dictates of merely instrumental or prudential reason, which moral reasons override. *Duty* is whatever you know you have most reason to do, and what you want to constrain yourself to do because you are aware of this. Kant gives the name 'duty' to all actions we have moral reasons to do, even meritorious actions that are not morally blameable to omit, because (human nature being what it is), we will occasionally need to exercise inner rational constraint if we are to perform these morally valuable actions.

Thus "the motive of duty" includes *all* the properly *moral* reasons we have to perform morally valuable (*pflichtmäßig*) actions. That makes motive of duty just as unitary, but also just as varied, as these moral reasons themselves. The single ultimate foundation of these reasons, as we saw in Chapters 3 and 4, is the value of rational nature as an end in itself, but there are many different ways that this value calls for acknowledgment and manifests itself in our motivation. "The motive of duty" is only the collective name for them. Many misunderstandings of Kant's notion of duty involve the mistaken thought that acting from duty is action whose motivation somehow excludes both desire and feeling. As we saw in Chapter 2, for Kant that would be nonsense. Acting from duty *always* involves desire, even a desire to do the action *for its own sake*. That is precisely why Kant thinks acting from duty is easy to distinguish from actions done for some further end, such as self-interest, but hard to distinguish from actions done from an immediate inclination to do them (G 4:397). The difference is whether the desire is rational and actively self-effected or merely empirical, a passive impulse. This is not a difference we can always be aware of merely by having the desire, and this easily allows us to perpetrate flattering self-deceptions on ourselves, as Kant is well aware (G 4:407).

Because it creates an immediate desire to do the action, the motive of duty is inevitably expressed not merely as an objective reason for wanting something and doing something but also as a *feeling*. In the First Section of the *Groundwork*, Kant highlights the feeling of *respect*, especially respect for the moral law. In the *Metaphysics of Morals*, as we have seen, he distinguishes four different kinds of such feelings. They include *moral feeling* (feelings of approval or disapproval directed at actions), *conscience* (moral feelings directed to oneself, in view of some action performed or contemplated), *love of human beings* (i.e., any form of benevolent caring or concern for the welfare of another as a person who is an end in itself), and finally *respect* (for the dignity of a person, or for the moral law as the basis of our own rational self-government) (MS 6:399–403). These feelings are the direct and natural acknowledgment of moral reasons. Visiting Aunt Maude at the Alzheimer's ward *from duty* (in the Kantian sense) is being motivated by the care and concern you owe her as your aunt, as someone with whom you presumably have a history of mutual affection, or maybe just as a suffering human being with whom fate has connected you in such a way that you have a decisive moral reason to show her some kindness and companionship. If members of your family take it upon themselves to interpose their dirty looks and nagging in place of your moral awareness and hijack your authority over your own actions, then that is only their officious infringement of your personal freedom. It has nothing to do with your acting from *duty* (in the Kantian sense).

Acting from duty, however, does involve self-*constraint*. To accept the Kantian concept of duty, you have to accept the paradox that what we have the best reasons for doing, what we most deeply, freely, and autonomously will to do, what Kant says we should always do gladly and with a cheerful heart, must also regularly take the form of self-constraint or "duty."

It is very beautiful to do good to human beings from love for them and from sympathetic benevolence, or to be just from love of order: but this is not yet the genuine moral maxim of our conduct, the maxim befitting our position among rational beings as *human beings*, when we presume with proud conceit, like volunteers, not to trouble ourselves about the thought of duty and, as independent of command, to want to do of our own pleasure what we think we need no command to do. (KpV 5:82)

That rational self-government often involves self-constraint follows from Kant's theory of human nature. As we saw in Chapters 1 and 2, it is an error (perhaps even a dishonest evasion) to ascribe this to some hostility on Kant's part to "the senses" or "the body." The real source of resistance to reason in us is our propensity to unsociable sociability in the social condition – especially in what Kant and Rousseau call "civilization" and what a subsequent social theory in the same tradition would call "capitalism" or "modern bourgeois society") (I 8:20, KpV 5:73, R 6:29–44). The irony of our fate is that the very historical conditions for developing our capacity for moral reason – which tells us that all rational beings are of equal (absolute) worth and that we ought to follow a moral law that brings all their ends into systematic harmony – are also conditions in which our empirical desires, as they are freely taken up by us in exercising our rational predisposition to humanity, naturally pressure us to behave contrary to that law of reason. As social (and especially civilized) creatures, therefore, we have a corrupt need to think better of ourselves than we do of others, and our natural impulses all cater to our self-conceit.

It may be that some of our resistance to Kantian duty is only resistance to Kant's dark, unflattering picture of human nature as he thinks our modern bourgeois civilization has made it. To the extent that this is true, we should reflect on the fact that this resistance partly is due to an unattractive complacency about ourselves and our society. When it masquerades as something more healthy than that, it may even deserve to be called (using, once again, a later terminology) a kind of "ideological mystification." Once Kant's conception of duty is properly understood in this social–historical context, we may begin to see that Kantian ethics has some powerful rejoinders to make against people's understandable reluctance to accept the centrality of "duty" in Kantian ethics.

2. The System of Duties

Right and ethics. Kant's most basic division of duties is between juridical duties and ethical duties, which determines the division of the *Metaphysics of Morals* (*Sitten*) into the Doctrine of Right (*Recht*) and the Doctrine of Virtue, which he calls "ethics" (*Ethik*). Right and ethics constitute separate "legislations" (MS 6:219–20) – that is, separate systems of duties, each with its own distinct fundamental principle, expressing the worth of humanity in a different way.

Right underlies the political state and its external legislation, constituting a rational structure of juridical duties that is distinct from the system of ethical duties. Many juridical duties are supposed to be enforced externally and coercively, as by civil or criminal laws. But Kant does not regard all duties of right as coercible. He thinks of duties of justice based on equity as unenforceable. (An informal promise, such as the one discussed in the *Groundwork*, is most naturally thought of as falling under this heading.) Even some juridical duties that rulers owe their subjects are such that no one can rightfully coerce their performance (MS 6:234–5, TP 8:289–306). An important (and partly original) aspect of Kant's theory of right is his theory of international and cosmopolitan right, pertaining to the relations between nations and between people of different nations (TP 8:307–13, EF 8:354–60, MS 6:343–53). Kant hopes there will someday be ways of enforcing at least some of these parts of right, but he thinks the relevant duties of right are valid even when there are no enforcement mechanisms. We therefore misunderstand the Kantian conception of "right" if we think of it as merely a philosophy of law and the state. Instead, right is a system of rational moral (*sittliche*) norms whose function is to guarantee the treatment of humanity as an end in itself by protecting the external freedom of persons according to universal laws. Most of the moral issues on which we will be focusing in Chapters 11–14 (issues about economic distribution, punishment, sex, and lying) are mainly issues of right, not of ethics. Many discussions in the literature of the supposedly "Kantian" approach to these issues are vitiated by their failure to appreciate this.

By contrast, the duties belonging to *ethics* have the function of treating humanity, in our own person as well as in the person of others, as an end in itself in ways that go beyond the mere protection of external freedoms. They perform this function by rational self-constraint that perfects human nature and promotes human welfare and happiness. Ethical duties, in contrast to duties of right, must *never* be coercively enforced. Whoever tries to do so violates the right of the person coerced, and such injustice should itself be coercively prevented. Ethical duties are performed only through the agent's own rational inner constraint involving the moral feelings already mentioned. Every juridical duty, however, for Kant counts also as an ethical duty, in the sense that the worth of humanity, which grounds ethics, requires us also to respect the right. We should perform juridical duties too through inner self-constraint, from the motive of duty – more specifically, one supposes, mainly from the feeling of respect directed to the right and to the external rights of persons.

The main division within *ethical* duties is between duties to oneself and duties to others. Within each of these main kinds, there is a further distinction between duties that are strictly owed, requiring specific actions or omissions, and whose violation incurs moral blame; and duties that are wide or meritorious, where specific actions are not strictly owed but rather deserve moral credit or merit. Kant treats these latter as *duties* (making no use of any category such as "supererogation") because, once again, 'duty' refers most fundamentally to rational constraint, and he thinks the meritorious actions in question are fit objects of inner rational self-constraint.

We can constrain ourselves, that is, through love of human beings as well as respect for them, and through the thought that our actions are meritorious as well as through the thought that omitting these actions would be blameworthy. Generosity toward others, or increasing our own perfection, is something we can *make ourselves do* through moral reasons and rational feelings. That is why not all duties are strict or perfect duties, and also why it is appropriate to speak at all of wide or imperfect duty.[2] Regarding duties to oneself, this division is described as between "perfect" and "imperfect" duty; regarding duties to others, the strict duties are called 'duties of respect' while the wide or meritorious ones are called 'duties of love'.

Conflicts of duty. Kant is widely regarded as denying that there can be conflicts of duty and is frequently made the target of those who want to insist that there can be, and are, "moral dilemmas" – that is, cases in which no matter what agents do, they act wrongly. This means they incur what is sometimes called "moral residue" – such as justified feelings of guilt or further duties, such as a duty to "make it up" to a person when they have broken a promise to them, even if they had to break the promise in order to fulfill another obligation.[3] Kantian moral theorists, such as Alan Donagan, have admitted that such conflicts can arise in consequence of the agent's own wrongdoing (for instance, making promises one should not have made),[4] but as others have pointed out, if moral dilemmas can arise in that way, there is no reason why they might not also arise as a result of the misconduct of other people, or even unfortunate circumstances for which no one is responsible.[5]

The principal passage in which Kant addresses the question is this:

A conflict of duties (*collisio officourum s. obligationum*) would be a relation between them in which one of them would cancel the other (wholly or in part). – But since duty and obligation are concepts that express objective practical necessity of certain actions and two rules opposed to each other cannot be necessary at the same time, if it is a duty to act in accordance with one rule, to act in accordance with the opposite rule is not a duty but even contrary to duty; so a *collision of duties* and obligations is inconceivable (*obligationes non colliduntur*). However, a subject may have, in a rule he prescribes to himself, two obligating grounds (*Verpflichtungsgründe*) one or the other of which is not sufficient to put him under duty. – When two such grounds conflict with each other, practical philosophy says not that the stronger obligation takes precedence (*fortior obligatio vincit*) but that the stronger *obligating ground* prevails (*fortior obligandi ratio vincit*). (MS 6:224)

Here Kant denies (in so many words) that there can be such a thing as a "conflict of duties." But we must pay close attention to what he means by this: He means that there can be no case in which one duty might so come into conflict with another as to "cancel" it (wholly or in part). Thus Kant does not necessarily disagree with those who insist that there can be real "moral dilemmas," because their claim is that there can be conflicting duties that *do not* "cancel" others (but instead give rise to "moral costs," or to other duties). Kant does explicitly recognize that there can be moral conflicts between obligating reasons (*Verpflichtungsgründe, rationes obligandi*) – that is, the grounds or reasons why we have a duty or obligation.

A better reason to complain is that in this passage Kant simply fails to address some other issues on which debates about "moral dilemmas" usually center. One of these is a point of deontic logic. From the fact that I am obligated to ϕ, it follows that it is false that I am not obligated to ϕ. But it does not follow that I am not obligated not to ϕ. Or if this is supposed to follow, that requires a separate deontic principle, one that would be questioned by those who believe in "moral dilemmas" (or "conflicts of duty," though in a different sense from the one Kant means). What Kantian ethics should say about this issue in deontic logic is not clear. Kant says nothing explicitly about it. If having a duty to ϕ is equivalent to determining rationally, all things considered, that you must ϕ, then that would seem to provide a good reason for thinking that you cannot, in this same sense, have a duty not to ϕ. But if duties fall under Kant's classification, and some of them are "strict," "narrow," or "perfect" duties, then there seems no good reason in principle why there could not be conflicts (in the above logical sense) between two duties falling under the latter heading. One thing should be clear: Kant does not deny this in the passage quoted above.

Kant allows that there could be a conflict between the two *grounds* of obligation (or obligating reasons) in question. In other words, the reason why you have a strict duty to ϕ might come into conflict with the different reason why you have a strict duty not to ϕ. His only rule here is *fortior obligandi ratio vincit* – the stronger reason prevails. This seems analytic, however, and analyticity is a feature that leads Kant to scorn other moral principles, such as Wolff's *fac bonum et omitte malum* (VE 27:264, 276–7). So we ought to wonder whether it really tells us anything informative at all. Kant gives us some guidance (but probably not enough) as to which obligating reasons are stronger than which others. Wide or imperfect duties succumb to strict or perfect duties; for example, the wide duty to aid a stranger is overridden by the duty not to let my parents starve (VE 27:537–8), and you must testify truthfully in court even if a lie would help your benefactor (and thus fulfill a wide duty of gratitude) (VE 27:508). This tells you *what to do in this case*, but it leaves most alleged "moral dilemmas" entirely unaddressed.

Kant also does not ask the following questions: When obligating reasons conflict, and we act on the stronger, is there ever a "moral residue" or "moral cost" left over from the weaker obligating reason? In which cases? And what would it consist in? (Justified feelings of guilt? A further obligation to make restitution to those to whom you would have owed the duty having the weaker ground?) That Kant does not raise such questions often leads people to conclude that he must deny there is any "moral residue." That conclusion seems overhasty and is clearly not required by any principle of Kantian ethics.

Or again, in cases of conflict *is* there always a stronger obligating reason? Might there be "ties"? Worse yet, might there be cases of conflict in which the obligating grounds are different, but it is impossible to establish any priority of one over the other? A negative answer to these questions is sometimes also inferred from Kant's claim that there can be no conflicts of duty. But the inference once again seems invalid, and Kant never says any such thing. In Chapter 3, §6, I suggested that an affirmative answer would cohere better with the basic conception of ethical theory appropriate to Kantian ethics.

The main reason Kant did not discuss any of these questions is that they are chiefly issues of moral judgment involving duties that are more circumstantial and relational than the duties falling under a "metaphysics of morals." He might have taken them up under the heading of "casuistical questions," but it would have been inappropriate to deal with them in the context of the passage where the issue of a *collisio officourum s. obligationum* arises. In short, once we understand what Kant means by his denial that there can be a "conflict of duties," there seems no good reason for the common habit of citing Kant as the paradigm case of a moral philosopher who stubbornly takes the negative side on all questions concerning whether there can be "conflicts of duty." For Kantian ethics, many of these questions seem to be open.

Duties that do not belong to the "metaphysics of morals." It is also important to appreciate that Kant's *Metaphysics of Morals* does not attempt to cover all the ethical duties we have. This is because Kant confines the "metaphysics" of morals only to those duties that are generated by applying the principle of morality to empirical human nature in general. But Kant recognizes that (as the ordinary use of the term "duty" reflects) many of our duties arise from the special circumstances of others, or our relations to them, and from the contingent social institutions defining these relations. In Kant's German idealist followers, Fichte and Hegel, the system of ethical duties came to be defined, or even superseded, by an account of a rational social order.[6] Not only these social duties but also the general duties that are the object of moral rules must be distinguished from the fundamental principle of morality in that they are empirically conditioned and subject in principle to variation with time and circumstances. Kantian ethics can thus allow some limited truth to those doctrines that fall under the name of "cultural relativism" regarding such duties. The objective content of people's duties, in other words, can change with social or historical circumstances, and also with the growth of our knowledge about what respect for humanity requires of us. But this does not in the least imply that the content of duty is ever merely a matter of subjective opinion or that it is determined by what people happen to believe their duties are.

Kant thinks the general duties we have merely as human beings are the foundation of all our duties. It is within their framework that we *also* acquire duties in consequence of social customs, institutions, and relationships. Some of these duties might be to ourselves, though most no doubt will be to others; some will be narrow and others wide; and some may in effect convert wide duties into narrow duties, as when particular responsibilities to others convert our wide duty of beneficence into a narrow duty to look after the welfare of our family or friends, or to provide for the interests of our clients in some professional relationship. Kant holds that we have duties based on social institutions and relations, and that they are important; but they fall outside the scope of what he intends to cover in the *Metaphysics of Morals*.

Kant regards the universal formula of the fundamental principle of duty as the law that is given universally by the idea of the will of every rational being (FA). This proposition, however, like all the formulations of the moral law presented in the *Groundwork*, is only about the philosophical foundations of morality. As we saw in Chapter 3, every such formula is distinct from the moral rules or duties that are to be directly applied in everyday moral reasoning, which result from the interpretation of it when it is applied to the empirical facts of human life. As Kant presents things in his final work on moral philosophy, the *Metaphysics of Morals*, our everyday moral reasoning depends on the constraints of our various duties, both wide and narrow, and not on some moral formula of permissibility such as FUL, applied procedurally to whatever situation presents itself. The need for a theory of duties, based on a different formulation of the principle of morality, is explicitly stated early in the Doctrine of Virtue:

[In] the formal principle of duty, in the categorical imperative "So act that the maxim of your action could become a universal law," ... maxims are regarded as subjective principles which merely qualify for a giving of universal law, and the requirement that they so qualify is only a negative principle (not to come into conflict with law as such). – How can there be, beyond this principle, a law for the maxims of actions? ...

For maxims of actions can be arbitrary [*willkürlich*], and are subject only to the limiting condition of being fit for a giving of universal law, which is the formal principle of actions. A *law*, however, takes away the arbitrariness of actions. (MS 6:389)

3. The Principle of Ethical Duties

Kant explicitly acknowledges in this passage that neither FUL nor FLN can give rise to any positive duties. Neither formula could possibly constitute any "CI-Procedure" for the derivation of a system of duties. The law that goes beyond the merely formal principle of duty has to do with the "matter of choice," namely with its *ends*. In other words, the foundations of a Kantian theory of ethical duties are *teleological*. The theory is based not on the inherent 'rightness' or 'wrongness' of actions but on which actions promote certain obligatory *ends* (our own perfection and the happiness of others).

Only the concept of an *end* that is also a duty, a concept that belongs exclusively to ethics, establishes a law for maxims of actions by subordinating the subjective end that everyone has to the objective end. (MS 6:389)

The supreme principle of the doctrine of virtue is: act in accordance with a maxim of *ends* that it can be a universal law for everyone to have. – In accordance with this principle a human being is an end for himself as well as for others, and it is not enough that he is not authorized to use either himself or others merely as means; . . . it is in itself his duty to make the human being as such his end. (MS 6:395)

Here it becomes clear that the "supreme principle of the doctrine of virtue" is something much closer to FH than to FUL. It is also clear that this principle will establish duties mainly by appealing to the fact that there are certain ends it is our duty to have. Kant gives these ends the collective name "duties of virtue" (MS 6:394–5).

The ends that are duties to have in accordance with this principle are of two kinds: Our own perfection, and the happiness of others. Regarding the former, Kant says:

The capacity to set oneself an end – any end whatsoever – is what characterizes humanity (as distinguished from animality). Hence there is also bound up with the end of humanity in our own person the rational will, and so the duty, to make ourselves worthy of humanity by culture in general, by procuring or promoting the capacity to realize all sorts of possible ends. (MS 6:392)

This argument rests our duty to make our own perfection into an end firmly on FH. Regarding our duty to make the happiness of others our end, the argument is different:

The reason it is a duty to be beneficent is this: since our self-love cannot be separated from our need to be loved (helped in case of need) by others as well, we therefore make ourselves an end for others; and the only way this maxim can be made binding is through its qualification as a universal law, hence through our will to make others our ends as well. (MS: 6:393)

This argument, while clearly alluding to the idea that humanity is an end in itself, also has evident parallels with the argument used in the fourth illustration of FLN in the *Groundwork*, where appeal is also made to the fact of human interdependence, the fact that our self-love cannot be rationally separated from our need to be helped by others (G 4:423).

A closer look, however, reveals that the two arguments are decisively different. With FUL or FLN, the question is only whether the maxim of refusing (on principle) to make the welfare of others our end can be willed without conflicting volitions to be a universal law (or law of nature). Because it cannot, it is impermissible. But even if the maxim of principled nonassistance is impermissible, it might still be permissible to adopt no maxim at all about helping others or making their happiness an end. Neither FUL nor FLN could possibly rule out this policy (or nonpolicy), because they test for permissibility only maxims (not the absence of a maxim). If we are to have a wide duty of beneficence, then we are required to include the happiness of others among our ends. Kant argues that we have such a duty by asking not whether the maxim of principled nonassistance can be thought without volitional conflict to be a universal law but instead what *we necessarily will to be an actual universal law* consequent on our rationally necessary volition that we be an end for others. To identify a maxim as one that we necessarily will as a universal law is to bring that maxim not under FUL or FLN, but under FA: the principle that we should act on those maxims that contain in themselves the volition that they be universal laws (G 4:440; cf. 4:432, 434, 438).

The basic divisions of the taxonomy: Duty towards . . . , Perfect and imperfect duty.[7] In the *Groundwork* Kant claims that maxims violating perfect duties cannot be thought of as universal laws, while those violating imperfect duties may be thought of but not willed as universal laws (G 4:424). This claim is unconvincing, however, because as we saw earlier, the maxim of killing others whenever convenient, which involves the violation of a perfect duty if any maxim could, might be thought of as a universal law, though it could not be willed as one (Herman, pp. 113–31). Kant never even tries to derive from his first formula the distinction between duties to oneself and duties to others. So FUL and FLN are not up to the task of explaining the taxonomy of duties.

FH provides by far the easiest way to make out the distinctions needed for this taxonomy. A duty *d* is a duty toward (*gegen*) *S* if and only if *S* is a finite rational being and the requirement to comply with *d* is grounded on the requirement to respect humanity in the person of *S*. A duty is wide or imperfect (or, if toward others, a duty of love) if the action promotes a duty of virtue (that is, an end it is a duty to set); an act is required by a strict, narrow, or perfect duty (or a duty of respect to others) if the failure to perform it would amount to a failure to set this obligatory end at all, or a failure to respect humanity as an end in someone's person. An act violates a perfect duty (or duty of respect) if it sets an end contrary to one of the ends it is our duty to set, or if it shows disrespect toward humanity in someone's person (as by using the person as a means without treating the person at the same time as an end).

The distinction between duties of respect and duties of love also shows how there might be narrow or perfect ethical duties, even though all ethical duties, as duties of virtue, are fundamentally wide duties. For the duty to promote an end involves not only a duty to refrain from adopting the maxim of refusing in principle to promote it but also a duty to refrain from setting all ends that oppose the obligatory end – specifically, any end of *decreasing* one's own perfection (or doing anything that makes you less worthy of your humanity), or making the unhappiness of any person your end (as happens in the "vices of hatred": envy, ingratitude, and malice) (MS 6:458–61). We thus have a perfect duty to avoid any action that involves these forbidden ends, and also a narrow or perfect duty to perform any action whose nonperformance would amount to the principled renunciation of the obligatory end. Regarding most narrow duties, including perfect duties to ourselves and duties of respect to others, however, Kant seldom appeals to the ends of our own perfection and the happiness of others. He more often appeals directly to the worth of humanity as an end in itself, and the requirement that we show respect for it in our actions.

Duties of virtue. In grounding duties of virtue on *ends* – the ends of our own perfection and the happiness of others – Kant does *not* mean to say that we have a duty to *maximize* our own perfection or the happiness of others. These ends are not conceived as summable quantities at all. The duties we have regarding them are not duties regarding anyone's happiness or perfection regarded as collective totalities. Rather, they are duties to include all the instances of our own perfection and the happiness of others among our ends, but they allow us to set our own priorities among these instances and to pursue some rather than others if they fit better into our lives. Thus they are *wide* duties, duties that determine us to make something our end but leave us with latitude (or "play room") regarding how far we promote the obligatory ends and which actions we take toward them (MS 6:390–4). Such actions are meritorious; their omission is not blameworthy unless it proceeds from a refusal to adopt the kind of end at all (MS 6:390).

Kant's theory regards the active pursuit of any end of these descriptions (the development of any talent or gift or capacity in ourselves, the contribution to anyone's happiness, or any component of their happiness) as in general meritorious (unless, of course, it proceeds by way of the violation of a strict or perfect duty). It is up to us to decide which such ends actively to include in our lives. As I have mentioned already, our relation to others in determinate social institutions may in effect turn some of these wide duties into narrow duties.

The crucial thing about this latitude is that it is partly up to us to decide for ourselves how wide or narrow to make a duty of this kind: "The wider the duty, therefore, the more imperfect is a human being's obligation to action; as he nevertheless brings closer to narrow duty (duties of right) the maxim of complying with wide duty (in his disposition), so much the more perfect is his virtuous action" (MS 6:390). This remark is obscure, but one possible reading of it is this[8]: If I commit myself to perfect myself in certain determinate ways, that commitment creates something approaching a perfect duty to actions that promote this perfection. A devoted musician or athlete might be blameable for failing to practice or keep in condition in ways that a casual amateur at these pursuits would not be. We ought to have expected that an ethics of autonomy would leave a lot of discretion to individuals in determining the shape of their lives, including the content of their moral duties. Kantian ethics fulfills this expectation.

These thoughts might lead us to a surprising conclusion. There seems to be much less rigor and system to our duties than we might have expected from Kant, based on his notorious reputation for moral strictness and his preoccupation with rational architectonic. I think it is true that Kantian ethics, as compared with many fashionable theories, is far more permissive and leaves a lot more to the free volition of individuals in determining what their own duties are. In short, Kantian ethics (contrary to its reputation) is in greater danger of being too lax than of being too strict. I think this reflects Kant's typically Enlightenment view, that morality, religion, politics, and other things that might appear to require total commitment from us can better be thought of as claims on us that, except for highly unusual circumstances, can be rationally integrated into a civilized and modestly comfortable mode of human life.

The downside of this humane attitude is inseparable from its upside. This is that Kant is cautious in requiring immediate changes in social relationships – such as marriage and the family, or the constitution of the state – even when existing institutions seem deeply at odds with basic moral values. Thus those who want to criticize Kantian ethics for being too rigoristic and also for being too politically conservative need to make up their minds: Kantian ethics could be modified in either direction, but whichever way it goes, these critics can't get everything they want, for reasons that have nothing to do with Kantian ethics. If Kantian ethics is not excessively lax, that has to be because it might decide to leave more to the empirical and social side of ethics than was indicated by Kant himself. That is the path taken, as I have already said, by both Fichte and Hegel.[9]

The crucial step in Kant's derivation of his system of duties is from the fundamental principle of morality, not as FUL or FLN but rather as FH and as FA, to duties of virtue – the ends that are also duties to have, namely, one's own perfection and the happiness of others. On the basis of these obligatory ends, together with the rights and dignity of rational beings as ends in themselves, Kant attempts a taxonomy of the kinds of duties we have. We may represent the major divisions of Kant's system of duties in the accompanying diagram.

Duties

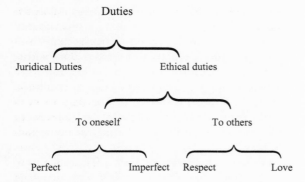

4. Duties to Oneself

In the Anglophone tradition of moral philosophy, the concept of a duty to oneself is commonly applied to alleged duties to promote one's own welfare.[10] For Kant, the rational claims of our own happiness rest on prudential reason, not moral reason. Because our own happiness is something we inevitably pursue from prudence without the constraint of duty (MS 6:386), we have no direct duty at all to promote our own happiness. If a "duty to oneself" means a direct duty to promote one's own welfare, then Kant denies in principle that we could have any duties of that kind. Prudential reason advises us to promote our own happiness whenever doing so does not violate duty. Kantian duty, as we have seen, is relatively permissive on this point. And as we saw in Chapter 1, Kantian ethics endorses the principle he calls "rational self-love" – a pursuit of one's own happiness that is moderated enough to accord with duty and to allow for the moral claims of others (KpV 5:73, R 6:45n), though this principle is a morally permissible counsel of prudential reason and not a direct moral duty.

In Kantian ethics, then, the concept of a duty to oneself has nothing to do with self-interest or any duty to promote one's own happiness. "Self-regarding duties do not depend on the relation of actions to the ends of happiness" (VE 27:343). "All such duties are founded on a certain love of honor consisting in the fact that a human being values himself, and in his own eyes is not unworthy that his actions should be in keeping with humanity" (VE 27:347). Instead, duties to oneself are about promoting self-perfection and maintaining the conditions for self-respect. They are duties to act in such a way as to be worthy of one's humanity.[11]

We also have an indirect duty to make our happiness an end – that is, a duty we might incur in the course of fulfilling other duties, such as the duty to maintain a temperament conducive to fulfilling our other duties (G 4:399). You could also put it this way: I *do* have a duty to promote my own happiness, but only when it falls under the heading of promoting either my own perfection or the happiness of others. Further, although duty may sometimes require us to sacrifice our happiness, Kant thinks it cannot be permissible to adopt the general maxim of sacrificing one's own happiness for the sake of others, because this maxim would destroy itself (by frustrating the happiness of all) if it were made into a universal law (MS 6:393).

One common objection to the concept of a duty to oneself is that it should be possible for the person to whom a duty is owed to release the subject of the duty from the obligation. Thus duties to oneself would be duties from which you could release yourself whenever you liked – hence they would not be duties at all. Of course there might be duties of which this is not true, such as those corresponding to inalienable rights. Kant provides an even more fundamental reply to this objection: He asks whether the concept of a duty to oneself is contradictory, because it seems to make a constraining person (or *auctor obligationis*) the same as the person constrained (the *subjectum obligationis*), which would permit the subject of the obligation (in his person as its author) to release himself from the obligation, concluding that this would make such a duty fundamentally null and void (MS 6:417). His perhaps surprising response is to deny that the author of the obligation to oneself is identical to its subject.

As we saw Chapter 6, §4, what is distinctive about the concept of an imperfectly rational and self-governing being (a being with 'personality' in the Kantian sense) is that this concept involves a relation between two moral persons who are combined in one and the same being. In regarding myself as an autonomous moral being, I consider myself both in the person of the rational legislator, whose law is necessary, objective, and binding on all rational beings, and also in the person of the finite, imperfect rational being who has both the capacity to obey this law and the possibility of failing to obey it.

Kant again employs here the distinction between the sensible and the intelligible (the *homo noumenon* and *homo phaenomenon*) (MS 6:418). As with the notions of phenomenal and noumenal possession in Kant's theory of what is yours and mine by right, to understand the distinction here with the "two worlds" metaphysical baggage would make no sense. The point is rather that as a subject of obligations to myself I think of myself as an empirical agent, while when I think of myself as the being to whom the obligation is owed I bring myself under a moral idea grounded on an *a priori* moral principle. No noumenal metaphysics is needed for that distinction.

Division among duties to oneself. Kant divides duties to oneself into duties to oneself as an *animal* being (MS 6:421–8) and as a *moral* being MS 6:429–37).

Suicide. The first relates to our predisposition to animality: self-preservation, nourishment, and reproduction. Kant's basic argument here is that it is a requirement of self-respect that we should respect the natural teleology involved in our animal instincts. Some of his judgments about what that teleology consists in, and what respect for it requires, now seem at best highly questionable. Some are even in fundamental conflict with Kant's own best insights on these topics. We will return to this point regarding sexual morality later on, in Chapter 13.

Regarding self-preservation, Kant's argument is that suicide is an act that shows blameable self-contempt (MS 6:422–3). This is sometimes doubtless true. When it is true, it supports a Kantian prohibition on suicide when it constitutes a denigration of one's person and a case of treating it as a mere means (G 4:422, MS 6:422–3). But it is equally true that in other cases suicide might be not only compatible with the preservation of our own dignity but even required by its preservation – as when we face the prospect of a life deprived (by disease or by the mistreatment by others) of the conditions under which our human dignity can be maintained. Kant himself sometimes seems to be aware of this point, though he never wholly accepts it (MS 6:423, VA 7:258, VE 27:374).

In the "casuistical questions" regarding suicide, Kant considers at least five cases in which it might be argued that killing oneself is justified. There he leaves the question open, for the reader to think about (MS 6:423–4). From remarks in his lectures, however, it would appear that he rejects all attempts to justify the deliberate ending of one's own life (VE 27:369–78, 603, 627–30). Kant considers suicide in many cases also a violation of one's ethical duties to others (such as one's spouse or children). He even regards suicide as a case of *murder* (*homocidium dolosum*), hence a violation of a duty of right (the right of humanity in one's own person) (MS 6:422). This would presumably underwrite the criminalization of both attempted suicide and assistance to another in committing suicide.

Suicide is a topic on which I think the position Kantian ethics should take is quite distinct from (in many cases diametrically opposed to) the position Kant himself takes. The principle that suicide is wrong when it expresses self-contempt or violates duties to others (who are materially or emotionally dependent on you) seems quite correct. Kant appears stubbornly resistant to the fact that suicide can sometimes be a way of defending one's human dignity, which might ground both a right to it (and therefore a right to assist others in it) and an ethical justification for it, at least in many cases. He claims correctly that only "a worthless man values his life more than his person" (VE 27:376) but is fainthearted in drawing the obvious conclusions on the subject of suicide. His principles on the subject of suicide seem to be correct, but some of his conclusions do not follow. A more flexible and permissive position seems required.

Duties to ourselves as moral beings in effect are duties regarding our *humanity*: our rational capacity to set ends and treat ourselves as ends. These duties concern lying, avarice, and servility. The first of these will be discussed in Chapter 14. I will say a little now about the other two.

Avarice. The duty to avoid avarice is in effect a duty to respect our own capacity for instrumental rationality. Kant distinguishes "miserly avarice" (*karger Geiz*) from "greedy avarice" (*habsüchtiger Geiz*) (MS 6:432). The latter is adopting the end of having more possessions than others do. (Note how "un-American" Kantian ethics is – *the mere end* of having more than others have is contrary to ethical duty!) Greedy avarice is a violation of a duty of beneficence (MS 6:432). Miserly avarice, however, is a propensity to hoard one's possessions with no intention to use or enjoy them. This is a violation of a duty to oneself, because it involves a failure to respect one's rational capacities to employ the means of one's own happiness to their proper end.

In his lectures, Kant makes some perceptive remarks about the psychology of this brand of self-contempt, which exhibits its close alliance to a kind of self-deception. Misers "go poorly clad; they have no regard for clothes, in that they think: I might always have such clothes, since I have the money for it . . . Possession of the wherewithal serves them in place of the real possession of all pleasures, by merely having the means thereto, they can enjoy these pleasures and also forego them" (VE 27:400). "The invention of money is the source of avarice, for prior to that it cannot have been widely prevalent"

(VE 27:402). For money gives the illusion of material substance to our imaginary power over the goods of life that we forgo in order to possess and retain it. The imagination of what we might enjoy serves as the substitute for what we do not enjoy and even multiplies our imaginary power of enjoyment in direct proportion to our deprivation in reality: "While still in possession of the money, we would have to expend it disjunctively, in that we could use it for this or that. But we think of it collectively, and fancy we could have everything in return" (VE 27:403).

In the same way, misers have the illusion of power over others, even of their admiration, because they possess the means to influence others and to be the objects of their envy: "Miserly people are scorned and detested by others, and they cannot understand why" (VE 27:401). "The miser is thus a stranger to himself; he does not know his own nature," and this makes avarice a vice that is especially difficult to correct (VE 27:402). Misers, Kant says, are fearful and anxious, because their riches are so important to them; they also tend to be superstitious and religiously devout, because they regard the fetishism of religious observances as a substitute for the good conduct pleasing to God in the same way that they regard money as a substitute for the goods of life: "In their anxieties, they wish to have comfort and support; and this they obtain from God, by means of their pieties, which after all cost nothing... [The miser] pays no heed to the moral worth of his actions, but thinks that if only he prays earnestly, which costs him nothing, he will already be on his way to heaven" (VE 27:401). Kant's discussion of miserly avarice, both in its psychology and in the social analysis surrounding it, contains much that anticipates Marx's critique of the fetishism of commodities.

Servility. The duty to avoid servility is a duty to treat one's own humanity as an end in itself. The proper measure of our self-worth is the fundamental issue for Kantian ethics. Kant's conception of human nature also makes this measure deeply ambiguous. As sensible beings, we seem to have little worth or importance; but as moral beings, we have a dignity beyond all price (MS 6:434–5; cf. KpV 5:161–3). All human beings share alike and equally in this incomparable worth, yet we have a powerful natural tendency to self-conceit, to value ourselves, our welfare, and our inclinations above those of others, and to treat other human beings as mere means to our own ends. This makes the moral feeling of respect – especially, self-respect – profoundly ambiguous (MS 6:437, KpV 5:72–5). Hence we must value ourselves simultaneously by a low and by a high standard (MS 6:435).

Comparing ourselves with the moral law results in humility, Kant thinks, and even humiliation (MS 6:435–6). But it elevates our value beyond every other we can even conceive to regard ourselves as both authors and subjects of that law (MS 6:436, G 4:393). In relation to others, therefore, our duty is twofold: first, to avoid the arrogance of rating our comparative worth above anyone else's, and second, to avoid the servile disposition that subordinates us to others, whether in order to gain some benefit from them or because of the self-contempt that may result from our failure to achieve competitive superiority over them.

The complexity of the duty to avoid servility or "false humility" may be briefly indicated by the variety of different requirements Kant regards as falling under it: (1) "Be no man's lackey. – Do not let others tread with impunity on your rights." (2) Avoid excessive indebtedness to others, which make you dependent on and inferior to them. (3) Do not be a flatterer or a parasite. (4) Do not complain or whine, even in response to bodily pain. (5) Do not kneel down or prostrate yourself to show veneration, even for heavenly objects. On Kantian principles it is a blasphemous insult to think of God as a childish despot before whom it is permissible for rational beings to grovel merely to gratify his vanity. Such degrading self-abasement is for Kant the essence of "idolatry" (MS 6:436–7).[12]

The duties to oneself just mentioned are all perfect (or narrow) duties. They are signified chiefly by citing kinds of actions or patterns of behavior that are contrary to duty. Kant also recognizes imperfect (or meritorious) duties to oneself, namely duties of self-perfection. These include perfection of our natural powers (our various talents, our "powers of spirit" or rational faculties; "powers of soul," including memory, imagination and taste; and "powers of the body," which Kant calls "gymnastics in the strict sense") (MS 6:444–5). They also include the duty to increase one's moral perfection (or virtue, which we discussed in the previous chapter) (MS 6:446–7). Again, in Kantian ethics we have no strict duty to maximize our perfection (even our moral virtue). Kantian ethics does not think in terms of maximization or optimization and (contrary to its undeserved reputation) does not make excessive or inhuman demands of moral agents.

We also have a duty to ourselves regarding our predisposition to *personality* – in other words, as self-legislating and morally accountable beings. This duty is that of conscience or self-examination, which we will consider in the next chapter.

5. Duties of Love and Respect

Duties toward others are divided into duties of *love* and duties of *respect*. As Kant notes, this distinguishes them in accordance with the *feelings* that accompany their performance, but the content of these duties is to conduct ourselves in certain ways, not a duty to feel anything (MS 6:448). On the contrary, susceptibility to the feelings in question, arising directly from reason, is not a duty but rather a condition for having any duties at all (MS 6:399). Duties of love are duties to benefit others (MS 6:450), while duties of respect are duties to avoid humiliating them and enabling them to maintain their self-respect (MS 6:449).

The distinction between duties of respect and duties of love parallels, in our conduct toward others, the distinction between perfect and imperfect duties to oneself. Duties of respect are narrow or strict duties not to behave in certain ways toward others, while duties of love are wide or meritorious duties, allowing for latitude regarding, how, how much, and toward whom we act benevolently. Where they lose this meritorious character, that is to be explained either by some special circumstance – for instance, if I come upon a child drowning whom I can save, it would be blameable not to save it – or through some special relationship I have to the person – such as the parental duty to care for one's offspring.

Duties of love. Kant further divides duties of love into duties of benefi-cence, gratitude, and sympathetic participation (*Teilnehmung*) (MS 6:451). We have a duty to place the happiness of others among our ends, and the wide duty to return benefits to those who have benefited us. Kant thinks that receiving benefits from others tends to humiliate us and can even lead us to resent them, so that we harm them in return for doing good to us. It is our duty to resist this common (but vicious) human tendency, which is all too natural to us in our social (especially in a "civilized") condition. Duties of love, though they are wide duties, also involve a strict duty never to make the unhappiness of others directly our end. Kant thinks these "vices of hatred" take three basic forms: envy, ingratitude, and malice – including vengeance (MS 6:458–61). Because they arise from self-conceit and arrogance, these vices are also especially characteristic of "civilized" human beings.

The duty of "sympathetic participation" deserves special mention, because the conception itself is perhaps not an obvious one and because appreciating its role in Kantian ethics will help to correct important ele-ments in the prevailing false image of Kantian ethics.[13] Kant also calls this duty by the name "humanity" (*Humanität, humanitas practica*) (MS 6:456–7). It includes the duty to cultivate the feeling of sympathy (which in this con-nection Kant calls *humanitas aesthetica*) in order to strengthen our sensitivity to the needs of others and strengthen our capacity to perform duties of beneficence. But to see only this is to miss the main point, as well as the meaning of the German word *Teilnehmung* ("sharing" or "participation") when it is used in this connection.

Kant emphasizes that there is no duty just to *feel* sympathy for the joys and sorrows of others, at least if the feeling is ineffectual (*tatlos*). It was a sublime way of thinking, he says, when the Stoics rose above such feelings of "compassion" (*Mitleid*) and "pity" (*Barmherzigkeit*) (MS 6:456–7). Kant does not think we have a duty to *avoid* such feelings, only no duty to *have* them or to make ourselves have them when they can have no beneficial effect. The duty of "participation" or "humanity," however, is also not merely the same as the duty to *benefit* others or show them "practical love" (both rather come under the earlier heading of the duty of "beneficence").

"Participation" is distinct both from "practical love" and from feelings of compassion. It is the active sharing in the situation of others, seeing things from their point of view, that will then usually give rise both to compassionate feelings and to beneficent actions that are both informed by the active sharing in the others' situation and undertaken from a standpoint aligned with theirs, so that it is not a standpoint of cool detachment or condescending superiority. If we are looking for colloquial English expressions for what Kant means by "participation," the terms 'understanding', 'involvement', and 'empathy' all come to mind. *Teilnehmung* is the Kantian term for what Jodi Halpern says physicians fail to give their patients when they adopt the emotionally costless (and personally phony) stance of "professional detachment" instead of the "humanizing empathy" they owe their patients as genuine caregivers.[14] It means taking part in the life of another, in ways that include simultaneously a cognitive and an emotional achievement. Its opposite would be cold indifference, detachment, and unconcern – in other words, the very attitude that invidious caricatures of Kantian ethics typically ascribe to the emotionally repressed Kantian moral agent.

Our duty to cultivate sympathetic feelings, when these are active and effective, should be looked upon as merely one aspect of our duty of participation or humanity. These feelings are aids in being open to communication with others and sharing in their situation, but it is this sharing (and not merely having certain feelings) that this duty requires of us. The duty of humanity or participation is a duty connected with our sociability, and closely related to the duties involved in friendship (VE 27:677–8). It is related, Kant says, to the *humanitas aesthetica et decorum* that cultivates our sociable relations with others, which it is a duty of virtue for us to bring about (MS 6:473). Beautiful art, in Kant's view, can contribute to this by the way it makes feelings "universally communicable" – even across great distances of historical time and culture (KU 5:355–6).

Participation, along with love, is also something Kant says we all *need* from other human beings. In the fourth example from the *Groundwork*, it is precisely this sympathetic participation (*Telnehmung*) that we may not refuse to others because we cannot rationally will that others should be unwilling to give it to us (G 4:423). This duty is in part a duty to be in active communion with others, "to participate actively in their fate" (MS 6:457, cf. VE 27:421–2, 692). This is something Kant regards as indispensable to valuing others as ends in themselves (G 4:430). In that sense, it is also good in itself, apart from any further benefit we may render others in consequence of it. So active sympathetic participation, unlike mere compassion or pity, is something we have a duty to give even when it will be ineffectual. But when we do come to act beneficently toward others, participation is what enables us to do so with intelligence and sensitivity.[15] Critics frequently take Kant to task for failing to realize that sympathizing with others is a necessary part of helping them intelligently. When the only part of Kant they know is the opening pages of the *Groundwork* (and they misread even that in the customary ways), they may even think that Kant is committed to rejecting in principle the idea that sympathetic participation is a duty, simply because it involves an emotional relation to others.[16] By now I hope we can see that such criticisms are seriously in error. Kant even sees better than many proponents of virtue ethics and moral sense theory that sympathetic participation is a matter not of what we passively feel, but of what we actively do.

Duties of respect. Because these are strict duties, they are classified according to the kinds of actions that would constitute violations of them: arrogance, defamation, and ridicule (MS 6:465). Respecting others requires us to moderate our own self-esteem to allow for proper recognition of the dignity of others – something we need to do on account of our natural social propensity toward self-conceit or arrogance (MS 6:462, 465–6). "Defamation" does not mean "slander" (*false* reports injurious to others, which is a violation of their rights) but the willful spreading of *true* reports about them that may bring them into disrepute. Kant condemns this because he thinks we take malicious pleasure in defaming others in order to advance our interests or flatter our self-conceit. This duty also includes a prohibition on "offensive inquisitiveness" that fails to respect the privacy of others (MS 6:466). "Ridicule" consists in exposing others to being laughed at, by making their faults an immediate object of amusement. Kant realizes that there is a fine line, calling for an acute exercise of judgment, between ridiculing others and preserving one's own self-respect through brushing aside someone else's attack in a jocular manner (MS 6:467).

Kant also includes under duties of respect the duty not to "give scandal" – not to tempt others into acts for which they will later have reason to reproach themselves (MS 6:394, 464). This is distinguished from the duty of respect not to "take scandal" – to exhibit excessive disapproval of others for bad conduct, or disapproval of conduct that is merely unconventional (MS 6:464). Regarding ethical duties, of course, even justified disapproval must never be employed as a form of coercion, because coercion is permissible only regarding duties of right, and applied to ethical duties it would itself be a violation of right (MS 6:220).

Is there a tension between love and respect? Kant claims that love and respect are opposites: the first drawing us toward people, the second keeping us at a distance (MS 6:449, VE 27:406–7). As Marcia Baron has pointed out, this may not seem right: The opposite of love is not respect but hatred or indifference; the opposite of respect is not love but contempt. It may be true that love should bring people closer together, but respect does not have to keep them apart.[17] Baron also notes another puzzle. Kant says: "One can love one's neighbor, though he might deserve but little respect, and one can show him the respect necessary for every human being regardless of the fact that he would hardly be judged worthy of love" (MS 6:448). But, Baron asks, "Does not everyone deserve respect, and does not Kant think so?"[18]

In my view, the solution to both puzzles lies in the fact that Kant's system of duties involves the application of the moral law to the empirical circumstances of human life, which involve a set of prevailing social attitudes that reflect our unsociable sociability. The moral law does indeed regard every person as deserving of equal respect, and the ground for this respect, humanity as an end in itself, is also the reason why all are objects of love – in Kant's sense of the "love of human beings" (MS 6:401–2). For Kant, love (properly speaking) is pleasure in the perfection of another leading to a desire to benefit the other (MS 6:449, KU 5:276, VE 27:416, R 6:45–6).[19] Hence the proper ground of love is always the ground of respect, so Kant emphasizes that without respect, no true love can occur (ED 8:337–8).[20] Yet to show respect for a person is to behave toward them in a manner consistent with others' showing respect for them, and consistent with their maintaining their self-respect.

Given the corrupt attitudes prevalent in our society, to have been dependent on another for benefits you need often deprives you of the respect of others, and also of your self-respect. This is the main reason that there is a tension between love and respect. Kant therefore insists that we must be careful to love others in a way that maintains respect for them, as by making them feel that they have honored us by receiving our beneficence (MS 6:453). When dealing with people who are oppressed and exploited, it is always more important to empower them and show solidarity with them than merely to bestow benefits on them. Proponents of the American "welfare reforms" of the past decade (an obscenely benign name for so outrageously ugly a thing) sometimes try to appeal to this point, but their fundamental hypocrisy is shown by the fact that these measures do nothing to empower the poor (and were never intended to do so) but were inflicted on the poor precisely on behalf of the interests of their political enemies and economic oppressors. The same threat to self-respect is also why people are prone to the vice of ingratitude, since "good deeds make us ungrateful because we fear being despised" (R 1471, Ak 15:649; MS 6:454–5, 459).

Can Kantian ethics allow for "appraisal respect"? More generally, under the influence of our corrupt civilization, people usually value themselves, and one another, for the wrong reasons. They respect others, for instance, not for their human dignity but for their power or wealth or because they are honored more than others for one thing or another. And because showing respect for others means maintaining the conditions under which they are respected by others and by themselves, we cannot simply ignore these prevailing social valuations. These valuations, considered on their true merits according to Kantian principles, are usually shameful and vicious (though when people consider these issues philosophically, they often prefer to dwell complacently on the exceptional cases where they are not). When Kant says that we should love our neighbor "though he might deserve but little respect" and should respect him "although he would hardly be judged worthy of love," I suggest he is referring to these prevailing standards, with which Kantian ethics disagrees in principle but whose influence it cannot afford to ignore in practice.

Stephen Darwall has distinguished "recognition respect" (his name for the minimal respect we think everyone is owed) from "appraisal respect" (the surplus respect we give to those whose qualities or deeds we think have especially deserved it).[21] This distinction may well be in line with our moral "intuitions" (i.e. our cultural prejudices), but properly speaking, Kantian ethics *recognizes* only that respect which is grounded in human *dignity* (a value that cannot be surpassed or added to), and therefore it *appraises* all human beings as of equal (absolute) worth – which, because it is the maximal degree of worth conceivable, cannot be exceeded by any other appraisal. Because "respect" is in general the attitude we take toward objective value, we do respect good things associated with others – power, wealth, honor, talents, accomplishments, moral virtue. Kantian ethics does not deny their value, but it does deny that the *self-worth of a person* in the eyes of others should ever depend on them (even on virtue or goodness of will).

The basic principle of Kantian ethics is that all human beings have equal dignity as ends in themselves. Kantian ethics should therefore radically oppose all social attitudes that involve comparisons between people regarding self-worth, comparisons that value some people more than others, on any ground whatever (even on moral grounds).[22] In the corrupt social life we lead, however, it is doubtless true that people do not look at their own self-worth or that of others in the way they should. Because of this, in order to fulfill our duty of respect for others we must at times show them "appraisal respect" as well. If we do not, we cannot share in their own self-valuation even to the minimal extent that this is required in order for us to show respect for them at all. We need not always share these grounds, of course, and sometimes we should reject them in principle. We should not, for example, agree with a person whose positive self-valuation is based on thinking he was born a member of the "master race" or on his ability to intimidate or manipulate other human beings. But if we do not respect people for some achievements in which they have shown themselves superior to others, especially when these achievements themselves have moral merit, then they won't regard us as respecting them at all, and we cannot refuse to take this into account.

No doubt many will think that there is no need here for compromise. If people simply do better than others, it may be thought, their self-worth should be considered greater. For better or worse, Kantian ethics rejects that view on principle. Kantian ethics holds that where morality is concerned, we should compare ourselves with the moral law or the idea of virtue, but never with others (VE 27:349, 462, MS 6:435–6). Human achievements have value, but they give the achiever no higher self-worth. On this point, Kantian ethics is radical, requiring us to think very differently about ourselves and other people from the way we are accustomed to doing. Or at least it asks us to try to integrate this new way of thinking into customs and practices with which it may have to make compromises in order to be true to Kantian principles at all. In a fully realized realm of ends, people would think and act very differently from the way they do here and now. We cannot immediately transport ourselves into the realm of ends, but we must grope our way toward it, making the best of the necessity to adapt fundamental moral principles to the imperfect condition in which we find ourselves. Appraisal respect is one of those cases in which Kantian values such as human dignity and the realm of ends must, given existing social institutions and attitudes, compromise with corrupt social customs and ways of thinking in order just to be true to itself.

This is a tension that Kantian ethics must live with. It is not a tension *within* Kantian ethics, however, but one between Kantian principles and the morally imperfect *real social world* to which they must be applied. La Rochefoucauld famously said that "hypocrisy is the tribute that vice pays to virtue."[23] In light of the point I have been trying to make in the last several paragraphs, it could equally well be said that for Kantian ethics, appraisal respect is the tribute virtue is sometimes forced to pay to vice.

10

Conscience

Philosophical theories of conscience might be categorized under three headings: *moral knowledge* theories, *motivation* theories, and *reflection* theories. People speak of their conscience "telling them to do" such-and-such. Such talk might imply that conscience is a source of moral knowledge about what to do. *Moral knowledge* theories of conscience try to explain how conscience affords us such knowledge. Some religious theories of conscience, for instance, interpret the voice of conscience as the voice of God within us. People also speak of "prickings" and "proddings" of conscience, or of their conscience urging them to do the right thing or bothering them if they have done (or are thinking of doing) the wrong thing. This suggests that conscience *motivates* us to do the right thing and to avoid the wrong thing. Conscience seems also to involve a certain way of *thinking reflectively* about what to do. This is usually a way of reflecting that gives first priority to moral considerations.

The three kinds of theory are not mutually exclusive. For example, Christian scholastic theories of conscience often distinguish *synderesis* (a notion derived from St. Jerome), which is a supposed source of moral knowledge, from *conscience*, which for some (e.g., St. Bonaventure) is an affective or volitional response to moral knowledge, while for others (e.g., St. Thomas Aquinas) it is the application of moral knowledge to action.[1] St. Bonaventure's theory, therefore, combines knowledge and motivation.[2] An early modern example of a reflection theory is that of Joseph Butler, for whom conscience (also sometimes given the names "reason" and "the moral faculty") consists in calm, rational reflection on what we ought to do.[3] Reflection theories obviously don't deny that both knowledge and motivation are needed for moral action, but they regard these as either presupposed by the reflection of conscience or else subsumed by it. An example of a pure motivation theorist would seem to be John Stuart Mill, for whom conscience consists in a painful feeling associated through our moral education with what we have been taught is the violation of duty (Mill, pp. 28–9). The association, he thinks, tends with the intellectual progress of humanity to be diminished in motivational power by "the dissolving force of analysis," so that for Mill, it would seem that the ultimate sanction of the utilitarian morality is (or, with further intellectual progress, will eventually be) not conscience at all but "the social feelings of mankind" (Mill, pp. 31–4).

In the terms I have just been using, Kant's conception of conscience is a motivation theory set in the context of a reflection theory. Kant regards conscience as distinct both from our awareness of moral principles (through *practical reason*) and from the *faculty of moral judgment*, which are the sources of the moral knowledge that is to be implemented in the process of self-examination (and associated motivation) that is conscience (MS 6:438). In the *Metaphysics of Morals*, Kant treats conscience under two main headings: (1) as one of the moral feelings presupposed by our susceptibility to duty (MS 6:400–1) and (2) as a crucial aspect of a fundamental duty to ourselves, the duty of self-examination and self-knowledge as our own moral judge (MS 6:437–42). Kant's principal theory of conscience is (2) the process of self-examination and self-judgment, but it will help us understand his moral psychology better if we begin with (1) conscience as a morally motivating feeling.

1. Conscience as Feeling

As we saw in Chapter 2, and again in the two preceding chapters, Kant is misread when he is seen as denying any role to feeling, emotion, or desire in those actions done from duty that have authentic moral worth. Moral action proceeds from desires produced in us by rational choice, grounded on principles of reason. In sensible creatures such as human beings, these purely rational desires, like inclinations, manifest themselves in the form of feelings – feelings resulting directly from the operation of reason on our sensibility. Susceptibility to these feelings is essential to our capacity to act rationally, and a being that was not susceptible to them could not be a responsible moral agent at all. In the *Groundwork*, the feeling of this kind that Kant emphasizes is *respect*, especially respect for the moral law (G 4:401). As we have already observed more than once, Kant distinguishes four distinct feelings that arise from pure reason: (a) moral feeling, (b) conscience, (c) love of human beings, and (d) respect (MS 6:399–403).

The last two feelings, (c) and (d), correspond to the two classes of our duties to others: duties of love and duties of respect (though the emphasis in that particular discussion of respect is on *self*-respect). (a) *Moral feeling* consists in a feeling of pleasure or displeasure (approval or disapproval) attached to actions, either performed or contemplated, and whether performed by another or by ourselves. (b) *Conscience* is a feeling of pleasure or displeasure associated with *myself*, in view of some action I am either contemplating or that I have already performed. In the former case, the feeling

is one that may motivate me either to perform the action or to refrain from
it. In the latter case, it is a feeling either of self-contentment or of moral
remorse. Because of its motivational force, Kant sometimes calls conscience
as feeling an "instinct," meaning that it is capable of impelling us to action
and not merely of judging actions (VE 27:351). Conscience as a feeling,
however, is the outcome of a specific process of moral *reflection*, and Kant's
proper theory of conscience consists in his account of this process.

2. The Inner Court

Kant's theory of conscience, as a reflection theory, is characterized by Kant's
conception of conscience as an inner court or judicial proceeding:

> Conscience is practical reason holding the human being's duty before him for his
> acquittal or condemnation in every case that comes under a law. (MS 6:400)

> Every concept of duty involves objective constraint through a law (a moral imperative
> limiting our freedom) and belongs to practical understanding, which provides a
> rule. But the internal *imputation* of a *deed*, as a case falling under a law (*in meritum
> aut demeritum*), belongs to the *faculty of judgment* (*iudicium*), which, as the subjective
> principle of imputing an action, judges with rightful force whether the action as
> a deed (an action coming under a law) has occurred or not. Upon it follows the
> conclusion of *reason* (the verdict), that is, the connecting of the rightful result with
> the action (condemnation or acquittal). All of this takes place before a judicial
> proceeding [*Gericht*] (*coram iudicio*), which, as a moral person giving effect to a law, is
> called a court [*Gerichtshof*] (*forum*). – Consciousness of an inner court in the human
> being ("before which his thoughts accuse or excuse one another") is **conscience**.
> (MS 6:437–8)

> The inner judicial proceeding of conscience may be aptly compared with an external
> court of law. Thus we find within us an accuser, who could not exist, however, if
> there were no law; though the latter is no part of the civil positive law, but resides
> in reason...In addition, there is also at the same time in the human being an
> advocate, namely self-love, who excuses him and makes many an objection to the
> accusation, whereupon the accuser seeks in turn to rebut the objections. Lastly we
> find in ourselves a judge, who either acquits or condemns us. (VE 27:354)

It is easy to take Kant's talk about conscience as a court to be a mere
metaphor, and in certain respects it obviously is. (There is no witness box,
no judge's gavel, no wooden-paneled room in a public building; and the
judge – the moral agent himself or herself in a self-judging capacity – wears
no robes.) But it is not as metaphorical as it might seem. The persons of the
accuser, the defender, and the judge are literally accusing, defending, and
judging, and though they are all the same natural person, they are literally
distinct *moral persons* – as are the imposer and the subject of duties to oneself,
and also the legislator and the subject of the moral law. To say that the court is
"inner" means only that the relations between these persons are *self*-relations.

For Kant, *inner* sense is our intuition of our own conscious states rather than of objects distinct from us; *inner* moral worth is the worth we have in relation to our own self-given moral law rather than in comparison to other people. In the same way, the different persons involved in the inner court are all roles played by a single moral agent in a process of self-reflection.

In one way, however, it would seem that the image of a criminal court, taken literally as a forum for determining only guilt or innocence, seems inadequate to capture everything Kant needs conscience to do. Conscience, as pronouncing guilt or innocence, cannot be the only kind of moral self-reflection, however, because some acts can be morally meritorious, and the judgment as to whether they are is not a judgment of guilt or innocence. This is a modification of Kant's conception of conscience that seems to be required in Kantian ethics merely in order to make it self-consistent.

Kant's "legalisms." Whether or not the image of a court is a metaphor, the fact remains that Kant chooses this image quite deliberately, and this choice is worth some reflection. In every area of philosophy, not only in ethics but even in theoretical philosophy, Kant habitually uses metaphors, images, and analogies derived from laws and legal processes. In the title of the *Critique of Pure Reason*, the word "critique" is based on the Greek word for "judge," and in the preface to the first edition, Kant describes the "Critique of Pure Reason" itself metaphorically as a "court of justice" (*Gerichtshof*), before which "reason may secure its rightful claims while dismissing all its groundless pretensions, and this not by mere decrees but according to its own eternal and unchangeable laws" (KrV Axi–xii). The principle of morality too, as we have seen, is for Kant a "moral law," which we may regard as legislated within each of us by our own reason. Even the crucial idea of "judgment," which plays such a vital role in Kant's epistemology, involves reference to the image of a judicial forum.

Based on these metaphors, Kant's moral philosophy is sometimes criticized as "legalistic." As we saw in the previous chapter, however, Kant draws a sharp distinction between right, which is concerned with protecting external freedom and admits of coercive enforcement, and ethics, which is concerned with human perfection and happiness and involves only inner self-constraint. He is careful to observe the distinction between standards of right and standards of ethics in his moral philosophy, even if his interpreters too often ignore the distinction and run roughshod across it. Kant's use of legal and juridical metaphors is better seen as an expression of the values that would be displayed in an ideal judicial process: A judicial proceeding should be a public forum in which important matters are to be decided freely and fairly according to objective standards, with all sides being given the best opportunity to present their case. Kant's attraction to these metaphors depends on the open-mindedness and freedom of the process of inquiry, the objectivity and universality of reason's standards, and the importance, to any exercise of reason, of public communication about these objective standards, operating under their authority. The same values also determine Kant's basic theory of conscience as an inner court of moral judgment. For Kant, the moral reflection of conscience must be rational, not merely a response to inchoate, prerational (or still less socially conditioned and inculcated) feelings. Conscience as feeling is to be the response of our sensibility to reason. Both the accuser and the defender within us must be seen as articulating their arguments on explicit grounds, and the verdict of the judge must equally be a reasoned one. The standards of argument are to be objective and universal, fair to both the prosecution and the defense, and the judge within us is to follow this law with integrity, allowing neither irrational self-hatred nor coddling favoritism to oneself to influence the decision. It is easy to deride Kant's use of judicial imagery, based on the pompous formalism of courts of law and the fact that in the real world they often perpetrate injustice rather than do justice. But once we understand the substantive values that underlie Kant's use of such images, it would be no joke to treat these values as lightly as our derision is in danger of doing.

Conscience and society. Kant is aware of theories of conscience that treat its voice as merely that of society, or of "art and education," but he distinguishes conscience in that sense (calling it *conscientia artificialis*) from self-judgment based on genuine rational principles (*conscientia naturalis*) (VE 27:355–6).

Insofar as what a person calls his "conscience" reflects only what society and upbringing have instilled in him, it can claim no rational or moral validity. Such a theory might understand conscience as a form of contingent, external motivation to morality (as Mill apparently does). In that case, however, the theory cannot also regard conscience as playing any role in moral *rationality* (as Kant, along with the entire tradition that includes Bonaventure, Aquinas, and Butler, thinks it should do). Because the court of conscience is an inner one, it is not literally a public forum but the moral law that all the inner parties recognize as one that has been legislated by the idea of the will of every rational being, and in that sense the rational standards used in the inner court are the same as would apply in a public forum.

In this respect, Kant's conception of conscience stands in striking contrast, for example, to the conception of conscience found in Martin Heidegger's in *Being and Time*. For Heidegger, the call of conscience is not articulate, or properly articulable, but consists in a discourse of silence. Conscience for Heidegger is Dasein calling itself back out of the public realm – which Heidegger dismisses in this context as merely the realm of *das Man* – to its own uncanny authenticity that recognizes no public standards.[4] Heidegger explicitly considers, and rejects, Kant's image of conscience as a court, precisely on the ground that conscience does not put a "self" up for trial according to an explicit norm. That is why its discourse can involve no articulate utterances but consists only in "keeping silent" (*schweigen*).[5] This is a deliberate rejection of the entire Enlightenment rationalist view of human life (discussed in Chapter 1, §4), according to which the ultimate norms to which we are answerable are always to be seen in an ideal context of free human communication according to universal standards.

3. Conscience, Guilt, and Punishment

Conscience as a duty. We saw in the previous chapter that Kant regards conscience as our primary duty to ourselves in regard to our moral predisposition to personality. This duty to oneself, "the duty to oneself as one's own innate judge," Kant regards as fundamental to morality as a whole and to our observance of all ethical duties whatever class they may belong. "The human being has a general duty of so disposing himself that he may be capable of observing all moral duties . . . This, then, is the primary duty to oneself" (MS 6:348). It is in virtue of this duty that Kant regards duties to oneself as taking "first place" and as "the most important of all" (MS 6:341).

There is no duty to *have* a conscience, Kant argues, because unless we do, we are not moral beings at all and cannot be held responsible for our actions (MS 6:400). "Having a conscience," in this sense, seems to mean having the fundamental *capacity* to carry out the kind of moral reflection conscience consists in. This capacity, for Kantian ethics – like the susceptibility to certain feelings and emotions, such as respect and love of human beings – is essential to human rationality itself. Our duty in regard to conscience consists in constraining ourselves to exercise these capacities and then attend to the verdict of our conscience. Of course many human beings fail to do this sometimes, or even all of the time. The duties involving conscience appear to be narrow or perfect duties. That is, it is not morally optional that we exercise the capacity for self-judgment whenever we face (or have made) a morally significant decision. Rather, in every morally significant choice, we are required to place ourselves before the inner judge and heed the verdict of the judge. To do this is not meritorious, but to fail to do it is blameable. Conscience has two distinct functions regarding our actions. It *warns* us (before we act) and it *pronounces a verdict* (of guilt or acquittal) over the actions we have already performed (MS 6:440).

Does conscience punish? The thought that conscience, or I myself as self-judge, sometimes renders a verdict of *guilty* might make us think that Kant would view us also as having the duty to punish ourselves for our misdeeds (as by depriving ourselves of the happiness of which we judge ourselves unworthy).[6] Kant says that conscience may "judge us punishable" (or not, if it finds us not guilty), but he insists that our happiness or misery is left for the ruler of the world to decide (MS 6:439n, 440, 460). It would even be a fundamental misunderstanding of Kantian ethical theory, and of the role in it of the idea that morality is the condition of worthiness to be happy, to think that we are required or even entitled to punish ourselves. Kant holds that it can *never* be our duty to deprive ourselves of happiness (whether we judge ourselves worthy of it or not) as long as no direct violation of duty is involved in the happiness itself or in the means of acquiring it. If we think we enjoy (or are hoping for) some happiness of which our conduct has not made us worthy, our only duty is to strive to improve our conduct so as to make ourselves less unworthy of that happiness.

Kant denies that it is even *possible* to punish oneself (MS 6:335). When he says this, I do not think he means to deny that people can deprive themselves of happiness or inflict suffering on themselves while thinking that they are undergoing punishment at their own hands. He does mean to deny, however, that such conduct could ever constitute *genuine* punishment, that it could count as an act rationally justified in the way legitimate acts of punishment are justified. Kant condemns the religious practice of penance, for example, as "slavish" and "hypocritical" (R 6:24n). It is slavish because it depicts us as trying to win the favor of the divine being by irrational acts of sycophancy. This is the only way Kant can understand such acts, because he thinks it is never our duty to deprive ourselves of any happiness unless the happiness itself or the means to it violate the moral law. It is also hypocritical because it is contrary to reason to deprive oneself of any happiness that does not directly involve immorality in its acquisition, and so human beings cannot honestly and wholeheartedly will to deprive themselves of happiness, even if they pretend to do so in their shameful attempts to humiliate themselves before God (whose goodness they also insult by supposing that this degrading behavior pleases him).

The only suffering we rightly undergo before the inner court of conscience consists in the painful feeling – a moral feeling, not an empirical one – that arises necessarily from the influence of reason on sensibility, attendant on the recognition that we have violated the moral law. But that pain is inseparable from the judgment itself, which is why conscience is counted among the feelings we can have no duty to have, because susceptibility to it is a presupposition of being morally accountable at all (MS 6:400–1). For Kant, however, *punishment* would have to be some *further* pain whose infliction is somehow due to us in consequence of the fact that we have done something wrong (MS 6:331). Or as Kant says: "*Moral remorse is the first outcome of the legally binding judicial verdict* [of conscience] . . . [But] even in *foro humano*, guilt is not assuaged by remorse, but by payment" (VE 27:353–4).

Kant's view on this point, it seems to me, contains an important insight into what it means to have guilt feelings. To *feel guilty* is to *judge oneself punishable* – but it is not to *undergo punishment* or to inflict it on oneself. (Guilt feelings are painful, but it is an error – sometimes even a piece of culpable self-deception – to represent this pain as *punishment*.) On the contrary, our guilt feelings are sometimes assuaged when we are punished, for then we think justice has been done to us and we need no longer judge ourselves punishable. Kant's view also affords us a way of drawing the distinction between guilt and shame. Moral shame, at any rate, is the feeling that we have failed to live up to our humanity; it is what Kant means when he speaks of our feeling "self-contempt and inner abhorrence" (MS 6:426). This feeling might be prompted not only by the verdict of conscience that holds us guilty of some transgression of duty but also by awareness of a mere lack of moral merit in our character, a bad moral disposition, or even the absence of any good disposition. Guilt, by contrast, is the judgment that we have committed some actual deed that violates the moral law and renders us punishable.

4. The Duty of Self-Knowledge

The first command of duty regarding conscience, Kant says, is to "know (scrutinize, fathom) yourself" regarding your own maxims and the incentives on which you act (MS 6:441). This is a duty Kant regards as impossible to fulfill completely. As civilization (or modern bourgeois society) has made us, our developed reason and self-conceit have made us skilled in all forms of flattering self-deception, and in any case the truth about ourselves is often too abysmal for us to face. Even the striving after self-knowledge is attended with some serious dangers. One of them is "enthusiastic contempt" for oneself (or of the entire human species), leading either to fanatical self-hatred or to a misanthropy that violates our duty to promote the welfare of others. The antidote to it is keeping alive our awareness of the moral predisposition in us (the absence of which would signify not evil but simply a lack of moral personality altogether) (MS 6:441).

Kant's target here is the morose self-scrutiny of certain religious self-examiners (such as Haller and Pascal) that leads sooner to madness than to truth (VA 7:133). This morbid attitude is closely allied in Kant's mind with the pietistic religiosity in which Kant himself was raised, which "reduces [the moral agent] to a state of groaning passivity, where nothing great and good is undertaken but instead everything is expected merely from wishing for it" (R 6:184). The contrary danger – which actually bears a striking resemblance to its opposite – is the "egotistical self-esteem that takes mere wishes – wishes that, however ardent, always remain empty of deeds – for proof of a good heart" (MS 6:441). The self-knowledge Kant insists is a duty must avoid both these extremes. It is the sober resolve, as far as we are able, not to deceive ourselves about our deeds or about their sources within us and seeks a knowledge whose sole aim is constructive moral self-improvement.

Can conscience err? One arresting claim Kant makes about conscience is that an *erring conscience* is impossible. The question of whether conscience can err is often raised by moral philosophers in the tradition in which Kant is working, and there is great reluctance to admit that an erring conscience is possible. But there are also large differences over the question of what an erring conscience would have to consist in. In Kant, Fichte, Fries, and Hegel, for example, we find four different conceptions of what an erring conscience would have to be, and thus four different propositions asserted

as each philosopher denies that conscience can err.⁷ Because Kant regards
conscience as distinct from moral judgment, he can (and does) hold that
this judgment can err without holding that conscience errs. "An erring conscience," he declares, is "an absurdity."

> For while I can indeed be mistaken at times in my objective judgment as to whether
> something is a duty or not, I cannot be mistaken in my judgment as to whether I have
> submitted it to my practical reason (here in its role as judge) for such a judgment;
> for if I could be mistaken in that, then I would have made no practical judgment at
> all, and in that case there would be neither truth nor error. (MS 6:401)

According to Kant, it is quite possible for me to err in my objective moral
judgments – thinking, for instance, that it is my duty to fight in a war, or
to refuse to fight in it, when in fact my duty is just the opposite of what
I think it is. This may also result in a conscience that condemns us based
on false judgments (such as overly demanding standards – a notion some
people may be surprised to find Kant employing at all). Kant calls this a
"morbid conscience": "But there is also a morbid conscience, where [the
human being] seeks to impute evil in his actions, where there is no ground
for it; but this is pointless. Conscience should not be a tyrant within us. We
can always be cheerful in our actions, without offending it" (MS 6:356–7).

Because Kant does not identify conscience with moral judgment, he
declines to infer from such cases that *conscience* can err. Conscience is the
process of moral reflection that makes use of such moral judgments in deliv-
ering on myself a verdict of guilt or acquittal for some action I have done or
am contemplating. The duty of conscience is therefore the duty to engage
in this reflection. Its judgment proper is that I have applied the standards
of moral judgment to myself (whether or not I have rendered the right
substantive judgment in doing so). An errant judgment of guilt or acquittal would be an error of understanding, or of practical judgment, not of
conscience. An *erring conscience* would have to be a mistaken judgment concerning whether I have held my actions up to the rational standards of moral
judgment: It would have to be, so to speak, the mistaken judgment that the
inner judicial process has taken place. It is this error that Kant apparently
regards as impossible.

> Conscience can also be defined as *the moral faculty of judgment, passing judgment on
> itself*... Conscience does not pass judgment on actions as cases that stand under
> the law, for this is what reason does so far as it is subjectively practical... Rather,
> here reason judges itself, whether it has actually undertaken, with all diligence, that
> examination of actions (whether they are right or wrong), and it calls the human
> being to himself to witness for or against himself whether this has taken place or
> not. (R 6:186)

This seems clear enough, but in some ways it is hard to reconcile with
what Kant plainly believes about people. Kant certainly realizes that many

people do not submit their actions to such a process of self-judgment, and he also often insists that people are extremely prone to self-flattering and self-exculpating illusions of all kinds. One such illusion would obviously be that I have submitted my act to the judgment of conscience when I have not. ("Hypocrisy" in the literal, etymological sense – that is, "deficiency in judgment" – might be regarded as the failure to pronounce conscientious judgment on one's actions when one ought to, while cherishing the illusion that one has properly judged them.) So it would seem quite inconsistent of Kant to deny that errors of this kind can occur. He knows they occur all the time:

There are tendencies in the souls of many to make no rigorous judgment of themselves – an urge to dispense with conscience. If this lack of conscientiousness is already, in fact, present, we never get that person to deal honestly with himself. We find in such people that they are averse to any close examination of their actions, and shy away from it, endeavoring, on the contrary, to discover subjective grounds on which to find a thing right or wrong. (R 6:616–17)

Kant is especially sharp in condemning the habit of thought that self-deceptively confuses the self-reproach–based imprudence with the verdict of conscience (R 6:24, VE 27:352–3). On the one hand, we perpetrate such confusions in the course of misinterpreting the moral law to ourselves so as to adapt it to our inclinations (G 4:405). On the other hand, we lend a certain air of dignity to our foolish (imprudent) acts by representing them as moral transgressions. Kant thinks that this is often a major ingredient in the hypocritical frame of mind of the self-torment of the sinner who inflicts religious penance on himself (R 6:24n). In both cases, we substitute a judgment of prudential reason for the verdict of conscience while persuading ourselves that we have made a conscientious examination of ourselves.

In view of all this, how can Kant consistently maintain that we cannot err in our judgment that I have submitted myself and my action to my practical reason in its role as judge? I suggest that what Kant might mean in denying an erring conscience is not that we cannot deceive ourselves in thinking that we have properly judged our actions when we have not but rather that if we do in fact genuinely submit ourselves to the judgment of conscience, then we cannot fail to be aware of doing so: "for [he says] if I could be mistaken in that, I would have made no practical judgment at all, and in that case there would be neither truth nor error" (MS 6:401). Kant's argument is this: In the self-deceptive belief that I have acted conscientiously when I have not, there has been no genuine judgment of conscience at all, so there cannot have been an erroneous one either. In other words, where conscience has actually operated, we cannot be mistaken in thinking that it has. That is the only sense in which conscience cannot err.

The duty to pass judgment on oneself in conscience is for Kant our most fundamental duty. Without fulfilling it, we cannot honestly represent ourselves either to others or to ourselves as having fulfilled any of our duties. Conscience would be unnecessary for an innocently good being, one that acts by a kind of inborn good nature or through some sort of training or upbringing, as a dog might be taught to do tricks. Such a being could also not rationally judge its actions good, and this means it could not be considered a moral being at all. It is an important claim of Kantian moral anthropology that the very social and historical processes that develop our capacity for moral reason also involve us in moral corruption. We never begin as moral agents with a clean slate, and our most fundamental moral action must always therefore be to struggle against ourselves (R 6:44–5, 72, 93–5). The most indispensable element in this struggle is the capacity for *conscience* – that is, honest self-judgment. We begin to see here why *truthfulness* – with others, but even more with oneself – is a fundamental *ethical* duty in Kantian ethics. (This is a theme to which we will return in Chapter 14, §4.)

11

Social Justice

A liberal political theory is one that views the protection of individual rights and property as the fundamental task of the state. It is often thought that a liberal theory so conceived also has a strong propensity toward political-economic *libertarianism*. That is, it must view the state as having few responsibilities for overseeing and regulating the economic life of society, and especially for providing for the welfare of the poor or redistributing wealth in an egalitarian direction. A liberal state, so the argument goes, because its preoccupation is solely with protecting individual freedom and property, ought to leave economic distribution entirely to the free market. If there are any countervailing tendencies to this within the liberal tradition, they are usually thought to lie in another side of liberalism – its consequentialist or utilitarian side, which adds to the state's charge of protecting individual rights a concern to promote the general happiness (or even reinterprets that first charge as a way of serving its utilitarian function).[1]

Kant is a theorist within the liberal tradition who provides a good test case for this argument. He views the state exclusively as a mechanism for protecting individual rights and property through coercive force. It is not the responsibility of the state to make people happy, but only to protect the external freedom they require to pursue their happiness (as they alone, and never the state, are responsible for conceiving it). For Kant, therefore, the "utilitarian" side of liberalism does not exist at all. Kant draws a sharp distinction between "right" and "ethics" – that is, between the sphere of normative concepts and activities concerned with the state and its coercive powers and the sphere concerned with the duties of individuals that are to remain externally uncoerced and wholly free of legal or state power and interference. He views the aim of human happiness, including duties of beneficence to be performed by the well-off on behalf of the less fortunate, as a concern exclusively of the ethical sphere, not at all the proper business of the state. So Kantian ethics should be especially hospitable to libertarian objections to such things as a welfare state, state interference in the economy, and state-administered economic redistribution that seeks to transfer wealth from the rich to the poor. Only a contrasting utilitarian strain within liberalism could possibly provide any corrective to such conclusions.

For a long time this was the dominant reading of Kant. F. A. Hayek saw Kant as one of the great historical champions of the political values he favored.[2] A similar reading of Kant's political theory has also been presented even by scholars who had no libertarian axe to grind.[3] More recently, however, several scholars have taken issue with this interpretation of Kant, arguing that his theory of right allows for welfare and redistributive activities of the state and even provides a cogent rationale for them.[4] This chapter will endorse the position of these more recent scholars. Then it will explore the continuity between Kant's theory of social justice and the closely contemporaneous, and similarly motivated, theory of natural right proposed by that greatest of all the Kantians, J. G. Fichte. No one could possibly view Fichte's political theory as hospitable to political-economic libertarianism.

1. Taxing the Rich to Support the Poor

Readings of Kant's political philosophy that see it as leaning in a libertarian direction take rise from two principal points of doctrine. The first is that Kant regards the basic function of the state as the coercive protection of the right of individuals to external freedom. He explicitly and emphatically denies that the purpose of the state is to provide for the welfare or happiness of its citizens. The welfare of a state consists not in the happiness of its citizens – which it is no business of the state to provide for – but in the conformity of its constitution to principles of right (MS 6:318). "A government established on the principle of benevolence toward the people like that of a father toward his children – that is, a *paternalistic* government (*imperium paternale*) . . . – is the greatest despotism thinkable" (TP 8:290–1).

The second point is that in Kant's view, "civil equality" (one of the three basic principles, along with "freedom" and "independence," of the civil expression of the innate right to freedom belonging to every citizen) has nothing to do with equality of wealth or income and is "quite consistent with the greatest inequality in terms of the quantity and degree of their possessions" (TP 8:291–2). Kant is an egalitarian about *human worth* – every human being has equal dignity (or absolute worth). But Kant is not an egalitarian in the sense that he thinks distributive justice requires the distribution to everyone of an equal amount of something (welfare, opportunity, wealth, capabilities, or anything else). Civil equality consists rather in the fact that no one among the people has "any superior with the moral capacity to bind him as a matter of right in a way that he could not in turn bind the other" (MS 6:314). "Civil equality" as Kant means it is a prohibition on a certain kind of asymmetry of power or hierarchy within the political system or system of right. It prohibits involuntary servitude and relations of dependence that are not voluntarily entered into.[5] But it places no *direct* restrictions, for example, on how much wealth or property some may own or on how little others may own.

Permissible grounds of redistribution. What these points show is only that whatever role the state may have in providing for the welfare of its poorer citizens or in redistributing wealth among its subjects, that role is not to be based either on providing for people's happiness or on achieving equality between them. They do not show that the state may not, *on other grounds*, be permitted by right to redistribute wealth, for instance, from the rich to the poor. And there is no question but that Kant thinks the state is entitled to do just that.

To the supreme commander there belongs indirectly, that is, insofar as he has taken over the duty of the people, the right to impose taxes on the people for its own preservation, such as taxes to support organizations providing for the *poor, foundling homes* and *church organizations*, usually called charitable or pious institutions.

The general will of the people has united itself into a society which is to maintain itself perpetually; and for this end it has submitted itself to the internal authority of the state in order to maintain those members of the society who are unable (*die es selbst nicht vermögen*) to maintain themselves. For reasons of state the government is therefore authorized to constrain the wealthy to provide the means of sustenance to those who are unable to provide for even their most necessary natural needs. The wealthy have acquired an obligation to the commonwealth, since they owe their existence to an act of submitting to its protection and care, which they need in order to live; on this obligation the state now bases its right to contribute what is theirs to maintaining their fellow citizens. (MS 6:325–6)

Those who favor the libertarian reading of Kant's theory of right do two main things with this passage. One is to claim that it is not (or that it may not be) consistent with Kant's doctrines as a whole.[6] The other is to hold that even if the passage is not inconsistent with Kant's principles, the rationale it provides for taxation of the rich to support the poor is extremely narrow – consisting solely in the fact that such conduct on the part of the state is necessary to maintain the survival of the state itself as an institution and the condition of right.[7]

The charges of inconsistency pretty clearly rest on fallacious reasoning.[8] As we have just noted, from the fact that welfare or redistributive conduct on the part of the state is not grounded on considerations of happiness or equality, it obviously does not follow that it can have no other legitimate ground. From the fact that Kant forbids the state to engage in paternalistic conduct aiming at the happiness of citizens, it obviously does not follow that it is forbidden to do anything to provide for their welfare in ways that do not involve paternalism. As Allen Rosen points out, from the fact that the state's basic rationale is to protect the individual's right to external freedom, it clearly does not follow that state coercion can be justified only when it is being used directly to protect individual freedom in particular cases.[9]

Further, Alexander Kaufman shows that Kant's objections to paternalism are really directed against a contemporary position in political philosophy, known as "cameralism" (represented by Christian Wolff and some of his followers, such as J. H. G. Justi). Cameralists advocate quite repressive governmental policies on the ground that left to themselves, people will not choose the correct means to happiness. They hold that it is the responsibility of the state to provide for both the virtue and the happiness of its subjects, and that only the wise and benevolent coercion of the government can achieve such desirable ends (Kaufman, pp. 39, 50–60). To interpret Kant's objections to this quite extreme position as general prohibitions on all social welfare activity by the state is badly to misread him.[10]

But what of the claim that the passage justifies taxing the rich to provide for the poor only for very narrow purposes – such as to ensure the survival and stability of the state itself? I think it has to be admitted that Kant's reasoning in the passage about taxing the rich for the benefit of the poor is far from transparent. But those who read it as providing only very narrow grounds for welfare or redistributive conduct on the part of the state have to understand Kant as saying that the rich may be taxed to support the poor only when, and to the extent that, the very existence and stability of the state itself requires it. This is how they have to read the words "the right to impose taxes on the people for its own preservation." That reading, however, is highly dubious. A much more natural reading of the passage is that Kant regards it as a legitimate interest of the state to provide, as far as possible, for the physical survival of its individual citizens. His argument, after all, rests on the claim that the wealthy "owe their existence to the act of submitting to [the state's] protection and care" and that this imposes on them the obligation to pay for "the sustenance of those who are unable to provide for even their most necessary natural needs." Clearly in both these cases, what Kant means is not the survival of the state as an institution but the survival of the individuals who are its members. It is reasonable to read the earlier language "the right to impose taxes on the people for its own preservation" in a similar way, so that "the people" does not mean the institutional structure of the state or the rightful condition it guarantees but rather the physical preservation of the individuals who are members of the state. If we wonder how the state's concern with the physical survival of its individual members can be reconciled with its fundamental task of protecting their external freedom, then we should reflect on the obvious fact that physical survival is a necessary condition for any human being to exercise free agency. Kant endorses this obvious thought in a *Reflexion* where he counts the means necessary for the preservation of my existence as belonging to my innate right to freedom (Ak 23:286).[11]

It is not difficult to see how a just concern with maintaining the freedom of citizens, quite apart from utilitarian or eudaimonistic considerations, might lead a Kantian to favor welfare legislation that goes well beyond providing as far as possible for the basic physical survival of all citizens. After all, if physical survival is a necessary condition for the exercise of externally free agency, it is certainly not a sufficient condition for it. Not mere survival, but a decent life, under conditions of self-respect and the respect of others, free from dependency on their arbitrary will, would seem also to be needed for the free status of a person.

If the protection of rightful freedom is the rationale for taxing the wealthy in order to maintain the poor, surely the rationale equally justifies doing more for them than satisfying their basic physical needs and doing more to regulate the economic life of society to prevent people from losing their free status to others and to prevent people from gaining economic control over the lives of others. As Wolfgang Kersting has cogently argued:

> When one considers the dangers that threaten right, freedom and the dignity of humans from a market place unsupervised by a social state and from radical libertarianism's politics of minimal state restriction, then one sees that the philosophy of right must require a compensatory extension of the principle of the state of right through measures toward a social and welfare state in the interest of the human right of freedom itself.[12]

The state as supreme proprietor. Kant's discussion of the state's right to tax the wealthy to support the poor occurs immediately following, and in the context of, his discussion of the sovereign (*Beherrscher*) as the "supreme proprietor" (*Obereigentümer*) of the land (MS 6:323).[13] This is regarded by Kant as the ground of the state's right to tax citizens in general, and Kant understands the state's role as "supreme proprietor" as guaranteeing it "the right to assign to each what is his" (MS 6:324). Kant's doctrine on this point must be further understood in the context of his theory of private property, and especially his crucial distinction between "provisional" and "peremptory" rights of property (MS 6:256–7).

Kant treats private property as the foundation of the state to such an extent that he holds that if we do not assume any rights of property that need to be determined and protected, then there would be no command to leave the state of nature and found a civil society coercively protecting rights (MS 6:312). But the rights of property presupposed by the command to leave the state of nature have to be regarded as merely "provisional" in the sense that they are neither determinate as to their content nor enforceable against others. A determinate right of property requires not only the proprietor's claim over the thing but also the unanimous declaration of all others to respect that claim (MS 6:255); and the only actual form this declaration can take is the recognition by the general will of a civil society of the thing as his (MS 6:256). Only this makes a person's property right "peremptory" – that is, actually valid and enforceable against others.

This means that all peremptory rights of property are held subject to the general will and the legislation made by it, including the laws (if there be such) saying that the rich are to be taxed for the benefit of the poor. There is therefore no natural right of property that anyone could legitimately assert against the general will, or any claim to property rights that could override the law. The point is not merely that the wealthy survive through the protection of the state and that they must therefore be prepared to be taxed to ensure the survival of their fellow citizens. For Kant, all property is held by citizens only subject to the laws that have been made by the general will, the will of the sovereign whose right it is "to assign to each what is his."

Laws governing the distribution of wealth, like all laws governing the lives of citizens, are just only by conformity to the idea of the social contract, the criterion that they might without contradiction have been rationally adopted by the unanimous consent of all (MS 6:340, TP 8:297, 304–5). But within this constraint, it would seem that for Kant, any form of taxation or economic redistribution approved in the legislation made by the people's representatives would be just. Those taxed or otherwise deprived of property for the benefit of others could have no ground for complaint.

If this is the true foundation in right for the taxation of the rich to provide for the basic needs of the poor, then it implies that legislators for a commonwealth have a great deal of latitude regarding laws governing economic regulation and redistribution. It also implies that Kant's argument for taxing the wealthy to provide for the poor does not have the status of asserting a basic rightful claim on the part of the poor to such support. Rather, it is merely a legitimate rationale that the legislative power might have for instituting taxation of the rich for that purpose. In the Kantian state, the legislative body might also rightfully choose to provide *no* support for the poor (in that sense, Kant's theory – as I read it – could at least be made consistent with libertarian policies). Alternatively, Kant's theory equally allows that the legislature might justly tax the wealthy quite heavily to benefit the poor far beyond what is needed for the satisfaction of their basic physical needs. The legislature might even without injustice do as U.S. legislation currently does and tax the poor for the benefit of the wealthy, or it might engage in various other forms of economic redistribution. It would be constrained only by the general criterion of justice: the regulative idea of the original contract.[14]

2. General Injustice

We might sooner wonder whether this last conclusion is consistent with Kant's theory, and whether the innate right to freedom of all human beings might *require* the state to redistribute wealth so as to protect the external freedom of the less well off. If physical survival is a condition for exercising free agency, perhaps the idea of the original contract renders any society fundamentally unjust unless it taxes the wealthy to maintain the poor. If further conditions beyond physical survival are required for free agency, perhaps the idea of the original contract requires going well beyond what

Kant proposes, in the direction of economic redistribution and state regulation of the economic life of society.

There is even some textual support for this way of putting pressure on
Kant's views. In some of Kant's early lectures and notes, there are suggestions that poverty itself represents a form of social injustice, even when it
results from a distribution of property and from transactions that are none
of them in themselves unjust. On this account, there is such a thing as a
"general injustice" that proceeds not from particular unjust acts but from
the unintended results of free human actions that are not unjust considered
separately and singly. Kant's use of this idea is chiefly to cast in the right light
certain practices that portray themselves as condescending beneficence but
that (in Kant's view) do not deserve to be considered meritorious.

> In accordance with [benevolence], people are merciful to others and show benefi-
> cence to them after they have earlier taken from them, even though they are con-
> scious of no injustice to anyone. But one can participate in the general injustice
> even if one does no injustice according to the civil laws and institutions. Now if one
> shows beneficence to a wretch, then one has not given him anything gratuitously,
> but has given him only what one had earlier helped to take from him through the
> general injustice. For if no one took more of the goods of life than another, then
> there would be no rich and no poor. Accordingly, even acts of generosity are acts of
> duty and indebtedness, which arise from the rights of others. (VE 27:416)

> In our present condition, when general injustice is firmly entrenched, the natural
> rights of the lowly cease. They are therefore only debtors, the superior owe them
> nothing. Therefore, these superiors are called "gracious lords." But he who needs
> nothing from them but justice can hold them to their debts and does not need to
> be submissive. (Ak 20:140–1)

> Many people take pleasure in doing good actions but consequently do not want to
> stand under obligations toward others. If one only comes to them submissively, they
> will do everything: they do not want to subject themselves to the rights of people,
> but t view them simply as objects of magnanimity. It is not all one under what title
> I get something. What properly belongs to me must not be accorded me merely as
> something I beg for. (Ak 19:145)

The same thoughts find their way into at least one of Kant's mature published
texts, in the form of the following remark from the "casuistical questions"
in the *Metaphysics of Morals*:

> Having the resources to practice such beneficence as depends on the goods of
> fortune is, for the most part, a result of certain human beings being favored through
> the injustice of the government, which introduces an inequality of wealth that makes
> others need their beneficence. Under such circumstances, does a rich man's help
> to the needy, on which he so readily prides himself as something meritorious, really
> deserve to be called beneficence at all? (MS 6:454)

These remarks indicate how fundamentally deceptive it is to portray welfare legislation as "charity" motivated by "compassion." They also show how

reprehensible it is to suggest that it might be "degrading" for the poor to be "dependent on state handouts." The issue is whether the state has provided every citizen with the conditions for a free life, one in which they do not have to beg for a living and are not vulnerable to exploitation by those who think providing for them is an act of charity. These conditions are *theirs by right.* To represent them as a degrading form of charity would be natural only to the sort of mindset that might consider it demeaning to you if the police protected you from being assaulted by muggers on the street instead of leaving you to fight it out with them.

Kant's suggestion that inequality of wealth is consequent upon the "injustice of the government" is most naturally understood as asserting that it is the responsibility of the government either to prevent or remedy "general injustice." This would imply that redistribution in a more egalitarian direction is not merely something the state is authorized to engage in but also something it *must* engage in if it is not to behave unjustly. If, therefore, there is an inconsistency in Kant's views, it is not introduced by his provision for taxing the wealthy to satisfy the basic needs of the poor but rather by his failure to require that the state do more than this. In Fichte we will find a Kantian liberal political theorist whose views are more consequent.

3. Fichte on Economic Justice

Fichte is usually thought of as a follower of Kant, and he generally thought of himself that way too. Kant's chief work on political philosophy is the Doctrine of Right, the first part of the *Metaphysics of Morals*, which was first published in 1797. Fichte's chief work on the same subject, however, is the *Foundations of Natural Right*, published in 1796. The economic implications of this theory were then further developed in the *Closed Commercial State* (1800).

Through his exceptional talents and tireless application, Fichte achieved a position of academic and cultural prominence that was at least the equal of that of any of his contemporaries. But the circumstances into which he had been born were those of poverty and degradation. His family had been serfs, until his father (a poor linen weaver) was emancipated. Kant too was from a poor family, and he rose to a position of academic prominence, associating with leaders of the community and members of the nobility. Fichte was less comfortable in his upward social mobility. He never forgot his origins, and he never became reconciled to such conditions of existence for any human being. He regarded it as an elementary question of justice that no human being should ever be vulnerable to the oppression of another, and hence that no human being should ever be subject to poverty, from which, he realized, vulnerability to oppression is inseparable. With the same ruthless consistency Fichte brings to every philosophical question, his political theory is animated throughout by the conviction that it is the first responsibility of the political state to secure the well-being of each individual as the most elementary condition for free activity, hence the first demand of right.

Rights of property. All property, according to Fichte, depends on a social contract, called "the property contract," through which people apportion their respective external spheres for free action. Social contracts for Fichte are not actual agreements (whether tacit or explicit), nor are they merely ideas of reason, as they are for Kant, to be used as a criterion for the justice of laws (TP 8:297–8). They are more like transcendental conditions for the possibility of human community – the fundamental terms on which people can live together subject to conditions of right. The fundamental purpose of entering into the property contract is to acquire a sufficient external sphere to perpetuate one's free activity in the future – that is, to satisfy one's external needs (GA I/4:21, SW 3:212–13, *Foundations of Natural Right*, pp. 185–6). Fichte infers that only they are parties to the property contract who thereby acquire *some* property; but not only that – they must also have *enough* property that they can live independently by what they own (GA I/4:8–9, 20–2, SW 3:197–8, 210–12, *Foundations of Natural Right*, pp. 170–2, 183–5). The state's fundamental responsibility of protecting the private property of every citizen thus requires it to distribute property in such a way that no individual falls into destitution. Conversely, every citizen must have an occupation, one that is known to the state and that the state can guarantee as a sufficient means of livelihood (GA I/4:23, SW 3:213–14, *Foundations of Natural Right*, pp. 185–6).

All property rights are grounded on the contract of all with all which says this: We all retain this on the condition that we allow you what is yours. Thus as soon as someone cannot live from his labor, that which is absolutely his is not being allowed him, and regarding him the contract is cancelled completely, and he is not bound by right to recognize the property of any other human being. (GA I/4:22, SW 3:213, *Foundations of Natural Right*, pp. 185–6)

Fichte does not intend, of course, that this should ever actually result in the cancellation of all property rights. Fichte's point is rather that the fundamental legitimacy of the state in enforcing property rights is conditional on its meeting the responsibility to distribute (if necessary, to redistribute) property in such a way that all able-bodied citizens can live freely from their own labor. This means at the very least that the poor have an absolute right against the state that they should be supported:

Every one possesses his civil property only insofar and on the condition that all citizens of the state can live from what is theirs; and insofar as someone cannot live from it, it ceases to be theirs and becomes his; of course according to the determinate judgment of the state authority. The executive power is responsible for this as for all other branches of state administration, and it is self-evident that the poor who have concluded the civil contract have an absolute coercive right on its support. (GA I/4:22, SW 3:213, *Foundations of Natural Right*, p. 185)

The point of saying that poverty cancels all rights to property is that the right of every citizen to earn a basic living takes absolute precedence over the right of the rich to enjoy the fruits of their greater good fortune. It is not only that the property of rich may justly be taxed to support the poor. In fact, it is even in a sense a misnomer to describe the situation this way, because that description seems to concede that what is taxed rightfully belonged to the wealthy in the first place before it was taxed. This, however, is precisely what Fichte denies:

First all must be well-fed and securely housed before any dwelling is decorated; first all must be comfortably and warmly clothed before any can be dressed finely...It counts for nothing that someone may say: "But I can pay for it." For it is an *injustice* that anyone can pay for luxuries while there are some of his fellow citizens who cannot acquire necessities or cannot pay for them; that with which the former pays is not rightful property; in a rational state, it would not be *his*. (SW 3:409)

Fichte's position implies, for example, that if a farmer does not have enough land to make a decent living, the state is required to redistribute land to rectify the situation (GA I/4:26). Fichte provides the state with redistributive rights, responsibilities, and resources in other ways as well. He maintains that because the dead are no longer parties to the social contract, there is no natural right of inheritance – none whatever. The property of those who die reverts to the state, and wills or testamentary dispositions are valid only if *the state* should choose to recognize them as ways in which *it* chooses to distribute *its* property among its citizens (GA I/4:55–6, SW 3:255–7, *Foundations of Natural Right*, pp. 222–4).

Regulation of the economy. Further, Fichte infers from these principles that the state has the right, and even the duty, strictly to regulate all trade and commerce. It is to fix prices on all necessities of life so that all may afford them, and it must guarantee that there are sufficient but never excessive numbers of people in each economic branch of society, so that every citizen is required to work and guaranteed a decent living from that work (GA I/4:37–41, SW 3:232–7, *Foundations of Natural Right*, pp. 202–7).

Fichte proposes a market economy, but one very strictly controlled by the state; external trade is to be carried out by the state itself, never by private citizens. This is the meaning of the title of Fichte's treatise of 1800: *The Closed Commercial State* (SW 3:387–513). Within the closed commercial state, it is the state that determines how many citizens are recruited to perform each kind of labor, and in what ratios commodities are to be sold, so as to guarantee that all live decently from their labor. These requirements, which are basic requirements of justice, cannot be left to chance, or (what is the same thing) to the mercy of the "free" market. For the state to leave the *market* "free" in these respects would be to infringe on the basic *freedom of human beings*, to prevent them from appropriating what they have a right to appropriate, and therefore to violate their basic right as persons.

It would be much the same if the state did nothing to prevent others from stealing or making use of their property, except that even in a state in which theft is widespread, undeterred, and unpunished, at least the state might have allowed people to appropriate what was rightfully theirs in the first place. In an economy that allows poverty to exist, and in a state that does nothing to guarantee all citizens enough property to live freely from their own labor, the individual's right of property has already been violated at its very foundation.

It is tempting to compare Fichte's recommendations with the system that prevailed in Eastern Europe for most of the twentieth century and went under the name of 'communism' or 'socialism'. Fichte's proposals certainly do not invite such names, because they allow for – and are even founded on – the right of private property. But it is doubtful that the "really existing" "communism" (or "socialism") of Eastern Europe ever really merited these names either. What is quite clear is that that system certainly bore a closer resemblance to Fichte's economic proposals than it did, for example, to anything one could find proposed in the writings of Karl Marx or Friedrich Engels. It is all the more noteworthy, therefore, that Fichte's proposals of an essentially state-run market economy are advanced solely on the ground that the state's task is to secure all citizens their rightful property.

4. Kantian Ethics and Economic Right

In view of the fact that a system of this kind is now the object of almost universal abhorrence, we are bound to ask where Fichte's argument has gone wrong. But there is no easy answer to this question. Eastern European "communism" is abhorred in large part because its political institutions were highly undemocratic and it was severely repressive of individual rights to free expression and freedom of action in matters having nothing to do with the economic sphere. Fichte's political philosophy involves no endorsement of these objectionable practices. He advocates representative government and quite liberal policies regarding personal freedom. (Fichte's position might well be called "libertarian" on many noneconomic matters; he even holds that the state has no *right* to prohibit suicide, adultery, prostitution, or even infanticide by an unwed mother – although Fichte strongly condemns all these acts as violations of *ethical* duty.) Our defense of personal liberty and democratic institutions is therefore not a good reason for objecting to Fichte's conception of economic justice. At most we might wonder (and ought to worry about) whether economic justice is possible in practice without unacceptable consequences in other areas of life (and if it is not, about why this is so).

We might also wonder whether Fichte's basic principles really entail his specific economic proposals. Fichte's basic thesis is that individual freedom and the right to property require that no one should be condemned to an existence of destitution, and that all must have property that makes them able to earn an independent living on the basis of their own labor. This thesis is also apparently the rationale for Kant's more timid proposal that the state ought to tax the wealthy to maintain the poor (though the basis in right for this proposal is the sovereign's position as supreme proprietor). It seems a separate question what kind and degree of redistribution, taxation, or state control over or regulation of the economy is required in practice to enforce these individual property rights.

Kant and Fichte deal with issues of poverty and redistribution entirely at the level of the right established within a single nation-state. Twenty-first-century issues about these matters are bound to involve also questions of justice between nations and within an economy that is essentially and irrecoverably global in scale. We cannot expect people to deal adequately with issues of global justice, however, if they are unwilling even to face up to issues of justice within a single nation-state as it is conceived in the liberal tradition. The positions and arguments we have been examining, therefore, are of fundamental relevance to issues of economic justice as we face them, even if they do not encompass important parts of what we must take up under the heading of economic justice.

What the arguments of Kant, and even more of Fichte, establish is that there is no basis in natural right for claiming that political institutions lack the authority to engage in whatever redistribution of wealth, or to exercise whatever degree of control over the economy, turns out to be necessary to protect its citizens from the loss of freedom attendant on their falling into a condition of poverty. Fichte further establishes this point entirely on the basis of the state's essential function of protecting individual freedom and quite independently of any possible state concern with people's *welfare* or *happiness*, also without any appeal to any principle of economic *equality*. Fichte's liberal state has no legitimate business even caring about whether people who are protected from poverty live happy, flourishing, or virtuous, lives or miserable and depraved lives – that is entirely their own business. The state also has no business seeking to equalize individuals' fortunes, incomes, or capabilities. It must, however, limit the economic inequality of its citizens to the extent that none has so little property as to be incapable of leading a free and independent life, and none has so much property as to be in a position to reduce any other to a position of dependence or unfreedom.

Precisely what system of taxation, or of redistribution of property, or state regulation of the economy, will best satisfy these demands in practice remains today an open question. Fichte's proposals in the *Closed Commercial State* might well turn out to be ineffective or even counterproductive to achieving the social justice he expects them to achieve. What Fichte's proposals show is that there is a profound problem with the very legitimacy of modern society regarding issues of wealth and poverty. If these proposals, or similar attempts in Eastern Europe during the past century, are unacceptable, we must nevertheless acknowledge that they were responses to real moral problems lying at the ground of the present economic regime of society. If laetrile does not cure cancer, it does not follow that cancer has no cure, still less that it is a condition of health. The best that can be said for capitalism is that it is a disease for which we have yet to find a cure.

No society that presently exists (or that has ever existed) has ever fully achieved what is required for a condition of right. People perhaps still do not know, or at least they still cannot agree upon, what political measures will achieve this condition. The main message we ought to take away from the study of theories of right such as Kant's and Fichte's is that it is imperative for us to discover these measures, reach agreement about them, and implement them. Until we do, we cannot claim to be living in a free or a just society, and our entire legal and political order will continue to lack fundamental legitimacy.

Fichte puts the point this way: "Any constitution of the state is in accord with right which does not make it impossible to progress toward something better . . . Only that constitution is completely contrary to right which has the end of preserving everything as it presently is" (GA I/5:313–14, SW 4:361, *System of Ethics*, p. 341). One can only wish that such sentiments were today more widespread regarding the political-economic order of society.

Punishment

Kant is widely regarded as holding a retributivist view of punishment. I think this common opinion is obviously correct, supported explicitly by many texts. But Kant also devised an entire practical philosophy, a theory about the foundations of right and ethics, and a theory of justice and ethical duties and a theory of justice based upon it. If we are to do Kantian ethics properly, we must constantly ask how Kant's own moral convictions relate to his practical philosophy as a whole – for instance, how, or even whether, these convictions can be supported by his theory. It cannot be a foregone conclusion that everything Kant says follows validly from his fundamental principles or is even consistent with them.

It is a sound hermeneutical principle that in studying any philosopher we should at the start provisionally assume that the philosopher's thought constitutes a coherent unity. Thus if Kant emphatically asserted a retributivist theory of punishment, then we should begin with the assumption that this retributivism can be supported by, or somehow integrated into, his larger theories of right and morality. Our first task should be to look for a way that Kant's retributivism can be seen to fit into his practical philosophy. Yet it is an equally valid hermeneutical principle that this assumption of unity and coherence should be only provisional or tentative. For it is always possible that careful investigation will show some of a philosopher's doctrines not to be as well supported by, or as consistent with, his basic theory as we were justified in provisionally assuming. This is the possibility for which I will argue regarding Kant's retributivism. I do not think Kant's retributivist convictions are supported by any arguments he suggests on behalf of them. The theory of punishment that arises naturally out of Kant's theory of right turns out not to be retributivist. The chief attempt others have made to effect an integration of Kant's retributivism into his ethical theory is unsuccessful both exegetically and philosophically. Kant's retributivism is even in serious tension with some of his most fundamental moral doctrines.

Any discussion of the ethics of legal punishment ought to begin by facing up to some obvious facts. If philosophical theories about punishment are viewed as providing a moral defense of what our criminal justice system actually does to criminals, then it should be admitted from the start that their task is hopeless. There is just about as much prospect for its success as there would be if we attempted a moral justification of the acts of theft, rape, and murder that are to be punished. It is no doubt reasonable to think that some sort of social response to criminal acts is morally justifiable, either with a view to preventing future criminal acts or doing justice to the criminals for their past acts. But no sensible person could think that a morally justifiable response would bear much resemblance to the organized system of brutality and abuse that is systematically practiced by existing courts and prisons. Historically, in the United States one of the main functions of criminal imprisonment has been to oppress racial and ethnic minorities, especially African-Americans. The prison system, in fact, functions for these minorities as a dehumanizing alternative to a system of higher education, which (given similar resources) could easily provide them with fulfilling lives and make their talents available to the rest of society. In our courts the poor receive little justice, while the rich are treated leniently. Children are often punished as if they were adults. Drug addicts and the mentally ill are punished rather than provided with the medical treatment they need. The system as a whole is outrageously wasteful of both economic and human resources. In our prisons, inmates are systematically subject to rape and sexual abuse by both other inmates and corrections officers. In several states, attack dogs are routinely used to "pacify" uncooperative inmates. Such outrages on human dignity are far too numerous and too varied for me even to begin to list them here.

The only defensible idea behind philosophical justifications of punishment is therefore to say what a justifiable response to crime *would* be (in a society very different from any that has ever existed on earth). Even this, however, has its dangers, because it leads to the pretense that our criminal justice system might come close enough to it to be morally justified, especially in view of the evident political impracticality of any more humane or more just response to crime that might be proposed in its place. It is the same with theories of just war, which lay down conditions under which a war might be justified and then are used to silence people's consciences over actual wars, none of which (even the "best" wars) have ever come close to meeting the conditions. In both cases, these mystifications work well enough to help sustain indefinitely some of the worst forms of wrongfulness and inhumanity practiced by the human species.

Among theories of punishment, retributivism often leaves an especially bad taste in people's mouths, perhaps because it appears to be merely an apology for vengefulness, or else because it declines to salve our guilty consciences with the prospect of some future benefit to be obtained through the act of punishment. Kant's retributivism, especially combined with his conspicuous insistence that death is the only just punishment for willful murder, makes his theory seem particularly odious. But as I have already indicated, I will argue below that Kant's retributivism is not in fact the justification of punishment that fits best with his theory of right, and also that it is doubtful whether Kantian ethics is even compatible with retributivism. I will also conclude, however, that this conclusion should not be entirely welcome to Kantian ethics, in view of certain advantages, seldom sufficiently appreciated, that retributivism enjoys over all rival theories.

1. What Is Retributivism?

The concept of punishment. Our first task must be to understand clearly what Kant's retributivism consists in. In order to do this, we need to begin with a few general remarks about the concept of punishment and theories of the justification of punishment. Punishment is a harm inflicted on a person by an appropriate authority because the authority ostensibly believes the person is guilty of doing something wrong or illegal.[1] This is offered here as a purely conceptual or analytic truth. It is also contained in the concept of punishment that punishment can be just or unjust. First, a punishment is unjust when the authority's belief that the person is guilty of the thing for which they are being punished is false (or feigned). And second, punishment can also be unjust because it is excessive (because the harm inflicted is greater than the wrongdoing deserves), and punishment can also be unjustly lenient (because the harm is less than the wrongdoing deserves). The points just made pertain to the very concept of punishment, in the sense that to the extent that they do not hold, we are not talking about cases of *punishment* at all. Someone who does not accept an institution with the conceptual structure just outlined does not accept any institution that could be correctly called 'punishment'.

The conceptual points I have just been making, however, admittedly have a retributivist sound to them. So it might be thought that retributivism about punishment could be defended on purely conceptual grounds. But that would be a serious error. It would betray a fundamental misunderstanding both of retributivism and the philosophical alternatives to it. For retributivism is not a conceptual view about what punishment is but one theory alongside others about how an institution with these conceptual features is to be *justified*. The fact that punishment has these conceptual features does not explain why any actual social or legal institution should have them.[2]

Theories of punishment. The differences between retributivism and alternative theories of punishment depend on answers to the following questions:

1. What is the justification for having an institution of punishment at all?

2. What is the nature of the reason (the "because") that justifies the authority in inflicting harm on a person *because* the person has done something wrong or illegal?
3. What are the standards that make a punishment "too severe" or "too lenient," and how are these standards to be justified?

Regarding question (1), the retributivist position is that the institution of punishment is justified by the fact that justice itself requires that some appropriate harm be inflicted on the doers of wrongful or illegal acts.[3] The most direct form of retributivism says that punishment is justified because persons guilty of crimes inherently deserve to be punished. Following Thomas Hill, I call this the "Intrinsic Desert Thesis" (Hill, p. 315). An alternative version of retributivism might hold that the justice of inflicting punishment is further explicable based on a scheme of distributive justice (but not, for example, on a method for maximizing the general happiness, which would render the justification nonretributivist).[4] Kant, as we will see presently, emphatically accepts the Intrinsic Desert Thesis.[5]

There are clearly *nonretributivist* alternatives to the Intrinsic Desert Thesis. Some theories hold, for instance, that the institution of punishment is justified by (a) the way it deters acts of wrongdoing or otherwise ensures law-abiding behavior, or (b) the way it morally improves wrongdoers, or (c) the way it makes the public feel safer, or (d) the way it satisfies the public's desire for vengeance against wrongdoers, or (e) the way it expresses the public's disapproval of acts of wrongdoing.

It is important to see that answers (d) and (e), in particular, are *not retributivist* answers to question (1). It is possible, of course, that punishment satisfies the public's desire for vengeance or expresses the public's disapproval at least in part because members of the public hold retributivist convictions. But this need not be so. The public might desire vengeance against the criminal without having to think its act of vengeance is inherently just. Even if many individual members of the public do think this, those who offer (d) and (e) as justifications of punishment need not endorse these retributivist convictions in order to offer (d) or (e) as answers to question (1). They might hold instead that allowing the public to satisfy its desire for vengeance or express its moral disapproval is justified as a way of maximizing the general happiness, or they might hold that the public is entitled to satisfy its desire for vengeance or express its disapproval, whether or not it has good reasons for these attitudes.

One retributivist answer to question (2) – an answer that might even be inferred from the Intrinsic Desert Thesis – is what I will call the "Directness Thesis," namely that the reason-giving connection between wrongdoing and the infliction of harm is *immediate* and *necessary*, not indirect or contingent. It would be indirect and contingent if it went by way of an appeal to such alleged facts as that punishment deters crime, or morally improves criminals, or has some effect on the public's feelings, or effectively expresses the public's moral attitudes, or plays a role in some social scheme of distributive justice. (From this last point we see that some possible versions of retributivism that are based on some further appeal to a scheme of distributive justice would not accept the Directness Thesis.)

One standard retributivist answer to question (3) is a third thesis, which I will call by its Kantian name: *Ius Talionis*. This is the claim that a punishment is just (neither excessive nor too lenient) only when the harm inflicted on the wrongdoer is *equal* to the wrong done. Alternative (nonretributivist) answers to question (3) might be that a punishment is neither too lenient nor too harsh when it suffices to achieve the relevant aim of punishment (deterring crime, making the public feel safe, assuaging the public's vengeful passions, etc.), but without inflicting more harm on the wrongdoer than is needed to achieve the aim. (On these views, punishment would be too lenient if it were insufficient to accomplish the chosen aim and too harsh if it harmed the criminal more than was necessary to achieve it.) A retributive theory of punishment that did not accept the *Ius Talionis* might derive its standards for just punishment from a system of distributive justice, so that the just measure of punishment would be determined by factors other than, or in addition to, the mere gravity of the crime itself. Thus there clearly are theories of punishment that someone could reasonably call "retributivist" without endorsing any of the Intrinsic Desert Thesis, the Directness Thesis, or the *Ius Talionis*. However, I think anyone who endorses *any* of these three ideas surely deserves to be called a "retributivist"; and someone who holds all three holds retributivism in a particularly strong or extreme form.

I now document the claims that Kant is such an extreme retributivist, and that he explicitly rejects most of the obvious alternatives to retributivism. In the Doctrine of Right, Kant's discussion of the ruler's right to punish begins: "The *right to punish* is the right a ruler has against a subject to inflict pain upon him because of his having committed a crime" (MS 6:331). As we have seen, this could be taken as merely a conceptual point about punishment, and that would not entail retributivism. But Kant soon follows this up with a number of assertions that certainly are retributivist.

Punishment by a court (*poena forensis*) . . . can never be inflicted merely as a means to promote some other good for the criminal himself or for civil society. It must always be inflicted on him only *because he has committed a crime.* . . . He must previously have been found *punishable* before any thought can be given to drawing from his punishment something of use for himself or his fellow citizens. The law of punishment is a categorical imperative. (MS 6:331)

In punishments, a physical evil is coupled to moral badness. That this link is a necessary one, and physical evil a direct consequence of moral badness, or that the latter consists in a *malum physicum, quod moraliter necessarium est*, cannot be discerned through reason, nor proved either, and yet it is contained in the concept of punishment that it is an immediately necessary consequence of breaking the law. The judicial office, by virtue of its law-giving power, is called upon by reason to repay, to visit a proportionate evil upon the transgression of moral laws . . . Now from this it is evident that an essential *requisitum* of any punishment is that it be just, i.e. that it is an immediately necessary consequence of the morally bad act; and this, indeed, is what its quality consists in, that it is an *actus justitiae*, that the physical evil is imparted on account of the moral badness. (VE 27:552–3)

But what kind and what amount of punishment is it that public justice makes its principle and measure? None other than the principle of equality (in the position of the needle on the scale of justice), to incline no more to one side than the other. Accordingly, whatever undeserved evil you inflict on another within the people, that you inflict on yourself. If you insult him, you insult yourself; if you steal from him, you steal from yourself; if you strike him, you strike yourself; if you kill him, you kill yourself. But only the law of retribution (*ius talionis*) – it being understood, of course, that this is applied by a court (not by your private judgment) – can specify definitely the quality and quantity of punishment; all other principles are fluctuating an unsuited for a sentence of pure and strict justice because extraneous considerations are mixed into them. (MS 6:332)

Although he who punishes can at the same time have the kindly intention of directing the punishment to [the end of happiness] as well, yet it must first be justified in itself as punishment, that is, as mere harm, so that he who is punished, if it stopped there and he could see no kindness hidden behind the harshness, must himself admit that justice was done to him and that what was allotted him was perfectly suited to his conduct. (KpV 5:37)

Woe unto him who crawls through the windings of eudaimonism in order to discover something that releases the criminal from punishment. (MS 6:331)

Intrinsic Desert. The first, second, and fourth of these quotations endorse the Intrinsic Desert Thesis; the second is particularly clear and emphatic in endorsing the Directness Thesis. What Kant calls "the law of punishment" seems to involve both the Intrinsic Desert Thesis and the Directness Thesis. The third asserts the *Ius Talionis*. The fourth and fifth are emphatic rejections of any alternatives to retributivist principles, regarding both the fundamental justification for punishment and the measure of just punishment. To claim that "the law of punishment" is a categorical imperative is to say that the justification of punishment is independent of any end not contained in the rational obligatory nature of the action itself. This claim is therefore a denial that the grounding of punishment could depend in any way on the public welfare, or the prevention of crimes, or the improvement of the criminal, or on any other effect that the institution of punishment or particular acts of punishment might have. It thus entails both the Intrinsic Desert Thesis and the Directness Thesis and rejects all justifications of the institution of punishment that depend on its conduciveness to any further ends, whatever they might be.

It is true that Kant hopes authorities will *also* use punishment to achieve other good ends, for the public or for the criminal, but he is clear that all such attempts must presuppose, and be constrained by, the essential justice of the punishment, as specified in the "law of punishment" and the *Ius Talionis*. In the first, third, fourth, and especially the fifth quotations, Kant roundly condemns modifying (especially lessening) punishments from the standard of the *Ius Talionis* in order to achieve other ends.

The equality of crime and punishment. Kant's talk, in connection with the *Ius Talionis*, about the "equality," "sameness," or "likeness" (*Gleichheit*) of crime and punishment will no doubt raise eyebrows. It certainly raises questions about what *Gleichheit* means in this context. The only case in which Kant himself seems to take the *Gleichheit* literally involves his notorious thesis that the crime of willful murder always calls for the death penalty. But I think critics of retributivism have generally exaggerated this problem. The basic idea behind the *Ius Talionis*, and its notion of "equality" between crime and punishment, is simply this: Just as offenses differ in their gravity, so punishments differ in their severity, and the just measure of a punishment depends chiefly, if not entirely, on the proportionality between them. A defender of the *Ius Talionis* need not be naïve or simple-minded about how this proportionality is to be determined. Hegel, who favors the same retributivist idea, correctly observes that the proper measures of crime and punishment vary historically, depending on the civil society of a nation and an age, so that a just penal code is a product of the society to which it is to be applied. Penal legislation is therefore a matter calling for good judgment, and taking the social and historical context into account. He thinks that as civil society becomes better ordered and people's customs become more enlightened and rational, the severity of just punishments will tend to diminish (Hegel, PR §218R). As I will indirectly indicate near the end of this chapter, the *Ius Talionis*, so understood, seems to me the most attractive part of retributivism.

A nonretributivist Kant? It may seem like belaboring the obvious to document in such detail the claim that Kant is a retributivist, even an extreme one. But in recent years Kant's commitment to retributivism has actually been questioned by some of the leading scholars who work on the topic, such as Sharon Byrd and Thomas Hill. Their general approach follows Rawls's distinction between justifying an action according to the rules of a practice and justifying the practice, to which I have already in effect appealed in distinguishing between the concept of punishment and theories justifying the institution of punishment (Rawls, TCR). Byrd and Hill want to read Kant's retributivist-sounding remarks as if they were intended only to justify the acts of sentencing judges or other officials from within the practice of criminal justice. Accordingly, in Byrd's formulation, they read Kant's theory of punishment as "Deterrence in Its Threat, Retribution in Its Execution."[6]

Presently I will suggest some reasons for regarding this interpretation as far less misguided than it might at first appear – its motivation actually lies in the most defensible theory of the state's right to punish that is available to Kantian ethics. Nevertheless, as an interpretation of *Kant* it seems to me untenable, simply because it is flagrantly at odds with what Kant says, considered in the contexts in which he says it. When Kant endorses the Intrinsic Desert Thesis, Directness Thesis, and *Ius Talionis*, he is plainly writing and lecturing *not* from within the practice of punishment but rather from the standpoint of philosophers and philosopher-citizens who are reflecting critically on punishment as part of a general philosophical theory of right and ethics. Sometimes Kant asserts retributivism in general moral or religious contexts. These passages cannot possibly be read as statements from within a legal practice. Even when Kant might be addressing himself to judges, as he occasionally does in the passages quoted, his admonitions clearly mean more than this reading allows. For Kant is there concerned with the fact that a judge's function is not merely to follow (by rote) a set of legal statutes but also to *do justice*. Plainly Kant thinks that if the law of punishment and the *Ius Talionis* are correct at the philosophical level, then judges who are doing their job ought to rule in ways consistent with them. That is what he obviously means, for example, when he sternly warns against "crawling through the windings of eudaimonism in order to discover something that releases the criminal from punishment" (MS 6:331).

2. Kant's Best Justification of Punishment

Right and the law of punishment. The next task is to see how Kant's retributivist principles might be rooted in his practical philosophy. The most natural place to begin this inquiry is with Kant's theory of the state and its right to punish crime. This is an area of Kantian doctrine that has not been as well studied as it should have been, especially in Anglophone literature, which deplorably often attempts to draw a "Kantian" theory of law and politics from Kant's ethical theory, especially from applications of FUL. All such attempts however, are not just wrong, but wildly wrong.

A *state* [Kant says], "is a union of a multitude of human beings under laws of right, insofar as these are *a priori* necessary as laws, that is, insofar as they follow of themselves from concepts of external right as such (are not statutory), its form is the form of a state as such, that is, of *the state in idea*, as it ought to be in accordance with pure principles of right. (MS 6:313)

The right of the ruler (*Befehlshaber*) to punish crimes is listed among the powers belonging, jointly or severally, to the three powers or authorities (*Gewalten*) that constitute the "idea of the state" or "the state in idea" that is to serve "as a norm (*norma*) for [a commonwealth's] internal constitution" (MS 6:313). The "ruler" is the *executive* authority, which is charged with carrying out the laws made by the *legislative* authority or "sovereign" (*Souverän, Herrscher*) representing the united general will of the people (MS 6:313–14). In particular cases, the ruler is charged with carrying out the decisions of the *judicial* authority, which is the third power belonging to the state in its idea.

The "law of punishment," the categorical imperative to inflict on a criminal a harm "equal to" his offense, would thus seem to be one of the "laws of right" or "*a priori* laws" that are supposed to "follow of themselves from concepts of external right as such" that constitute the "idea of the state." Thus Kant claims that "every murderer must suffer death" because "this is what justice, as the idea of judicial authority, wills in accordance with universal laws that are grounded *a priori*" (MS 6:334). Yet Kant fails to provide any explicit account of how the law of punishment "follows from concepts of external right" – that is, any explicit argument *why* it is immediately necessary that the perpetrator of wrongdoing or crime should be visited with a harm "equal" to the crime.

In one of the five quotations presented above, Kant even suggests that it is *impossible* to provide any proof of such propositions. Perhaps he thinks that the mere concept of punishment as "the right of the ruler to inflict pain upon [a subject] because of his having committed a crime" already involves the thesis that this "because" is "immediate and necessary," and this is why he thinks the Directness Thesis is one of the "concepts of external right as such." If so, then the thought is confused and erroneous. For we have already seen that although it may be contained in the concept of punishment that the ruler should punish a criminal *because* he committed a crime, it is not contained in the very concept of punishment that this "because" has to be immediate and necessary. The concept of punishment, which is neutral between retributivist and nonretributivist justifications of punishment, could of course be regarded as a "thin" concept of punishment, in contrast with a "thicker" concept that Kant might regard as belonging among the "concepts of external right" that go to make up "the state in its idea." (On the whole, this is the view I think we have most reason to ascribe to him.) But the retributivist elements included in this thicker concept would then need to be defended by some sort of argument, whether or not they are capable of "proof" in whatever strict sense Kant intends to deny that they admit of proof.

In any event, if the "law of punishment" is supposed to be self-evident but unprovable ("incapable of being discerned through reason"), then Kant's retributivism seems already doomed by his own declarations to lack any real support from the rest of his theory of right and ethics, which is precisely the theory he claims is based on practical reason. The correct reaction to Kant's retributivism would then seem to be Fichte's, when he concludes that Kantian retributivism is "grounded on a categorical imperative which is inscrutable (*unerforschlich*)."[7]

The coercive protection of right. Our first attempt to link Kant's retributivism to his larger practical philosophy, by starting with the ruler's power to punish and tracing it back to the idea of the state, thus reaches a dead end. However, we might try beginning elsewhere, not with the idea of a state but with the universal principle of right from which the idea of a state is to be derived. The principle of right is: "Any action is *right* if it can coexist with everyone's freedom in accordance with a universal law" (MS 6:230). The basic referent of 'right' is *uncoerced external freedom*, and the condition of universally valid laws in which everyone equally enjoys such freedom. The opposite of *right* in this sense is *wrong* (*unrecht*), meaning: "injustice." Thus Kant's concept of a "right" action is very different from the notion of a "right" action as it standardly figures in Anglophone moral philosophy. As we saw in Chapter 9, §2, right (*Recht*) represents a moral (*sittlich*) standard that is independent of the *ethical* (*ethisch*) standard whose principle is the supreme principle of morality formulated in the *Groundwork*.

The value of right is nevertheless deeply grounded in Kantian practical philosophy. For external freedom, independence from constraint by another's will (as long as your will leaves them externally free in accordance with universal law) is the sole innate right possessed by human beings and is grounded on their dignity as ends in themselves and self-governing agents (MS 6:237). For Kant, the function of the state is to establish a general condition of right (*Rechtzustand*) – in contrast to a "state of nature" (*Naturzustand*) (MS 6:305–6). A rightful condition is one in which everyone's rightful freedom of action is protected by a coercive authority that limits everyone's external actions to those that are right and prevents people from doing wrong (or injustice) to others – that is, doing acts that infringe on their freedom to do acts that are right.

A rightful condition is imperative because even if all happened voluntarily to limit their actions to what is right, no one would truly enjoy a condition of rightful freedom. This is because rightful freedom would still have no determinate boundaries (there would be no way to settle disputes about it, such as disputes over property) and also no coercive protection or guarantee for it. Even if people's rights weren't in fact violated, they would not be protected, as justice requires. Thus a state of nature is already a state of injustice, no matter what people in it might choose to do with their lawless freedom (MS 6:312).

It is fundamental to the powers of the state, therefore, that it be able rightfully to coerce its subjects to respect the right of others and limit themselves to actions that are right as determined both by pure principles of right and by the state's own laws and statutes. Kant derives this right to coerce from something fundamental to externally free (or right) action in general. He takes it to be an analytic proposition that any act of coercion which prevents wrong (*unrecht*) (i.e., prevents the interference with an action that is right) is consistent with everyone's freedom according to universal law. Such coercion is therefore right. So the concept of right involves, analytically, the authorization (*Befugnis*) to use coercion against wrong (MS 6:231).[8] In a condition of right, however, the authorization to exercise rightful coercion resides not in individuals but exclusively in the ruler (the state's executive power) acting under the laws made by the sovereign (the united general will of the people).

This line of reasoning provides a clear and cogent account of the state's right to punish.[9] Punishment is justified as a form of coercion used to protect right. But it is not a retributivist justification at all. In the context of Kant's practical philosophy, it seems to be a much better-grounded justification of punishment than Kant's retributivism. The insight into this fact is what I think motivates those, such as Byrd and Hill, who want to treat the deterrence of wrong as Kant's real justification of punishment and interpret away his retributivism as merely a conceptual analysis of punishment from within the practice.[10] Thus their interpretation is not only charitable but even grounded in the deep structure of Kant's theory of right. That makes it profoundly sad that this interpretation is textually indefensible.[11]

Punishment as the coercive deterrence of wrong is clearly not by itself *inconsistent* with retributivism. The problem is that Kant's theory of right makes the coercive deterrence view fundamental and turns retributive punishment into merely a way of administering it (as Byrd and Hill want to do). Kant is emphatic that the relationship between the two is just the reverse: "All means of punishment, therefore, which merely aim at protecting the person and property of men are but means and signs of the punishment itself" (VE 27:556).

3. Punishment and Universal Law

We therefore seem to be at an impasse in the attempt to relate Kant's retributivism to his practical philosophy. But there still might be a way out if Kant's retributivism could be derived in some other way from something deep within his practical philosophy. Inevitably there have been hermeneutically charitable attempts to do this. The best known of them has been presented (in slightly different forms) by Edmund Pincoffs and Samuel Fleischacker.[12] It starts from Kant's Formula of Universal Law in the *Groundwork*, employing this formula in ways Kant never does in an attempt to justify conclusions Kant apparently endorses. In particular, Pincoffs and Fleischacker attempt to use the Formula of Universal Law to justify Kant's version of the *Ius Talionis*, in which the criminal "draws on himself" the very wrong he perpetrates (or at least something "equal" to it).

We show, exhibit, wrongness [in the criminal's maxim] by taking it at face value. If the criminal has adopted it, he is claiming that it can be universalized. But if it is universalized, it warrants the same treatment of the criminal as he has accorded to his victim. So if he murders, he must be executed: if he steals, we must "steal" from him . . . To justify the punishment to the criminal is to show him that the compulsion we use on him proceeds according to the same rule by which he acts. This is how "he draws the punishment on himself." In punishing we are not adopting his maxim but demonstrating its logical consequences if universalized. (Pincoffs, p. 9)

Retributive punishment serves a moral function for Kant by making the criminal live under the law he implicitly sets up in his criminal act. The criminal acts on a maxim that he would not will as a universal law; we apply the law of that maxim to him, as though he had willed it universally . . . We are merely following out the rational interpretation of his irrational act, and he should have no reason to complain. (Fleischacker, p. 442)

Neither Pincoffs nor Fleischacker ever claims that the line of reasoning they present in these quotations was stated by Kant himself. (They would be wrong if they did.) Their aim is apparently to present an argument they think Kant *could* have given that *would* support his assertion of the *Ius Talionis*: "If you steal from him, you steal from yourself; if you kill him, you kill yourself," and so forth.

The fallacy in this form of retributivism. Their line of reasoning begins with one correct premise, namely that for Kant the criminal acts on a maxim that cannot be willed as a universal law. Kant does hold that wrongful acts violate juridical duties, that every act violating a juridical duty also violates an ethical duty, and also that an act which violates an ethical duty involves a maxim that cannot be willed as a universal law. But how are we supposed to get from this true premise to the conclusion that someone (presumably, the state's executive authority) is entitled to act toward the criminal in a manner that accords with what his maxim *would* imply *if it were universalizable* (which it necessarily is not) and *if the state acted (justly) on that maxim* (which it necessarily could not)? We should be struck here by the fact that the argument involves as premises two counterfactuals whose antecedents Kant holds to be *necessarily* false. It is hard to see how one could justify in Kantian terms *anyone's* acting on a maxim (or on the presumptive universalized form of a maxim) unless it is possible for *someone* to will that maxim as a universal law. By Pincoffs and Fleischacker's own admission, it is not possible, either for the criminal or for anyone else, to will the criminal's maxim as a universal law. So the natural conclusion is that *no one* has a right to act on either the criminal's maxim, or on its presumptive (but necessarily bogus) universalized form. It would harmonize with Kant's procedure in the *Groundwork* to *argue* to someone who proposes to act on a maxim that can't be universalized that if he tried to will it as a universal law, he would have to will to be treated in ways that he cannot rationally will to be treated. But it would not harmonize – or even be minimally consistent – with Kantian principles to claim that we are justified in *actually treating* the person in the way no one can rationally will to be treated. Yet precisely this is the conclusion the argument is supposed to establish.

There are also difficulties in this view arising from the fact that Kant's justification of punishment is supposed to apply to a principle of *right*, while

FUL is one formula of the principle of *ethics*. If it were consistent with FUL to treat a doer of wrong (*unrecht*) in accordance with the universalized form of his immoral maxim, then the same argument ought to hold equally for maxims that violate merely ethical duties. So we would have a right to enforce ethical duties by coercion – which is fundamentally contrary to Kantian ethics. Thus if we found someone who adopted the maxim of refusing charitable help to others (as in Kant's fourth example in the *Groundwork*), then we would apparently have a duty *not* to provide charitable help to this stingy person when he needs it, as a way of compelling people to be charitable. That nasty conclusion would contradict both the letter of Kant's ethics and the fundamental spirit of Kantian ethics.[13]

Hegel's retributivism. The argument put forward by Pincoffs and Fleischacker on Kant's behalf does resemble in certain respects an argument that is actually found in the writings of Hegel (and which I have sympathetically expounded in Chapter 6 of *Hegel's Ethical Thought*).[14] But Hegel's version of the argument is defensible only given certain Hegelian theses that Kant does not (and could not consistently) endorse. Hegel uses a complex theory of mutual recognition and personhood to argue that we can distinguish the *actual* will of the criminal from a "rational will" or "will in itself," to which the criminal is committed as a participant in this system of mutual recognition and which may be at odds with his actual or empirical will. It is this "will in itself" that sets up the criminal's wrongful maxim as a universal law and justifies our treating his criminal act as involving the volition that the wrongful maxim be applied to him.

Hegel's view thus justifies punishment by claiming that the criminal wills his own punishment, that punishment is the actual carrying out of the criminal's own rational will (i.e., the criminal's "will in itself"). Kant, however, explicitly denies that criminals do (or even can) will their own punishment: "For it is no punishment if what is done to someone is what he wills, and it is impossible to *will* to be punished" (MS 6:335). Further, an argument like that of Pincoffs and Fleischacker that detours through the criminal's maxim and the criminal's will would be inconsistent with the Directness Thesis as Kant explicitly interprets it. "No one suffers punishment because he has willed *it*, but because he has willed *a punishable action*" (MS 6:335).

Hegel's argument and the one used by Pincoffs and Fleischacker do have in common one significant and very serious *limitation*. Even if your doing something to me gives me a *right* to do it to you, it does not necessarily give me a *reason* to do it to you, still less does it *require* me to do it to you. To say that the criminal "sets up" or "wills" an act as if it were a universal law might justify saying that we are *permitted* to treat the criminal according to that law, just as my permission might grant you the right to cross my property. (Pincoffs speaks of our being "warranted" in applying the criminal's law to him; Fleischacker says he "has no reason to complain.") Yet nothing in the argument could justify saying that we *must* apply the criminal's law to him, that we are obligated to apply it to him, any more than my granting you permission to cross my property (which would "warrant" your crossing it and give me "no right to complain" if you crossed it) imposes on you a *duty* to cross my property.[15] Thus the argument can never justify the full Kantian retributivist position that the ruler is *required by right* to visit the criminal with a harm equal to the wrong he has inflicted and does an *injustice* if he fails to do so.[16]

4. Is Retributivism Consistent with Kantian Ethics?

Thus far I have argued that Kant's retributivism receives no real support from the rest of his practical philosophy. Now I present two reasons for thinking that Kant's retributivism is inconsistent with fundamental elements of his ethical theory.

Retributivism and the basic duty to others. The *first* reason is this: Kant argues in the *Metaphysics of Morals* that our ethical duties are all founded on certain "duties of virtue," or ends it is our duty to have. The two fundamental such ends are our own perfection and the happiness of others (MS 6:385–8). Kant might also be seen as deriving these ends from the formulas of universal law and humanity, when he argues (in the third and fourth examples) that the maxim of refusing to set them is impermissible under these formulas (G 4:422–3, 430). The fact that the happiness of others is a duty of virtue makes it equally impermissible to adopt any maxim setting a contrary end – namely, one that makes anyone's unhappiness directly my end – as occurs, for instance, in the maxims characterizing the vices of envy, ingratitude, and malice (or hatred) (MS 6:458–60).

There is in Kant's texts never any suggestion, much less an argument, that there ought to be an exception to this duty of virtue in the case of wicked people or criminals.[17] Yet Kant's "law of punishment" tells us that if someone has committed a crime, then the judicial authority is both permitted and required to make its end the infliction on the criminal of a pain or harm that is commensurate with the crime. Kant asserts the "law of punishment" to be a categorical imperative and a law of reason, but he never derives it in any way from his practical philosophy, and he even suggests that it does not admit of any derivation. However, the law of punishment seems to be in direct conflict with the basic ethical principle that the happiness of others is a duty of virtue. It is true, of course, that this is a conflict between retributive punishment and an ethical duty (not a duty of right). And it would be consistent within Kantian ethics to hold that we are permitted by right to do something that violates an ethical duty. Kant holds, however, that both duties of right and duties of virtue are duties in the sense that compliance with them is a categorical imperative (MS 6:219, 222–3). Therefore, it could not be consistent to say that we are *required* by a duty of right to do something that violates an ethical duty. And Kant's retributivism does threaten us with precisely this inconsistency.

There is no such problem about the justification of punishment as coercive protection of right. It does not involve making the unhappiness of others an *end* but merely permits the ruler to inflict unhappiness – in ways that accord with right – as a *means* of coercively protecting the rightful freedom of all. So not only is the justification of punishment as coercive enforcement of right validly derived from Kant's theory of right (as the retributive justification is not) but it is also consistent with his moral theory (while the retributive justification is inconsistent with it).[18]

Retributivism and the coercion of ethical duties. Here is the *second* reason: Kant draws a distinction between juridical duties or duties of right, which it is permissible to enforce through external coercion, and ethical duties, which are to be fulfilled through inner rational constraint but which it is impermissible for anyone to try to coerce the agent to fulfill. Punishment, however, whatever else it may be, is clearly a form of external coercion. Yet in his statements of the Intrinsic Desert Thesis, the Directness Thesis, and the *Ius Talionis*, Kant quite often claims that what deserves punishment is not so much the external injustice of the criminal's act as more properly the "inner wickedness" (MS 6:333) or the "moral badness" of the wrongdoer (VE 27:308). Understood in this way, Kant's retributivism directly conflicts with the Kantian doctrine that ethical duties may not be coerced.[19]

Kant famously claims that goodness of will constitutes the indispensable condition of the worthiness to be happy (G 4:393). We clearly need not interpret this as authorizing anyone to punish any person at all simply for having a bad will. And basic principles of Kantian ethics forbid us to read it as instructing us to remove happiness from anyone we think of as unworthy of the happiness they enjoy. For such a reading would again directly contradict the fundamental principle of Kant's theory of duties that the happiness of others must always be an end for us, hence that their unhappiness may never be among our ends.

Worthiness to be happy and the highest good. If the famous claim about the good will and worthiness to be happy is to be even minimally consistent with the spirit of Kantian ethics, then it has to be viewed as an effective way for us to represent to ourselves the inner worth of our own will – especially to the extent that we find our will less than perfectly good. We are to think of both the happiness we enjoy and the happiness we hope for and then ask ourselves whether we have made ourselves worthy of it through our conduct. This gives us a vivid measure, one that insatiably self-loving creatures like ourselves can all too easily understand, of our *inner* worth (where 'inner' means: as compared not with others, but with the moral law).

The point of this measurement would not be to deprive ourselves (still less to deprive others) of any happiness anyone might otherwise lawfully enjoy but instead to excite either self-contentment or shame (more likely, the latter) when we consider honestly whether we have made ourselves worthy of the happiness we continue to enjoy and lawfully pursue. The point is to make us behave better, not that we should pointlessly violate prudential rationality by making ourselves unhappy for no good reason. Recall that for

Kant, religious penance is roundly condemned. He can interpret it only as a hypocritical attempt to curry favor with the Deity (represented unworthily as a vain tyrant) through substituting a set of morally indifferent displays of sycophancy for the good conduct God actually requires of us.

Occasionally Kant does try to link the idea that the good will is a condition of worthiness to be happy with his retributivism about punishment (VE 27:552). This is chiefly (or even exclusively) when he is thinking about God as a judge of the world. When we regard human beings as under *moral* laws, he says, then "God alone" is entitled to inflict punishment (MS 6:460).[20] Kant even sometimes represents God's proportioning happiness to worthiness as the doing of punitive justice, not only on those who act contrary to right but even on those whose wills are not as good as they should be (R 6:140–1; VpR 28:1084–8; VE 27:553).

I think these retributivist-inspired doctrines about God directly conflict with the basic spirit and central tenets of Kant's moral theory. I think they also contradict some of the most prominent things Kant says explicitly about God's justice. Here Kant asserts his retributivism as a doctrine about divine justice and then curiously backs away from it.

The feeling of freedom in the choice of the final end is what makes [God's] legislation worthy of love. – Thus although the teacher of this end [Christ] also announces punishments, that is not to be understood – or at least it is not suited to the proper nature of Christianity to explain it – as though these should become the incentives for performing what follows from its commands; for to that extent it would cease to be worthy of love. (ED 8:338)

The religion of Zoroaster had these three divine persons, Ormuzd, Mithra and Ahriman, the Hindu religion had Brahma, Vishnu and Shiva ... The Goths revered their Odin (father of all), their Freya (also Freyer, goodness) and Thor, the judging (punishing) god ... The religion of Egypt had its Ptha, Kneph and Neith, of whom, so far as the obscurity of the reports from those ancient times permit us to surmise, the first was to represent spirit, ... as the world *creator*, the second, a generosity which sustains and *rules*, the third a wisdom which limits this generosity, i.e. *justice* ... It is hard to give a reason why so many ancient peoples hit upon this idea, unless it is that the idea lies in human reason universally whenever we want to think of the governance of a people and (on the analogy with this) of world governance. (R 6:140–1)

But the expression *poenae vindicativae*, like the expression *iustitia ultrix* [both expressions used by Baumgarten] is really too hard. For vengeance cannot be thought in God ... So it is better to regard the punishments inflicted by divine justice on sins in general as an *actus* of *iustitiae distributivae*, that is, a justice limiting the apportionment of benevolence *by the laws of holiness* ... God's justice must limit benevolence so that it distributes good only *according to the subject's worthiness*. (VpR 28:1086–7)

In the first of these quotations, Kant insists that divine punishment must not be an incentive to morality – in other words, it may not act coercively on us, as punishment necessarily does. In the second and third quotations, Kant not only rejects the biblical idea of God as vengeful but also describes God's punitive justice as consisting only in the way divine holiness sets limits to God's generosity. But limited generosity is obviously still *generosity*. It is not retributive punishment. Limited benevolence still aims at the person's happiness, whereas retribution aims at harming the person, taking away some portion of the person's happiness or inflicting unhappiness for its own sake, simply because justice requires it. So this account amounts to a more than tacit (as well as an *inconsistent*) *rejection of a retributivist theory of divine justice.*

If we are to think about God as proportioning happiness to worthiness, the only way to do so consistently with Kantian ethics is as follows: God *owes* happiness to no one, but as a benevolent being he is in general disposed to make his creatures happy. How he benevolently distributes happiness is up to him, but we are justified in supposing that he will distribute it in the morally best way. Because one of Adam Smith's rational impartial spectators will be pleased when seeing someone with a good will enjoying happiness but displeased to see those enjoying uninterrupted prosperity who are adorned with no trait of a pure and good will (G 4:393), we suppose it fitting that God should show greater benevolence toward those with a good will than toward those with a bad will. Thus we think of him as proportioning happiness to worthiness in his benevolent distribution of it.

There is no reason, however, to think (and every reason to deny) that God (who is a morally perfect being) would employ *coercion* to enforce ethical duties. Neither a just state nor a private person could permissibly use coercion to enforce *ethical* duties. But punishment is coercion, so it is not fitting to represent God's withholding of benevolence from people with bad wills as a form of punishment. To think of God as doing so is directly inconsistent with basic Kantian doctrines. Virtually always, when Kant suggests such a picture, he is trying to integrate traditional religious representations of divine justice and world government into his own moral theory (as a way of making that theory more appealing to people with traditional religious beliefs and attitudes) (cf. R 6:140–1, VpR 28:1085–8, and also ED 8:328–30). More self-consistently, however, Kant also occasionally criticizes the idea of divine punishment, arguing that this idea is especially unworthy of Christianity, which is a religion that is supposed to promote love of humanity (ED 8:338–9).

Neither in this world nor beyond it, therefore, can the basic principles of Kantian ethics be made consistent with Kant's retributivism.

A final word on behalf of retributivism. As a defender of Kantian ethics, however, I take little comfort from this last conclusion and actually find it quite troubling. For I think retributivism gets right at least one important thing that all alternative theories probably get wrong. By focusing attention almost exclusively on what the criminal deserves, retributivism enables us to set strict rightful limits on what it is permissible to do to criminals in the name of justice – something that not only nonretributivist theories but also popular moral opinion and actual penal institutions seem deplorably unable to do.

In nineteenth-century England, pickpockets were publicly hanged, even though the jubilant crowds witnessing these gruesome demonstrations of public bloodthirstiness were at great risk of having their pockets picked while reveling in the grisly festivities. In many places in the United States today, draconian prison sentences are mandatory for helpless drug addicts. "Three strikes" laws, such as we have here in California (passed and then later confirmed by popular referendum), sometimes result in someone's receiving a life sentence even for a minor theft. There is no rational standpoint from which these unspeakably barbarous practices could be justified. They do nothing except display how mean-spirited and vindictive the public can be and how shameless politicians are in appealing opportunistically to everything that is worst in their constituents. They are all damning indictments of the radical evil in human nature, at least as bad as the crimes to which they are an unjust response.

Such laws can certainly be criticized as ineffective deterrents, just as even in the eighteenth century enlightened philosophers such as Montesquieu and Beccaria already presented the empirical evidence to show that it is the certainty of punishment, not its severity, which serves as an effective deterrent to crime. But to a person of decent moral sensibilities, this seems a strangely cold-hearted and irrelevant point to make about them. The first and most obvious thing to say about these penal practices is rather that they are outrageously *unjust* – that the severity of the punishments is grossly disproportionate to the gravity of the crimes – and that this would be true even if they did serve as effective deterrents, or whatever other welcome consequences they might have. As far as I can see, only a retributive theory of punishment, and especially a reasonable interpretation of the *Ius Talionis*, could adequately justify this immediate reaction. That is why I am reluctant to expel retributivism from Kantian ethics, despite the evident conflict between it and basic Kantian principles. In other words, I think that contrary to its undeserved reputation for harshness, a retributivist theory of punishment seems to offer the best way of justifying greater leniency than is shown by our monstrously unjust penal institutions. It troubles me that Kantian ethics, by not being able to embrace retributivism, might not be (in the words of our fashionable political slogans) as "soft on crime" as we would need to be if we are to deal justly with criminals.

13

Sex

Sexual morality is probably the very last topic on which a sensible person would want to defend Kant's views. On many subjects, a better understanding discovers Kant's position to be more defensible than it seemed at first, but here honest inquisitiveness does little to improve the overall situation and in some ways only makes it worse. Some of Kant's views about sex are so extreme as to be either ridiculous or abhorrent to all enlightened people. However, not everything Kant said on the subject of sexual morality deserves such scorn. And if we look a little beneath the surface and also pry into some corners of Kant's work that seldom get much attention, we will find that even on this topic there is more originality and insight in some of Kant's thoughts than is usually appreciated. There is even one adventurous strand in Kant's texts that might permit Kantian ethics to correct most of Kant's own wrongheaded official pronouncements.

1. Sexual Desire

Kant's treatment of sexual morality depends on two principal ideas, both of which must seem at best highly dubious to any enlightened person today: The first idea is that respect for rational nature requires respect for the natural teleology of our desires, joined with the traditional doctrine that the sole natural purpose of sexual desire is procreation. Kant uses this traditional doctrine as a ground for condemning, with appalling harshness, what he regards as "unnatural" sex acts, including homosexuality, bestiality, and masturbation.

Lust is called unnatural if one is aroused to it not by a real object but by his imagining it, so that he himself creates one, contrapurposively; for in this way imagination brings forth a desire contrary to nature's end ... But this does not explain the high degree of violation of the humanity in one's person by such a vice in its unnaturalness, which seems in terms of its form (the disposition it involves) to exceed even murdering oneself. (MS 6:424–5)

Kant even considers "unnatural" sexual acts a violation of the right of humanity in one's own person, hence a *crime* that may be prohibited by law and punished (MS 6:277).[1]

Kant's second idea is that sexual activity itself threatens rights and the dignity of human beings, because it involves treating the person of a rational being not as an end in itself but merely as a means.

The human being has an impulse directed to others [merely] as objects of enjoyment ... This is the sexual impulse ... Love as human affection is the love that wishes well, is amicably disposed, promotes the happiness of others and rejoices in it. But it is plain that those who merely have sexual inclination love the person from none of these motives, are quite unconcerned for their happiness, and will even plunge them into the greatest unhappiness, merely to satisfy their own inclination and appetite ... As soon as the person is possessed, and the appetite sated, she is thrown away, as one throws away a lemon after sucking the juice from it. The sexual impulse can admittedly be combined with human affection, and then it carries with it the aims of the latter, but taken in and for itself, it is nothing more than mere appetite. So considered, there lies in this inclination a degradation of the human being; for as soon as anyone becomes an object of another's appetite, all motives of moral relationship fall away ... This is the reason why we are ashamed of possessing such an impulse, and why strict moralists, and those who wish to be taken for saints, have sought to repress and dispense with it. To be sure, anyone who did not have this impulse would be an imperfect individual ... ; yet such has been the pretension, and people have sought to refrain from this inclination because it debases the human being. Since the sexual impulse is not an inclination that one has for another qua human but an inclination for their sex, it is therefore a *principium* of the debasement of humanity, a source of the preferring of one sex over the other, and the dishonoring of that sex by satisfying that inclination. The desire of a man for a woman is not directed to her as a human being; on the contrary, the woman's humanity is of no concern to him, and the only object of his desire is her sex. (VE 27:384–5)

According to Kant, sexual desire is not a form of love, because love seeks the good of its object whereas sexual desire does not. Sexual desire aims merely at using the other person's sex organs for your pleasure, even if this results in their extreme unhappiness. Kant regards sexual pleasure, for both sexes, as the strongest possible pleasure the senses afford (MS 6:426); and it is also capable of becoming a "passion" – that is, an inclination, shaped by ends adopted through free choice, that resists rational control (VE 7:251, 132–266). According to Kant's anthropological theory, all passions arise from desires that have other human beings as their objects and seek some form of superiority or domination over them (VE 7:268–70, 25:733, 1141, 1359).

The *natural* passions include, besides sex, the natural desire for freedom from all the restraints that the existence of others imposes on us (including all the claims they make on us through right and morality). The *social* passions are tyranny, greed, and ambition – which are directed, respectively, at dominion, wealth, and honor – as well as the desire for revenge (VA 7:265–75). Our passion for freedom is the desire to be rid of all limitations imposed on us by the existence of others (such as their rights against us) (VE 7:268–9, 327). So the ultimate object of our passion for freedom is to enslave others (VE 25:1355). It is chiefly on account of the passion for freedom that Kant declares that in the context of political life, "the human being is an animal who needs a master" – not in the sense that he is born for slavery but that people require a coercive power in order to be protected from their becoming the slaves of one another. This also creates an insoluble problem, however, because whomever we grant power over others on account of this will also be an animal that needs a master (I 8:23).

Sexual desire is also a passionate desire – namely, to subject the body of another to ourselves for the purpose of satisfying our animal appetites (VE 27:384–5, MS 6:278). Kant concedes that sexual appetite can be combined with human love and thus carry with it the aims of love, but he thinks this combination is always contingent and unstable. Because in his view sexual pleasure inherently involves degrading another person, Kant argues it is also degrading to the one who feels it (MS 6:424–5).

Most of us feel strong resistance, if not outright revulsion, in the face of both these ideas about sex. In the second idea, however, there is at least a partial truth, however twisted it may be in Kant's application of it. As Barbara Herman has rightly emphasized,[2] much of the strictness in Kant's sexual morality is dictated by the need to restrict sexual activity in ways that will protect human beings – especially women – from degrading treatment. Though Kant regards sex as supremely pleasurable for both sexes, the principal form it takes, as a result of the universal dominance of men over women in society, is the enjoyment of women by men. Given the nature of sexual desire as a passion, this fact of male dominance threatens women with the greatest possible violations of their rights as persons. Kant holds that the right of humanity can be protected, and the natural reproductive purpose of sex fulfilled, only through a civil contract giving two people of different sexes possession of each other's sexual capacities and making this right both lifelong and exclusive. Outside such a contract, he thinks, sexual activity reduces human beings – especially women – to mere things for another's use.

Sexual union in accordance with law is marriage (*matrimonium*), that is, the union of two persons of different sexes for lifelong possession of each other's sexual attributes...For the natural use that one sex makes of the other's sexual organs is *enjoyment*, for which one gives itself up to the other. In this act a human being makes himself into a thing, which conflicts with the right of humanity in his own person. There is only one condition under which this is possible: while one person is acquired by the other *as if she were a thing*, the one who is acquired acquires the other in turn; for in this way each reclaims herself and restores her personality...Hence it is not only admissible for the sexes to surrender to and accept each other for enjoyment under the condition of marriage, but it is possible for them to do so *only* under this condition. (MS 6:277–8)

Sexuality as unsociable sociability. This view of sex may seem repellent (or ridiculous), but it has close affinity to views that are still with us. It is essentially the view taken, for example, by Andrea Dworkin.[3] The idea that sexual pleasure is bound up with treating both the other and oneself as mere things or objects was the main theme of Sartre's treatment of human sexuality in *Being and Nothingness*. The same account, but emphasizing women as the primary focus of objectification and degradation, was given by Simone de Beauvoir in *The Second Sex*.[4] It would not naturally occur to us to dismiss Sartre's or Beauvoir's views about sex by citing their lack of sexual experience or their unhealthy religious upbringing; such condescending thoughts are equally out of place when assessing similar views as they appear in Kant.

The obvious point to make against such a view of sexual desire, whether in its eighteenth- or twentieth-century expression, is that it appears to be extremely simplistic and one-sided. Plainly there is far more to sex than the desire to use another's body in a degrading manner for your selfish pleasure. Even the elements in sexual desire closest to this are combined, at least in healthy people, with other elements of human emotion that radically transform their meaning. So it appears pointlessly reductive to dwell on only one aberrant aspect of sexual desire, as Kant does.

In evaluating philosophical theories, however, we should always beware of obvious criticisms, especially when the aim of the theory was never to deny surface complexity but rather to reveal it to us in light of what the theory claims to be deeper and more essential. When we try to understand a philosopher's theoretical account of one area of human life, we should never overlook the way it serves to express the more basic principles that unify his thinking.

Kant's view of sex is part of his larger theory of empirical anthropology, according to which the development of our rational capacities takes place alongside of, and even chiefly by means of, a propensity to what Kant variously calls "radical evil," "unsociable sociability," or "self-conceit" (I 8:20, KpV 5:73, R 6:28–32). The natural development of reason in human beings takes place in a social context and further drives people to depend on one another. At the same time, it involves a fundamentally irrational desire for superiority over others – over those very beings whom our reason shows to have the same dignity or absolute worth that we have. Thus what may at first look like merely some one-sidedly nasty ideas about sex are really only consistent applications of Kant's theory of human nature. In such a theory, what might seem like an aberration may serve as the key to deeper understanding – as happens, for example, in Nietzsche's theory of the will to power or

Freud's theory of the struggle between libido and the death instinct. Kant's claim is that however sexual desire may express itself in combination with other ends and feelings, its fundamental natural-social meaning, like that of all our inclinations, includes the evil propensity to treat others as our inferiors and as mere means to our ends.

2. The Subjection of Women

In applying the concept of unsociable sociability to sex, Kant especially emphasizes the fact, which he appears to regard as an irremediable feature of human life, that men systematically stand in a decisively superior relation of power – physical, social, economic – over women. This is for him the chief determinant of the fact (as he sees it) that sexual desire is degrading to our humanity and its satisfaction a threat to human rights and dignity. Our understandable objections to some of Kant's opinions about sex should not cause us to ignore the truth present in his theory at this point or to underestimate the importance of that truth.

That truth may be put as follows: Sexual violence against women has always been, and remains, a pervasive and systematic feature of all human culture. In one way or another, it is built into virtually every system of family life, every form of the marriage relation, every traditional moral or religious code regulating people's sexual behavior. It belongs especially to the patterns of systematic violation of these official codes that attaches to the codes themselves as part of their cultural meaning. Thus women throughout the world have always been driven through economic need into sexual slavery. Rape has always been one of the chief instruments of military conquest. In the United States, one girl in three will be sexually molested before she reaches the age of sixteen – usually by her father or by some other male whom society has placed in a position of power over her.[5] Further, in virtually all human cultures, traditional sexual morality is morbidly fixated on the woman's body. The chief aim of sexual morality has always been to remove from the woman power over her own sexuality and give it to some male – her father until she marries, after that her husband. "Promiscuity" – a woman's having sex with anyone other than her male sexual proprietor – is considered the worst crime she can commit; in some cultures it is routinely punishable by death. In this context, homosexuality (whether gay or lesbian) is "unnatural" not because it does not lead to procreation but because it does not involve dominion of a man over a woman. Female genital mutilation, forced marriages, and honor killings are characteristic of more brutal cultures in which the basic cross-cultural principle of traditional sexual morality is acknowledged more frankly and innocently.

What we find in Kant's traditionalist views on sexual morality is more characteristic of what he would call "civilized" (that is, modern European) cultures, where there is more pretense and less candor. One of Kant's chief errors was to think that traditional monogamous marriage is an effective way of protecting women from sexual degradation, when in fact it has always functioned mainly as a powerful mechanism for inflicting it. Kant himself was clearly a representative of traditional sexual morality and its implicit assumption that it is only just for women to be subordinated to men.

The first lesson we ought to learn from this is that even those philosophers who are clear-minded, consequent, and farsighted enough to articulate certain basic moral principles – such as the equal dignity of all rational beings – are often confused and fainthearted when it comes to seeing the consequences of these truths for the social customs around them and the moral prejudices they have come to accept. It is therefore only as a result of the Enlightenment values Kantian ethics represents, and a long struggle to apply these values more consequently to our moral beliefs, attitudes, and practices, that the equal personhood of women has attained some limited degree of recognition. This recognition has come very late in the historical development of Enlightenment ethics because Kant, along with many of the chief representatives of this radical view, refused to draw the conclusions that plainly follow from their egalitarian principles and found some way or other of embracing the traditional sexual morality whose most fundamental principle is the unequal social status of men and women, and the coercive power of men over women.

Today we see a strong backlash against the egalitarian values of the Enlightenment, and specifically on the part of traditional sexual morality. In Western cultures we see this primarily in the extreme and willful interpretation of the inherently gradual character of human biological development that dogmatically declares the rights of personhood, and the entitlement of these rights to coercive social protection, to begin at conception. This strangely arbitrary and nonsensically extreme view about the beginning of personhood suddenly acquires intelligibilty once we understand that its real but unacknowledged aim is the reassertion of traditional social control over a woman's sexuality. The decision that a fetus has the status of personhood is simply a declaration that a pregnant woman's womb does not belong to her but belongs to another person, whose rights society is entitled to protect. When you consider the close association in real life of this arbitrary decision with a hypocritical "abstinence only" code of sexual morality and with policies of callous disregard for the fate of the weakest members of society (once they are born), it is an affront to human intelligence to pretend that such views are anything but an attempt to confine women, as far as possible, to their traditional status of sexual subordination as less than free persons.

Of course those who reassert traditional sexual subordination in this form seldom acknowledge that this is the meaning of their position. Most of them even pay lip service to human dignity, equality, and other Enlightenment values – for example, by representing their attack on the personhood of women as really a defense of the human rights of fetuses, hence analogous to the movement for the abolition of slavery. But this only indicates the depth of the social illusion and self-deception built into their world view. This is the main reason why the so-called "debates" in our culture over abortion and stem-cell research, over birth control and other issues regarding women's reproductive health, and over sexual morality more generally are so heated and intractable. It is very difficult to reason with people who cannot level with you about their own position because even in their own minds they are in denial, in moral and historical terms, about its fundamental meaning.

3. The Meaning of the Figleaf

Kant's most insightful remarks about sex, in my view, occur in none of his official pronouncements about conjugal right or ethical duties to ourselves. They are found instead in the course of a short, satirical occasional essay entitled *Conjectural Beginning of Human History*. In the remainder of this chapter I am going to explore and develop a single thin and wayward strand of Kantian thinking present in this sadly neglected text, setting its implications in direct opposition to some of Kant's official views about sexual morality.

Sexuality as the human transcendence of our animal nature. In the *Conjectural Beginning*, Kant is responding to his erstwhile student Herder, whose imaginative yet pious interpretation of the *Genesis* narrative became a vehicle for his counter-Enlightenment speculations about the early development of the human race on Earth. Kant replies to Herder's piety and enthusiasm with his own wry and sometimes irreverent commentary on the same scriptures. He first makes fun of Herder's attempt to use scripture as the basis for historical conjectures. Then, with more serious intent, Kant uses scriptural interpretation as a vehicle for his own pro-Enlightenment account of the meaning of human faculties of reason, and some conjectures in a mythic spirit about their earliest development in history that tantalizingly skirt the line between the facetious and the serious.

What Kant says here about the *Genesis* story is sometimes unorthodox, to say the least. He interprets Adam and Eve's eating of the forbidden fruit not as an act of sinful disobedience but as an act of liberation, in which our first parents decisively separated themselves from the rest of nature as free and rational beings. While the "divine voice" (of animal instinct) had previously confined their nourishment only to certain fruits, nascent human reason devised a new way of satisfying this natural need by choosing the fruit of another tree, replacing the safe slavery to instinctual impulses with a new and dangerous mode of life based on freely setting their own ends and the invention of means to them.[6] This was followed, he says, by a second, even more momentous change. The natural impulses associated in other animals with reproduction were transformed through imagination into desires that fundamentally altered both people's self-awareness and their relation to other members of their species:

The human being soon found that the stimulus to sex, which with animals rests merely on a transient, for the most part periodic impulse, was capable for him of being prolonged and even increased through the power of the imagination, whose concern, to be sure, is more with moderation, yet at the same time works more enduringly and uniformly the more its object is *withdrawn from the senses*, and he found that it prevents the boredom that comes along with the satisfaction of a merely animal desire. The figleaf (*Genesis* 3:7) was thus the product of a far greater manifestation of reason than that which it had demonstrated in the first stage of its development. (MA 8:112)

The claims made in this passage, if accepted, require the radical rejection of the traditional ideas that ground Kant's official position on sexual morality. Kant is claiming that only among nonrational animals – not among humans – is the natural function of sex limited to the reproductive. This, he says, is why sexual desire remains a merely transient and periodic impulse for other animals, while for human beings it takes on a very different and far greater significance.

When the human imagination gives sexual desire a new and social character, both its aim and object are radically transformed. The meaning of *human* sexuality, as Kant recognizes here, transcends not only reproduction but any merely animal purpose. Sexual desire has far more to do with people's most intimate relationships to one another, and the role in them of some of the psychological features that are most fundamental to morality. The essence of human sexual desire is that it is desire directed at another human being, regarded as a rational or self-conscious agent. It therefore becomes a vehicle for the most basic human attitudes of other-admiration and self-respect that ground moral relationships between human beings. And it is these attitudes and relationships that are at stake when a human being becomes an object of sexual desire and reciprocates or refuses it. In the *human* meaning of sexuality, the biology of reproduction has been reduced to a merely contingent occasion. It is almost incidental.

Clearly Kant never fully appreciated the full significance of this insightful idea. Once we accept this idea, however, there is no longer any ground for condemning as "unnatural" those forms of sexual activity that have no relation to procreation. Or, if you prefer, it is the very nature of human sexuality that it should be "unnatural" – that is, that its meaning should no longer be constrained by its reproductive function. Instead, the significance of sexual desire undergoes a kind of free expansion through the imagination. In that sense, it is traditional sexual morality – with its notion that the sole legitimate purpose of sex is reproduction – that is guilty of perverting human sexuality and of reducing human beings to the level of nonrational animals. In this passage Kant clearly saw through this perversion, even if he lacked the vision or the courage to develop this insight elsewhere in his ethical thought.

Sexuality and self-respect. Kant's second remarkable insight in the passage is the way he develops the first idea, seeing sexuality as an essential ingredient in the psychological foundation of human sociability, and even of morality itself:

For to make an inclination more inward and enduring by withdrawing its object from the senses, shows already the consciousness of some dominion of reason over impulse and not merely, as in the first step, a faculty for doing service to those impulses within a lesser or greater extension. *Refusal* was the first artifice for leading from the merely sensed stimulus over to ideal ones, from merely animal desire gradually over to love, and with the latter from the feeling of the merely agreeable over to the taste for beauty, in the beginning only in human beings but then, however, also in nature. (MA 8:112–13)

For Kant in this passage, the biblical fig leaf is chiefly a device through which men and women excited each other's sexual desires, by refusing immediate access to their object and thereby transforming that object into one of the imagination. In other words, Kant is irreverently suggesting that the fig leaf was not so much the first expression of shame as the first striptease, and paradoxically at the same time the earliest expression at the level of feeling and desire of the human capacity to relate to others over time according to enduring principles. Further, he is asserting a close connection between the ambivalent enticement-refusal structure of properly human (that is, imaginatively determined) sexual desire and the ambivalent structure of the basic moral feeling of respect, which leads us to value the person respected, while also requiring us to keep our distance.

This is a striking account of the psychological-historical origins of our respect for persons. An account we might expect from Hobbes, for example, or from Nietzsche, might locate the origin of respect in the combination of awe and fear we would feel toward someone who has the power to harm us. By contrast, Kant views the respect for persons as originating in the enticement-refusal structure of imaginatively transformed sexual desire.

If the insights of this passage in the *Conjectural Beginning* undermine Kant's first main idea about sexuality – that its moral significance must be grounded in its "natural" reproductive function – they tend to strengthen, and even provide a deeper insight into, his second main idea: that sexual desire, under the conditions of unsociable sociability, threatens the worth and dignity of human beings. For if our dignity is originally based on the enticement-refusal structure of sexual desire, then voluntary sexual self-bestowal is crucial to maintaining human dignity.

This explains, for instance, why the right of humanity is violated whenever sexual activity is compelled, and the option of refusal taken away, whether by rape, social subordination, or extortion through economic dependency. No doubt forcibly compelled sexual activity would even without this be a restriction of a human being's external freedom. But this alone could not explain why rape is any worse a violation of human dignity than, say, a simple act of assault involving moderate, or often only minor, bodily injury.

In traditional sexual morality, the humiliation of rape consists above all in the fact that the violated woman has become "damaged goods." She is a cause of shame and humiliation rather than pride to her male possessor, and if she is not already a man's possession, ownership of her becomes a less attractive prospect. In some cultures, attachment to a raped woman is so degrading to her father, brother, or husband that she is in danger of being murdered to expunge their shame. From this point of view, more enlightened sexual attitudes would seem merely to make rape a less serious crime, by making the woman's sense of self-worth independent of the need to be valued by some man as his sexual and reproductive property.

However, once we accept Kant's idea that your option of sexual consent or refusal is fundamental to others' respect for you as a person, then it becomes evident quite independent of these traditional customs why any form of extorted sexual activity is a denial of the basic self-worth of a human person, and an encroachment on the person's fundamental rights. If our relation to our sexuality is also one of the psychological bases of our sense of self-worth, there is even room in sexual morality for the idea that our sexual behavior might constitute a violation of duties to oneself based on self-respect. But the conclusions it suggests about all these matters may be very different from the traditionalist ones highlighted in Kant's official position.

The *Conjectural Beginning* account might also help to explain why the social acknowledgment and acceptance of someone's sexual identity – including, for instance, the identities of people as gay, lesbian, or transsexual – is fundamental to their being respected as a person. As we reflect further on the close connection Kant sees between our awareness of ourselves as sexual beings and the self-respect that grounds Kantian morality, we might also begin to see (as Kant apparently could not) how the sexually repressive tendency in traditional morality – its denigration of our sexuality as a whole – consorts well with those forms of unenlightened religious temper that attempt to annihilate the human sense of self-worth and encourage people to adopt a slavish attitude in relation to the Deity.

Sexual propriety as origin of the moral law. In this same passage Kant also introduces yet a third surprising theme. He extends his second insight – about the relation of sexuality to human self-worth and mutual respect – representing human sexuality as also the foundation of the earliest historical form of moral legislation, namely the morality of custom, respectability, and social propriety:

Propriety (Sittsamkeit) an inclination by good conduct (*guten Anstand*) to influence others to respect for us (through the concealment of that which could incite low esteem), as the genuine foundation of all true sociability, gave the first hint toward the formative education (*Ausbildung*) of the human being as a moral (*sittlichen*) creature. – A small beginning, which, however, is epoch-making, in that it gives an entirely new direction to the way of thinking – and is more important than the entire immeasurable series of extensions of culture that followed upon it. (MA 8:112–13)

Here Kant's provocative claim is that the original form of rational control over desire was not over *one's own* desire, but over *another's* (sexual) desire. Rationally controlling our own desires, as through the moral motive of duty, turns out to be a derivative application to oneself of a control that is in its origin both interpersonal in form and sexual in content. This passage therefore develops an original and distinctive side of the Kantian theme that certain forms of sociability are conditions for the development of reason. The basic principle of Kant's moral anthropology is the rich though oxymoronic idea of unsociable sociability. The *sociable* side of this idea is that human beings are profoundly dependent on one another. One basic sociable impulse that makes them so, as Kant presents things, is the powerful need, even with no further object in view, to reveal ourselves to others – to communicate to them our thoughts, desires, and feelings (MS 6:471). The unsociable side of our nature, however, makes these self-revelations extremely dangerous to us, because other human beings seek dominance over us and are disposed to think less of us, to lose their respect for us, because of them.

Sociability, intimacy, and the human need for friendship. These two contrasting features of human sociability lead, in Kant's view, to a profound need to find another person to whom we can reveal ourselves on conditions of mutual trust. This for Kant is the foundation of our need for *friendship* – which he describes as "the human being's refuge in this world from the distrust of his fellows, in which one can reveal his disposition to another and enter into community with him. [This] is the fundamental condition under which it is possible for a human being to enjoy his existence" (VE 27:428). It is obvious that sexuality, as Kant describes it in the *Conjectural Beginning*, is also fundamentally a matter of human intimacy or self-revelation. For on this account, human sexuality is not basically about reproduction but about the interplay of self-concealment and self-revelation, self-withholding and self-bestowal, both in imagination and in reality. It is therefore very much about the possibility of communication between people on terms of mutual trust and respect. Kant's theory also suggests that this need for intimacy must constitute a fundamental element in human sexual desire.

4. Kant's Defense of Marriage

Unfortunately Kant never brings his theory of intimacy in friendship together with any theory of sexual intimacy in marriage. But there is a clear explanation for this failure that also affords us some insight into the way Kant understands the social realities around him. For Kant denies that marriage partners can ever be friends in the true sense. He thinks the mutual trust needed for the intimacy of true friendship cannot exist unless the friends are on terms of equality. The conditions for this trust are destroyed if one person is, for instance, economically dependent on the other, as Kant takes it for granted that a wife will be on her husband (VE 27:683). In keeping with the prejudices and practices of his time, Kant sees this state of affairs as "natural" and unavoidable. He regards women as weaker than men, physically, socially, and even intellectually. However, he also regards women as more self-controlled emotionally than men. The woman is therefore able to use the man's sexual desire and emotional needs to bend him to her will (VA 7:306–7).

This is the way Kant integrates sexual love into his theory that we love only what we regard as inferior to us: "We love everything over which we have a decisive superiority, so that we can toy with it, while it has a pleasant cheerfulness about it: little dogs, birds, grandchildren. Men and women have a reciprocal superiority over one another" (R 1100 Ak 15:490). It is difficult to avoid the impression that Kant regards most marriages as operating by a dynamic of mutual exploitation, in which men take advantage of women through their greater physical, intellectual, social, and economic power but women take advantage of men through their manipulation of the man's emotional vulnerability and lack of sexual self-control. Kant's view of marriage may help to explain why, after being twice engaged in his youth, he later chose to remain a lifelong bachelor.

Whatever else we may say about Kant's view of marriage, the reasoning behind his claim that husbands and wives can never be true friends seems shrewdly consequent – at least up to a point. The unequal relationship of two human persons represented by traditional marriage surely does pose a formidable obstacle to the kind of trust, intimacy, and total unification of personality that other early modern theorists of marriage – Hegel, for instance – made the basis of their conception of the family as an institution (Hegel PR §161). Hegel ridicules Kant for reducing marriage to a contract between two people for the mutual use of their sexual organs (MS 6:277–8, Hegel PR §161A). But Kant is only being consistent, based on the institution of marriage as both he and Hegel knew and accepted it. An association on such unequal terms in which the dignity of humanity is under threat because of this inequality could never represent a true model of human intimacy or (in Hegel's terminology) "spirit's immediate feeling of its unity." Within such an unequal relationship in which personal dignity is at stake, it makes sense that the right of humanity could be protected only by subjecting the entire relationship to some coldly contractual conditions.

Complete consistency, however, should also have required Kant to conclude that marriage, if it is truly to be a relation of right that protects the dignity of the woman, is also impossible under the traditional conditions of her economic dependence and social subordination to her husband. For in Kant's picture of the reciprocal power struggle between husband and wife, the coercive powers, the powers that should be curbed and regulated by right, are all the husband's powers.

What Kant can and cannot defend in traditional marriage. Some elements in traditional marriage are quite intelligible on the basis of the Kantian conception of human sexuality I have been developing out of his remarks in the *Conjectural Beginning*. It is easy enough to understand how, at least for many people, sexual exclusivity and the permanence of their relationship might be necessary conditions for mutual trust. It is therefore understandable on Kantian principles why an understanding involving mutual fidelity might be part of *most people's* sexual relationships, and why the observance of this understanding might, *in those cases*, be an important principle of sexual morality. It is less clear, however, why these conditions of trust should be coercively enforceable by a contractual arrangement, as Kant thinks they are.

By no stretch of the imagination could Kant's views about women be considered "liberationist," and "misogynistic" seems the only appropriate word for some of his opinions about the female character. At the same time, Kant is concerned about the defense of the rights of women as persons, and he thinks societies are more civilized to the extent that in them the traditional oppression of women has given way to customs in which women have some defenses against their inferior social position. Kant's intellectual gifts also include social perceptiveness about the customs of his own time. He was aware of the ways in which the economic weakness of the woman in the marriage relation, taken together with her capacity to allure, please, and manipulate men, explains the way married women behave and even the way it makes sense for them to behave. Some of Kant's views here may surprise us, or (conceivably) even shock us:

In marriage, the man woos only his own wife; but the woman has an inclination for *all* men. (VA 7:307)

Where civilization has not yet ascended to feminine freedom in *gallantry* (where a woman openly has lovers other than her husband), the man punishes his wife if she threatens him with a rival. But when gallantry has become the fashion and jealousy ridiculous (as never fails to happen in a time of luxury), the feminine character reveals itself by extending favors toward men, woman lays claim to freedom and, at the same time, to the conquest of the entire male sex. – This inclination, though it indeed stands in ill repute under the name of "coquetry," is nevertheless not without a real basis of justification. For a young wife is always in danger of becoming a widow, and this causes her to extend her charms over all men whose fortunate circumstances make them marriageable; so that should this situation occur, she would not be lacking in suitors. (VA 7:304–5)

Here again, we may see why Kant decided late in life to remain a bachelor. His official position was to defend the traditional institution of marriage, but on several counts his attitude toward it was far from uncritical.

On the basis of the account of human sexuality we have drawn from the *Conjectural Beginning*, many aspects of traditional sexual morality no longer seem justifiable, conspicuously including some that appealed to Kant himself. If human sexuality differs from sexuality in other animals by the fact that human sexual desire has been essentially transformed by imagination and the meaning and function of sexuality is no longer bound up with reproduction, then Kant no longer has any reason to object to masturbation, homosexuality, or other allegedly "unnatural" sexual practices as "crimes against nature."

Yet even as we reject Kant on these matters, there is still room in Kantian ethics for his more basic idea that some sexual activities might violate duties to oneself by exhibiting a lack of self-respect. I suggest that these can be found not so much where Kant looks for them but chiefly in cases where people take pleasure in being degraded or humiliated, or in degrading and humiliating others. In fact, some of the attitudes toward ourselves as sexual beings exemplified by Kant, and by "conservative" sexual morality even today, might themselves be seen as violations of duties of self-respect, through the way they fail to accept human sexuality as a full part of our humanity or limit the scope of the kinds of sexuality they find acceptable in accordance with unenlightened prejudices about what is "natural" and "unnatural." It is important to realize that Kantian ethics, when made consistent with Kant's own best insights, can make these points against some of Kant's own backward attitudes and opinions with as much justification as (or even more than) any other ethical view.

One aspect of Kant's traditional conception of marriage that seems not at all justifiable is the idea that mutual trust should be possible *only* within a relationship defined by a single uniform set of rules and understandings (especially one that can be coercively enforced, particularly against women). On that picture, the dynamics of sexual desire and modesty concern the tension between intimate self-disclosure and the capacity to withhold it, which forms the erotic basis for a morality based on the respect of others and self-respect. In this account, there is no foundation for the tediously traditional requirement that every sexual relationship *must* serve the biological end of procreation. So if marriage is to be founded on it, this relationship need not be heterosexual, or between one man and one woman. In fact, the connection between sexuality and intimacy on terms of mutual trust does not justify restricting sexual activity for everyone to any single kind of relationship – such as a lifelong exclusive commitment.

The *Conjectural Beginning* account provides no reason why sexual activity (whether heterosexual or homosexual) might not take place in the course of establishing a relationship of mutual trust, rather than after it has already been established. Even casual sexual encounters for mutual pleasure might be regarded as permissible, as long as they involve no kind of coercion or exploitation or the betrayal or degradation of anyone. All these matters, from the standpoint of a more consistent Kantian ethics, should be left to autonomous individuals to decide freely for themselves. The only problems arising for such a permissive sexual code would be due to the fact that these last conditions may not be easy to fulfill in a society beset with inequalities of power and in which people's thoughts and feelings are still under the morbid influence of traditional sexual morality. Yet coercively limiting people's options to traditional monogamy, especially with its provisions involving the subordination of the wife to the husband, would cure none of that. We know that it often only makes matters worse. There is a lot in Kant's views about sexuality that is true and insightful, and that he wants to use in favor of traditional marriage (for instance, the need to protect the right and dignity of the woman against the threat of sexual violence) that might better be used to draw up an indictment against traditional marriage – to demand its abolition, or at least its radical reform.

What is now called the "defense of marriage" (namely, the exclusion of gay and lesbian couples from it) is not really a *defense* of anything at all, any more than it would be a "defense of property" to declare Jews ineligible to possess any, or a "defense of free status" to condemn all dark-skinned people to slavery. Instead, it is simply an attempt to coerce universal conformity to a set of unenlightened prejudices, hence an attack on the rights of individuals in an area of their lives that (according to Kantian principles) lies at the core of their dignity and self-worth.

Kant's own defense of monogamous marriage can best be understood as an attempt to protect the rights of persons, especially women, within sexual relationships that Kant accepted as inherently coercive because of what he saw as a fundamental natural, social, and economic inequality and consequent subjection of one party to the other. This is the best way, for example, to understand Kant's prohibitions on polygamy and concubinage. Kant's defense of monogamous marriage is therefore analogous to later attempts to regulate slavery or child labor, which were no doubt aimed at alleviating the worst abuses of these odious practices but always ended up lending support to the fundamental injustice.

One of Kant's best friends was Theodor Gottlieb Hippel, the Bürgermeister of Königsberg. Hippel helped Kant buy his house on Prinzessinstraße, in the shadow of the royal castle that gave the city its name. He also wrote whimsical novels in the style of Laurence Sterne, as well as widely known treatises advocating civil equality for Jews and, what is more relevant to our present interests, provocative tracts advocating radical reform of both marriage and sexual morality with the aim of securing full social, professional, and economic equality between men and women. It was sometimes rumored in Kant's day that he was either a ghost writer of or a silent collaborator on Hippel's "feminist" writings.[7] The intent of these rumors may sometimes have been friendly to Kant, but some of it was certainly hostile, because Hippel, like William Godwin and other male defenders of women's rights in that age, was also calumniated as an unprincipled sexual libertine. Kant refused to participate in the attacks on his friend's character, but he also publicly denied any association with Hippel's writings. I think it would be mere wishful thinking for us not to take these denials at face value.[8] But a parallel conclusion is, I think, entirely warranted – namely, that Kant's best thoughts about sexuality, instead of leading to the official position he held and defended in his writings, sooner lead to radical conclusions about sexual morality that are much more like Hippel's.

14

Lies

Kant's strict views on lying have been regularly cited as a reason for thinking there is something fundamentally wrong with Kantian ethics. Some of Kant's statements here seem so excessive that most Kantians who have dealt with the topic have tried to distance themselves from them, usually claiming that they do not (or need not) follow from Kant's own principles. In this chapter, I will do a little of that, partly by questioning whether the famous example of the "murderer at the door" really fits the principles Kant applies to it, but mainly by claiming that some of what Kant says about lying as a violation of an ethical duty to oneself should be taken as warranted rhetorical exaggeration rather than as literal doctrine. By and large, however, I will argue that Kant's views about veracity are reasonable or at least defensible, if not self-evident. This is mainly because I also think some of them – especially his position in the brief, late, and famous (or notorious) essay *On a Supposed Right to Lie from Philanthropy* (1797) – have been badly misunderstood. My first task will be to correct that misunderstanding.

1. Intentionally False Declarations

Let's begin with an elementary point of terminology. 'Lie' (*Lüge, mendacium*) is a technical term for Kant. It means: an intentionally untruthful statement *that is contrary to duty*, especially contrary to a duty of *right*. An intentional untruth, when it violates no duty of right, is called a *falsiloquium*, a term I will translate here, for the sake of convenience, as "falsification" (MS 6:238n, VE 27:447). In Kant's usage, therefore, it is an analytic proposition that a lie is contrary to duty and hence analytic that lying is always wrong. (Actually, there is one possible exception to this last assertion, the case of the "necessary lie," which we will discuss later). However, it is by no means analytic that every falsification is contrary to duty (or wrong), and Kant does not believe that every falsification is contrary to duty. That it is an analytic truth that lying is contrary to duty tells us nothing about the conditions under which a falsification becomes a lie. It therefore implies neither strict nor lax moral views about veracity.[1]

The next point to consider is not terminological. It is that Kant considers the prohibition on intentional untruthfulness in relation to two (and only two) kinds of duty. It is either a violation of a duty of *right* or a violation of a perfect ethical duty to oneself (though of course Kant may regard many lies as violating both duties at once). Here we will first consider lying as a violation of a duty of right and then turn to lying as a violation of a perfect ethical duty to oneself.

This brings to our attention once again Kant's basic distinction between right and ethics. The fundamental principle of morality derived in the *Groundwork* (in all its formulations) is the principle of ethical duties. But duties of right fall under a different principle: "Any action is right if it can coexist with everyone's freedom in accordance with a universal law, or if on its maxim the freedom of choice of each can coexist with everyone's freedom in accordance with a universal law" (MS 6:230). It is unclear (and controversial in the literature on Kant) whether the principle of right is based on the principle of morality or is independent of it (my own view, argued elsewhere, is that it is the latter).[2] Every duty of right, however, in Kant's view also generates an ethical duty, because respecting the innate right to freedom possessed by all persons is an ethical duty grounded on the right of humanity (according to FH) (MS 6:237).

Because the prohibition on lying, when lying is regarded as the violation of a duty of right, is a matter of right rather than of ethics, it is not natural for Kant to think about this duty by trying to derive it from the principle of morality (in any of its formulations), as a great deal of the existing literature on this subject tries to do – for instance, by considering this prohibition via the example of the lying promise discussed in the *Groundwork* (G 4:402–3, 422, 429–30).[3] I think this error alone vitiates most of the arguments found in that literature, regarded either as interpretations of Kant's views in the right-to-lie essay or even as properly Kantian views on the subject of veracity.

Not every intentionally false statement is a lie, in the sense of a violation of a duty of right. Many such statements are merely falsifications. In order to understand how a falsification can become a "lie" (in the technical sense that it is a violation of a duty of right), we need to understand yet another crucial piece of technical terminology – the term "declaration" (*Aussage, Deklaration*, Latin *declaratio*). All these terms, in Kant's vocabulary, refer to statements that occur in a context where others are warranted or authorized (*befugt*) in relying on the truthfulness of what is said, and make the speaker liable by right, and thus typically subject to criminal penalties or civil damages, if what is said is knowingly false.

The fact that (in juridical contexts) *Aussage* and *Deklaration* are technical terms for Kant is usually missed by readers of the essay on the right to lie. But this is quite clear from his consistent use of the term throughout his writings, and especially in the *Metaphysics of Morals* (KpV 5:44, MS 6:254, 258, 304, 366). Sometimes Kant appends the adjective "solemn" (*feierlich*) to "declaration," to emphasize the special significance of the term (R 6:159, MS 6:272, 304). One paradigm case of a declaration would be a statement made under oath in a court of law, where it is to be taken as probative (KpV 5:44, MVT 8:268, MS 6:272). Another clear case of a declaration would be a promise or warranty contained in the terms of a contract (MS 6:254, 272). However, because in Kantian ethics right is the larger rational system of morals (*Sitten*) that grounds mere positive legislation and the enforceable rights it secures, declarations are not limited only to statements with specific legal consequences. For example, Kant thinks that a person's solemn avowal of religious faith counts as a declaration (R 6:159, MVT 8:268).[4]

Declarations must be truthful. Kant's main principle governing the prohibition on untruthfulness regarded as a violation of duties of right is this: *An intentionally untruthful declaration is a lie, hence a violation of a duty of right.* This applies chiefly to cases of untruthfulness that deprive someone of something that is rightfully theirs – such as a piece of property, or a choice it is their right to make. "The only kind of untruth we want to call a lie, *in the sense bearing upon right* (*im rechtlichen Sinne*), is one that directly infringes upon another's right. e.g. the false allegation that a contract has been concluded with someone, made in order to deprive him of what is his (*falsiloquium dolosum*)" (MS 6:238n). Such a *false declaration* or "wrongful falsification" contrasts with a mere falsification – that is, an intentional falsehood that involves no infringement of right:

[One is] authorized to do to others anything that does not in itself diminish what is theirs, so long as they do not want to accept it – such things as merely communicating his thoughts to them, telling or promising them something, whether what he says is true and sincere or false and insincere (*veriloquium aut falsiloquium*); for it is up to them whether they want to believe him or not. (MS 6:238)

The test for whether it is up to the person whether to believe me or not is whether it is he or I who assumes responsibility, in relation to matters of right, for his believing what I say. For instance: If I casually volunteer the information that my car has 35,000 miles on it, and you take some action on the basis of that, those actions are up to you and you bear the responsibility for them. But if in a contract of sale of the car I state to you that the mileage is 35,000 when really it is 135,000, then you can sue me, and I bear the blame for any other actions you take based on my declaration.

The basis of all duties of right, according to the principle of right, is the protection of unhindered external freedom according to universal laws. What is rightfully mine includes property (MS 6:260–70), or various other things that can be made the objects of contracts, including the promised performances of others (MS 6:274–6), or also a choice that is mine to make unhindered by coercion or by the deception of others as to the consequences of my options. What belongs to me by right is regarded by Kant as falling under principles and duties of right because it bears on my external freedom under universal law. I am externally free only insofar as I can make use of what rightfully belongs to me, including the performances others have contracted and the unhindered choices that are rightfully mine to make.

In the context of right, a *declaration* is a statement made by another on whose truthfulness I am authorized to rely. If a declaration made to me is knowingly false, my freedom is wrongfully restricted. More generally, however, truthfulness in declarations in general is something on which all persons are authorized to rely, within a system of right (or external freedom of persons under universal laws). If someone lies in a court of law, for example, it is not only his adversary whose right is violated but the entire system of right, which must presume the truthfulness of declarations made in legal processes. If someone is defrauded in a contract, it is not only this person whose right is violated but the entire system of contract right, which is structured around the truthfulness of the declarations involved in contracts. (As we will see, this is what Kant regards as the crucial point of disagreement between himself and Benjamin Constant.)

Kant also puts this point in the following way: When I make a lying declaration, "I bring it about, as far as I can, that declarations (*Aussagen* [*Declarationen*]) in general are not believed, and so too that all rights which are based on contracts come to nothing and lose their force" (VRL 8:426). The claim here is *not* that some particular lie might *in fact* shake people's confidence in trials or contracts (as if it by itself would cause them no longer to believe anyone, or had no other reason to mistrust what people say).[5] It is rather that the system of right is constituted by a set of laws that are universally valid – actions are right only if they can coexist with everyone's freedom under this system according to a universal law. A statement counts as a declaration whenever reliance on its truthfulness is required to secure people's rightful freedom under universal laws. Hence it is contrary to the very concept of right that it could be right to make an untruthful declaration when the truthfulness of that declaration is required by rational laws of right. By making such a declaration, I am in that sense acting in a way that, if its permissibility were generally allowed, would deprive all declarations of their validity, whether or not I intend that result and whether or not it actually occurs. Kant also puts it this way: "It cannot hold with universality of a law of nature that declarations should be allowed as proof and yet be intentionally untrue" (KpV 5:44).

We could put this point in the terminology of John Rawls (Rawls, TCR) if we said that for Kant, right is a "practice" (the rational practice involving what is necessary to guarantee people rightful freedom under universal law). Truthfulness in making declarations is one of the rules of the practice. "Right" is, in effect, a rational framework for understanding, justifying, and correcting not only state and legal institutions but also other kinds of understandings between people guaranteeing their external freedom under universal laws. Kant attempts to justify the practice of right by showing the necessity of different aspects of it for protecting something regarded by Kantian ethics as of fundamental value – namely, the guarantee to persons of their external freedom according to universal law. The requirement that there be "declarations" at various points in the system of right is to be established by presenting contract law, judicial trials, informal promises, and so on, as requiring them. Once the making of truthful declarations is established as part of the "practice" of right, the rule of right requiring that declarations be truthful goes with the practice of making them. The duty always to be truthful in declarations needs no further defense.[6]

2. Kant and Constant

History of the famous example. In the famous late essay, untruthfulness is being considered (as the title of the essay, as well as its content, clearly indicates) solely as a violation of a duty of *right.* That essay is part of a controversy between Kant and the French writer Benjamin Constant. As I have said, the brevity of the essay, along with the common neglect of Kant's entire theory of right, often prevents readers from appreciating the precise nature of the question being addressed in it. They are so fixated on the famous example (chosen by Constant) that is discussed in it, and by Kant's apparently unreasonable position on that example, that they never even notice certain unusual, artificial, or even dubious features the example must take on if it is to be an illustration of the point Kant is trying to make.

The moral principle "it is a duty to tell the truth" would if taken unconditionally and singly, make all society impossible. We have proof of this in the very direct consequences drawn from this principle by a German philosopher, who goes so far as to maintain that it would be a crime to lie to a murderer who asked us whether a friend of ours whom he is pursuing has taken refuge in our house. (Constant, *Des réactions politiques,* quoted by Kant, VRL 8:425)[7]

Constant is perhaps[8] responding to an example Kant was to use in the Doctrine of Virtue – a servant lies to the police in saying that his master is not at home, and this lie enables the master to slip away and commit a crime:

For example, a householder has ordered a servant to say "not at home" if a certain human being asks for him. The servant does this and, as a result, the master slips away and commits a serious crime, which would otherwise have been prevented by the guard sent to arrest him. Who (in accordance with ethical principles) is guilty in this case? Surely the servant too, who violated a duty to himself by his lie, the results of which his own conscience imputes to him. (MS 6:431)[9]

If this is the example Constant has in mind, then he radically modifies it, transforming the servant of a would-be criminal into the friend of an innocent man who is trying to escape someone intending to murder him.[10] What shocks people is that Kant's position about Constant's example is that the friend must not lie to the murderer:[11]

Truthfulness in declarations (*Aussagen*) that one cannot avoid is a human being's duty to everyone, however great the disadvantage to him or to another that may result from it; and though I indeed do no wrong to him who unjustly compels me to make the declaration if I falsify it, I nevertheless do wrong in the most essential part of duty in general by such falsification, which can therefore be called a lie . . . ; that is, I bring it about, as far as I can, that declarations (*Aussagen* [*Declarationen*]) in general are not believed, and so too that all rights which are based on contracts come to nothing and lose their force; and this is a wrong inflicted upon humanity generally. (Kant, 8:426)

What the dispute is about. It is clear both in Constant's essay and in Kant's reply that the real issue is the duty to speak truthfully in declarations in *political* contexts, and the alleged limits on this duty.[12] This point is easy to miss because the example of the murderer at the door is not at all about the speech of politicians or statesmen. Constant's thesis is that moral principles can be applied to politics only by means of intermediate principles. Specifically, he claims that the principle of truthfulness in declarations must meet the condition that those to whom one speaks have a right to the truth. Kant's counterthesis is that the duty of right to be truthful in declarations is not limited by that condition.

Kant is usually interpreted as holding that while it may be permissible to refuse to answer the murderer's question, if you cannot avoid answering it (as Constant stipulates you cannot), then it is not permissible to lie to him, even if your truthfulness directly enables him to murder your friend (VRL 8:425–7). The natural reaction to Kant's position, so understood, is that it is a piece of rigoristic craziness. It is regularly used to call into question the moral sanity of any philosopher who could take such a position, and sometimes also to back up the crudely fallacious argument, discussed in Chapter 4, §1, that the very notion of a categorical imperative commits Kantian ethics to a set of rigid moral rules. (That Kantian ethics should in principle admit possible exceptions to any moral rule was argued in Chapter 3, §4.)

The usual interpretation of Kant's position gives no thought at all to the fact that he would see no violation of right whatever in a mere falsification uttered to the would-be murderer. Although the category of "declaration" includes more than assertions made under oath or in a contract, it is no part of Kant's theory to hold that just anyone who knocks on your door is automatically in a position to require from you a solemn declaration regarding the present whereabouts of some person. Perhaps a police officer, as in Kant's original example, might be in such a position. That is why Kant argues that the servant would be criminally liable as an accessory to his

master's crime (MS 6:431). But someone merely appearing at your door
with murderous intent normally would not. Of course, if the murderer could
not require a *declaration* from you, then telling him an intentional untruth
would not count as a *lie* (*mendacium*). Kant explicitly allows that no lie, and
no violation of right, occurs if we commit a falsification in order to prevent
another from making wrongful use of the truth:

I can also commit a *falsiloquium* when my intent is to hide my intentions from the
other, and he can also presume that I shall do so, since his own purpose is to make
a wrongful use of the truth. If an enemy, for example, takes me by the throat and
demands to know where my money is kept, I can hide the information here, since
he means to misuse the truth. That is still no *mendacium*. (VE 27:447)

Sometimes Kant describes this situation, or one very much like it, in terms
that make it permissible even to make a false *declaration*, and thus to tell a lie.
This is the one possible exception to the proposition Kant seems otherwise
to regard as analytic – namely, that lying is wrong, as being contrary to a
duty of right. For there are passages in his lectures in which Kant invokes
the traditional concept of a "right of necessity" (*Notrecht, ius necessitatis*), in
which under compulsion in an extreme case of need or distress, a person
is permitted to do something that would normally violate a rule of right.
A "necessary lie" (*Notlüge*) occurs where someone forcibly compels you to
make a declaration of which you know they will make wrongful use.

Yet since men are malicious, it is true that we often court danger by punctilious
observance of the truth and hence has arisen the concept of the *necessary lie*, which
is a very critical point for the moral philosopher. So far as I am constrained, by
force used against me, to make an admission, and wrongful use is made of my
statement, and I am unable to save myself by silence, the lie is a weapon of defense;
the declaration that is extorted and then misused permits me to defend myself, for
whether my admission or my money is extracted is all the same. Hence there is no
case in which a necessary lie occurs except where the declaration is forced from me
and I am also convinced the other means to make wrongful use of it. (VE 27:448)

In Constant's example it is stipulated that you have no alternative to making
the declaration. Yet because the murderer has not forcibly extorted the
declaration from you, a lie to him under these circumstances would not
count as a necessary lie.[13]

Can the murderer demand a declaration? It might be argued that in the
example of the murderer at the door, there could be no question of making
a statement having the rightful import of a declaration. Tamar Schapiro
has argued that a Kantian has good grounds to make an exception to a duty
when the duty is based on a practice between people, but the understanding
on which the practice rests has been reduced to a sham, as through the
systematic misconduct of some of the parties to it.[14] To put it in the Rawlsian
terms already mentioned, we might argue that the murderer at the door,
through his wrongful intentions, has undermined the practice of right, and

therefore that the concepts of "declaration" and "lie" that presuppose the rules of this practice no longer apply to what I tell him.

I think Schapiro's theory of excuses or exceptions is entirely cogent within a Kantian theory of right, and so is its application to this case. Yet Kant himself clearly rejects that argument, at least as applied to this example. The reason is that he holds that even when someone intends to use a declaration unjustly, it might nevertheless be possible in principle for him to be entitled to a *declaration*. Thus Kant allows Constant to assume that this is true in the case of the murderer at the door. When someone unjustly requires a declaration of you, Kant holds, you do no wrong to *him* in falsifying your declaration, but you nevertheless do wrong to humanity generally by violating your unconditional duty to be truthful in all your declarations:

Truthfulness in declarations (*Aussagen*) that one cannot avoid is a human being's duty to everyone, however great the disadvantage to him or to another that may result from it; and though I indeed do no wrong to him who unjustly compels me to make the declaration if I falsify it, I nevertheless do wrong in the most essential part of duty in general by such falsification, which can therefore be called a lie . . . ; that is, I bring it about, as far as I can, that declarations (*Aussagen* [*Declarationen*]) in general are not believed, and so too that all rights which are based on contracts come to nothing and lose their force; and this is a wrong inflicted upon humanity generally. (VRL 8:426)

This point is closely related to one of the main issues between Kant and Constant, Kant's rejection of Constant's claim that we owe truthfulness only to those who have a "right to the truth" (VRL 8:426). It might seem that Kant should agree with Constant here, because the Kantian distinction between a lie and a mere falsification might seem to amount to the distinction between saying something false to someone who has a right to the truth from you and saying something false to someone who has no such right. Yet Kant rejects any such account of the distinction because he holds that the duty not to lie attaches to every declaration as such and is not owed only to the person to whom it happens to be made.

On this issue, moreover, Kant seems clearly to be right. As we have already seen, the duty to make a truthful declaration under oath in court is not owed merely to the attorney who asks you the question but involves you in a relation of right to the judge, the jury, and the entire process of justice. In relation to what ultimately interests Kant the most, the duty of politicians to be truthful in their public declarations is a duty whose performance must be relied upon by the public at large.[15] In the essay on the right to lie, Kant sometimes distinguishes between a lie in the strict sense of the jurists, where the untruthful declaration violates the right of an assignable individual or individuals, and a lie in a broader sense, in which it violates the right of humanity (VRL 8:426; cf. VE 27:448). His main point in that essay is to insist on the validity of this broader conception, making an untruthful declaration wrongful (a lie, the violation of a duty of right) even where no assignable individual (with a "right to the truth") is wronged by it. This point seems especially pertinent if the real target is lies in a political context, where statesmen or politicians make untruthful declarations to the public. For here it is the public at large, or humanity in general, and no assignable individual, whose right is infringed by the lie.

Kant's *further* view here, that you might be *unjustly* required to give a declaration that you nevertheless have no right to falsify, seems more questionable. This is a first cousin of his also questionable view that you are required to obey even the unjust commands of a civil authority, as long as they do not require you to do something that is in itself wrong. But this questionable view clearly plays a role in his willingness to regard it as conceivable that the murderer at the door, even with his plainly unjust intent, might in principle be in a position to demand a declaration from you.

Once we appreciate all these points, we should begin to see how extreme and artificial (or even dubious) is the kind of case in which Kant's principles require him to say that it would be wrong to lie to the murderer at the door.[16] If our statement to the would-be murderer is not a declaration, then we need not speak truthfully, because that would be a mere falsification, not a lie. If he *extorts* a declaration from us, intending to use it unjustly, then that would be a case of a "necessary lie" and would again be permissible. It is only where a declaration is unavoidable yet not extorted that lying to the murderer at the door would violate the right of humanity. Most people who read Kant's essay seem bedazzled by the thought that Kant is willing to say about *any* case of the murderer at the door that you may not rightfully lie to him. The glare prevents them from seeing anything else about the case, including any of the more specific principles involved.[17]

What seems to me most implausible about Kant's claims about the murderer at the door is not that it would be wrong to make a lying declaration to him, given the conditions stipulated, but rather that the stipulated conditions could ever obtain in the case of a murderer at the door. That, however, is not the error with which Kant is usually charged. It would be an error merely about whether this example could really fit his principles, not an error infecting Kantian principles themselves. With two centuries hindsight, and in light of how often and how badly Kant's claims in this essay have been misunderstood, it seems clear that he would have done better to reject the example itself as unsuited to illustrate the issue on which he and Constant disagree. Even Kant's tactical decision to accept the example is defensible, however, at least to this extent, that there are certainly cases very much like that of the murderer at the door, where it is by no means unreasonable to hold that one must not lie even in order to prevent a great harm or wrong. Hence in order to gain a better appreciation of the issue Kant means to address, we might do better to consider a different example, in which the necessary assumptions would be less artificial or implausible.

Suppose you are a witness under oath in a court of law. You are asked by the prosecutor a question the truthful answer to which will predictably result in the conviction of your friend (or in Kant's example, your brother), whom you know to be innocent, on a charge of murder. Here an unscrupulous prosecutor might play the role of the murderer at the door, the innocent defendant the role of his intended victim, and again you are faced with the choice between telling the truth and saving him.[18]

No one should deny that this would be a deeply troubling predicament to be in, but a decision can be troubling even though you know how it has to be made (and all the more troubling just *because* you know this). And my own considered view about it is the Kantian one: Unless I think the legal process is illegitimate, or a mere sham, I think I had better tell the truth and be prepared to live with the consequences. Otherwise (as Kant himself suggests), *I* am the one turning the process into a sham, by behaving according to a principle that, if generally followed, would bring all solemn testimony and all legitimate legal processes into discredit (VRL 8:426).[19]

Political lying. As I have mentioned, the issue that appears to have really concerned both Kant and Constant is the duty of politicians and statesmen to be truthful in their official declarations. Here we surely need no "trolley problems"; there is no shortage of crying examples all around us in real life.

Stephen Holmes persuasively describes Constant's position in the dispute with Kant as the outcome of his experiences during the French Revolution, where the line separating police officials from murderers was not necessarily well defined and where declining to lie (even, we may suppose, in a declaration to a policeman or in solemn declarations in a political context) might easily result in you, or your friends, being sent to the guillotine.[20] Under those circumstances, Constant's position is certainly understandable. Looking at the dispute from this angle, Kant might be faulted for failing to appreciate the extreme conditions that motivated it.

Kant's contrary view, however, belongs to his insistence in *Perpetual Peace* that for rulers and statesmen, political expediency must always be subordinated to principles of right and that high office and political power – and the need to confront the kinds of decisions that go with the possession of such extraordinary power – earn no one an exemption from these principles. Maxims involving deception, moreover – denying the wrongs you have done, for example, or concealing your true aims and policies from the public – are prominent in that discussion (EF 8:375–6, 381–2).[21] Considered in historical context, the dispute between Kant and Constant is one in which each of the parties is making a valid point but about quite different issues, though issues that can interact in real life. If Constant's position is understandable as a reaction to the extreme conditions he faced during the Revolution, Kant's position is the fundamentally correct one about the duties of statesmen and politicians in the context of political life in general.

More recent real-life examples of lying declarations by political leaders and government officials leave me feeling far less ambivalent. Outrageously wrong political lying has played a decisive role in the political life of the United States certainly as far back as most of us can remember, and since the beginning of the new millennium (January 2001) it has become the chief determinant of governmental policy in virtually every area, from foreign policy to law enforcement to health and environmental policy.[22] But perhaps what should perhaps be uppermost in our minds is the outrageous political manipulation and falsification of intelligence leading up to the U.S.–British invasion of Iraq in 2003. This involved systematically untruthful declarations to the public by many officials of both governments, including the president's State of the Union Address in 2003 and that of U.S. Secretary of State Colin Powell before the United Nations delivered on February 5 of the same year. These officials have since claimed that they did not deliberately lie, but were only misinformed by their intelligence sources. But it has also been well documented that they carefully picked and chose among what those sources told them, ignoring stronger evidence in favor of weaker when it suited their purposes, and that they even manipulated the gathering of intelligence with a view to rationalizing the policies they had already decided upon. In light of this, such excuses are obviously nothing but further lies compounding the wrongs they have committed. Reflection on recent history, I think, should increase our sympathy with the supposedly extreme position Kant takes in the right-to-lie essay.

Rules and exceptions in philosophy and real life. Philosophers are always looking for counterexamples to general theses, and this makes them look hard for exceptions to every rule of right or morality that might be proposed. As I have argued in Chapter 3, §4, Kantian ethics says they are right. For in moral philosophy it is an important truth that because of the great complexities of human life, no moral rule simple enough to be practically useful can be framed so delicately as to be free of exceptions. But alongside this truth, philosophers should also appreciate another truth, one that was always vividly before Kant's mind and that I think explains some of the things he says about lying as well as other subjects.

The following is a true empirical generalization about people's behavior in real life: People have a powerful tendency to use the fact that there are exceptions to moral rules in order to rationalize making exceptions when they should not. For this reason, the speech act of asserting truly that there are exceptions to rules is more often than not used to justify wrongdoing, while the speech act of asserting falsely that there are none is most often a rhetorical attempt (probably unsuccessful) to prevent wrongdoing. Sometimes, on the contrary, the opposition is between inflexible moral prejudice and an open-minded reasonableness that is trying to take circumstances into account. Philosophers prefer to imagine the latter situation, because it flatters them by making their subtle reasonings a force for good rather than for evil. But if we take human beings as they are, we must admit that this is not the typical case.

If we take proper account of this true generalization, it tends to justify those moralists who rhetorically exaggerate the strictness of important moral rules and to cast doubt on the wisdom and even the moral integrity of philosophers who derive conceptual titillation from devising counterexamples to them and treat such counterexamples as reasons for relaxing strictness of the rules. Kant shows himself to belong to the former class of moralists, for example, when he denies we should teach children that there can be "necessary lies," because (he says) "they would soon take the smallest excuse for a necessity, and often allow themselves to tell lies" (VP 9:490).

In this respect, people in power tend to be far worse than even the naughtiest of children.[23] When they argue for exceptions to important rules restricting their conduct – using murderer-at-the-door arguments to justify lying, or ticking-bomb arguments to justify torture, or weapons of mass destruction in the wrong hands to justify preventive war – then you can be certain that they will lie to your face when there is no murderer at the door, use torture on prisoners when there is no ticking bomb, and start wars of aggression when there are no weapons of mass destruction.

Constant claimed that Kant's position would make political life impossible. The charge seems exaggerated, but the decisive Kantian rejoinder, which is surely no exaggeration, is that the policy of politicians to permit themselves lying declarations for supposedly worthy ends is precisely what *does* make possible much of what is utterly intolerable in our actual political life.

3. Truthfulness as an Ethical Duty to Oneself

A *lie* (*Lüge, mendacium*), in the strict sense of the term, is an untruthful *declaration*. Except perhaps in the case of necessary lies, all lies, in that sense, are (analytically) contrary to a duty of right. Kant considers the topic of untruthfulness also in the context of ethics, and here a "lie" (let's call this a "lie in the loose sense") is any intentional untruth that violates a duty – in ethics, a perfect duty to oneself, grounded in self-respect. As before, to call an untruth a "lie" is to say already that it is contrary to duty, so the claim that lying is always wrong turns out once again to be analytic. The terminological points just made do seem to be functioning in Kant's discussion of lying as a violation of a perfect duty to oneself.

The greatest violation of a human being's duty to himself regarded merely as a moral being (the humanity in his own person) is the contrary of truthfulness (*aliud lingua promptum, aliud pectore inclusum genere*). In the doctrine of right, an intentional untruth is called a lie only if it violates another's right; but in ethics, where no authorization is derived from harmlessness, it is clear of itself that no intentional untruth in the expression of one's thoughts can refuse this harsh name. (MS 6:429)

This statement is far more extreme than anything Kant says in the essay on the right to lie. Taken literally, he is saying that any intentional untruth whatever violates a duty to oneself by displaying contempt for oneself as a rational being. Kant seems further to be claiming that all such lies are of equal gravity and "the greatest violation of a human being's duty to himself as a moral being." But should we take such statements literally?

Although Kant repeats similar claims in his lectures (e.g., VE 27:701), I do not think they can be taken at face value as expressions of his considered views. I think they have to be understood as the rhetorical exaggerations on the part of a moralist who is not only motivated by the philosophical aim of systematizing moral rules for theoretical purposes but also – or even instead – concerned to have what he sees as the proper effect on his audience.

Moral doctrine and moralistic rhetoric. Kant would be contradicting himself if he said that every intentional untruth, regardless of context, is a worse expression of self-contempt than servility, or than the refusal to pay attention to one's conscience (MS 6:434–5, 437–40). Further, only two pages later, in the "Casuistical Questions" pertaining to this section, he clearly entertains an example in which intentional untruthfulness seems justified.

Can an untruth from mere politeness (e.g. the "your obedient servant" at the end of a letter) be considered a lie? No one is deceived by it. – An author asks one of his readers "How do you like my work?" One could merely seem to give an answer, by joking about the impropriety of such a question. But who has his wit always ready? The author will take the slightest hesitation in answering as an insult. May one, then, say what is expected of one?" (MS 6:431; VA 7:151–3)

Though Kant's "casuistical questions" are intended more as invitations to the reader's reflections and exercises in judgment than as firm statements of doctrine, in this case it is clear that Kant regards an affirmative answer to the final rhetorical question as entirely understandable. It is hard to see how self-respect could require that we be impolite to people even to the point of violating the conventions of letter writing. Nor would the self-respect of the great Professor Kant seem to be at risk if he gave a kind rather than a frank reply to the overconfident question asked him by a foolish young author at one of Kant's famous dinner parties. Indeed, Kant might sooner lose his self-respect if he gave a bluntly truthful answer – which might cruelly damage the questioner's career, as well as his self-esteem. In discussing "necessary lies," or *falsiloquia* that violate no duty of right because they are told under constraint in a case where it is known that the person spoken to intends to make wrongful use of the truth, Kant never suggests that these intentionally false statements should be avoided because they violate a duty to oneself. Obviously that suggestion would be absurd in these cases.

I think Kant was well aware that for many truths, there is a right time and place to tell them. In a situation where they must not be told, sometimes the only other option is to tell an untruth. Kant shows this in a passage from his lectures that once again follows hard upon some of his most extreme and apparently unqualified condemnations of all forms of intentional falsehood: "A moral casuistic would be very useful, and it would be an undertaking much to the sharpening of our judgment, if the limits were defined as to how far we may be authorized to conceal the truth without detriment to morality" (VE 27:701). Thus when we consider all the evidence, it seems clearly not to be Kant's real opinion that all intentionally false statements display self-contempt and are violations of a duty to oneself. His statements that they are should be read as rhetorical exaggerations rather than as literal doctrinal pronouncements.[24]

The claim that speaking falsely to another violates your self-respect contains a truth that far too many people ignore far too often. This may be why Kant feels justified in stating it so boldly and without qualification. If taken as a universal rule, however, it is obviously subject to many exceptions, and even entire classes of exceptions. We have seen that Kant acknowledges some of these himself. In addition, there are many cases in which telling intentional falsehoods is even the best way of exhibiting and retaining your self-respect. Kant condemns behavior that is overly inquisitive – prying into the secrets of others that are none of your business (VE 27:451–2). Sometimes the most effective way to protect yourself from such misconduct and assert your self-respect is to answer a prying question untruthfully. Sometimes the aim may be to deceive (as when a truthful answer, or even a refusal to answer, would divulge damaging information you have a right, or even a duty, to conceal), but sometimes it will be merely to convey impudently to busybodies (and to anyone else overhearing the conversation) that they are not going to get trustworthy information by asking questions they should not ask.[25]

This is one point Constant may have had in mind when he argued that we have a duty to tell the truth only to those who "have a right to the truth." Kant may be correct in rejecting Constant's defense of untruthfulness in the special case of solemn declarations, but in its proper context, Constant's point is correct.[26] I don't think Kant is unaware of this. In his lectures and in the *Metaphysics of Morals*, where he sees himself as playing the role of moral instructor as well as that of moral theorist, he feels entitled to indulge in the rhetorical exaggeration of truths to which, as moral philosopher, he should have recognized (and even does recognize) some important limitations and exceptions.[27]

Deception and the social condition. Why did Kant feel it so necessary to indulge in rhetorical exaggeration here that makes him so vulnerable to misinterpretation? We have already looked at one reason: Kant thinks people tend to make exceptions to rules in their own interest when they should

not, and this often makes the speech act of asserting the unexceptionable-
ness of moral rules morally justified even when it is an error theoretically.
But there is also something special for Kant about the moral issues involved
in truthfulness that might have made rhetorical exaggeration even more justified in this case. Kant regards deception and duplicity as the systematic vice
most characteristic of human nature in the civilized condition (R 6:33–4,
VA 7:149–53, 332–3). Whereas brutality is the characteristic vice of human
beings in the premodern (or "savage") condition, the vice endemic to civilization is deceitfulness (R 6:33–4). Civilized people, as Rousseau pointed
out, always "live outside themselves" in the opinion of others, and this gives
them powerful reasons not only to manipulate that opinion but even to
falsify the truth to themselves, because a condition of self-honesty is not fundamentally where they live in the first place (Rousseau, *Discourse*, pp. 68–71).

The third and most definitive formula of the moral law, presented in its
most intuitively graspable version, is FRE: All rational beings should regard
themselves as part of a single community united by a "realm" (or mutually
furthering system) of the ends of each member. In such an ideal community,
no one would have a reason to conceal the truth from anyone, either from
fear of what the other might do with it or from the hope to gain something
at the expense of others by imposing falsehoods upon them. Actual human
society, however, is for Kant a site of nearly universal competitiveness and
mistrust, as people try to make others (and even themselves) think they
are better than they really are and also to manipulate one another in the
attempt to get the better of them.

We order our behavior in such a way that in part we conceal our faults, and in part
also put a different face on them, and have a knack for appearing other than we
are; so other people see nothing of our sins and weaknesses beyond the appearance
of well-being ... Hence nobody, in the true sense, is open-hearted. Had it been as
Momus wanted, that Jupiter should have installed a window in the heart, so that
every human being's disposition might be known, then human beings would have
had to be better constituted, and have good principles, for if all human beings were
good, no one could hold anything back; but since this is not so, we must keep our
shutters closed. (VE 27:445)

Kant thinks that in the social condition, our inclinations themselves
become deceptive, especially those directed toward other people and aimed
at some kind of superiority over them. They then lead to "delusion" (*Wahn*),
"an internal practical deception of taking what is subjective in a motive for
what is objective" (VA 7:274, cf. R 6:168). Delusive inclinations easily become
passions – that is, inclinations difficult or impossible for reason to control.
Inclinations that have become delusive "are apt to become passionate in
the highest degree, especially when they are applied to competition among
human beings" (VA 7:273). Human cleverness itself, as it develops in society,
is originally not a faculty for seeking truth but a faculty for deceiving. "To

obscure something is the art of clever brains" (VA 7:151). "It belongs to the basic constitution of the human creature and to the concept of his species to explore the thoughts of others, but to withhold one's own – a nice quality that does not fail to progress gradually from *dissimulation* to *deception* and finally to *lying*" (VA 7:332).

The most basic kind of lie, closely associated with the radical evil in human nature, is "the secret falsity we see even in the closest friendship" and the portrayal of ourselves to others as better than we are – "many vices concealing themselves under the appearance of virtue" (R 6:33–4). Kant condemns lying so vehemently because he sees it everywhere and sees it as the foundation of the evil we find in the social condition.

For just these reasons, however, Kant regards the moral ideal of complete honesty between people, despite the fact that may be difficult or even impossible to achieve perfectly, as one that should be held up to them in its purity. Thus in reluctantly conceding the force of such excuses for untruthfulness as "jest, politeness, and necessity," Kant concludes the thought wistfully, saying that "here too we perceive the regrettable weakness of human nature, which sets bounds to the sublimity of an unconstrained openness of heart" (VE 27:701).

An untruthful person, in Kant's view, is someone who lacks the courage to deal with people truthfully. So he is despised by everyone (MS 6:429, VE 27:449, 700). Kant seems to think that the liar's willingness to put himself in such a position in the eyes of others betrays a profound disrespect for himself. Lying in Kant's view betrays a profound error, itself based on deception, about the nature of one's own worth. The liar places that worth in what others (or he himself) can be deceived into thinking about him, but he also acts in such a way that others are likely to despise him (and so however arrogantly he may conduct himself, his conduct always also betrays a profound self-contempt). On both counts, he fails to live up to his true worth, to his dignity as a human being.

4. The Inner Lie

In the section of the Doctrine of Virtue that deals with lying as a violation of a duty to oneself, Kant begins with the eye-catchingly exaggerated condemnation of all untruthfulness as a violation of a duty to ourselves grounded on self-respect. Nearly half the text of this section, however, is devoted not to lies told to others but to what Kant calls "the inner lie" – the lie to oneself, or what we would now call "self-deception."[28] We miss much of Kant's discussion – and an important reason he has for indulging in hyperbole – if we do not appreciate the importance for him of the inner lie, and even the way he thinks the outer lie is often rooted in the inner lie.

Kant notes in passing that it is difficult to explain how such lies are possible, because a lie seems to require a second person whom one intends to deceive (MS 6:430). Kant notes the puzzle but apparently has no doubt that inner lies do occur. If anyone were seriously to deny that self-deception actually occurs, the only correct response would be to accuse that person of it.

Such paradoxes may point to the fact that self-deception is only partly voluntary, because one reasonable conclusion from them is that it may be impossible for an inner lie to be entirely conscious and deliberate. At the same time, there is clearly something culpable about the motivated inattention to evidence, or incongruous policies in the weighing of evidence that we see in cases of self-deception.[29] Even the aspect of involuntariness involved in the inner lie may be part of what is culpable about it. If in self-deception we are passive victims of our own psychic processes, then it is also we who perpetrate this same victimization, as well as the ones who willingly compound that culpability by viewing ourselves as passive in relation to the inner lie, as if to disclaim responsibility and also win sympathy for ourselves.[30]

Kant thinks that human beings have powerful motives to lie to themselves. As we have already seen, the social condition as Kant understands it is one in which even our desires are deceptive. They interfere with our judgments about reality, enticing us to see the world not as it is but as we wish it to be. Self-conceit makes us want to place our needs and inclinations systematically ahead of those of other people, who before the bar of reason are our equals as ends in themselves. Contrary to reason, we will that others should put our desires ahead of their own, and to this end we portray our vices as virtues – not only to them, but even to ourselves.

Religious inner lies. Kant makes some very pointed remarks about certain forms of self-deception that avail themselves specifically of certain religious beliefs:

Someone tells an inner lie, for example, if he professes belief in a future judge of the world, although he really finds no such belief within him but persuades himself that it could do no harm and might even be useful to profess in his thoughts to one who scrutinizes hearts a belief in such a judge, in order to win his favor in case he should exist. Someone also lies if, having no doubt about the existence of this future judge, he still flatters himself that he inwardly reveres his law, thought the only incentive he feels is fear of punishment. (MS 6:430)

The second kind of inner lie condemned here applies to the way of thinking advocated in some of the most commonly accepted arguments that holding religious beliefs has morally good effects on people. The effect of these beliefs may actually be (and often is) exactly the reverse of this, as when religious fanatics attack those they regard as infidels or heretics, or corrupt the intellects and characters of others by converting them to the faith. But here, as elsewhere, we seek to portray our bad conduct to ourselves as good and regard both these kinds of wrongful behavior as obedience to the will of God.

The first kind of inner lie includes various styles of religious apologetics, such as Pascal's wager and James's will to believe. We wish to believe something (because we wish it were true, or because it would be flattering to us if it were true), and we satisfy the wish by telling ourselves we believe it, acting as if we believe it and associating with others who are lying to themselves in the same way until eventually we do come to believe it. Whatever advantages (real or imagined) we may acquire in this way are purchased at the cost of our integrity and self-respect.

The inner lie is always wrong. Kant therefore condemns inner lies in the harshest terms: "By an outer lie a human being makes himself an object of contempt in the eyes of others; by an inner lie he does what is still worse: he makes himself contemptible in his own eyes and violates the dignity of humanity in his person" (MS 6:429).

When Kant condemns the "inner lie" absolutely, there is no longer any need to take him to be indulging in rhetorical exaggeration. That the inner lie is a violation of an ethical duty to oneself is a principle as unexceptionable as any in ethics, and it makes good sense from the standpoint of Kantian ethics. This does not mean that we need to ignore how difficult (or even impossible) it is for human beings to escape self-deception, and so it need not imply a harsh or unforgiving attitude toward it, especially in others. Even in oneself, too harsh an attitude toward our faults may easily lead us to deceive ourselves by pretending we do not have them, which could, ironically, easily lead to our being more and not less susceptible to self-deception in consequence of recognizing that it is a moral fault, and that there are no exceptions to this. It is always one thing to realize that conduct is wrong and another thing to decide what attitude we should take toward some example of wrong conduct. Sometimes the best way to deal with wrong conduct, or even the best way to minimize it, is to take a liberal and tolerant attitude toward it rather than to treat it with strictness and severity. Kant seems to have recommended such a tolerant attitude toward some of the deceptions that he recognized as ineradicable in our unsociably sociable social life (VA 7:151–3).

Truthfulness with oneself is an especially important value to an ethical theory grounded on the value of rational self-government in accordance with objective ethical truth. For Kantian ethics grounds all value on the dignity or absolute worth of our rational nature. Deceiving oneself is a betrayal of that rational nature at its very foundation. Those who falsify what they know even before their own minds are undermining their rational functioning in the most basic possible way. When people do it in order to avoid the painful consciousness of their own faults and failings or to put their own actions in a more flattering light than they deserve, this also amounts to a subversion of moral conscience at its very foundation (MS 6:437–40).

To Kantian ethics, lying to yourself corrupts moral values at their very foundation, so that it empties of value any other value in whose name we might try to justify self-deception. Ethical theories that place ultimate value elsewhere – in pleasure or happiness, for instance (especially if these are located merely in conscious states rather than in any successful activities in the real world) – might perhaps license a milder attitude toward the inner lie. For there is no doubt that concealing the truth from ourselves sometimes contributes to our contentment, by saving us from the grief of having to confront bitter realities, especially about ourselves. Still others may regard the high priority placed on truthfulness by Kantian ethics as a hopeless naïveté. Kant was painfully aware that self-honesty is difficult and elusive, and complete self-honesty is unattainable by us. Recent postmodernist views regard this as a reason, or at least an excuse, for not even making the attempt, or even for giving up on the whole idea of truth, in favor of a more relaxed and less serious orientation to life, one that is more relativistic, more aesthetic, adorned with all the civilized graces of intellectual sophistication and ironic detachment.

Yet when either of these alternatives is set alongside the unrelenting Kantian insistence on human dignity and the supreme value of honesty and integrity in all our thoughts and volitions, the comparison reveals quite mercilessly the basic shallowness of all such competing philosophies.

15

Consequences

1. Kantian Ethics vs. "Consequentialism"

Conventional labels put Kantian ethics under the rubric of "deontology," which is contrasted with "consequentialism." The referents of both labels, however, are usually caricatures, used to oversimplify philosophical positions for the sake of convenience and less innocently to provide people with a plausible pretext for rejecting ideas they do not understand. There are in fact a number of quite different reasons why Kantian ethics distances itself from most positions that go by the name "consequentialism," and the chief effect of the caricatures is to erase the distinctions among these reasons.

Fundamental values are distinct from methods of ethical reasoning. One basic issue in ethical theory – which arises at least for the kind of ethical theory I have ascribed in Chapter 3 to both Kant and Mill – is the nature of the fundamental value and the kinds of entities in which this value is to be found. Many ethical theories take these entities to be *states of affairs*, especially regarded as consequences of actions. These theories share with Kant the view that purposiveness, the setting of ends to be produced, is the most fundamental feature of all action, but they differ from him in taking this feature also to determine the nature of the values grounding ethical theory. As we saw in Chapter 5, the basic value for Kantian ethics is not a state of affairs but the dignity or absolute worth of rational nature as an *end in itself*. It is this which opens up the possibility that certain actions can be required or forbidden in themselves, irrespective of their consequences, whether an action respects the worth of rational nature in persons need not depend, at least in principle, on its consequences or on whether it achieves some end to be produced. But this feature of the basic value grounding Kantian ethics does not, all by itself, directly entail that in moral deliberation, the choice of actions must depend on something other than the value of the states of affairs that are produced by them. There is a distinction between what an ethical theory might take as the *fundamental value* and how that theory represents the ethical reasoning that proceeds from this value.

This point applies not only to Kantian ethics but also to theories that do take the grounding value for ethical theory to lie in states of affairs. Such a theory might think of moral deliberation exclusively as instrumental reasoning about the most efficient way to produce good states of affairs and avoid bad ones. But it need not do so. The wiser and more circumspect versions of utilitarianism, for example, ask not merely which actions (considered singly and severally) produce the most pleasure and the least pain but instead about which set of moral rules, which moral code, would (if generally taught and practiced) be most conducive to the general happiness. Mill's utilitarianism is one of these theories. It takes moral rules from the received moral code but also recommends their rational reform on the basis of utilitarian values. Moral reasoning then proceeds from there, in a decidedly "deontological" spirit, by considering the obligations imposed by moral rules, not merely from instrumental reasoning about how to produce the greatest happiness locally or in the short term.

Kant's views on the subject of lying, for example, are sometimes contrasted with "consequentialist" views that would allegedly justify lying to the murderer at the door. Such a contrast is shallow and without substance. It confuses consequentialism with culpable disregard of the long-term consequences of practices and policies, while confusing Kantianism with a fetishistic attitude toward rules against lying. In this way, it underestimates both theories. For Kant's theory grounds the prohibition on lying declarations needed to protect external freedom under universal law in the system of right. And any consequentialist who can see beyond the end of his nose could give an entirely satisfactory account of why it is wrong to make a lying declaration even to prevent some great immediate harm. (For example, see Mill, pp. 22–3.) More generally, a consequentialist theory will usually make the right judgments about what to do if it is careful to do two things: First, it must judge the moral rightness of actions by their predictable or reasonably expected consequences rather than by their actual consequences; and second, it must give sufficient weight to the importance, as regards their consequences, of human practices that involve agents' selecting their actions not on the basis of the foreseen consequences of those actions but rather in accordance with the moral rules built into the practice. Practices of this kind include virtually all those aimed at securing trust between people and the benefits of such trust.[1]

A common moral error that sometimes passes for "consequentialism" is one we might call 'self-congratulation in the future perfect tense'. People are sometimes tempted to violate an important moral principle by the lure of some great good to be gained in the relatively near future (or the prevention of some terrifying evil). For example, people holding great political power use it in ways they ought to know are wrong, but they imagine future generations contemplating with gratitude the bold vision that led them to lie, or start an aggressive war, or violate the rights of others. This is the state of mind which, combined with the short-sightedness and incompetence that usually attends such enterprises, has led to most of the terrible deeds for which their perpetrators are in fact remembered only with revulsion. Are philosophical consequentialists more prone to such illusions than the adherents of other theories? Mill thought not (Mill, pp. 22–3, 25–6), and I agree with him.

What may lead people into these illusions is that there certainly are actions which are clearly wrong or immoral but which, viewed in retrospect, we are glad took place. Perhaps Bernard Williams's portrayal of Gauguin's abandonment of his family so that he could go off to the South Seas and paint is such a case.[2] But I worry more about someone like Catherine the Great of Russia, one of the greatest and most enlightened political reformers in that country's history, who, however, came to power by conspiring with her lover in the murder of her husband, the tsar. We feel ambivalent about such cases, and we ought to do so. Our feelings here are, and ought to be, in a permanent state of unresolved (even irresolvable) tension. There would be something wrong with someone who regretted that Catherine's reforms had occurred, but something even more wrong with someone who thought they provide a moral (or even a supra-moral) justification for murder.

If there is any fault to be found with consequentialism in this area, it is the mistake of believing that we could ever identify that course of action which would lead to "the best consequences overall and in the long run." Part of the problem here is that we often do not know the consequences of our actions, beyond the immediate ones that might fall under our intentions. But the deeper error is believing that there could be clear sense, and even a determinate reference, to a phrase like "the best consequences" – so that the ultimate rationale for any course of action could be seen as that it contributes to them. This is an error Kantian ethics avoids, a point to which we will return in a moment. The thing to appreciate right now is that locating basic values in states of affairs to be brought about does not preclude a method of moral reasoning that places emphasis on conformity to the right moral rules.

A precisely analogous point can be made about Kantian ethics. Given its value basis, Kantian ethics might in theory require us always to reason wholly "deontologically" – that is, directly from the dignity of rational nature to those actions that show respect for this dignity. In that case we would attend only to the "rightness" or "dutifulness" of those actions in relation to that value and we would never consider the consequences of our actions at all. In fact, however, Kantian ethics does nothing of the kind. As we saw in Chapters 8 and 9, moral reasoning in Kantian ethics is based on "duties of virtue" – ends to be produced, which it is our duty to set out of regard for the dignity of humanity and the worth of rational nature as an end in itself. These ends consist in our own perfection and the happiness of others. Kantian ethics therefore requires us to concern ourselves with producing good states of affairs. Recently David Cummiskey and Shelly Kagan have even defended the thesis that Kantian ethics, if carried out consistently, would result in a kind of consequentialism as regards moral reasoning.[3] I think this thesis is erroneous, but in order to see what is wrong with it we need to raise issues that are quite independent of the way Kantian ethics conceives of the basic value grounding ethical theory.

The "greatest good." One such issue is whether, in the context of moral reasoning, good states of affairs, as ethics regards them, are the kinds of things that admit of meaningful pursuit as wholes, or of optimization. Consequentialist theories, in order to yield determinate results, usually need some way of ordering the values of possible future states of affairs, so as to use the differences among those values in deciding which actions we should perform. The most traditional way to do this is to treat the good as something like a single measurable whole that our actions might try to maximize. This is the point, for instance, of the utilitarian conception of "the general happiness." The pursuit of this maximum provides consequentialist theories with a method of moral reasoning that corresponds to the fundamental value. But it is questionable whether the good to be produced by actions is the sort of thing that can be correctly thought about in this way.

Whenever we set any end, the concept of the end establishes some criterion for distinguishing (relative to that end) between consequences that are more and less desirable. Some ends specify an optimal consequence (namely, the full attainment of the end). Most ends also provide a rationale for some rank-ordering among possible outcomes (those that are closer to the end's attainment). Some ends are conceived in an open-ended manner, so that the point of actions directed to them is simply to get "the greatest possible amount" of something. When you are gambling, for instance, you want to end up with the maximum amount of money you can, and outcomes can be rank-ordered according to their actual or probable payoffs. Other ends are conceived in terms of some "optimal" state of affairs, and the idea is to reach that and not fall any further short of it than you have to. If our end is to satisfy the preferences of a group of people, we aim at frustrating no one unnecessarily, and an idea like Pareto optimality will be appropriate to use.

Not all the ends we set are like these cases, though. Suppose I leave my house with the end of taking a pleasant and interesting walk in the woods. Among the events that would constitute the achievement of my end are my seeing various animals, birds, and wildflowers along the way. But my concept of the end furnishes me with no conception of what a maximally best set of such experiences would be and only a very crude sense of an ordering among the events I am hoping for. Obviously a walk on which I see no birds or animals at all would fulfill my end less than one on which I do see some.

But to ask about finer discriminations (whether it would be better to see one deer or to see two downy woodpeckers) might make no sense. This is not the sort of end that is conceived in terms of "optimality" or involves a precise rank-ordering of all states of affairs as more and less desirable.

It is not the least bit evident that there is any concept of "the good" apart from the concept of a specific end (or ends) and a specific context of goal-directedness. Such a general conception of "the good" might be thinkable if there were some single encompassing end that everyone does (or should) propose for their actions, and if, further, this was the kind of end that admits of something like maximization, or at least a precise rank-ordering of outcomes relative to it. I think this is Bentham's picture when he proclaims that we are subject to two sovereign masters, pleasure and pain.[4] He thinks of everyone as aiming at the greatest preponderance of pleasure over pain, and he also thinks there is some fundamental standard (such as "intensity") for clearly comparing and measuring sensory states. If we also had some way of making interpersonal comparisons between the states of different people, then we might have some use for the notion of a "greatest overall good" and also for the concept of a rank-ordering of states of affairs relative to it. The forms of hedonism that would justify such presuppositions are no longer as popular as they used to be, but philosophers and decision theorists often still suppose that the value grounding ethics is some state of affairs ("the good") which shares the formal properties that Benthamite hedonism would ascribe to pleasure. This assumption casts what Scanlon aptly describes as the "shadow of hedonism" over much ethical theorizing in the consequentialist tradition (Scanlon, pp. 100–3). Scanlon is correct to call the assumption into question.

Kantian ethics does not think in this way about the ends to be produced that we are morally required to set. It takes these ends always to be *particular instances* falling under the general concepts of 'my own perfection' and 'the happiness of others'. I have no duty to make myself "as perfect as possible" or to make others "as happy as possible." Kantian ethics is not even committed to the proposition that such phrases have any determinate meaning or any possible reference. More generally, it is not committed to the idea that there is any single standard (which might go by a name such as "maximization of the good") which applies across the board to all the variety of possible ends we might set on moral grounds.

Instances of a person's perfection, or parts of a person's happiness, regarded as determinate ends of action may have local standards of measurement. There may be standards according to which a person measures his progress in the development of a talent. But there is no reason at all to think it even makes sense to set up standards of "perfection" that apply across different talents or perfections – enabling me to decide whether I perfect myself more by learning to play Brahms's Intermezzi, op. 117, or running a marathon, or mastering string theory in physics, or becoming an expert on the history of the American Civil War. And it is similar with happiness, which is, as Mill points out, a "concrete whole," made up of qualitatively different parts (Mill, p. 38). Unless you are a Benthamite hedonist or have arbitrarily assumed that human happiness shares the formal features he ascribed to pleasure and the absence of pain, there is no sense to the idea of "maximal" happiness.

From each individual's point of view, decisions about what would make that individual better or worse off – decisions that might be reported in terms of the individual's "preferences" – will be based on that individual's conception of the various ends that the individual thinks of as constituting "my happiness." As we saw in Chapter 1, Kant himself thinks of prudential reasoning as involving an idea of my satisfaction with my state or condition considered as a whole. This creates an implicit standard, set up by each individual, for what would make that individual more and less happy. But the kinds of reasons that might go into determining the content of my happiness, and the values that enter into its conception, are not limited to value assignments attached to *states of affairs*. For instance, I may value devoting my life to scholarship or artistic endeavors because I regard this as a fulfilling way to live and not solely on account of the specific states of affairs (books published, paintings sold, etc.) that I hope will result from the activities I engage in.[5] And my choice of this way of life may have more to do with facts about my family history, or the values that this choice honors (rather than promotes), than with anything about the future states of affairs that result from it. Even if the fulfillment of my projects in this way of life does take the form of states of affairs, the reason why I value those states of affairs may have more to do with other values than with the valuable properties of those states of affairs. It might have more to do with the meaningfulness to me of the activities that take those states of affairs as their ends than with any desirable properties of the states of affairs themselves. My desire for those states of affairs might, in Rawls's terminology, be 'principle-dependent' (Rawls, *Lectures*, pp. 46–9). And of course those states of affairs themselves need not have any internal standard of "maximization" that grounds my choice to give some good states of affairs priority over others in declaring my self-interested preferences.[6]

Formal theories of rational choice offer us only an uninterpreted calculus. How and even whether its formal parameters fit our conception of the ends we pursue is a contingent matter. Welfare economists, and some ethical theorists, are accustomed to accept the judgments of individuals about which states of affairs are best for them, treating their expressed preferences as if they were reports of an objective ordering of happiness or utility that might provide inputs into some formal calculus for maximizing the good. Their decision to interpret such reports in this way often reflects some substantive ethical value, such as that we ought to respect the rights of individuals to determine for themselves what counts as good for them for the purpose of the fair distribution of benefits. This "antipaternalistic" policy, though perhaps perfectly correct in many contexts, needs moral justification. Kantian ethics would ground such a policy on our duty to respect the rights of rational beings as ends in themselves. Any ethical theory that is not Kantian should provide some alternative justification. It is a serious error from the standpoint of ethics simply to build this policy into the formal structure of some theory purporting to tell us about "the good."

What counts as "consequences"? Some consequentialists think they can include "deontological" considerations in their ethical theories by treating such "states of affairs" as "a promise's having been kept," "a right's having been respected," and so on as having great positive value, or "a promise's having been broken," "a right's having been violated," and so on as having great negative weight when we calculate the overall value of consequences. If the values assigned are large enough, then it will apparently be possible for consequentialist theories to accommodate the conclusion that we should not break promises or violate rights merely in order to achieve other good consequences, such as a greater tendency of pleasure over pain. Such theories, however, miss the crucial point that it matters to practical deliberation not only what possible states of affairs we value and how much comparative value we assign them in relation to others but also *why* we assign those values. A theory misleads rather than clarifies if its assignment of values to states of affairs is really nothing but a roundabout way of representing a kind of practical consideration that in fact does not take the form of *valuing states of affairs*. This way of looking at the matter, for example, sometimes invites the distorted interpretation of doing the right thing as being concerned with a certain kind of consequence – one's own "moral purity" (see Scanlon, p. 388, note 28). And trying to capture such moral considerations as duties of right or other strict duties in this way easily leads to interpretive awkwardness, or worse.

Suppose the federal Department of Homeland Security offers me a large sum of money if I betray my friend to them so that he may be detained indefinitely without charge or trial and tortured at Guantánamo Bay under the pretext that he is a terrorist. Suppose I know further that if I do not betray my friend, several other people will betray their friends in a similar way or even worse (suppose these friends may suffer extraordinary rendition to distant countries whose secret police tortures prisoners far better than do the clumsy Americans at Gitmo). And suppose, finally, that if I betray my friend, I know these other people will all lose the opportunity to betray their friends.

In such a situation, can I use the negative moral value of a "bad consequence" (such as "friend-betrayal") to articulate the "deontological" thought that *I must not betray my friend*? If I consider merely the overall negative value assigned to states of affairs involving "friend-betrayal," then it actually looks as if I *should* betray my friend, because doing that will minimize the overall negative value of "friend-betraying states of affairs." Unless I have been rendered morally bankrupt through the study of philosophical ethics, this will surely seem a highly unsatisfactory result. I could avoid it, of course, by assigning a much higher negative value, *ceteris paribus*, to *my* acts of friend-betrayal than to such acts when they are performed by others. But this seems ad hoc and arbitrary, not to mention somewhat self-indulgent – as though I thought that *my* acts of friend-betrayal are much more important than the (objectively worse) friend-betraying actions of others. "Consequentialist" renderings of the simple "deontological" claim that it is wrong to betray your friend, and the distortions of thought and speech required to produce them, are likely to appeal mainly to those philosophers who are so hopelessly committed to certain doctrines that they have come to prefer the abstract theoretical elegance of these doctrines to the correct interpretation of people's words and actions.

The greatest good versus the realm of ends. Sometimes it provides a useful way to think about choices to assign positive or negative values to various outcomes and calculate which actions maximize the value of the states of affairs that result from them. This way of thinking about both individual and social choice, where it makes sense, should be open to a Kantian as much as it is to any rational agent. It might, for instance, be the most rational way of deciding what to do in pursuit of some determinate part of the happiness of some person or persons that the Kantian agent has made an end. It is a nontrivial question how far the nature of human goods and the teleological reasoning involved in the setting of ends required by morality permit such consequence-based modes of practical reasoning to be employed either by individual moral agents or as a way of making social choices that are morally grounded. This seems the most promising strategy for defending something like a "Kantian consequentialism." Some of the features of Kantian ethics, however, such as the strictness of duties of right, might set principled limits on the use of consequentialist-style practical reasoning. And of course Kantian ethics regards the use of such modes of reasoning as having moral presuppositions not grounded on the value of states of affairs that need to be articulated.

The Kantian notion that comes closest to the utilitarian idea of the "general happiness" is that of the realm of ends. But it is significant that the realm of ends is conceived not as a single state of affairs aimed at, but a system of purposive activity shared by different rational beings who stand in social relationships to one another – they respect one another as ends in themselves and choose to live according to a common set of objective moral laws expressing this mutual respect. This is why they choose to share a common set of ends that brings the happiness of each into harmony with the happiness of all the others, and why each one chooses to limit the pursuit of her own happiness in such a way that it can belong to such a shared, purposive system. There is no reason to suppose there is a single standard for maximizing the achievement of the end (or rather the shared system of ends) that is pursued by the members of the realm of ends. Instead, the ideal of the realm of ends is a way of representing the *maxims* to which each member is bound in belonging to the realm.

Bringing about the good and individual agency. This feature of the realm of ends points to yet a third issue on which Kantian ethics parts company with any ethical view that would model ethical reasoning solely on the rational instrumental pursuit of good states of affairs. Kantian ethics is based on the idea that rational requirements in general, and moral requirements in particular, are always addressed to particular rational agents. If there is a moral demand that something should be done, then it is a demand that makes sense when addressed to some agent in particular who has the duty to do it. Even if there were a single standard for the goodness of states of affairs (e.g., a utilitarian "greatest happiness"), there would arise a nontrivial question, not decided by the content of this maximally desirable state of affairs, about how this end is to be promoted, who is to promote it, and what each agent is required to do.

Is there any agent who is in a position to promote the optimal state of affairs, and whose business it is to do so? Perhaps Leibniz's God, in choosing the best world from among all the possible worlds, would be such an agent. Or there might be one or more human agents (albeit with less knowledge and power) who would be in a position to pursue this end, if we imagine a society that is governed by a single benevolent despot, or one that is being designed from scratch by a privileged coterie of utilitarian social engineers. But whether despotism or social engineering should even be permitted seems morally questionable and is certainly in need of justification. So such a picture cannot be allowed to determine in advance our basic framework of moral reasoning.

Kantian ethics differs from ethical theories whose style of practical reasoning is oriented to producing the best states of affairs by making the primary thing the relationships between rational beings, and the terms on which rational beings relate to one another. The basic thing is that rational beings should follow a common set of laws or principles expressing their self-respect and their respect for one another as ends in themselves and the idea that they are legislators in common of the laws to which they are subject. These laws are what determine, for each individual, the demands morality will make on that individual, including the states of affairs that individual has moral grounds to set as ends and to consider good from a moral point of view. Because these matters are determined for each individual independently of any notion of a single greatest good or best state of affairs, there is no need in Kantian ethics for such a notion to serve as any sort of standard for determining the goodness of states of affairs as possible ends of action.

Moral philosophers like to reflect on cases in which people's interests are deeply at odds and we must choose among them – cases where there is a

lifeboat shortage, or a trolley running out of control, or where you can save
five people only by killing someone else. Some ethical theories seem to hold
that we should at least consider deciding such cases based on which course
produces the greatest total good (or the least harm). Kantian ethics takes a
different approach to them, inquiring instead into the process of collective
decision making that properly respects the rights and dignity of all those
affected by it, how far it harmonizes the necessary ends of all involved,
whether all affected have consented or reasonably could consent to it, and
so on. Kantian ethics, however, need not specify any single "right answer"
or "right decision procedure" for such cases. These matters would depend
on the interpretation of the fundamental principles of morality and right
under a set of empirical circumstances, and they might also depend on
how moral judgment applies the set of moral rules or duties that would
result from such an interpretation. It is neither trivially true nor obviously
false that decisions made on Kantian grounds would be the same as those
made on the basis of the best overall consequences (even assuming that the
notion of "best consequences" has a clear and applicable sense in the case
in question). Kantians and optimizing consequentialists may or may not,
therefore, reach the same decisions. But Kantian ethics will not reach them
by the same route, or on the same ultimate value basis, as the optimizing
consequentialist.

The highest good. Kant does have something like a conception of the
maximally best state of affairs or "greatest good overall," in the form of his
ideal of the highest good (*summum bonum*). This is, for each individual,
morality of conduct combined with the happiness of which this conduct has
made the individual worthy, and for a world as a whole, it is the greatest
moral perfection of the rational beings belonging to that world, combined
with the happiness such perfect beings would thereby deserve (KrV A804–
19/B832–47, KpV 5:108–13, KU 5:434–6, TP 8:279–82, R 6:5–6, VA 7:277–
8). The *summum bonum* is a systematic conception of the final end that all
rational beings should share. It can be equated with the ideal of the realm
of ends – as the state of affairs that would result if the realm of ends were
fully actualized. It can also be thought of as an end ascribable to God in his
creation of a world (KpV 5:124–33, VpR 28:1061–2, 1073–6, 1084–8).

It is significant, however, that in Kantian ethics, the highest good is never
thought of as something that a finite rational being has a duty to set as the
kind of end from which moral laws and duties are to be derived. I take this
to follow from two distinct points of Kantian doctrine that we have just been
examining. First, we are in no position to know in practice what a phrase such
as "the greatest good overall" might refer to. We have no standard of measurement for determining "greatest" in this context, and we do not know
enough about the future to make judgments about what would lead to "the
greatest good overall" even if that phrase made sense. Second, even if we
knew this, none of us is in a position to be responsible for directing the course
of things toward such a maximal good. Our task is to respect the rights of

persons (and the right more generally) and to set as ends those instances of goods falling under the rubrics of our own perfection and the happiness of others toward which we are capable of making a meaningful contribution with our limited powers in our limited lives. The larger practical context for our action is not the highest good (regarded as "the greatest good overall") but the realm of ends. That is to say, it is not an encompassing consequence to be brought about but a web of relationships between rational beings in which all their particular ends can be shared and all are respected as ends in themselves.

2. Good versus Evil

The realm of ends would be a society of free and rational beings whose fundamental ends are not individual ends, isolated from and possibly in competition with one another, but rather a system of consciously shared ends. As a member of such a realm, I would govern all my actions by the principle that my deepest ends must not conflict with the deepest ends of other rational beings but these ends must be drawn from the rational system of ends that I ought to pursue in common with others. The realm of ends would therefore be, as we saw in Chapter 4, a free association in which (as the *Communist Manifesto* puts it) the *free development of each would be the condition for the free development of all.* In the realm of ends, the freedom and dignity of each member is respected as an end in itself, and each of us consciously finds satisfaction in working for the good of others. Once again, the essential Kantian idea is well expressed by Marx: "In my individual life I would have directly created your life; in my individual activity I would have immediately *confirmed* and *realized* my true human and social nature."[7]

For Kant, however, the realm of ends is "obviously only an ideal" (G 4:433). The unsociable sociability of human nature renders us unfit to live at present in a manner that comes anywhere close to this ideal. This provides no excuse for our corrupt maxims and practices, but the duties we have are at present not the same as they would be if human beings were equal to the lofty demands of the ideal of the realm of ends. It is our moral task to regulate both our individual lives and our collective life in such a way as to honor the ideal of the realm of ends and to embody a striving, however pitifully small and imperfect, toward that ideal.

From one point of view, this involves an attempt to transform human nature itself in accordance with the ideas of mutual respect, autonomy, and human community that are grounded in the moral principle of reason. From this standpoint, the human condition is one of continuous hoping and striving "until perfect art again becomes nature, which is the ultimate goal of the moral vocation of the human species" (MA 8:117–18). It is always a question of learning to live with maxims, practices, and ways of life that fall dismally short of the ideal realm of ends but make possible both human life as it is and the striving toward the ideal.

There is an immense gap between what human life is and what it would be if individual lives, and the collective life of humanity, were governed by moral principles. In living with this gap, Kantian ethics requires that we take an attitude toward ourselves that is very different from the attitude we take toward others. Our duty of conscience (discussed in Chapter 10) requires us to be merciless in our self-examination – though always with the sober aim of moral improvement, not so that we may indulge "the self-torment of the remorseful sinner" – a self-deceived state of mind that Kant finds disgusting (R 6:24n). Toward others, however, our attitude should be basically tolerant and beneficent. If their merits seem greater than our own, we do best by regarding them as examples of what we should live up to and as evidence that it would be possible for us to live up to it. By thus transforming our comparison with others into such an "inner" comparison, we guard against our human tendency to competitiveness and envy (KpV 5:76–8, VP 9:491). Even more dangerous, however, is our tendency to dwell on the moral faults of others. In Kantian ethics it is always contrary to duty "inwardly to look down on some in comparison to others" (MS 6:463). The right way to look at the bad conduct of others is think about how little separates you from them: "How many people who have lived long and guiltless lives may not be merely fortunate in having escaped so many temptations?" (MS 6:392–3).

Kant's common reputation associates him closely with a harshly "moralistic" attitude toward life. But the theme just touched on sets Kantian ethics decisively against some of the principal traits associated with that attitude. "Moralists" tend to be people who revel in the sharp separation of good from evil, and right from wrong. Kant does think we should make such a sharp separation when the distinction in our own actions is clear and when we are tempted to blur it in order to make things easier for ourselves. But it is also considered unattractively "moralistic" to separate *people* in our thoughts as "good" and "evil," and even to *want* them to be neatly separated in that way. And we all have such moralistic tendencies. That is why we do not want to hear about the faults or the misconduct of our "heroes" and "saints," and why we are even more offended when people say anything good about a plainly reprehensible person. We are quick to accuse them of wanting to make excuses for the villain, perhaps even of wanting to be villainous themselves.

In fact, though, real people's lives and characters are, morally speaking, nearly always hopelessly complex and ambiguous. The human world is *not* divided neatly into "good" people and "bad" people. Our moralistic tendency to see it that way, born of wishful thinking that it should be like that, is usually associated in our minds with our sense of moral righteousness, but the worst things we do are done in the certain conviction that we are the good people and those we injure are malefactors who deserve what they get. In Kantian ethics, however, the most fundamental principle is that all rational beings (the stupid and the evil as much as the intelligent and the good) have equal dignity and are entitled to equal respect. We are all destined, both individually and collectively, to spend our lives trekking across a vast, bleak, disorienting moral landscape – the trackless desert separating our profoundly corrupt society from the realm of ends. We have to build our own roads across the wasteland and are condemned to uncertainty about whether, in our brief lives, we have seen our species advance even a single step closer to the ideal.

This view of things leads to some even simpler thoughts about the right moral attitude for people to take toward themselves and other people: Always attend to what you yourself ought to do, based on the moral principles and rules that apply to your situation, and the rights and interests of others that are involved in it. When you think about other people, think mainly about what they can demand of you by right, and what you have reason to do for them on account of their needs. When you think about what they might do to help or hinder your ends, think about it in the context of the ends you share with them or can share with them. Never content yourself with doing merely no worse than what you see the next guy doing. Instead, think about what *you* should do, and do that. Above all, don't let your attention be distracted from what you should do by the evil you see in others, or – especially – by the harm you fear from them. If you want to combat "evil," don't think first about the evil in *other* people. First look in the mirror and combat the evil you see right there. You will probably find at least enough of it staring you in the face to occupy all the antagonistic effort you are prepared to muster.

There are people who, when they see these ideas expressed as Kant expresses them, react by regarding Kantian ethics as excessively severe and even inhuman. But inhumanity is precisely what people seem to me to fall into when they think in the ways against which Kant is warning us. Or maybe the objection to these Kantian thoughts is that they are too simple-minded to be worthy of the analytical reflections of clever philosophers. But they seem to me to represent a kind of *wisdom*, the kind of which Kant says that it is more a way of acting than a kind of knowledge and that it needs philosophy not to tell it what to do but only to prevent us from subverting it in ourselves through too much self-deceptive sophistication.

3. The Limits of Ethical Theory

This book has been about a certain kind of *ethical theory* – *Kantian* ethics. It has also been about *ethics* – about ethical issues, such as those about lying, sexuality, and economic justice. These two points of focus are closely related, but they should not be confused. When Kant says that it is "a duty for everyone to have a metaphysics of morals, which every human being also has within himself" (MS 6:216), he should be taken to mean that it is a duty for me to frame for myself my own set of reflective thoughts about what is right and wrong, and how this applies to me and my life. This is a set of thoughts of whose perfect or ideal formulation no philosophical theory can ever be more than a provisional and imperfect approximation. It makes sense to have strong convictions about ethical issues – for instance, that it is always (or nearly always) wrong to falsify declarations or lie to oneself, or that the prevailing economic system or sexual mores are in need of radical reforms. But the same is not true of ethical theories.

The function of an ethical theory is to help us examine and criticize our ethical convictions, sometimes to reach new ones, to defend these convictions, and to understand the rational basis of them. But our powers of reason are so fallible that we can never hope to reach certainty or confidence about this basis. Kantian ethics may be (my own conviction is that it certainly is) the best kind of theory human beings have devised as a background for their moral reflections. But the ground of its principal value, which we explored in Chapter 5, is vulnerable to doubt. In Chapter 7 we saw that Kantian ethics depends on the conviction that our will is free, but it admits that we do not understand how this freedom is possible, and that the very idea of it may be in principle incomprehensible to us. Chapter 12 concluded that the Kantian position on the moral justification of punishment is threatened at the deepest level with inconsistency. On numerous topics dealt with throughout this book – the extent of human personhood, the nature of the moral virtues, the demands of duty, the nature of conscience, the conditions of social justice, the principles governing sexual conduct and the prohibition on truthfulness – I am aware that the Kantian position I defend remains deeply questionable and controversial. The study of ethical theory is nevertheless valuable to us as reflective moral agents, despite the fact that if pursued honestly and diligently, it will leave us in a state of hopeless perplexity about the foundations of morality from which there is no prospect of escape. Or rather – it is utterly indispensable to us as moral agents *precisely because* it is bound to condemn us to that state.

We justifiably believe that it would be wrong to tell a lie and that our present society is fundamentally unjust. But I do not think we are justified in *believing* any philosophical theory about ethics. The most we could be entitled to *believe* about Kantian ethics, for instance, is that the arguments in favor of it are stronger than the objections against it, that it is on the whole a better guide to philosophical reflection on ethics than any of the competing theories we know of, and therefore that we should assent to its claims and defend them when the occasion arises.[8] But even the best philosophical theory is one beset with doubts, and its competitors always have some relative advantages on certain issues. (This is just the way it is in philosophy.) So we should never allow these troubling considerations to drop so far out of our reflections as to permit ourselves to *believe* any philosophical theory.

There can be nothing more important to us in this brief flicker of life than whether we have acted as we should or have failed to do so (or as Kant would say: "in conformity to duty" or "contrary to duty"). Yet the ultimate basis of our judgments about this matter of supreme importance will always remain obscure and uncertain.

This is the way I propose that Kantian ethics should now think about the contrast that Kant himself drew between "the starry heavens" (the prospect of which humbles us to insignificance) and "the moral law" through which we gain a sense of our sublime dignity (KpV 5:161–3). Kantian ethics no longer needs (if it ever did) the supernaturalism implied in Kant's contrast, but in the contrast I am proposing in its place is also something that is earnest and uplifting yet at the same time frustrating, humiliating, frightening and comfortless. It is one of the tasks of philosophy to make us aware that neither religion nor science offer us any prospect of certainty or any consolation as we face the absurdity of the human condition.

Our chief business in life is that our thought and conduct should live up to the dignity of rational nature. But our human condition has arisen, and is sustained, by the merest cosmic accident. It can never have any greater meaning than we, with our feeble and errant rational powers, are able to give it by acting as we ought, according to reason.

Notes

Chapter 1. Reason

1. "Kant's ethics and Kantian ethics" is the title of a course given by Onora O'Neill at Cambridge University during Lent term, 2005. See http://www.phil.cam.ac.uk/u_grads/course_material/course_material_2.html and http://www.phil.cam.ac.uk/u_grads/Tripos/Ethics/course_material/1_kant_outline_05.pdf.
2. Simon Blackburn, *Ruling Passions* (Cambridge: Cambridge University Press, 1998), pp. 246–8.
3. Richard Taylor, *Good and Evil A new direction: A forceful attack on the rationalistic tradition in ethics* (Buffalo, N.Y.: Prometheus Books, 1984), p. xii. I am grateful to Simon Shengjian Xie for reminding me of Blackburn's and Taylor's vividly worded statements of the common image of Kant.
4. "Il n'est rien si dissociable et sociable que l'homme: l'un par son vice, l'autre par sa nature." Michel Eyquem de Montaigne, "De la solitude," *Essais*, ed. André Tournon. Paris: Imprimerie nationale Éditions, 1998, 1:388. "There is nothing more unsociable than Man, and nothing more sociable: unsociable by his vice, sociable by his nature," "Of Solitude," *The Complete Essays*, tr. M. A. Screech. London: Penguin Books, 1991, p. 267.
5. See Charles W. Mills, "Kant's Untermenschen," in Andrew Valls (ed.), *Race and Racism in Modern Philosophy* (Ithaca, N.Y.: Cornell University Press, 2005); Reinhard Brandt, *D'Artagnan und die Urteilstafel: Über die Ordnungsprinzip der europäischen Kulturgeschichte* (Stuttgart: Steiner, 1991); Tseney Serequeberhan, "Eurocentrism in Philosophy: The Case of Immanuel Kant," *Philosophical Forum* 27 (1996), pp. 333–56.
6. See Robin May Schott (ed.), *Feminist Interpretations of Immanuel Kant* (University Park: Pennsylvania State Press, 1997). Not everything in this collection fits neatly into one side or the other of the controversy as I have described it. But the papers by Schott, Sedgwick, Schröder, and Baier pretty clearly belong to the anti-Kantian side, while the paper by Baron weighs in on the Kantian side. See also Susan Mendus, "Kant: An honest but narrow-minded bourgeois?" in Howard Williams (ed.), *Essays on Kant's Political Philosophy* (Chicago: University of Chicago Press, 1992); Elizabeth Brake, "Justice and Virtue in Kant's Account of Marriage," *Kantian Review* 9 (2005), pp. 58–94; and Lara Denis, "Kant's Ethical Duties and

Their Feminist Implications, in Samantha Brennan (ed.), *Feminist Moral Philosophy*, Canadian Journal of Philosophy Supplementary Volume (2002), pp. 157–87.

7. Marcia Baron has pointed this out very effectively in her article in the collection cited in the previous note.

8. There is a good discussion of Forster on race in Frederick C. Beiser, *Enlightenment, Revolution & Romanticism* (Cambridge, Mass.: Harvard University Press, 1992), Chapter 7: Georg Forster, the German Jacobin, especially pp. 156–70.

9. See Emanuel Chukwudi Eze, "The Color of Reason: The Idea of 'Race' in Kant's Anthropology," in Katherine M. Faull (ed.), *Anthropology and the German Enlightenment* (Lewisburg, Pa.: Bucknell University Press, 1994), pp. 200–41; Robert Bernasconi, "Who invented the concept of race? Kant's role in the Enlightenment construction of race," in Bernasconi (ed.), *Race* (Oxford: Blackwell, 2001), pp. 11–36, and Bernasconi, "Kant as the ultimate source of racism," in Tommy Lott and Julie Ward (eds.), *Philosophers on Race* (Oxford: Oxford University Press, 2002), pp. 145–66.

10. It is sometimes observed that in his essay on teleological principles in philosophy (Ak 8:174 note) Kant quotes from a pro-slavery document, with apparent approval of something it says (though not directly of its defense of slavery). But it is sometimes nevertheless inferred from this passage that Kant must have favored the institution of slavery, or at any rate that he did not oppose it. But Kant explicitly regards free status as an innate and inalienable right (MS 6:237). He holds that all labor must be subject to a contract between employer and laborer (MS 6:285) and that the terms of such a contract can never include the ownership of the laborer by the employer or the relation of *dominus servi* (MS 6:283). In the Doctrine of Right, his condemnation of the institution of serfdom (which still existed in Prussia in his day) is repeated, emphatic, and unequivocal, and it is presented in terms that likewise condemn any system in which one person is owned by another (MS 6:241, 283, 324, 330, 454).

11. For example, Thomas Hill and Bernard Boxill, "Kant on Race," in Boxill (ed.), *Race and Racism* (Oxford: Oxford University Press, 2001), pp. 448–72; and Marcia Baron, "Reading Kant Selectively," in Dieter Schönecker and Thomas Zwenger (eds.), *Kant verstehen/Understanding Kant: Über die Interpretation philosophischer Texte* (Darmstadt: Wissenschaftliche Buchgesellschaft, 2001), pp. 32–46. But perhaps I say this is the position of "leading" writers only because I have defended it myself: See *Kant's Ethical Thought* (New York: Cambridge University Press, 1999), pp. 3–7, 335, 338–9.

12. Laurence Thomas has recently put forth an interesting argument that the usual position taken by Kantian philosophers is unstable. It is not possible, he thinks, consistently to maintain the principled egalitarianism that modern Kantians want to find in Kant along with accepting the degrees of intellectual superiority and inferiority that Kant himself thought obtained between the races. Laurence Thomas, "Moral Equality and Natural Inferiority," *Social Theory and Practice*, 31/3 (2005), pp. 379–404. But the plausibility of Thomas's argument would depend on the precise extent of the intellectual superiority and inferiority Kant ascribed to the races. The stability of the resulting position might be maintained if the degree of intellectual differences between races does not prevent the "inferiors" from being fully autonomous moral agents. (The same applies to gender differences.) But if Kant thought women and nonwhites were no more

capable of governing their lives than small children, then it would be difficult to maintain his moral egalitarianism in practice except between white males. Of course the whole issue would be moot for present-day Kantians who find Kant's empirical theories of gender and race every bit as false (not to mention offensive) as the critics do. For them there would be no problem of "instability" at all.

13. Pauline Kleingeld, "Kant's Second Thoughts on Race," *Philosophical Quarterly* 57 (2007), pp. 573–92.

14. C. C. Girtanner, *Über das Kantische Prinzip für die Naturgeschichte* (Göttingen, 1796).

15. This was a position that, down to the twentieth century, occasioned charges that Kant was culturally naïve and incapable of appreciating what "civilized" people have had to deal with in their encounters with "savages" in other parts of the world. See, for example, Fritz Medicus, "Kant's Philosophy of History," *Kant-Studien* 54 (1900), pp. 61–7.

16. Lizzie rudely rebuffs Darcy in Volume II, Chapter XI. See Jane Austen, *Pride and Prejudice*, Norton Critical Edition (New York: Norton, 1966), pp. 131–3. He is obviously beginning to rethink things already when he writes the letter to her in the very next chapter. By the time they meet at his estate in Volume III, Chapter I (p. 173), he has plainly decided to earn her better opinion, which he endeavors to do by saving her sister from disgrace (Volume III, Chapter IV, pp. 188–90) (though Lizzie does not learn of his part in it until later). So the full conversion of his opinion seems to take about a dozen chapters (the last eight of Volume II and the first four of Volume III). It is one of Austen's typical ingenious ironies that we first think the title of the novel refers to Darcy's pride and Lizzie's prejudice, but the deeper meaning refers to the change in Darcy – his abandonment of his irrational class prejudice, and his consequent need to win Lizzie by mending her wounded pride.

17. For example, if you are deliberating about what to do, you have, in a purely formal respect, the end of making a decision and acting on it. If it should turn out that the best reason for your deciding and then doing something (e.g. keeping a promise, helping a friend, going to your violin lesson) is that doing it is a moral duty that is commanded by a categorical imperative, then it will also be true (in this formal sense) that you follow the categorical imperative as a way of reaching your end in view – namely, of deciding what to do and doing what you decide. But this truth does not contradict Kant's claim that a categorical imperative constrains us independently of any independently given end. For of course he does not mean ends such as "deciding what I have best reason, all things considered, for doing" but some more material end, such as maximizing my perfection or happiness, pleasing God, and so forth. The ends of "deciding what to do" or "determining what I have the best reason to do" or even "doing what I should do, all things considered" are not pre-given material ends, grounding the determinate decision, but are already built into the very exercise of practical reason. So to say that reason is a matter of determining how to reach them does not decide either way whether there are categorical imperatives. I think many who say they find some fundamental incoherence in the very notion of a categorical imperative manage to make this momentous discovery by attending to some entirely formal end of this sort, supposing that categorical imperatives must be excluding even that kind of end, and then a bit later, in a

moment of felicitous confusion, they substitute their favorite material end for this formal one, thus enabling them for the first time really to disagree with Kant's view that there can be a kind of reason for action (the reason grounding a categorical imperative) that does not depend on any such pre-given ends' being achieved. Their argument, however, now rests on a fallacious inference, facilitated first by their failure to understand what Kant means by a "categorical imperative" and then by a convenient confusion between a purely formal end built into rational decision making and a determinate material end on the basis of which the decision might be made.

18. Reason is not "procedural" even in the looser sense John Rawls and some of his followers take it to be. See Rawls, Lectures Kant, especially Chapters II and VI, for this interesting but fundamentally erroneous understanding of Kantian practical reason. We will see in Chapter 4 why in this respect the Formula of the Law of Nature is not, and cannot possibly be, what Rawls's "Kantian constructivism" would make out of it.

19. But the essential intersubjectivity of reason applies critically to many less demented conceptions of practical reason, such as Rawls' notion of "deliberative rationality," which is more Sidgwickian than Kantian. See John Rawls TJ, pp. 416–24.

20. John Rawls sometimes draws a distinction between 'rationality' and "reasonableness" – awarding the first term to formal theories of practical reason, or alternatively, a Humean conception of reason (that restricts in certain essential ways what can count as a reason), and reserving the latter term for a less artificial notion – though one that he still thinks can be codified, at least loosely, in a "CI-procedure." (See John Rawls Lectures, pp. 46–7, 240–1.) I have been told by people who knew Rawls well that he sometimes thought better of this distinction and doubted whether he should have drawn it at all. I would like to believe these stories, because I think the distinction is fundamentally misguided. It grants legitimacy to false, formalistic theories of rationality and sometimes to the sophistical caricatures that contrast "rationality" with decency and humanity. T. M. Scanlon employs a similar distinction, even though he agrees that the theories with which the use of the term "rationality" is associated are mistaken (Scanlon, p. 192). I will use the terms "rational" and "reasonable" pretty much interchangeably. It is sometimes noted that the German word *vernünftig* covers all the ground occupied in English by both of them, so this practice can do no harm in giving an account of Kant's views.

21. See Christine Korsgaard, "The reasons we can share: An attack on the distinction between agent-relative and agent-neutral values," CKE, pp. 275–310.

22. This is of course exactly what was done to the Enlightenment notion of reason in Horkheimer and Adorno's famous (and utterly misguided) polemic *Dialectic of Enlightenment*, tr. John Cumming (New York: Continuum, 1999). Although the Enlightenment was never a monolithic movement, there is no philosopher whose views on reason are more definitively Enlightenment views than Kant, and there is no figure in the history of philosophy who was more firmly opposed to the reduction of rationality to instrumental reason that Horkheimer and Adorno take to be essential to "Enlightenment" when they identify its fundamental spirit as that of manipulation (of people as well as nature) for arbitrary ends. It is rather as if someone (ignoring the Pauline epistles and everything that flowed

from them) should locate the essence of Christianity in the view that salvation depends on following the law and should then attack Christianity as nothing but Pharisaism.

23. Kant, like some other early modern philosophers (especially Descartes and Locke), thinks about propositional attitudes and epistemology in a different way from the way we usually do today. For us, the generic attitude is "belief" and it is about *beliefs* that we ask whether they are true, justified, and so on. For these other early moderns, however, the generic notion is *assent*. See Locke, *Essay Concerning Human Understanding*, ed. P. Nidditch (Oxford: Clarendon Press, 1975), Book IV, Ch. XVI–XVII, pp. 657–88. This is an important difference, because belief (as we understand it) is both a more dispositional and a less active state of the mind than assent, which is occurrent rather than dispositional and to a considerable extent voluntary, as other actions are. In Locke and Kant, "belief" (or "faith" – or *Glaube*, which covers the range of both English words) is a different concept from the one designated by theories of knowledge where "belief" is the genus, and "knowledge" is something like justified true belief. For Locke and Kant, "belief" is a certain "degree" of assent, marked by a more objective mode of justification, and perhaps a greater degree of justified certainty, than mere "opinion," but a lesser degree of these than "knowledge." Neither concept of belief seems to me "right" (or "wrong"); they are different, both are legitimate, and it is important not to confuse them. But an epistemology based on assent is much better suited to a view of things, like Locke's or Kant's, that places great value on our rational regulation of doxastic states and activities. For *assent* is something we can do conditionally, for certain purposes or from a certain point of view. In the course of an argument from premises we may not think are true, we may assent (conditionally) to conclusions that follow from them. A scientist who does not believe a hypothesis (in our usual sense) may assent to it for the purposes of pursuing a certain line of inquiry. And for Kant, we may assent to certain judgments (about God, freedom, or immortality) from a practical point of view only. But none of this applies to *belief*, in the generic, dispositional, and perhaps mainly involuntary sense that we tend to use the term. In that sense, you either believe something or you don't; there may be degrees of certainty or confidence attaching to your belief, but believing is something you don't do only conditionally, for certain purposes or from a certain point of view. Kant may exploit this ambiguity illegitimately in dealing with issues of religious *Glaube*, because there may be relevant differences between the practical faith his doctrines purportedly justify and the religious faith he would like his audience to believe they justify. Religious faith may be a more unqualified, generic, and involuntary state than the rationally responsible form of assent for certain purposes that Kant offers us. On the other hand, it is arguable that a rational person should be especially careful about "belief" in the generic and passive sense, precisely because it is less subject to rational regulation. If we move from "faith" as a passive state to "faith" in the Kantian sense of subjectively justified assent, there may be a loss from an emotional point of view (because that sort of faith, when not based on objective arguments or evidence, involves an abdication of rational responsibility, permitting belief to be determined by wishful thinking and self-indulgent, self-deceptive motives of all sorts). But there is a big gain in rational autonomy and self-honesty.

24. This important concept in Kantian ethics, especially in relation to the conception of the highest good, is explored by Stephen Engstrom, "The Concept of the Highest Good in Kant's Moral Theory," *Philosophy and Phenomenological Research* 52 (1992).

25. There is a good discussion of this point in Scanlon, pp. 25–30. I think we would also call someone 'irrational' if the reasons they deliberately ignore are sufficiently obvious and important. For instance (contrary to what Hume says) it seems irrational for anyone to ignore the destruction of the world as a possible reason for allowing his finger to be scratched.That we may not consider moral reasons in general as sufficiently obvious and important for this to be true of them says something about our culture, its 'common sense', and consequently the common word usage that reflects these. But it does not provide an argument that there are no reasons to comply with moral demands.

26. This happens when such theorists say that rationality is only a matter of the aims and considerations that individual agents acknowledge – as though their declarations (possibly not in good faith) were the final arbiter. There is something here analogous to Pascal's famous satire of the Jesuit doctrine that no one can do evil unless he does it with a bad conscience: "They will all be damned, these half-sinners who retain some love of virtue. But as for those open sinners, hardened sinners, undiluted, complete, and consummate sinners, hell cannot hold them: they have deceived the devil by their complete surrender" (Pascal, *Provincial Letters*, tr. A. J. Krailsheimer. Harmondsworth: Penguin, 1967), p. 65. It is likewise with those who don't consider anything contrary to reason unless it runs afoul of the aims and preferences the agent acknowledges and endorses. The deepest forms of unreason, those that resolutely and systematically reject the strongest reasons – for example, the cool and meticulous planning of those who ran the Nazi death camps – come out on these theories as perfectly rational.

27. Compare the contrary pronouncement of Bernard Williams: "Can we define a notion of rationality where the action rational for A is in no way relative to A's existing motivations? No" (Williams, p. 112). Williams shows that he takes the question of whether something belongs to "A's existing motivations" as an empirical question, the answer to which might vary from agent to agent. No doubt it is an empirical question whether A is a *person* (a rational being responsible for her actions). But it is not an empirical question whether every person has reasons to respect the rights and dignity of rational beings, or to be concerned about their welfare. It is an essential property of a morally responsible rational being that it has such reasons, even if A refuses to be moved by them and even denies that they provide her with any motivation for action. This is not a point on which empirical investigations might reveal that some rational beings have such reasons and others do not.

Chapter 2. Moral Worth

1. I have argued in detail elsewhere for my interpretation of the opening pages of the First Section of the *Groundwork*. In this chapter I present only a brief version of that reading and the argument for it. See "The Good Will," *Philosophical Topics*, Vol. 31, No. 2, Fall 2003; "The Good Without Limitation," *Groundwork for the Metaphysics of Morals*, edited by Dieter Schönecker and Christoph Horn

in collaboration with Corinna Mieth (Berlin: Walter de Gruyter, 2006); *Kant's Ethical Thought* (New York: Cambridge University Press, 1999), pp. 19–47.

2. In Kant's own examples in this discussion (G 4:397–9), there is apparently a countervailing inclination in the case of the man tempted to suicide and the gout sufferer tempted to imprudent indulgence in unhealthful food or drink. But there is no countervailing inclination in the case of the grieving man who must tear himself out of this sad condition in order to help others from duty. This may be significant, because there is nothing inherently immoral, or indicative of a bad character, in the desire to live a happy life or the desire for gustatory pleasure, but it might well be a sign of bad character if we had a positive inclination not to help those in need. Sometimes Kant is taken to be denying these obvious facts, or even charged with thinking that beneficent actions are positively bad unless we had to overcome some positive inclination not to help others. A careful reading of his examples, however, exonerates him of such nasty charges.

3. Kant's view is that genuine moral worth pertains to character and is a worth we give ourselves, rather than a worth given us by nature or fortune. This should not be confused with the position, attributed to Kant by Bernard Williams (and plainly alluded to by Blackburn in the passage quoted in the Introduction), that there can be no such thing as "moral luck" and that our moral theory should be dictated by a view of ourselves and the world that locates moral value only in what is immune to luck. See Williams, pp. 21–2, 38. This latter position is, I think, quite alien to Kant's ethical thought. Kant does think that the worth we give ourselves – worth of character – is a higher worth than any that could come from the fortune of having a good temperament (G 4:398–9). But he does not hold that there is no moral value at all in a good temperament, or even that such a central moral quality as moral *virtue* can ever be entirely disentangled in practice from temperament. This point will be further discussed in Chapter 8. In the early pages of the *Groundwork*, Kant's aim is to elicit agreement from common rational moral cognition to the claim that when we think of good will or character in abstraction from temperament or its other empirical concomitants, it is valued more highly than any of them and regarded as having an authentically moral worth they do not have. This aim involves no claim that in real life good will or character can be known, or that it can even ever exist, entirely in separation from these other things. It is a misreading of Kant's aims as well as his position – a misreading as common as it is basic – to come away from the *Groundwork* thinking that the latter claim is what matters to him, or even that he wants to make that claim.

4. This is the invalid inference that someone might draw from a Kantian theory that is displayed in Schiller's famous epigram:

> Scruples of conscience
> I like to serve my friends, but unfortunately I do it with inclination
> And so I often am bothered by the thought that I am not virtuous.
> Decision
> There is no other way but this! You must seek to despise them,
> And do with repugnance what duty bids you
> (Friedrich Schiller, Xenien, The Philosophers in Goethe, *Werke*, ed. Erich Trunz (Munich: Beck, 1982), Volume 1, p. 28.

The Xenien were co-written by Schiller and Goethe. I will not try to decide whether Schiller thought Kant himself was a proper target of the satire here. My point is that if he did think it, the thought involved a fundamental misunderstanding of Kant's position.

5. For more of these, see the discussions cited in note 1.
6. Empiricist moral psychologies, of course, hold that all feelings and desires are of merely empirical origin. When Kant's views are being reported by empiricists, they often simply translate Kant's denial that action from duty is action from inclination (empirical desire) as the claim that action from duty involves no feeling or desire at all (because their theories refuse to acknowledge the very kind of desire and feeling Kant holds to be present in these cases). Consequently, the seemingly innocent translation (of 'inclination' as 'desire') actually involves a direct begging of the question against the most fundamental tenet of Kant's entire moral psychology. When Kant's assertions are subjected to it, this guarantees from the start that his position will appear repugnant, if not downright nonsensical – which is exactly how Kant himself would regard the "Kantian" position when so translated.

Chapter 3. Ethical Theory

1. Samuel Freeman has convincingly argued that Rawls came to regard Kantian constructivism as an unworkable doctrine and thought of it as only a transitional phase in his own thought. But he continued to think of Kant himself as a "Kantian constructivist." Freeman, "The Burdens of Public Justification," *Philosophy, Politics, and Economics*, Vol. 6, No. 1 (February 2007).
2. Rawls rightly reports that Kant is a "constructivist" about mathematics and parts of physics (Rawls, Lectures, p. 238). But I see no textual grounds at all for ascribing to him an analogous position in ethics. However, Rawls might be seen as sending us some mixed messages regarding what the "CI-Procedure" is supposed to accomplish in Kant. On the one hand, it is supposed to "present in procedural form all the requirements of practical reason" (Rawls, Lectures, p. 165) and constitute "a procedural representation of all the criteria that are relevant in guiding our moral reasoning" (Rawls, Lectures, p. 217). Thus its function is to "construct the content of the [moral] doctrine" (p. 239), which includes "specifying the content of the duties of justice and virtue" (p. 237). On the other hand, the CI-Procedure "is no algorithm intended to yield, more or less mechanically, a correct judgment" (p. 166). He also says that the content of moral doctrine "can never be specified completely" and is "always subject to error and correction" (p. 239n). Rawls does not make explicit with respect to what we are supposed to be able to correct a procedure that claims to include a complete specification of all the criteria of practical reason, or how its specification of duties could be incomplete or erroneous, if the content of the doctrine, and the system of duties, involves nothing except what is "constructed" according to the procedure. But the scales drop from our eyes as soon as we realize that the ultimate criterion here, which is being taken for granted without his even bothering to mention it, is still consilience with "intuitions" or "considered judgments." The dominant (Sidgwickian) model seems for Rawls to be the only game in town.

3. I do not agree with Rawls or his "constructivist" followers when they take it to be a Kantian position that "there are no moral facts" and that moral principles do not rest on real or objective values – or as they often like to put it, on any "independent realm or order of values" (Rawls, "Kantian Constructivism in Moral Theory," *The Dewey Lectures*, in John Rawls, *Collected Papers*, Samuel Freeman, ed. [Cambridge, Mass.: Harvard University Press, 1999], p. 307). Kant's explicit statements about the objective value of humanity or rational nature, for example, give the lie to Christine Korsgaard's assertion that "For Kant acts of valuing are the source of all value – all legitimate normative claims – not the other way around. Obligation does not arise from value: rather obligation and value arise together from acts of legislative will" (Korsgaard FC, p. 95).

I suspect that antirealist-sounding assertions may mean quite different things coming from different "constructivists." I don't say that the constructivists are unaware of this. For example, Thomas Hill admits that "'Kantian constructivism', unfortunately, is a broad label that has been used to characterize significantly different views." Hill, p. 61. Onora O'Neill speaks of "constructivisms" in the plural. O'Neill, pp. 206–18. We find Christine Korsgaard asserting that "Good maxims are the products of our legislative wills. In that sense, values are created by human beings" (Korsgaard, SN, p. 112) while Barbara Herman declares that "we are not to mistake the idea of construction for some form of creation" (Herman, p. 214). Both, however – and "Kantian constructivists" more generally – seem to want to find a middle path between possible positions: For Korsgaard (Korsgaard SN, pp. 164–6), it is between "voluntarism" and "realism," while for Herman, constructivism is "a way between the poles of naturalism and metaphysical realism about value" (p. 210). O'Neill acknowledges that constructivism has a problem "finding a stable third position" between "realism and relativism" (O'Neill, p. 206); there is no space here to consider O'Neill's proposal that constructivism must appeal to "the possible consent of actual agents" (O'Neill, p. 217), or to decide whether it avoids the Scylla of relativism and the Charybdis of realism. Although Herman denies that "construction" is "some form of creation," Herman also says that "the idea of construction suggests the bringing into being of a moral world that is intelligible to us and expressive of our nature as reasonable and rational beings" (Herman, p. 214). It is not clear what is "brought into being" (is it values, or maxims, or a social world conforming to them?) or how this "bringing into being" is not any "form of creation."

The problem with constructivism may be that this is an issue where there is no middle path, but only a hard choice (as between right and wrong). If so, then it would not be surprising that constructivists have to hem and haw, adopting ambiguous or self-contradictory formulations and never arriving at any clear position that avoids the extremes they find so odious. However, I doubt that "constructivism" even represents any distinctive position at all within metaethics. For a defense of this last claim with respect to Christine Korsgaard (the Rawlsian who has developed this metaethical position most extensively and prominently), see Nadeem J. Z. Hussain and Nishiten Shah, "Misunderstanding Metaethics: Korsgaard's Rejection of Realism," *Oxford Studies in Metaethics*, edited by Russ Shafer-Landau (Oxford: Oxford University Press, 2006), Volume 1, pp. 265–94. At any rate, no distinctive metaethics or metaphysics of value is implied in (or excluded by) Rawls's original idea that the dominant or Sidgwickian project in ethical theory should be carried out through an account of practical reason stated in terms of a set of procedural requirements. I will have more to say on the metaethics of Kantian ethics in Chapter 6.

4. Marc Hauser, Fiery Cushman, Liane Young, R. Kang-Jin, and John Mikhail, "A dissociation between moral judgments and justifications," *Mind and Language* (forthcoming). These authors appear to think that 90 percent is a great deal of agreement. But in some matters of moral judgment, it has to be regarded as entirely possible that 90 percent are wrong and 10 percent or fewer are right. Not long after September 11, 2001, George W. Bush had approval ratings of over 90 percent. (Now there's a counterexample for you!) The degree of consensus among many perceptual intuitions does not, therefore, seem to me sufficient to qualify them as trustworthy data for moral philosophy. See also Rebecca Saxe's review of scientific literature on morality in the *Boston Review*, http://bostonreview.net/BR30.5/saxe.html.

5. I have heard it said that when Republicans conduct opinion polls, they frame the questions so as to get the answers that support the policies they already favor, whereas Democrats tend to conduct polls in order to find out what the public wants, and then frame their policies so as to do the "will of the people." If so, then the Democrats might seem to have their hearts in the right place, and you might think their method would lead sooner to electoral victory. But given the way opinion polls work, and how people respond to them, it is not surprising that this difference might have led to Republicans' winning many more elections than Democrats.

6. The intuitional method has spawned an interesting empirical research project, championed by John Mikhail, in which empirical data on people's responses to trolley problems are used to argue for, and to investigate the principles of, an alleged innate moral faculty – analogous to the innate linguistic faculty postulated in Chomskian linguistics. John Mikhail, *Rawls' Linguistic Analogy* (New York: Cambridge University Press, forthcoming). See also Marc Hauser, *Moral Minds: How Nature Designed Our Universal Sense of Right and Wrong* (New York: Ecco/ HarperCollins, 2006). The ultimate aim of this project might turn out rather similar to what I will later claim (in Chapter 6) is Kant's own position: that moral principles rest on the *nature* of will or practical reason as a faculty. But some of the points being made in this section give me grounds for doubting that Mikhail's approach is the right way to investigate the nature of will or practical reason.

7. John Rawls, "The Independence of Moral Theory," *Proceedings and Addresses of the American Philosophical Association* 48 (1974–5), p. 9. It may be that under specific circumstances, different people will make different judgments about how a moral principle is to be applied, one deciding that it permits a given action, another that it prohibits it, or one thinking an exception to the principle is warranted and another not. I think we must assume even here that there is only one *correct* judgment (about a given action, under specific circumstances), because otherwise we are admitting a plural (or merely relative) moral *truth*, which would be nonsense. But it may be impossible that people should always agree in such cases and impossible to know who is right or wrong. It may also happen, in certain difficult cases, that there simply is no correct answer to the question of whether a given action is right – not all moral questions have a "right" answer. Such indeterminacies of moral judgment, however, are not matters of moral *theory* but only

of the *application* of the principles and rules that it is the business of moral theory to determine. We might be tempted to consider differing judgments about how moral rules apply, hence what to do under given circumstances, as different "intuitions," and differing ways of applying rules under given conditions as differing "reflective equilibria" between principles and intuitions. If we thought Rawls was talking about this, then his claim that "there is no single correct moral conception" – in the sense that there is no single way for moral theory to decide every particular case, or determine the detailed fit between principles and particular cases – would seem entirely correct and reasonable. But it is important to realize that this is *not* what he is claiming. For different "moral conceptions" in the sense he means would be different moral principles or moral rules, which might be justified with equal validity according to the method of reflective equilibrium. And that would introduce into moral theory a plural or relativistic notion of moral truth, which (once again) would be as nonsensical as a plural (or merely relative) truth about mathematics, or physics or history. Of course many questions in moral theory (as in other areas of philosophy, or in history or even in physics) will be forever debated. Sensible people will regard themselves as fallible about such matters even as they argue forcefully for one side or the other. And different positions (at least within very broad limits) should always be tolerated. But moral theory aims at deciding which fundamental moral principles, and which moral rules, are *the correct* ones. Here there can be acceptable disagreement between differing (incompatible) views, but no plurality of *true* or *correct* views on the same theoretical issue. To confuse the idea that there might be no determinable right answer about how moral rules apply with the very different idea that there might be a plurality of correct conceptions points to another way in which the dominant conception of ethical theory locates the relation between general moral principles or rules and particular moral judgments in the wrong place.

8. There are, of course, some who profess skepticism about moral truth, especially about the existence of fundamental moral truths. (Kantian ethics is not skeptical about this, of course, and we shall see why in Chapters 4–6.) Some seem to think there can be particular moral truths without any fundamental moral truth, while others are skeptics, relativists, or nihilists about all moral truth. The former position is superficial, unstable, unphilosophical. More radical moral skeptics usually see themselves as iconoclasts, but it is less often a position people seriously believe than one that nonphilosophers like to try out in discussions they do not take seriously with the aim of showing how bold and clever they are. This is Hume's view of the matter, for instance. He finds those who "dispute the reality of moral distinctions" to be "disingenuous," moved by "a spirit of opposition, or from a desire of showing wit and ingenuity, superior to the rest of mankind" (Hume E p. 169). I think Hume is right that moral skeptics usually seem intellectually self-conceited (often fatuously so). We should demand some proof, in the form of their actual conduct, that they really mean what they are saying. Of course, if their proofs are too convincing, this exposes them to moral blame (and they might even end up in jail). Few philosophers who undertake to defend radical moral skepticism (especially beginning students of philosophy) realize what a fine line they need to walk, if they want us to take them seriously, between being reprehensible and being merely silly.

9. It was also the way he thought about the metaphysics of morals, in relation to existing religious and political institutions (he was a republican and an outspoken opponent of standing armies and permanent armaments living under a military despotism, and a proponent of thinking for oneself in religious matters living under a regime that attempted to enforce conservative orthodoxy on clergy and academics by legal compulsion).

10. David Phillips, in a private communication, has pressed these points about Sidgwick and sees them as calling into question my claim that Sidgwick is really a proponent of what I am calling the dominant conception of ethical theory. He suggests that Sidgwick's approach may not really be different from the one I ascribe to Kant and Mill. I think this judgment gives Sidgwick too little credit for originality and fails to credit him with a historical influence he seems to me plainly to have had. But it would be quite correct to insist that it is entirely unjust to blame Sidgwick himself for some of the excesses of "trolley problem" ethics, or for some of the uncritical uses of the dominant method I have criticized above. And it would be quite correct to see him as appreciating some of the strengths of the more traditional kind of ethical theory I am associating with Kant and Mill. My point is that Sidgwick is the inventor of the now dominant model, but he was a lot smarter (and a lot more worth studying!) than many of those who now employ it.

11. As for the claim that moral judgments are easier to make than prudential ones, there is no reason to ascribe to Kant the general thesis that this generalizes beyond the example he is discussing here, in relation to which it plays a role in enabling him to derive the first formula of the moral principle. In many cases, it is obvious that prudential judgments are easier to make than moral ones. Suppose I am working for a corporation, or an agency of the government, and I see some of my colleagues beginning to engage in patterns of wrongdoing or illegality. I clearly realize it would be highly imprudent for me to bring their misconduct to light (through the press, or the criminal justice system), but it may be a much more difficult question to decide at precisely what point the gravity of their misconduct justifies my playing the role of whistleblower, outweighing the loyalty I owe to the organization or to my co-workers personally. Nothing in Kantian ethics requires me to see the moral question as easier than the prudential one in a case like this.

12. In calling the model "foundational," I do not intend to associate it (affirmatively or negatively) with "foundationalism" in epistemology (or moral epistemology). A foundational theory, as I understand it, recognizes a fundamental value and a fundamental principle. But it remains open how these might be discovered or justified, and in the model as I describe it there is considerable looseness in how the principle itself is to be employed in reaching and justifying moral conclusions.

13. Bush is famously no diligent student of universal human rights or the international legal documents that seek their protection. Therefore it is no surprise that he also misquotes the Geneva Convention. It speaks not of "outrages on human dignity" but of "outrages on personal dignity" (as among the "acts [that] are and shall remain prohibited at any time and in any place whatsoever with respect to ["persons presently taking no active part in hostilities,"

including – but not limited to – prisoners of war]" [*Third Geneva Convention* (1949), Article 3 (c)]). The point is that this prohibition covers *even persons who have been enemy combatants* (whether or not they have been part of a uniformed national army – a red herring invented by legal sophistry) at any time when they are *hors de combat,* as they surely are after having been detained.

14. It was an important question in the early reception of the critical philosophy whether the truths about our faculties that ground cognition and action are truths of empirical psychology or are somehow known to us *a priori.* Kant, along with most of later transcendental philosophers, seems to have taken the latter position, while the former one was argued by such Kantians as J. F. Fries and later Leonard Nelson. If the position of Fries and Nelson is correct, then the moral principle might be *a priori* in the sense Kant meant, and yet the constitution of practical reason, on which this *a priori* law depends, might itself be a matter for empirical investigation. Kant's official conception of the *a priori* is that cognition is *a priori* when it is wholly independent of experience. This formulation seems clear enough at first glance, but its meaning obviously depends on what we count as possibly contrasting with "experience." If we mean by "experience" only those data to which our faculty of reason is applied, then principles grounded in the nature of that faculty itself will count as *a priori* even if we think the faculty of reason is part of the empirical world and its nature (and principles) are known at least in part through experience – although then the experience through which the faculty of reason and its principles are known will not count as "experience" for the purposes of the claim that principles of reason are *a priori.* These considerations also point to a way in which Kant's use of "*a priori*" may sometimes deviate from his official formulation in the direction of an older conception of *a priori* knowledge: According to the older conception, to know something *a priori* is to know it from its ground rather than from its consequences or effects. (This is the sense in which Descartes considers the "ontological" proof of God's existence in the Fifth Meditation *a priori* – because it is drawn from God's nature – in contrast to the proof in the Third Meditation, which is drawn from our idea of God, which is argued to be possible only as an effect of God.) Desmond Hogan has argued that this older sense of *a priori* occurs far more often in Kant's arguments and theories than has been commonly appreciated and plays a crucial role in his claims about the unknowability of things in themselves. See Hogan, "How to know unknowable things in themselves" (unpublished at this writing). If we use "*a priori*" in this older sense, then the principle of morality is clearly *a priori* if it can be shown (as Kant plainly means to do) that it is grounded in the nature of our will or faculty of practical reason, irrespective of whether the nature of the will or practical reason can be known wholly independently of experience.

15. M. Baron, P. Pettit, and M. Slote, *Three Methods of Ethics* (Oxford: Blackwell, 1997), p. 6.

16. Scanlon, pp. 198–202, provides a good discussion of this point. The so-called "particularist" position that there are no such rules at all is intelligible only against the background of the dominant conception of ethical theory, and even of an exaggerated interpretation of what it thinks rules can do.

17. Sartre, "Existentialism is a Humanism," in W. Kaufmann (ed.), *Existentialism from Dostoevsky to Sartre* (New York: Meridian, 1956), pp. 295–8.

Chapter 4. The Moral Law

1. In his other writings, and especially in his unpublished reflections, Kant toys with a number of other ways of systematizing the three formulas:

Formula:	FUL (FLN)	FH	FA (FRE)	Text
Concept	Form	Matter	Thorough determination	4:437
Quantity	Unity	Plurality	Totality	4:437
Judgment form	Universal	Particular	Singular	A70, 79/B95,106
Transcendental	One	True	Good (Perfect)	B113–115
Faculty	Understanding	Judgment	Reason	R5734, 18:339–40
Principle	Contradiction	Sufficient Reason	Thorough determination	R5562, 18:234
Modality	Possibility	Actuality	Necessity	R5739–42, 18:341
One-All	All derived from the one	All connected in one	The one derived from all	R5734, 18:340

For further discussion of the items in this table, see "The Moral Law as a System of Formulas," in H. Stolzenberg and H. F. Fulda (eds.), *Architektur und System in der Philosophie Kants* (Hamburg: Meiner Verlag), 2001.

2. The classic treatment of these tests is found in Onora Nell (O'Neill), *Acting on Principle* (New York: Columbia University Press, 1975), especially Chapter 5.

3. Therefore, there is no conceivable way that FLN could be used by Kant, as Rawls asks us to accept, to construct the content of moral doctrine generally, or to specify the duties of justice and virtue. Rawls himself seems to realize this: "Now one [reason for studying the CI-Procedure] is to use it as a way of generating the content – the first principles along with the essential rights, duties, permissions and the rest – of a reasonable moral doctrine. I don't believe the CI-Procedure is adequate for this purpose" (Rawls, Lectures, p. 163). Yet he clings to a reading of Kant that, despite being quite deficient in textual support, makes this hopeless project fundamental to Kantian ethical theory. I can account for this only on the assumption that Rawls regards any version of the dominant model (however hopeless it might be in its execution) as a more charitable interpretation of Kant than an interpretation that does not permit us to force Kantian theory into that model.

4. This Kantian quest for the Holy Grail – an interpretation of FLN that makes the test "come out right" for all maxims – seems to me as pointless as the original Christian quest, based on an equally gross misunderstanding of what matters and what does not.

5. For example, in the very first critical discussion of the *Groundwork*, Gottlieb August Tittel, *Über Herrn Kants Moralreform* (Frankfurt: Pfahler, 1786). In 1798,

J. G. Fichte appears to be acknowledging these objections when he claims that "the moral law is purely formal and must receive its content from somewhere else" (Fichte, SW 4:166, cf. Fichte, *System of Ethics*, tr. D. Breazeale and G. Zöller [Cambridge: Cambridge University Press, 2006], p. 157). Of course Fichte, unlike many both then and since who raise such objections, does not view this fact as a serious problem for Kantian ethics. Fichte is right.

6. There is in fact even a problem with the text at this point. The word most editors render as *Ableitung* ("derivation") is actually *Abteilung* ("partition") in both the 1785 and 1786 editions of the *Groundwork*. This might suggest that Kant really means to say that it is the *division* (not the derivation) of the duties that is evident from FUL and FLN, except that if that were his meaning, he would have used a word like *Einteilung*, not *Abteilung* (which really cannot bear the sense this interpretation would require). So I agree with the consensus of the editors that the text should be emended to *Ableitung*.

7. Barbara Herman, *The Practice of Moral Judgment* (Cambridge, Mass.: Harvard University Press, 1993), pp. 116–19. Herman's argument was anticipated by Paul Dietrichson, "Kant's Criteria of Universalizability," in Robert Paul Wolff (ed.), *Kant's Foundations of a Metaphysics of Morals: Text and Critical Essays* (Indianapolis: Bobbs-Merrill, 1969). The same conclusion is supported by Christine Korsgaard, *Creating the Kingdom of Ends* (Cambridge: Cambridge University Press, 1996), pp. 82–4.

8. Marx and Engels, *Manifesto of the Communist Party*, in Allen Wood (ed.), *Marx: Selections* (New York: Macmillan, 1988), p. 158.

9. Some years ago, I recall Margaret Thatcher's charging her political opponents with preferring greater equality even if it means that we are collectively less well off. I conclude that Kant's fundamental principle of morality places him squarely on the side of Mrs. Thatcher's opponents.

10. The "from itself" (*von selbst*), I suggest, refers to the fact that FH is derived *solely* by combining FUL and FH, and that it has no content apart from the fact that it unifies the other formulas.

11. Klaus Reich, "Kant and Greek Ethics II," *Mind* 48 (1939), pp. 452–3.

12. Examples are H. J. Paton, *The Categorical Imperative* (London: Hutcheson, 1947), p. 130; O'Neill, p. 127; Paul Guyer, "The Possibility of a Categorical Imperative," in Guyer (ed.), *Groundwork of the Metaphysics of Morals: Critical Essays* (Lanham, Md.: Rowman and Littlefield, 1998), p. 216. Henry Allison suggests that Kant gives us reason to consider FUL the "universal formula" at the point where he first formulates it in the Second Section: "The categorical imperative [Kant says] is thus only a single one, and specifically this: [then he states FUL]" (G 4:421). But if we take this statement as a declaration that the categorical imperative can be formulated in only one way, namely as FUL, then this is massively contradicted by the fact that Kant goes on to formulate it in four other ways. It seems much more reasonable to take Kant's statement to mean that the categorical imperative can be only that "precisely same law" which receives three principal (and two variant) formulations in the ensuing pages. Which of these formulations might eventually deserve to be considered the "universal formula" has surely not been decided at this point in the exposition (indeed, it would not even be possible to raise the question, when so far we have only one formula before us).

13. It might also be thought to agree with the following claim: "One must be able to will that the maxim of our action should become a universal law: this is the canon of the moral judgment of this action in general" (G 4:424). This seems to say of FUL (or perhaps FLN) that it is the canon (or standard) of moral judgment – which is what Kant says about the "universal formula" at G 4:436. But it seems highly questionable to take this statement to be about FUL or FLN in particular, as distinct from other formulations of the moral principle, at a point in the exposition at which no other formulas have yet been introduced. It is similar in regard to Kant's statement a bit earlier that "The categorical imperative is thus only a single one, and it is this; . . . " followed by a statement of FUL (G 4:421). At a point where Kant has no other formulas with which to compare FUL or FLN, it seems a mistake to read him as speaking about these formulas as distinct from others yet to be introduced. It seems more reasonable to take both statements to be general ones about the principle of morality Kant is in the process of deriving. Which formula of this principle is the definitive one, or the one best suited as a canon of moral judgment, is at the time of these statements as yet undetermined. Later stages of the exposition clearly indicate that the definitive formula, and the canon of moral judgment, is FA rather than FUL or FLN.

Chapter 5. Humanity

1. It follows directly that metaethical antirealists can respect anything at all only by acting in a way that implicitly conflicts with their own doctrines.
2. Peter Singer is no Kantian, but I think a Kantian could (or even should) agree with a lot of what he has said against the doctrine of the sacredness of human life. See Singer, *Rethinking Life and Death* (New York: St. Martin's Griffin, 1996).
3. She first did so in the article "The Formula of Humanity," first published in *Kant-Studien* 77 (1986), later in Korsgaard CKE, p. 128. The idea is key to her subsequent writings, especially Korsgaard SN. Despite my disagreement with her on this point, my own interpretation of Kant's argument for FH obviously has some strong affinities to hers, as critics of both of us have frequently noted. But there are significant differences between us, which the critics have often failed to appreciate. I hope the present discussion may make some of this clearer.
4. For instance, in Korsgaard FC, pp. 92–3.
5. Kant also says here that this involves attributing to other rational beings the same property we attribute to ourselves: "It is not enough," he says, "to ascribe freedom to our own will, on whatever grounds, if we do not have sufficient grounds to attribute the same quality also to all rational beings" (G 4:447). And he concludes his argument by claiming that because any rational being must "act under the idea of freedom," it must extend the same thought to all: "It must regard itself as the author of its principles independently of alien influences: consequently it must, as practical reason or as the will of a rational being, be regarded by itself as free: i.e. the will of a rational being can be a will of its own only under the idea of freedom and must therefore with a practical aim be attributed to all rational beings: (G 4:448). We will return to this point in Chapter 7. For now, however, it should be clear that Kant is not in agreement

with those approaches that think we are to regard ourselves as free only from the "standpoint of the agent" or the "first person"; this would be insufficient to establish what his argument requires. For such approaches see Korsgaard, CKE, pp x–xii, and Hilary Bok, *Freedom and Responsibility* (Princeton, N.J.: Princeton University Press, 1998).

6. We may sometimes have to sacrifice some human being's interests, or even his life, but as we have seen, this is not necessarily the same as sacrificing the *dignity* of the person. There are several different senses in which Kant speaks of something as having "absolute" value. This is one of them. Another is that what has absolute value has it irrespective of any relations to anything else (in particular, irrespective of any relations to the way it is considered or judged – G 4:439). Yet another is the goodness without limitation that belongs to every good will (G 4:394). Kant also speaks of a certain kind of good will, one that is not only good but an "absolutely good will," when it does not merely act on good maxims but acts on the *principle* of acting only on maxims that are universally legislative (G 4:437). This plurality of senses of "absolute" may at times be confusing, but we need to be aware of it if we are not to make mistakes (or attribute to Kant mistakes that he does not make).

7. The one exception might be R 6:26n, where Kant says that from the fact that a being has reason it does not follow that it is capable of representing its maxims as universal laws or that its reason is capable of being unconditionally practical. If Kant's point here is merely that the concepts of humanity and personality are different, then what he says is correct. But if he is claiming that a being might have humanity without personality, then I think he is wrong, for reasons given in the text.

8. See Ludger Honnefelder, *Die Einheit des Menschen* (Paderborn: Schöningh, 1994). Christine Korsgaard has defended a similar view to me in conversation, though I have never seen her do it in print and cannot be sure I am understanding her correctly. But what I recall her saying, putting the matter in Kantian terms, is that we apply the same concept of noumenal personality to a newborn child as we do to the mature human being it will become. Honnefelder welcomes the possible consequence of such a view that it extends personality to embryos and fetuses, while I take Korsgaard to resist this consequence.

9. The issues we are discussing here are, in Kantian terms, issues of right, not of ethics. They concern duties and claims that may be coercively enforced. It is a separate question whether the value of a fetus, and of its development to the point of birth, might constitute a reason for a woman to regard as an ethical duty her carrying it to term even at considerable cost to her own health and welfare. Probably there is such an ethical duty, at least in many cases. But those who would deny a woman even the right to make a choice whether to comply with this duty have thereby utterly forfeited their standing to argue with them about such issues. Someone who would deny you the freedom to make a choice that is rightfully yours to make has no business trying to tell you how you ought to make it. The effrontery of those who picket abortion clinics should therefore be met with stony stares of contempt by the women in whose lives they are trying to meddle.

10. The word *Zeugung* can mean 'conception' or 'begetting' but also something more general, such as 'generation' or 'procreation'; hence it does not

definitively settle either way whether Kant thinks the fetus is a person prior to its birth. I do not deny that it might reasonably be interpreted to favor an affirmative answer to that question, but if Kant had intended to favor such a view, he certainly could (or even should) have expressed himself more explicitly. In any case, he never *argues* for this stronger view.

11. In a recent paper, Patrick Kain employs some of Kant's views about biology to argue that he thinks of personhood as belonging to every human being, beginning with conception, Kain, "Kant's Defense of Human Moral Status," *Journal of the History of Philosophy* (forthcoming). This would be an alternative route to something like the "unity of the person" view, and, if accepted, it would yield the conclusion that every member of the human species, from conception, is a person as regards its rights and moral status, even if this being never develops the capacities necessary to be a person in the strict sense. No doubt such a conclusion would be welcome to many people today, especially those on the conservative side of issues about the permissibility of abortion, embryonic stem-cell research, and so forth. Kain's reconstruction of Kant's position is informed and in some ways plausible, though it seems to me more a speculative reconstruction than a compelling account of what Kant actually thought. And the attempt to bring biology to bear on it seems to fly in the face of Kant's declaration that we can form no proper concept of the beginning in time of a free being. Even if what Kain formulates were Kant's actual view, however, this view would depend heavily on Kant's controversial version of what is for us a clearly outdated biology – and even involves a willingness on Kant's part to entertain the theory of "preformation" regarding human persons – a view he otherwise consistently rejects regarding the natural genesis of living things. The conclusion to be drawn from Kain's account for present-day Kantian ethics is that if this is Kant's own account of personhood and moral status, then it is no longer a viable option, and Kantian ethics should seek a different one that can be grounded on Kantian principles that might still be tenable. That, in effect, is what I am doing in this section.

12. Jeremy Bentham, *Principles of Morals and Legislation* (New York: Hafner, 1948), p. 311n.

13. It is not easy to say how, or how much, different living things do, or can, feel pleasure or pain. I have spoken to biologists who say that the nervous systems of most invertebrates are too primitive for us to ascribe much real pain ("in our sense") to them, but also to other biologists who have rejected such a judgment with horror. It is common for chefs to say that a lobster does not suffer when plunged into boiling water, but the heroine of the German film *Bella Martha* (2001) (English title: "Mostly Martha"), who is a master chef and hardly a sentimental character, holds that this is terribly cruel and insists on a different method of killing a lobster before boiling it. There may be deep conceptual confusion at this point in our entire way of thinking about mental states, perhaps of people as well as animals.

If mental states are real, then they must exist, be what they are, when known from a variety of perspectives, not a single perspective. "What can be known only from a single perspective" is almost a definition of the merely imaginary or unreal. So if our mental states are real, their reality is constituted in part by others' interpretations of them and justified attitudes toward them. But regarding mental states, especially states such as pain, we tend to think that the only perspective on it that matters is that of the being experiencing it. This would seem to be a *moral* stance on our part, or perhaps a premoral stance that enters into morality at a fundamental level as one of its ingredients – that, at any rate, is what Rousseau thought (Rousseau D 37–8, Rousseau E, 41–2, 181–92). But it also seems that for rational beings, their valuation of the being whose states are in question plays a role in the attitude they take – a state of affairs that Rousseau acknowledges in his typically provocative manner by imagining a civilized man whose neighbor is being murdered right under his window: "He has merely to place his hands over his ears and argue with himself a little in order to prevent nature, which rebels within him, from identifying with the man being assassinated" (Rousseau, D, p. 38). We miss the point if we see nothing more in this than a condemnation of the civilized man. For Rousseau's point is precisely that he and his audience are all beings of exactly that kind, in whom natural sympathy has necessarily been transformed by society and reason. We are supposed to see in the absurdly cruel conduct of the civilized man not merely something to be avoided but the very predicament to which we are all in one way or another condemned by our social condition. In other words, if there is to be any hope for any of us, it will have to depend on the quality of the arguments we give ourselves while standing there with our hands over our ears.

As it seems to me, "sympathy" in this sense plays a role not in our formulation of fundamental moral principles but in our interpretation of them in moral rules and in the application of these rules. But when we are unsure what our stance on the pain of some being is, because it is a being whose nervous system is very different from ours, we would seem to have lost our moorings. The line separating callousness from excessive sentimentality seems extremely hard to draw. Those who think anything is obvious here, or that it can be settled empirically in any easy way, seem to me very much mistaken.

14. I am grateful to Allan Gibbard for bringing this issue to my attention.
15. See Agnieszka Jaworska, "Respecting the Margins of Agency: Alzheimer's Patients and the Capacity to Value." *Philosophy & Public Affairs* 28(2) (1999), pp. 105–38.

Chapter 6. Autonomy

1. See Friedrich Schlegel and Friedrich Schleiermacher, in F. Beiser (ed)., *The Early Political Writings of the German Romantics* (Cambridge: Cambridge University Press, 1996), pp. 132, 155, 174–5.
2. "It is not such a very long step from Kant to Nietzsche, and from Nietzsche to existentialism and the Anglo-Saxon ethical doctrines that in some way resemble it. In fact, Kant's man had already received a glorious incarnation earlier in the work of Milton. His proper name is Lucifer." Iris Murdoch, *The Sovereignty of Good* (London: Routledge, 1970), p. 80.
3. The term 'theonomy' is most associated with the theology of Paul Tillich, though it was not original with him. See Tillich, *Systematic Theology*, Volume III (Chicago: University of Chicago Press, 1963), pp. 249–74. Cf. Franz Rosenzweig, *The Star of Redemption*, tr. W. W. Hallo (Notre Dame, Ind.: University of Notre Dame Press, 1985), pp. 28–30, 66–9, 112–16, 176–82. There is an interesting

attempt to reconcile an ethics of "theonomy" with one of "autonomy" in Robert M. Adams, *Finite and Infinite Goods* (Oxford: Oxford University Press, 1999), pp. 249–76. Its success depends, however, on adopting a realist (albeit supernaturalist) metaethics – which may displease both some proponents of divine command theory and some proponents of autonomy.

4. G. E. M. Anscombe, "Modern Moral Philosophy," *Collected Philosophical Papers* (Oxford: Blackwell, 1981), iii: Ethics, Religion and Politics, p. 27. The essay was first published in *Philosophy* 33 (1958).

5. Kant's terminology might be confusing here. Sometimes Kant distinguishes "laws of nature" from "laws of freedom": The former are laws according to which everything does happen; the latter, laws according to which things ought to happen (G 4:385, MS 6:214). But within laws that command what ought to be done, those that are *most* properly called laws of *freedom* are called "natural" laws as contrasted with "positive" or "arbitrary" laws (MS 6:224, cf. 6:227).

6. There are a few places (e.g., G 4:414, 419, 429, 431, 434, 437) where Kant does speak of good actions, categorical imperatives, or rational beings as ends in themselves in terms of being "thought" or "represented" as such. The verbs here, however, are usually different: *denken* and *vorstellen*. And the context shows that either they must be *thought* or *represented* that way because they *are* that way. Or sometimes this terminology is used to suggest that the moral truth in question might still be in doubt and still requires demonstration (which Kant promises it will receive in the Third Section of the *Groundwork*).

7. Some of these texts have been emended according to suggestions made by Patrick Kain, "Self-Legislation in Kant's Moral Philosophy," *Archiv für Geschichte der Philosophie* 86:3 (2004), pp. 277, 284. The present discussion more generally obviously reflects the influence of this excellent article, which changed my mind about some things and finally gave me the courage of my convictions on others. Compare the only half-correct view of Kant's discussion of the "legislator" and "author" of the moral law presented in *Kant's Ethical Thought*, pp. 160–1.

8. Perhaps this is a good place to set the record straight about something. Christine Korsgaard's reaction to some metaethical realist noises emitted by me in her presence was: "You can take the boy out of Cornell, but you can't take Cornell out of the boy." She has the history entirely wrong. My adherence to metaethical realism dates from my undergraduate days, as I have already indirectly confessed elsewhere: See "Attacking Morality: A Metaethical Project," in *Unsettling Obligations: Essays on Reason, Reality and the Ethics of Belief* (Stanford, Calif.: CSLI Press, 2002), p. 189, note 6. These were the halcyon days back at Reed College, when I detested everything about analytical philosophy and was especially grossed out by G. E. Moore's sophistical attacks on what he called "the naturalistic fallacy" as well as everything downwind from them (where I thought the stench only grew stronger as you followed out the tradition). (Like all Reed students, however, I always respected Marvin Levich, the great teacher who personified analytical philosophy to us and whom in retrospect I can see as having begun my conversion to it.) My mind had changed a lot about analytical philosophy before I ever set foot in Ithaca (my exposure to teachers at Yale who disliked analytical philosophy and attacked it at every turn had the effect of causing me to study it assiduously and to be forever after decisively influenced by it). But my sentiments

concerning antirealist metaethics remained the same as ever. At no time have I ever subscribed to "Cornell realism," as defended by such people as Nicholas Sturgeon, Richard Boyd, and David Brink (though I have always respected their work).

9. Here I agree with Kain, "Self-Legislation in Kant's Moral Philosophy," p. 287, note 80.

10. It has been common to heap scorn on "faculty psychology" as an outworn relic of a philosophical dark age, and Kant has often been the target of such scorn. This attitude, however (not to put too fine a point on it) is ignorant and wrong-headed. We often conceptualize activities, mental activities in particular, in the way I have just been describing. That way of thinking about them is often both useful and (if I may be blunt) *correct*. Attempts in psychology to replace faculty concepts with simple causal mechanisms often result in crudity, oversimplification, and error. They often amount to the application of a picture derived from elsewhere (for instance, from the natural sciences) to a subject matter where it does not belong. That Kant thinks about the mind in terms of normatively guided faculties is not a cause for shame – on the contrary, it is one of the glories of his philosophy.

11. Reath,, p. 134. Reath's discussions of autonomy, especially in the two papers "Legislating the Moral Law" and "Autonomy of the Will as the Foundation of Morality," are probably the best discussions of Kant's conception of autonomy I know of, especially in the "Kantian constructivist" tradition. They are attempts to reconcile the "rationalist" and the "voluntarist" aspects of the doctrine precisely through a conception of the law's rational validity that is explicated in constructivist terms. They illustrate that Rawlsian constructivism is not as one-sidedly voluntarist as I am perhaps depicting it here.

In the end, however, the question cannot be avoided: Are the procedures justifying the law's rational validity correct because they reflect a moral state of affairs lying absolutely in the nature of things, or are they something we ourselves create, so that their validity rests on that? Reath's account retains its balance by avoiding the question. In Christine Korsgaard's *The Sources of Normativity* (Cambridge: Cambridge University Press, 1996) there is again an attempt to mediate, to see Kant's conception of autonomy as capturing the truth in both voluntarism and rationalism (or "realism"), pp. 104–13, 164–6. But voluntarism seems to me to win out, in the form of what Korsgaard calls "reflective endorsement" (which she thinks we must bestow on certain actions and policies simply on account of the practical identities we have chosen, and ultimately on the identity as rational agents that we cannot renounce because of the structure of our rational agency; pp. 113–28). But Korsgaard refuses to take this structure to be any sort of reality on which the validity of our reflective endorsements depend. "Values are not discovered by intuition to be 'out there' in the world . . . Values are created by human beings . . . The form of realism I am endorsing here is procedural rather than substantive realism: values are constructed by a procedure, the procedure of making laws for ourselves . . . Of course we discover that the maxim is fit to be a law; but the maxim isn't a law until we will it, and in that sense create the resulting value" (p. 112). Kant agrees that values are not discovered by intuition and that they are not "out there" in the sense of being located somewhere external to our rational nature. But in every other respect, Kant clearly disagrees with what Korsgaard is saying. Neither the objective worth of humanity nor the moral law is created or constructed by human beings; they lie in the nature of things, they are "absolute" in the sense that they do not depend on any act or attitude of ours. In particular, it is not Kant's view that the moral law is not a law until we will it to be one. His clearly stated view is that the moral law's validity lies in the nature of things, independently of what we will, but once we come to appreciate this, we can find reasons for regarding it as proceeding from our will. Reath comes much closer than Korsgaard to appreciating this point.

I realize that Rawlsian constructivism takes different forms in different representatives of it, and sometimes it can be a slippery position, one that perhaps tries to be *too* "Kantian" in the sense that it attempts to harmonize elements in the traditional reading of Kant that are in tension, without making the hard decisions (or even looking too carefully at how Kant himself might have made them). Perhaps my characterizations of constructivism in this book are at times oversimplified, owing to the fact that my attempts to address this kind of position are peripheral rather than central to my concerns. But I do not think that on the whole they are unfair.

12. Notoriously, however, Kant himself, violating the strictures of his own critical philosophy, engages in this gratuitous supernatural metaphysics with annoying regularity, especially in the *Groundwork* (G 4:450–5) and the *Critique of Practical Reason* (KpV 5:48–57, 70–1, 89–103). In §5 of the next chapter I will give Kant the rap on the knuckles his inconsistencies deserve, and I will attempt to rescue his theory of freedom from the disgraceful supernaturalism that has always made it an object of obloquy among enlightened people everywhere.

13. In the *Religion*, Kant writes: "Between a shaman of the Tunguses and the European prelate who rules over both church and state, or (if instead of the heads and leaders, we only want to look at the faithful and their ways of representation) between the wholly sensuous *Wogulite*, who in the morning lays the paw of a bear skin over his head with the short prayer, "Strike me not dead!" and the sublimated *Puritan* and Independent in Connecticut, there certainly is a tremendous distance in the *style* of faith, but not in the principle; for as regards the latter, they all equally belong to the same class, namely of those who place the service of God in something (faith in certain statutory articles, or the observance of certain arbitrary practices) which cannot by itself constitute a better human being" (R 6:176). We should notice here the distinction drawn between statutory law and what is "by itself" good. But it was something else that annoyed the young Hegel, a pious young antinomian theologian, only a couple of years later. In his view, between any of these forms of religious slavishness and the Kantian autonomous moral agent, "the difference is not that the former makes himself into a servant, while the latter is free; instead it is that the former carries his master outside himself, while the latter carries his master within himself and is in bondage to himself" (Hegel ETW, p. 211). It is certainly possible to make sense of the notion of "bondage to oneself" if the part of you that is in charge is something like an addictive desire or irrational compulsion. It may be that in the rationalizations of some people, some such psychic force, or the internalized

injunctions of some external authority (the parent, the priest, social custom, or some misguided philosophical doctrine), might assume the name of "reason" or "the moral law." And if we impose this malicious interpretation on Kantian ethics (as we have already seen others do in Chapter 1), then Hegel's point is well taken. But if there is any such thing at all as reason and rational self-constraint through reason, then it would be an extreme form of moral blindness to think that constraint is no different from servitude to external authorities. The mature Hegel was plainly not blind in this way. See Hegel PR, §§11–27, 133, 149, 174–5, 187, 194, 197. The Hegelian suggestion that individual reason cannot play this role raises legitimate questions but does not stake out a position as different from Kant's as Hegel or his followers may think, for reasons just stated in the passage to which this note is appended.

Chapter 7. Freedom

1. For a defense of this reading of the *Groundwork*, see Dieter Schönecker, *Kant Grundlegung III: Die Deduktion des kategorischen Imperativs* (Freiburg und Munich: Alber, 1999). Cf. Schönecker and Wood, *Kants Grundlegung zur Metaphysik der Sitten: Ein einführender Kommentar* (Paderborn: Schöningh, 2002), pp. 170–206; and for an account of the development between the first Critique and the *Groundwork*, see Schönecker (with collaboration from Stefanie Buchenau and Desmond Hogan), *Kants Begriff transcendentaler und praktischer Freiheit* (Berlin: deGruyter, 2005).
2. This criticism of Kant was first published in *Mind*, Vol XIII, No. 51 (1888).
3. The 'Incorporation Thesis', as he calls it, is the cornerstone of Henry Allison's account in *Kant's Theory of Freedom* (New York: Cambridge University Press, 1990).
4. Twice in the Third Section, Kant speaks of providing a "deduction" of freedom (from pure practical reason) (G 4:447, 454). Then at the very end of the book, he speaks of having provided a "deduction" of the moral law (G 4:463). In the second Critique, he denies that "the objective reality of the moral law" can be "proved by any deduction" (KpV 5:47). But it is not in the least clear that he is denying here what he claimed in the *Groundwork*. On the contrary, what he is denying is that we can show there is any instance in experience of actual obedience to the moral law – as Kant thinks he has shown in the first Critique, by a transcendental deduction, that there are actual instances of the categories in experience (KpV 5:46–7). He continues to speak of a "deduction of freedom" from the moral law, as a principle of practical reason (KpV 5:48), and the entire section in the course of which these remarks occur is entitled "On the Deduction of the Principles of Pure Practical Reason" – a nominal phrase for which Kant's main task in the section is presumably that of showing how, and in what sense, we can supply it with a referent. Those who read the second Critique as denying that the moral law can be provided with a "deduction" in the sense in which that term was used in the *Groundwork* seem to be guilty of misreading the text.
5. The claim that Kant's views underwent a fundamental change is most associated with Karl Ameriks, *Kant's Theory of Mind* (Oxford: Oxford University Press, 1982), Chapter 6. This view has been widely adopted since, however, for example by John Rawls, Lectures, pp. 253–72.

6. But many people still find themselves in this sad condition. See Richard Dawkins, *The Selfish Gene* (Oxford: Oxford University Press, 1989): "We are all survival machines – robot vehicles programmed to preserve the selfish molecules known as genes. This is a truth that still fills me with astonishment. Though I have known it for years, I can still never seem to get fully used to it." This doctrine is astonishing to Dawkins only because he has apparently convinced himself of it, even though he also cannot help but realize that it is obviously false. It is a crude extrapolation from scientific results in accordance with certain equally crude philosophical dogmas. It is not true of other animals any more than it is of human beings. On the other hand, selfish behavior, in the usual sense, is action for a reason (not necessarily the best reason, but a reason just the same). So if Dawkins means literally what he says that our genes act selfishly in programming us, then he is attributing practical freedom to some of our molecules, even if not to us. But we have to suspect here that Dawkins is not speaking literally. If the doctrine is not meant literally but is merely some form of sublime scientistic poetry, then that would provide an alternative explanation of its capacity to awe and astonish him.

7. See Patrick Suppes, *Probablilistic Metaphysics* (Oxford: Blackwell, 1984).

8. A good discussion of such theories, and the scientific methodology behind them, is found in Michael Strevens, *Bigger Than Chaos: Understanding Complexity Through Probability* (Cambridge, Mass.: Harvard University Press, 2003).

9. I say "something like" because I do not want to try to decide whether cats or birds have the capacity to act for reasons. Perhaps they do, but not in the same sense in which human beings do. How these senses might differ is not relevant to my present concerns.

10. Leibniz, *Discourse on Metaphysics* §13, *Philosophical Essays*, ed. R. Ariew and D. Garber (Indianapolis: Hackett, 1989), pp. 44–6; Locke, *Essay Concerning Human Understanding*, ed. P. Nidditch (Oxford: Clarendon Press, 1975), Book II, Chapter XXI, §§47, 51–2, 71, pp. 263–6, 282–4.

11. Jean-Paul Sartre, *Nausea*, tr. Lloyd Alexander (New York: New Directions, 1964), p. 10. Of course in the novel, Roquentin does not think that the muddiness was a reason for not picking up the paper. In fact, he thinks he is looking forward to clasping the pulpy mess in his hands. That only makes the sudden inhibition the more shocking to him. Of course sometimes compulsions and inhibitions can be overcome, but then the agent does after all have the possibility of acting against them and is not necessitated. The difference between Roquentin's deciding for a reason either to pick up the paper or not to pick it up and his finding himself *unable* to pick it up still marks a fundamental conceptual distinction.

12. Kant seems to think that this conceptual truth does not hold in the case of the holy will, such as God's will. "One might raise the objection that God cannot decide otherwise than he does, and so he does not act freely but from the necessity of his nature. The human being, however, can always decide something else, e.g. a human being, instead of being benevolent in this case, could also not be that. But it is precisely this which is a lack of freedom in the human being, since he does not always act according to his reason; but in God it is not due to the necessity of his nature that he can decide only as he does, but rather it is true freedom in God that he decides only what is in conformity with his highest understanding" (VpR 28:1068). This is a consequence of the fact

that Kant regards freedom as only the capacity to act according to reason (and not the possibility, where this is also present) of acting contrary to reason (MS 6:213–14). Perhaps Kant and I can just agree to differ about God, but to me it seems clearly a conceptual truth that a being that acts for reasons never acts as it does necessarily but can always decide otherwise, even in cases where it is quite certain that it will not do so.

13. Many of our beliefs, for example, cannot be changed just by our arbitrarily choosing to change them, and the reasons we have for these beliefs certainly play a role in this fact. But it does not follow that "believing something for reasons" ever involves the causal necessitation of the belief. Sometimes we speak of "reasons" for a belief meaning justifying reasons, not reasons for which we first formed the belief or reasons that play a causal role in our maintaining it. These justifying reasons may instead be part of the explanation for why it never occurs to us to raise any question about the belief (which would be a free action, if we did it), or why, if the occasion arises to put the belief in question, we (freely) decide not to do so. Here the reason for our decision explains our refusal to put the belief in question but does not necessitate it (we certainly *could* consider the matter further, even if we choose not to – and this follows simply from the fact that our refusal is motivated by a reason). We will do better to think here not so much about beliefs (which are usually not, after all, voluntary actions done for reasons) but about acts of assent to propositions we believe. Unless they have been forcibly extorted from you by torture, acts of assent are done for reasons, which may be constituted partly by your belief in what you are assenting to (and the reasons for holding these beliefs), and partly by the pragmatic appropriateness of assenting to it under the circumstances. Assent in such cases may be certain to occur, if the reasons for it are strong enough and you are motivated by them, but it is a matter of choice and never causally *necessitated.*

14. Sometimes people say "I cannot do otherwise" in cases where they do take themselves to be acting for reasons. (Here philosophers sometimes like to quote Martin Luther: "Here I stand, I can do no other.") This is not a counterexample to what I have just been saying. For one way to articulate a particularly strong (we even say: "compelling") reason to yourself is to say: "You must do this." And when the person – Luther, for example – is steadfast enough in his volition that he has been successful in doing what he has a compelling reason to do, he reports simultaneously the strength of the reason and his own success by saying: "I had to do it." Or sometimes such talk represents a particularly obvious (and reprehensible) form of deception (or self-deception) – as when the CEO, in being "lean and mean" so as to make a modest improvement in the bottom line, says to a room of hapless employees: "I simply had to let you all go – oh, and yes, given my options under the new laws, I had no choice but to renege on our contract and cancel your pension plans as well."

Suppose I give what I think is a compelling reason for you *not* to do something. I might sometimes say (especially if it looks as if you might defy my reasoning): "You simply can't *do* that!" But the all too familiar response is: "Just watch me!" (And then you go right ahead and do the thing I just said you "can't" do.) You may behave this way when the reason is not so compelling after all, but as long as what I am doing is is offering you a reason (as opposed to tying you up, or giving you a drug that induces paralysis, compulsive inhibition, or some other incapacitating condition), then this response is always equally available to you no matter how compelling the reason is, as long as you are willing to be stubborn and unreasonable enough. Again, it is sometimes *dead certain* how people will act, and that they will act that way for certain reasons. But that can never mean they have been deprived of the *possibility* of acting in other ways. If what some philosophers mean by "practical (or volitional) necessity" is a case in which I am supposed to be acting freely, or acting for a reason, but it is literally impossible for me to act otherwise, or to against the reason – though free I literally lack the ability to act otherwise, or I am acting with necessity and truly have no alternative possibilities – then that is a nonsensical description of whatever case they have in mind. See Bernard Williams, "Practical Necessity," in *Moral Luck* (Cambridge: Cambridge University Press, 1981), pp. 124–32; Harry Frankfurt, "Rationality and the Unthinkable," *The Importance of What We Care About* (Cambridge: Cambridge University Press, 1988); and "Autonomy, Necessity and Love," and "On Caring," in *Necessity, Volition and Love* (New York: Cambridge University Press, 1999).

15. There may be a problem here arising from Kant's view that our freedom is incomprehensible to us. For if this view is correct, that means there is a limit to how well we can ever understand our own grounds for deciding when people have practical freedom and when they lack it. But this is not a problem only for Kant. On the contrary, quite apart from anything Kant says, it is simply a fact that we do not understand any of these matters very well. When psychologists are called as expert witnesses to determine the degree of imputability of people accused of crimes, they very often say that their knowledge does not enable them to answer the questions about responsibility that are posed by the law. Those who would claim that some psychological or neuroscientific theory has all the answers here are guilty of the very thing with which Kant's critique of reason charges traditional metaphysics. They pretend to understand something they do not understand. Two philosophers who have argued articulately – neither one from a superstitious or religious motive – that we may not be able even in principle to understand our own minds are John Searle and Colin McGinn. See Searle, *The Rediscovery of the Mind* (Cambridge, Mass.: MIT Press, 1992), and McGinn, *The Mysterious Flame: Conscious Minds in a Material World* (New York: Basic Books, 1999). I would like to think their pessimism will be proven wrong, but I think it is only ordinary human honesty to admit that neither psychology nor neuroscience nor any other discipline at present is very close to understanding many things about how minds work. Perhaps the most admirable thing about Daniel Dennett's *Consciousness Explained* (Boston: Little, Brown, 1991) is its title's virtual admission that the book's wildly ambitious aims amount to an unresisting invitation to the charge of intellectual fraudulence.

16. Henry Allison calls this the 'Reciprocity Thesis'; see Allison, *Kant's Theory of Freedom*, pp. 7, 201–13.

17. It is characteristic of Enlightenment thought generally to acknowledge human folly and also to laugh at it, while at the same time doing what one can to encourage people to be less foolish. In this respect, Don Alfonso of Mozart's *Così fan tutte* and Mr. Bennet of Austen's *Pride and Prejudice* are typical Enlightenment

heroes. They are also flawed characters, who are, however, aware of their own flaws. This too is typical of the Enlightenment hero.

18. "Your conscious life, in short, is nothing but an elaborate post-hoc rationalization of things you really do for other reasons." V. S. Ramachandran, *A Brief Tour of Human Consciousness* (New York: Pi Press, 2004), p. 1. This is no doubt true about a lot of what we think regarding our reasons for doing what we do. But here it is stated as if it held universally about every conscious thought of every person. Taken literally, in that sense, it would be self-undermining. Presumably when he makes this assertion, Ramachandran is implying that he has reasons for making and believing it, and he must think he knows these reasons and has reason to think they are good ones. But that implies that he thinks at least this part of *his* conscious life (if not ours) is not made up only of a post hoc rationalization of something he does for reasons other than the ones for which he thinks he says and believes this. And if he also expects us to agree with him for the same reasons, then he must think that when we do, at least that little corner of our conscious life is also not a mere post hoc rationalization of something we do for reasons other than the ones he has offered us. So just how often is what Ramachandran says true of us? I do not think it makes sense to suppose that we can answer this question. "More often than we like to think" seems right, but we cannot coherently give the answer "always," which is what his remark, taken literally, seems to assert.

19. Sometimes we act for reasons of which we are not aware, or about which we are in denial. People sometimes think cases like this count against freedom of the will. But clearly they presuppose practical freedom in the negative sense every bit as much as cases in which we act for the reasons we think we act. Freudian explanations sometimes ascribe to unconscious subsystems or agencies in the mind behavior that is motivated by reasons. For example, an obsessive-compulsive person might wash his hands frequently because this is the best way to reduce a psychic conflict of which he is not consciously aware (except in the form of a powerful need to wash his hands). To reduce this conflict is then not a causal but a reasons-explanation for his behavior, even if the behavior is in a larger sense "irrational" and even if the person is unaware of (or suppressing) the real reason why he is doing what he is doing. In general, "irrational" behavior is merely a species of rational behavior – it is not behavior that is to be explained like the behavior of a robot, according to mechanical causes, but is usually explained by a set of reasons of which the agent is not aware (and which usually would not be seen as good reasons for it, if they could be weighed rationally). Only beings that have the capacity to act for reasons, hence practical freedom in the negative sense, involving multiple possibilities, and an absence of external necessitation are capable of irrational behavior. This and the behavior of birds and cats are merely two respects in which those who think it is easy to deny freedom of the will, or who think they can rid themselves of the problem of freedom at zero metaphysical cost by some easy form of compatibilism, underestimate the difficulty of taking either of these positions.

20. In general, acting for reasons is not something we do for a reason. We are essentially beings who act for reasons (good ones or bad ones) and must think of themselves as acting for reasons. In that sense, we have no option but to act

for reasons. But whatever particular thing we do for reasons is something we always have the option of not doing. This point is closely related to the truth contained in Sartre's famous declaration that we are condemned to be free.

It is sometimes said that it "seems" to us that we are free (or even that it is "bound to seem" this way), even though we are not. The reason most often given why it is "bound to seem" this way is that we are ignorant of the causes determining us, so we are bound to think there are none. But that is clearly an insufficient explanation. We often are ignorant of the cause of something – for example, why only one sock out of a pair shows up after doing the laundry – without having any temptation to think there is no cause. Besides, thinking we are free is not thinking that our actions have no cause; it is thinking that we are their cause, acting for reasons. The fact that the argument for freedom we have just examined fails to exclude the possibility that we are not free might, however, be a reason for thinking that to those persuaded by this argument it "seems" we are free. For we do think that something "seems" a certain way to us if we have some ground for thinking it is that way, but the ground does not exclude the possibility that it is not that way. But I think the talk of "seeming" is nevertheless out of place here. For it is correct to say that it "seems" a certain way only when we might entertain the phenomena that make it seem that way while at least being able coherently to judge that it is not that way. But the point here is that we cannot coherently judge that we are not free. It is true that we can entertain a coherent picture of the world (and ourselves) that is internally coherent (perhaps even compelling to some people) according to which we are not free. But we cannot coherently represent ourselves as judging for good reasons that that picture represents the way things are. So it is actually out of place to say that it "seems" to us that we are free. It would be more accurate to say instead that although we cannot exclude the possibility that we are not free, we also cannot coherently judge that we are not free. That last point takes it a step beyond merely "seeming," though it definitely leaves us short of being able to offer theoretical grounds.

21. For example, see Rawls, Lectures, p. 264.
22. There is perhaps another reason why Kant's bold assertion that the moral law is a "fact of reason" may seem to people like a better approach than his attempt to derive the moral law from the practical presupposition of freedom. In the eighteenth century, it may still have been true that the denial of human freedom seemed to present the most profound challenge to morality as a whole. But I do not think this is any longer true – or at least not to the same degree. Moral skepticism today rests less often on the thought that we are mechanisms lacking in the conditions of moral accountability than on the thought that the ideas grounding moral value are illusions – for example, the idea that human beings have a dignity that gives every one of us a reason to respect and care for others that should rationally outweigh self-interested considerations.

The problem of freedom mattered so much to Kant because he thought morality requires our capacity to act for a certain special kind of reason – an *a priori* reason, grounding a categorical imperative. This was also a reason whose *a priori* status he associated with our being a special kind of natural being – one with supernatural capacities and even a supernatural destination that marks us out as having the value associated with our capacity to act on this special *a priori* reason. But if practical freedom is basically the general capacity to act for reasons at all, then as soon as it is conceded that we have this capacity, it is no longer an interesting question, from a psychological point of view, whether we have the ability to act from *a priori* reasons. For the question of whether a being capable of acting for reasons is free has already been answered (in the affirmative). If there are *a priori* reasons for acting, then a being capable in general of acting for reasons can act on them; if there are not (if all genuine reasons are empirical), then a being capable of acting on reasons would still have the capacity to act under the illusory impression that there are *a priori* reasons. So our *capacity to act on them* is the same either way. The interesting question, however, on which *we* are more likely to rest the question of whether morality is an illusion is whether distinctively moral reasons (whether we consider them empirical or *a priori*) are genuine reasons at all. The answer to that question does not depend on whether we have the general capacity to act for reasons but on what Kantian ethics regards as the normative structure of rationality itself and the reasons it recognizes – chiefly the absolute worth or dignity of rational nature as an end in itself. If this is correct, then the Kantian claim that probably matters most to us is the assertion that there is a moral law at all – that its validity for us is a "fact of reason." Rhetorically, then, if not argumentatively, the assertion that it is such a fact addresses, in Kantian language, the worry *we* are most likely to have about morality. That is perhaps why philosophers today are likely to think the revision that Kant's views underwent between 1785 and 1788 (if indeed this happened at all) is a progressive development. Yet argumentatively considered, in terms of the way Kant looked at things, the change they attribute to him would clearly be no improvement whatever. Whether or not Kant abandoned the argument of the *Groundwork* (which, as I have said, remains questionable), he had no good ground for doing so and no good reason whatever for moving from it to the new position commonly attributed to him in the second Critique.

23. "Kant's Compatibilism," in A. Wood (ed.), *Self and Nature in Kant's Philosophy* (Ithaca, N.Y.: Cornell University Press, 1984), pp. 73–101.

24. Or, as Schopenhauer colorfully puts it: "Whoever steals once is a thief all his life." Schopenhauer, *Essay on the Freedom of the Will*, tr. K. Kolenda (Indianapolis: Bobbs-Merrill, 1960), p. 52. Cf. Schopenhauer, *The World as Will and Representation*, tr. E. J. F. Payne (New York: Dover, 1958), pp. 286–307, 501–7. Occasionally, Kant says similar things himself (VA 25:438). But he never derives them from metaphysical theories of noumenal freedom, and his point seems only the empirical one that human characters (whether good or bad) tend to be constant over time, so that the struggle to improve one's character is apt to be an uphill battle. It is part of Kant's theory of the radical propensity (*Hang*) to evil in human nature itself that we always retain a "predisposition" (*Anlage*) to morality, which cannot be destroyed as long as we are moral agents (R 6:27–8). As long as we have it, we always retain the possibility of a radical conversion from bad to better – which is Kant's interpretation of the Christian doctrine of being "reborn" (R 6:49–66).

25. Friedrich Daniel Schleiermacher, "Anthropologie von Immanuel Kant," *Athenaeum* 2 (1799), Reprint ed. Bernhard Sorg (Dortmund: Harenberg, 1989),

pp. 684–7. See Brian Jacobs, "Kantian Character and the Science of Human-ity," in B. Jacobs and P. Kain (eds.), *Essays on Kant's Anthropology* (Cambridge: Cambridge University Press, 2003), pp. 118–19. A careful exposition of Schleier-macher's objection is presented by Patrick R. Frierson, *Freedom and Anthropol-ogy in Kant's Moral Philosophy* (Cambridge: Cambridge University Press, 2003), Chapters 1–4. Frierson's attempt to answer the charge on Kant's behalf (Chap-ters 5–6) attempts to show there is no contradiction between Kant's theory of noumenal freedom and the Kantian project of empirical anthropology as applied to moral action. This project can succeed if its aim is only to rescue from inconsistency the Kantian story of noumenal freedom when taken in con-junction with Kant's moral anthropology. But I fear that like Kant himself (at times), Frierson thinks the tale of noumenal freedom is also something we might find credible and integrate into our moral psychology in a positive way. How-ever, some tales that are free of contradiction are still not believable and should not be proposed to people's belief. Kant's theory of noumenal freedom, when employed as a framework for moral psychology, is one of these self-consistent but incredible fantasies, as all but the most uncritical readers of the Kantian texts can plainly see.

26. It is important, of course, that the concepts of witches, fairies, and noumenal causes of our actions, though they may refer to nothing that exists, are not self-contradictory. But as far as I know, this is true.

27. Kant's wholly illicit adventures into supernaturalist metaphysics are particularly noticeable in the *Critique of the Power of Judgment*, where he seems to invite us to interpret our experience of the sublime as a kind of awareness of the transcen-dence of our intelligible over our natural being and seems to resolve both the antinomy of taste and the antinomy of teleological judgment by appealing to the supersensible substratum of appearance (KU 5:266–8, 339–41, 411–15). It is beyond the scope of this discussion to decide how far these illegal excursions into the forbidden territory beyond the bounds of sense might be acceptably interpreted in a way that does not violate the critical philosophy's strictures on transcendent metaphysics. The point here must be simply that no acceptable interpretation could result in any positive doctrine concerning our freedom as supernatural or noumenal beings. Nothing in Kantian ethics could possi-bly require such a doctrine, because the critical limitation of reason positively forbids it.

28. This objection follows a familiar pattern. It is difficult for people to believe that certain things can arise entirely from the fundamental forces that modern nat-ural science recognizes. Chief among these things are three that we regard as fundamental to what (and who) we are: life, consciousness, and free agency. Yet there seems no reason in principle why natural processes cannot result in beings' having consciousness or even the capacity to determine their actions freely, entirely from themselves. In fact, doesn't it look for all the world as if we ourselves are just such wondrous products of nature? From the fact that *we* are the products of physiology and environmental conditions, it does not fol-low that our actions are causally determined by these, unless you assume that the two sorts of causality belong to the same series, within which transitivity of causation holds. This is a larger and more dubious assumption than many real-ize. Most educated people now accept that life can be explained naturalistically

(as the result of complex, self-reproducing chemical compounds and their amazing proliferation and adaptation through a process of natural selection). If so, why might not consciousness and free agency be the results of these processes too? Even in the case of life, however, there is still resistance even now on the part of those who think that life must somehow be a product of "intelligent design." Some philosophers of mind believe they can explain consciousness and even free choice as the results of brain processes, but all too often the ardent preaching of their scientistic faith meets with deep skepticism among the heathen.

I think the resistance in all three cases is due to cultural factors that are hard to understand and that, on a subrational level, determine our philosophical "intuitions." This perhaps makes it quixotic to attempt to rid ourselves of them through rational argument. The relevant intuitions seem to be ubiquitous and easily elicited, even through the shallowest rhetorical devices, such as the cavalier use of words like "merely," "only," and "nothing but." "Life can't possibly be *merely* a physical process." "If consciousness is *nothing but* a brain process, then all consciousness, even *this* sensation of red, or pain, or desire that I am having now must be some sort of illusion." "If human beings are *merely* the products of their heredity and environment, they cannot possibly be the kind of metaphysical *causa sui* that a truly free agent would have to be." Or, to cite one of my own favorite uses of this rhetorical device: "No one has ever actually *seen* the Brooklyn Bridge. It is merely the action of light waves on the retina of the eye." Robert Benchley, "Did You Know That –?", *My Ten Years in a Quandary, and How They Grew* (New York: Harper, 1936), p. 133.

29. Good examples of what I mean here are Daniel Dennett, *Elbow Room: The Varieties of Free Will Worth Wanting* (Cambridge, Mass.: MIT Press, 1984) and P. S. Churchland, "Feeling Reasons," in A. R. Damasio, H. Damasio, and Y. Christen (eds.), *Neurobiology of Decision-Making* (Berlin: Springer, 1996). It is noteworthy that most of the articles in this volume, which are by neuroscientists, take for granted the commonsense position that human beings and even animals (monkeys, even insects) make decisions, which unfold over real time, between real alternatives that are open to them. They do not worry about reconciling these commonsense assumptions with traditional assumptions about causal determinism. Churchland's appropriation of Humean arguments that do supposedly achieve this reconciliation makes surprisingly little attempt to adapt to neuroscience but leaves things at the psychological level of Hume's eighteenth-century mentalistic vocabulary of motives and sentiments. Less evasive approaches to free will, which very sensibly favor compatibilism but do not pretend that there is nothing perplexing about free human action, are to be found in Alfred Mele, *Autonomous Agents* (Oxford: Oxford University Press, 1995) and John Martin Fischer, *The Metaphysics of Free Will* (Oxford: Blackwell, 1994).

30. See http://www.the-brights.net/.

31. It is fairly clear that there is no single "center" in the brain in which volition and decision making are located. Decisions result from the interactions between many brain areas, with their input converging in the prefrontal lobes of the cerebral cortex. See H. Damasio, "Human Neuroanatomy Relevant to Decision-Making," J. M. Fuster, "Frontal Lobe and the Cognitive Foundation of Behavioral Action," and J. Altman, "Epilogue: Models of Decision-Making," in Damasio, Damasio, and Christen (eds.), *Neurobiology of Decision-Making*, previous note.

This sheds little light, however, on the nature of reasons and our capacity to respond to them. I suggest that is because reasons are primarily a social and communicative, not a neurophysiological, phenomenon.

Chapter 8. Virtue

1. An inspection of the *Metaphysics of Morals* shows that he is much more interested in listing determinate "vices" – such as arrogance, defamation, ridicule, envy, ingratitude, gloating (*Schadenfreude*), and hatred. But these are not so much traits of character as patterns of volition common among human beings that are opposed to duty.
2. MacIntyre, *After Virtue* (Notre Dame, Ind.: Notre Dame University Press, 1984), p. 149.
3. This distinction is one of the primary focuses in Felicitas G. Munzel, *Kant's Conception of Moral Character: The "Critical" Link of Morality, Anthropology and Reflective Judgment* (Chicago: University of Chicago Press, 1999).
4. A "sanguine" person, as Kant uses the term, is not more disposed to pleasant feelings than a melancholic person, but only disposed to more sudden and violent feelings, whether of pleasure or displeasure. A choleric person is more disposed to quick reactions, and a phlegmatic person to slower ones, whatever form the reactions may take. Thus a sanguine person might be disposed to sudden feelings of anger or grief as much as feelings of joy, and a choleric person is disposed to react more quickly, not only indignantly (as to insults) but also cheerfully (as to compliments). Kant also gives no credit whatever to the traditional idea that these temperaments are associated with four distinct bodily fluids. Clearly he is taking over the traditional theory of the four humors only terminologically, while devising a new theory of temperament that is quite alien to it.
5. Kant held some amusingly crotchety views about the influence of diet and medicaments on health, both physical and mental. But it would be a serious mistake to exaggerate the thought that he regards bodily remedies as determining our moral constitution. For, on the contrary, he also held crotchety views about the ways that voluntary resolve can influence bodily health – for instance, about how the pain of gout can be diminished by directing attention away from it, and how breathing with closed lips can diminish thirst (MCP 15:939–43; SF 7:97–116).
6. Hume is no doubt correct that people would think very differently about an *agent* depending on whether their bad action reflected an enduring trait or seemed to be only a slip committed in a rare moment of weakness. But that would not be relevant to whether they are to be held responsible for the action. (At a legal trial, it might come in at the sentencing phase, but it would be bizarre to hold that a person could not be held responsible for a crime that all the other evidence shows to be wholly voluntary simply on the ground that such behavior was uncharacteristic of him.) The context of Hume's remark, however, is precisely one of responsibility and accountability. Imagine what someone who believes Hume's theory might think about his own actions: "Everyone knows I am an extraordinarily trustworthy person, on whom his friends can always rely. So if I betray my friend to the Homeland Security people in exchange for the large reward they are offering, I can't be held responsible for it, nor could this

act redound to my infamy." It might be said that a truly trustworthy person would not have that thought. But that thought is justified, even required, by Hume's account of moral responsibility. So what would follow is that a truly trustworthy person (or more generally, a virtuous person) could not coherently believe Hume's account of moral responsibility.

7. Kant does distinguish the *abiding* maxim of the conformity of actions to the law (*virtus phaenomenon*), which can be acquired little by little over time, from the virtue of the intelligible character (*virtus noumenon*), which involves the right incentive and appears to be the same as or very close to what he means by a "moral disposition" (R 6:47). His point in that passage is to emphasize the importance of the need for a fundamental revolution in an agent's way of thinking in combating the propensity to radical evil, and that mere external changes in habitual behavior are not enough. I do not think this discussion, despite his use of the word *virtus* in the course of it, is really about the same topic as Kant's discussion of virtue as moral strength.

8. These points were made long ago by Paul Dietrichson, "What does Kant mean by 'acting from duty'?" in R. P. Wolff (ed.), *Kant: A Collection of Critical Essays* (Garden City, N.Y.: Anchor, 1967). It is a sad commentary on the way Kant is commonly misunderstood that they still have to be made today.

9. Michael Slote, "Agent-Based Virtue Ethics," in R. Crisp and M. Slote (eds.), *Virtue Ethics* (Oxford: Oxford University Press, 1997). The nineteenth-century British philosopher James Martineau is probably best known through Sidgwick's criticisms of him in Book III, Chapter of the *Methods of Ethics*.

10. This point is made by Stephen Engstrom, "Happiness and the Highest Good," in Whiting and Engstrom (eds.), *Aristotle, Kant and the Stoics: Rethinking Happiness and Duty* (New York: Cambridge University Press, 1996), pp. 125–6. There may be an element of truth, however, in the thought that Kantian virtue is like Aristotelian continence in this respect if it is correctly interpreted. Kant does not have a very high opinion of the virtue of actual human beings, sometimes wondering whether true virtue is ever found anywhere in the world (G 4:407). The view might be attributed to Kant that the best most of us can do in being virtuous is to achieve the weaker versions of virtue. But of course that does not mean that he would not count the stronger versions, which Aristotle would call "virtue," as something other than virtue. And it is in any case misleading to identify Kantian virtue with continence for the other reason I am about to give in the text.

11. Because what is bad about intemperate people is not their desire to act against the right decision *as such* but their desire to enjoy base pleasures, presumably continent people will be grieved not by acting according to the right decision but only by having to forgo the base pleasures they would enjoy if they indulged themselves. Continent people regret forgoing these pleasures more than they should, and more than virtuous people do. I am grateful to Terence Irwin for pointing out this distinction to me.

12. There are several possible explanations for someone's doing this. By comparison with many moral psychologists, Kant gives less credit to human innocence – to the kind of moral strength that might be due to a happy nature or to non-rational conditioning – and accordingly relies more on the moral strength that agents must acquire through reflection and struggling against their own

corrupted nature. To these other moral psychologists, Kantian virtue may seem less attractive than the kind they are accustomed to believe in, and this might cause them to give it an invidious interpretation. More generally, Kant takes a less charitable view of human nature than many moral philosophers, and so it might be understandable that they would regard even the best moral character, viewed through his eyes, as inferior to their depiction of it. Other explanations for this will be suggested presently in the text, when we consider what will happen if we mistakenly equate the Kantian distinction between rational and empirical desire with the Aristotelian distinction between rational and nonrational parts of the soul.

13. This famous formulation of this basic idea of Kantian ethics comes, of course, from Rousseau SC, Book II, Chapter VIII.

14. Here Kant is not at all far from Philippa Foot, "Virtues and Vices," in Crisp and Slote (eds.), *Virtue Ethics*, op. cit., pp. 166–8, though I do not think she realizes this, and she certainly thinks there is a more positive place for the ideal of wisdom in ethics than Kant does.

15. "I mistrust all systematizers and I avoid them. The will to system is a lack of integrity." Friedrich Nietzsche, *Twilight of the Idols*, Maxims and Arrows 26, in W. Kaufmann (ed. and tr.), *Portable Nietzsche* (New York: Viking Press, 1954), p. 470. Nietzsche apparently supposes that there could be such a thing as the *integrity* of a fragment, or even of an isolated impulse or insight, divorced from the whole of which it is a part. This gets things exactly wrong, by treating stubborn adherence to the isolated impulse in disregard of the whole as a necessary condition for integrity. But the name for this trait is not "integrity"; it is "irresponsibility."

16. For a fuller discussion of this, see "Kant's History of Ethics," *Studies in the History of Ethics*, 2005. Online journal: http://www.historyofethics.org/.

17. This point, along with many other cogent criticisms of virtue ethics, is effectively made by Robert Louden in "Some Vices of Virtue Ethics," in Crisp and Slote (eds.), *Virtue Ethics*, op. cit., pp. 210–13.

Chapter 9. Duties

1. It might be thought that Kant deserves some of the opprobrium suggested by these abuses, on account of his infamous view that there is no right of resistance to unjust authority and that we are obliged to obey even the unjust commands of the supreme commander of a state (TP 8:297–305, MS 6:318–23). After all, didn't Adolf Eichmann appeal to Kant at his trial, claiming that he was only acting from duty and obeying the law? And didn't Hannah Arendt think that there was some basis of truth in this appeal? (See Hannah Arendt, *Eichmann in Jerusalem: A Report on the Banality of Evil* [New York: Penguin, 1994], p. 137.) Kant's views on the topic of passive obedience are certainly questionable enough, but he clearly knew the difference between saying we are obligated to obey commands that are injust to give and saying that we are obligated to do wrong if commanded to do so. The latter thing he clearly refused to say and even explicitly denied. "Obey the authority who has power over you (in whatever does not conflict with inner morality)" (MS 6:371). He presents a clear example of this in his reference (though not by name) to the case of Henry Norris, groom

of the stole, who was put to death for refusing to give false testimony against Anne Boleyn when commanded to do so by Henry VIII (see KpV 5:30, 155). The example was drawn from Hume, *History of England* (Indianapolis: Liberty Fund, 1983), Volume 3, p. 118.

2. Marcia Baron has recently argued that properly speaking only strict or perfect duties can be done from the motive of duty, because for Kant duty requires "commands," "necessity," or "necessitation," and Baron thinks such talk is "mysterious" except in the case of strict or perfect duties. Baron, "Overdetermined Actions and Imperfect Duties," in H. Klemme, D. Schönecker, and M. Kühn, *Moralische Motivation: Kant und die Alternativen* (Hamburg: Meiner Verlag, 2006), p. 34. But I think such notions are perfectly in place, and not the least bit mysterious, wherever it might be in place to *constrain* or *make oneself* do something for a (moral) reason. If Baron were correct, then there could be no imperfect duties at all, regarded as consequent upon a *command* of reason, carrying with it a practical *necessity*. Or at least all such duties would have to be "mysterious" too. Perfect duties necessitate an action through the fact that if we do not perform them, we incur blame. If Baron were correct, then the morally grounded assertion that "I must do that" could mean only that if I do not do it, I will be subject to blame. But it seems to me not the least bit mysterious for me to think that I *must* help some people in need even if I do not think I would be to blame if I did not help them. I can see the help as morally "commanded" and "necessitated" by the fact of the need of those to be helped and their moral claim on me, without my having to think that helping them is the only way I can escape blame or self-reproach. People who perform heroic, saintly, or otherwise exceedingly meritorious actions often report feeling that they "had to" perform the action. I do not think all such people are showing such skewed moral judgment, or pathological susceptibility to guilt feelings, that they think they would have been blameworthy if they had not performed the action. On the contrary, I think there would be something the matter with your character if you could not *make yourself* do something, or decide you *had to do it*, on moral grounds, unless you are afraid you would be blamed (or blame yourself) if you *didn't* do it. If Baron is right about the way people think of duty, self-constraint, and necessitation on moral grounds, then that would only be another reason for regarding the whole idea of duty as odious. But I do not think that Kant thought this way about duty or related notions of moral self-command, moral necessitation, and the like. That he did not think this way is shown merely by the fact that he had a concept of imperfect, wide, or meritorious duty.

3. See Walter Sinnott-Armstrong, *Moral Dilemmas* (Oxford: Oxford University Press, 1988). Also, Terrance McConnell, "Moral Dilemmas," *Stanford Encyclopedia of Philosophy* online: http://plato.stanford.edu/entries/moral-dilemmas/.

4. Alan Donagan, *The Theory of Morality* (Chicago: University of Chicago Press, 1977), pp. 143–9. As he points out, this goes back to Gregory the Great, who described such cases in terms of the twisting of the devil's testicles. See also St. Thomas Aquinas, *Summa Theologiae* I–II, Q. 19, a.6, II–II, Q. 62, a. 2.

5. See Ruth Barcan Marcus, "More about moral dilemmas," in Mason, H. E. (ed.), *Moral Dilemmas and Moral Theory* (New York: Oxford University Press, 1996), pp. 23–35.

6. See Fichte SW 4:327–65, cf. *System of Ethics*, §§27–33, pp. 310–44; Hegel PR §§142–258, pp. 189–281. But because for Fichte the ends of the rational will are determined only through communication with others (Fichte SW 4:229–53, *System of Ethics*, §18, pp. 217–42) and because for Hegel the system of right is fundamentally the system of ethical life (Hegel PR, §33, p. 62), in a sense the whole of these works is nothing but an exposition of the nature of rational social life.

7. There might be some reason for distinguishing the "perfect/imperfect" distinction from the "narrow/wide" distinction, because the verbal formulations of these distinctions in different places do not seem to be the same (see G 4:421 and MS 6:227, 390–4). But Kant uses the "perfect/imperfect" distinction, in effect, to mark the distinction between narrow and wide duties to ourselves (MS 6:421, 444), and more generally, I do not think they count as two different distinctions in his mind. So I will treat the terms as interchangeable for present purposes.

8. Another possible reading might be one that emphasizes the importance of a pure moral disposition: The fulfillment of our imperfect duty to do our duty from duty (see Chapter 2, §3) would involve our taking an attitude toward even imperfect duties that increases the demand on ourselves: We think we should not merely fulfill them but fulfill them on principle and from a certain motive. This change of attitude on our part could be seen as "bringing closer to narrow duty our maxim of complying with wide duty," and the increased merit involved in this pure disposition could therefore be seen as rendering "so much the more perfect our virtuous action." I do not attempt to decide here which reading – this one or the one offered in the text – is correct. Perhaps both are. It would not be the first time a philosopher had succeeded in stating two distinct ideas, both having philosophical interest and merit, using the very same assertion.

9. This is a path I would recommend to Kantian ethics in any case. Too much philosophical energy has been wasted destructively by those who treat Kant and these followers as enemies. It would be much more profitable to emphasize the ways in which they depend on Kant, remaining faithful followers even where their enthusiasts foolishly think they are "going beyond" Kant, and equally the ways in which they creatively extend Kant's teachings in ways Kantians ought to welcome rather than to resist.

10. See, for example, Sidgwick, p. 7. In his posthumously published essay on suicide, Hume concludes without question that suicide can never violate a duty to ourselves, on the ground that people who commit suicide must always consider life a "burthen," hence worse (for them) than annihilation. See Hume D, p. 104. The considerations that might make suicide a violation of a duty to oneself (or – a possibility that Kant sometimes at least entertains – that might make suicide the fulfillment of a duty to oneself) seem never even to have been considered by Hume.

11. On this topic, see Lara Denis, *Moral Self-Regard: Duties to Oneself in Kant's Moral Theory* (New York: Garland, 2001); and Andrews Reath, "Self-Legislation and Duties to Oneself," in Mark Timmons (ed.), *Kant's Metaphysics of Morals: Interpretive Essays* (Oxford: Oxford University Press, 2002), pp. 349–70.

12. For further treatment of this theme, see Thomas E. Hill, Jr., "Servility and Self-Respect," in *Autonomy and Self-Respect* (New York: Cambridge University Press,

1991) and Jeanine Grenberg, *Kant and the Ethics of Humility: A Story of Depen-dence, Corruption, and Virtue* (Cambridge: Cambridge University Press, 2005).

13. On this topic I am grateful for the opportunity to read a paper (unpublished at this writing) by Melissa Seymour.

14. Jodi Halpern, *From Detached Concern to Empathy: Humanizing Medical Practice* (Oxford: Oxford University Press, 2001).

15. In a sensitive and thoughtful paper on this topic, Marcia Baron concludes that Kant's rejection of compassion and apparent admiration for Stoic indifference to the sufferings of a friend when you can do nothing about them are at odds with our way of thinking about these matters. Baron, KE pp. 195–226. But she seems to me to misread the following comment about the Stoic: "It was a sublime way of thinking that the Stoic ascribed to his wise men when he had him say: "I wish for a friend, not that he might help me in poverty, sickness, imprisonment, etc., but rather that I might stand by him and rescue a human being." But the same wise man, when he could not rescue his friend, said to himself, "What is it to me?" In other words, he rejected compassion" (MS 6:457). I understand the "but" that begins the penultimate sentence as a caveat that is being issued about the Stoic sage and his "What is it to me?" I do not read Kant as regarding this Stoic attitude as expressing an admirable or "sublime" way of thinking. In the following paragraph, Kant goes on to agree with the Stoic to the extent that he sees no point in letting yourself be infected with the pain of another, when this leads only to "an increase in the ills of the world" (MS 6:457). I see it as Kant's consistent position to reject those forms of sympathy that are sentimental and self-involved, but he is not rejecting active participation in the situation of another, which is not a mere passive state of one's own feeling. This is why he ends the paragraph by pointing out how this passive form of sympathy passes over into the pity that looks down on others, which "has no place in people's relations with one another" (MS 6:457). It is crucial to understanding these two paragraphs that they follow immediately on the discussion of the duty of participation we are discussing. The point of the first is to distinguish Kant's position from that of the Stoic sage who says, "What is it to me?" when he cannot help his friend. The point of the second is to distinguish the active participation that is our duty from a self-involved feeling of sadness that separates us from those we pity instead of bringing us closer to them. Whether or not this agrees with the way "we" regard these matters, it seems to me to display none of the "coldness" that concerns Baron about Kant's views on this topic.

16. "Kant more or less advises us to keep ourselves to ourselves, not to link our fate unnecessarily closely with that of other persons, to remain detached – respecting others, but not getting too mixed up in their lives. Kant does recognize a moral duty of philanthropy, love of our fellows, but he construes this as involving not feeling or emotion but solely goodwill, benevolence, willingness to do things for others, to draw only close enough to them to help them." Annette Baier, *Moral Prejudices: Essays on Ethics* (Cambridge, Mass.: Harvard University Press, 1995), p. 34. This version of the criticism is superior to most, in that Baier is aware of, and takes account of, what Kant says about friendship and intimacy. But even there she draws the wrong conclusions from what she finds. Kant agrees with Hume (with a passage Baier quotes at the beginning of this chapter, p. 33) that without friendship human life would not be worth living. She notes, however, that Kant

also warns us about the limits of friendship, and the dangers and painfulness of intimacy, and the fact that prudent self-interest is often better served by a policy of detachment from others than one of emotional involvement with their fates. She is right that Kant would *advise* us (from a prudential standpoint) that becoming too emotionally involved in the lives of others is not always conducive to our selfish welfare. What she misses, however, is the crucial point, which is that Kant thinks we *ought* to care about others just the same – we have a *duty* to do so. This caring does involve emotional sympathy or participation (*Teilnehmung*), and our duty of sympathetic participation is a duty independent of, and distinct from, our duty to show them goodwill, practical love, and beneficence, even if performing the duty of participation may *also* aid us in being more intelligently beneficent.

17. Marcia Baron, "Love and Respect in the Doctrine of Virtue," in Mark Timmons (ed.), *Kant's Metaphysics of Morals: Interpretive Essays* (Oxford: Oxford University Press, 2002), pp. 391–407.
18. Baron, ibid., p. 397 note.
19. Those who know only the *Groundwork* may think that Kant's chief (or only) conception of love is "practical love" – the maxim of benefiting others, which is a duty, and hence the only possible referent of the biblical command to love (G 4:399). But in fact Kant regards love, properly speaking, as a feeling, and therefore practical love as love in only a secondary or improper sense (MS 6:401–2).
20. Baron, ibid, p. 396–7, apparently missed this passage and even thinks Kant might deny that love depends on respect.
21. Darwall, "Two Kinds of Respect," *Ethics* 88 (1977), pp. 36–49.
22. For a further defense of this as a Kantian principle, and the argument that it is also Kant's position, see *Kant's Ethical Thought*, pp. 132–9.
23. François, Duc de la Rochefoucauld, *Reflections, or Sentences and Moral Maxims.* Dual language edition (London: Associated University Presses, 2003), No. 218.

Chapter 10. Conscience

1. St. Thomas Aquinas, *Summa Theologiae* II–1, Q. 1.
2. St. Bonaventure, *Commentary on the Sentences, Works* (St. Bonaventure, N.Y.: Franciscan Institute, 1979), II, Distinction 39.
3. Joseph Butler, *Five Sermons*, ed. Stephen Darwall (Indianapolis: Hackett, 1983), Sermons II and III.
4. Heidegger, *Being and Time*, tr. Robinson and Macquarrie (New York: Harper & Row, 1962), p. 316.
5. Heidegger, *Being and Time*, pp. 316, 318, 339. Heidegger's account of conscience displays in these ways a clear affinity with the Romantic conception of moral autonomy, for which the autonomous self is radically individualized and cut off from the public realm of rational discourse and becomes a matter either of feeling or of some other kind of inarticulable awareness, such as that of the Heideggerian "uncanny."
   Heidegger also denies that his own characterization of conscience as a "call" is a "picture," such as he takes Kant's characterization of conscience as an inner court to be. He may be correct about this, but I have already suggested

certain important respects in which the account of conscience as an inner court is not metaphorical – nor, therefore, "pictorial" either.

6. This is the chief error in an otherwise exemplary discussion of Kant's conception of conscience by Thomas Hill, in Hill, Chapters 9 and 11.

7. See Fichte, SW 4:173–5, cf. *System of Ethics*, pp. 165–7. J. F. Fries, *Handbuch der Praktische Philosophie, 1. Theil: Ethik* (Heidelberg: Mohr und Winter, 1818), pp. 214–15; Hegel PR, §§138–9.

Chapter 11. Social Justice

1. A reading of the liberal tradition that sees it as fundamentally utilitarian in motivation has recently been defended by Russell Hardin, *Liberalism, Constitutionalism and Democracy* (New York: Oxford University Press, 1999).

2. F. A. Hayek, *Law, Legislation and Liberty*, Volume II: *The Mirage of Social Justice* (Chicago: University of Chicago Press, 1976). A similar libertarian reading of Kant's doctrine of right had already been given by Mary Gregor, *Laws of Freedom* (New York: Barnes and Noble, 1963), pp. 35ff. Regarding Hayek, it is true that he shares with Kant one important principle – namely, that social justice should not be conceived primarily in terms of some distributive outcome that is designated as "just" and then acts, practices, and procedures are regarded as just merely because, and to the extent that, they result in that outcome. But a Kantian can agree with Kant on this point while holding that the state has very significant regulatory and redistributive responsibilities. It's only that the redistributive mandates must be motivated by something other than a prior conception of justice in terms of a certain distributive outcome.

3. See Jeffrie G. Murphy, *Kant: The Philosophy of Right* (London: Macmillan, 1970); Howard Williams, *Kant's Political Philosophy* (New York: St. Martin's Press, 1983). Even an interpreter favorable to socialism, and to the neo-Kantian tradition of socialist thinking, presents fundamentally the same picture of Kant himself: Harry van der Linden, *Kantian Ethics and Socialism* (Indianapolis: Hackett, 1988).

4. Leslie Mulholland, *Kant's System of Rights* (New York: Columbia University Press, 1990), especially Chapters 7–9; Allen D. Rosen, *Kant's Theory of Justice* (Ithaca, N.Y.: Cornell University Press, 1993), especially Chapter 5; Paul Guyer, *Kant on Freedom, Law and Happiness* (New York: Cambridge University Press, 2000), pp. 235–61; and Alexander Kaufman, *Welfare in the Kantian State* (Oxford: Clarendon, 1999).

5. Kant condones, however, certain kinds of hierarchies of power and authority that any self-respecting Kantian today will regard as an affront to human dignity. He thinks that in the public sphere, a woman must always be represented by a man (her father or husband) and in that sense remains in a permanent condition of civil minority or tutelage (*Unmündigkeit*) (MS 6:279, VA 7:303, 305–6). He thinks that only those who are economically independent should be "active citizens" with a right to vote or participate in political life (MS 6:314–15). He even thinks that family right forbids servants to leave the service of the family, and if they run away, the head of the household is entitled to compel them to come back and serve the family (MS 6:283). I think the wide gap here between what Kant thought and what we now think is due to the fact that we have had two centuries to reflect in practice on the idea of human dignity that is the basis of Kantian ethics, and

to acquire a better understanding of what kinds of social relationships respect it and what kinds do not. I hope that if people continue to attempt to put this idea into practice in their social lives, there will be social practices we now tolerate and even take for granted (such as the influence of wealth on political decisions or the commodification of labor) that people in the future will rightly come to regard as odious from the standpoint of human dignity, just as we regard some of the practices Kant approved of. In that way, I do not think the right reaction to Kant's errors on these matters is to treat his views with repugnance and to congratulate ourselves on our differences. The right reaction is rather to ask ourselves which other social practices that we now condone are really as repugnant to the idea of human dignity as are the civil minority of women, restrictions on the voting franchise, and the bondage of family servants.

6. The position that the substance of this passage is inconsistent with Kantian doctrine is taken by Murphy, who says that on Kantian principles "it is unjust to tax Jones in order to be benevolent to Smith" (p. 144). Gregor (pp. 35–6) says very much the same thing. Williams, who is more cautious, holds that the passage is at least not obviously consistent with Kant's theory of right and the state (pp. 196–8).

7. This claim is made by Williams (pp. 196–7) and by Bruce Aune, *Kant's Theory of Morals* (Princeton, N.J.: Princeton University Press, 1979), p. 159.

8. The passage does explicitly contradict Murphy's principle that it is unjust to tax Jones to benefit Smith, but Kant never subscribes to such a principle, so there is no contradiction within his views. Murphy's principle may sound like natural justice to libertarians, but on reflection it seems no more reasonable than the principle that the state should permit no economic activities or transactions that might allow Jones to appropriate more than Smith in the first place. (Neither principle, it seems to me, has much to be said for it.)

9. Rosen, p. 188.

10. Kaufman, pp. 39, 50–60.

11. The reading of "preservation of the people" in this passage as meaning the preservation of the state is sometimes supported by quoting another passage from *On the Common Saying*: "If the supreme power makes laws that are primarily directed toward happiness (the affluence of the citizens, increased population, etc.) this cannot be regarded as the end for which a civil constitution was established, but only as a means of securing the rightful state, especially against the external enemies of the people" (TP 8:298). But to see the two passages as parallel presupposes that the state practice of taxing the rich to support the poor would have to be motivated by a concern with happiness – an assumption we have seen is false. The aim of this passage is clearly to reject state paternalism or cameralism and to assert again the point that the fundamental end of the civil constitution is maintaining a condition of right and the external freedom of the citizens. There is no reason to deny, and a lot of reason to affirm, that this is precisely the aim Kant sees the state as having in taxing the rich in order to support the poor.

12. Kersting, "Politics, freedom and order," in P. Guyer (ed.), *The Cambridge Companion to Kant* (New York: Cambridge University Press, 1992), p. 357.

13. Here Kant is plainly following Rousseau SC, Book I, Chapter IX.

14. Alexander Kaufman has recently argued for a capabilities-based system of social welfare as the right Kantian model of welfare legislation within a just state (Kaufman, Chapter 6). He is careful, however, to propose this model on the basis of a Kantian theory of reflective political judgment and not on the basis of the fundamental Kantian conception of political rights (which is the sort of basis that has typically been alleged by those who have tried to give a libertarian interpretation of Kant's theory). Kaufman's proposal, as I understand it, would have the status of a rationale, grounded in Kantian moral and political theory, that might be offered to an enlightened legislature in support of a system of welfare laws that are broadly egalitarian and capabilities-based. It could not have the status of a claim, founded on basic principles of right, that a state must be unjust, or its conduct contrary to right, if it fails to adopt such a system. So understood, I think Kaufman's proposals are consistent with Kant's theory of right, property, and the state. Yet it would seem to be inconsistent with Kant's theory of the state as supreme proprietor and peremptory rights as entirely subject to the discretion of the general will to claim that this welfare scheme, or indeed any welfare scheme at all (even the taxation of the wealthy to support the poor, proposed by Kant himself), is absolutely required by right. In short, given Kant's theory of property, the wealthy have no cause to complain if they are taxed for the benefit of the poor, but the poor would equally have no cause to complain if the state chose not to tax the wealthy to provide for their basic needs.

Chapter 12. Punishment

1. Many wrongful acts are made illegal because they are deemed wrongful, and some people believe that it is inherently wrong to break the law. But if there are wrongful acts that are not illegal, or illegal acts that are not wrongful, then it is possible to take different positions on whether an authority is justified in punishing them (or whether the laws ought to be changed so that the act which is not wrongful is no longer illegal, or the act which is wrongful should be illegal). The *concept* of punishment cannot settle this issue.

2. This error is basic to J. D. Mabbott's influential article "Punishment," *Mind* 48 (1939), pp. 152–67. The error was correctly diagnosed in John Rawls TCR, which distinguishes between justifying an action under a practice and justifying the practice. Once the practice of punishment is accepted, we are justified within it in punishing people because they have done something wrong and to the degree of severity their conduct is held to deserve. These are conceptual points about the practice. It is a separate question why we should have the practice at all. Retributivism is a distinctive view about how the practice of punishment is to be justified.

3. The retributivist who takes this line might be asked why this harm should be inflicted by (or only by) certain authorities. Various answers could be given to this question – for example, that social order and justice require that there be a reliable way of determining who is really guilty of wrongdoing and of settling possible controversies about this in a way that all agree to abide by. Kant's argument that punishment is one of the powers of the state's executive authority is a version of this argument (MS 6:331–7). There is nothing specifically retributivist

about this answer, nor does a retributivist's answer to the question even need to appeal to anything specifically retributivist.

4. This distinction between two kinds of retributivism is drawn by Anthony Ellis, "Critical Study of Recent work on Punishment," *Philosophical Quarterly* 45 (1995), pp. 225–33. An example of the kind of retributivism not based on the Intrinsic Desert Thesis is Herbert Morris, "Persons and Punishment," J. Feinberg and H. Gross (eds.), *Punishment: Selected Readings* (Encino, Calif.: Dickenson, 1975).

5. An interpretation of Kant on punishment that might be viewed as taking him in the opposite direction, grounded not on the Intrinsic Desert Thesis or the Directness Thesis but on the "construction of right" mentioned at MS 6: 632–3, is presented by Susan Meld Shell, "Kant on Punishment," *Kantian Review* 1 (1997), pp. 115–35. My reasons for thinking that Kant's retributivism is not as Shell portrays it are given below, in the texts where I find him endorsing the Intrinsic Desert Thesis and also the Directness Thesis. See also next note. The support for Shell's reading, which seems to me extremely slim (but not entirely nonexistent), consists in a few scattered passages (none of them occurring, it should be noted, directly in contexts where the justification of punishment is being given) where Kant compares the reciprocity of right to the reciprocity of physical forces. See P 4:358 and note, possibly also KU 5:464–5. In the place where you might expect Kant to make Shell's point – his discussion of the "construction" of right as equal reciprocal coercion in the *Metaphysics of Morals* (MS 6:232–3) – it is striking that he does not explicitly mention criminal right at all but mentions only cases of private right (the right of a creditor to coerce payment of a debt, the precise determination of rights of property). Hence those who want to regard Kant's theory as involving a "construction" of penal right involving something like the *Ius Talionis* are left entirely to their own devices. Nothing in Kant's explicit treatment of penal right lends support to their project. But the fact that Kant endorses the Directness Thesis is my main reason for thinking that he is not the kind of retributivist who bases the justice of punishment on some further scheme of distributive justice.

6. B. Sharon Byrd, "Kant's Theory of Punishment: Deterrence in Its Threat, Retribution in Its Execution," *Law and Philosophy* 8 (1989), pp. 151–200; others who have defended a similar idea are Don E. Scheid, "Kant's Retributivism," *Ethics* 93 (1983), pp. 262–82 and Thomas Hill, *Human Welfare and Moral Worth*, Chapter 10.

7. Fichte, SW 3:282–3, *Foundations of Natural Right*, p. 245. Fichte is no retributivist at all. In the theory of punishment, as in many other areas of philosophy, he proves himself to be a better friend to the critical philosophy than Kant ever realized, by drawing conclusions from the Kantian philosophy more consequently than Kant does.

8. The idea here is that if I coercively prevent only actions that are wrong (not right), then my act of coercion cannot be inconsistent with everyone's freedom to perform right actions according to a universal law. There may, of course, be difficulty in framing particular laws in such a way that their enforcement involves the coercive prevention *only* of actions that are not right. Can we limit verbal or written expression (in the form of pornography or racist propaganda) in such a way as to prevent women or minorities from having violence incited against

them without also including in our prohibition some acts of expression that are consistent with everyone's freedom according to universal law? To many of us, it seems that all attempts to do this have so far failed. British laws against libel and slander (though they are part of civil rather than criminal law) are notorious in this respect, in imposing excessive requirements on those who speak or write to prove the truth of what they say and thus restricting freedom of speech in ways that are plainly recognized as unacceptable by all reasonable people beyond that provincial island. Nevertheless, despite the difficulties in applying the principle Kant is maintaining here, I think his fundamental point remains cogent.

9. By this I do not mean that this justification of punishment is free from problems. There are, I think, some fundamental difficulties with any attempt to justify threats of harm as a way of coercing rightful behavior. Such threats can be justified, for example, only insofar as they *successfully* prevent wrong. Where they do not do so, the presumed justification vanishes. Kant is aware of this in his discussion of so-called "equivocal rights," those that cannot be coercively enforced because no coercive threat can suffice to prevent the wrong – as in the case of the "right of necessity," where one man in a shipwreck kills another by pushing him off the plank; here even the threat of the death penalty would not prevent him from committing the homicide, because he would die immediately if he did not commit it (MS 6:235–6). This plays a role also in Kant's discussion of infanticide by an unwed mother and one military officer's killing another in a duel (MS 6:335–7). These, he says, are crimes deserving of the death penalty, but the act of killing is so bound up with the killer's need to preserve her or his honor that the threat of death cannot prevent the killing. More generally, what is to prevent us from using an analogous argument to say that no punishment is justified in the case of a terrorist fanatic who will not be deterred by any penalty whatever? Or consider any crime that is actually committed despite the law's threat to punish it: If the threats had been sufficiently coercive to prevent the crime, it would not have occurred. May we not conclude, by reasoning analogous to that used in the case of the right of necessity, that it is always and necessarily wrong to punish any actual crime whatever? Perhaps these objections will be deemed sophistical, but I think they point to a serious problem involved in morally justifying any form of coercive prevention that operates by means of threats.

10. It is quite natural to express this approach to punishment in Kant (as Thomas Hill and Sharon Byrd have done) by saying that Kant has not a "retributivist" justification of punishment but rather a "deterrence" justification. I admit this is basically correct, but I am uncomfortable with the term "deterrence" because I think it can be misleading. The aim of punishment, on Kant's theory, is not merely to deter violations of right but *coercively* to *prevent* them. Only the state has the right to coerce in this way, and it is justified in coercing only to prevent violations of right (or violations of laws whose collective purpose it is to secure a rightful condition). Not all deterrence is coercive prevention. I might "deter" you from making a rude remark to a friend of mine that I see you are about to make by throwing you a grimace that indicates it will displease me if you continue as you are doing. Now I have a perfect right to grimace in this way, and my grimace (even if it succeeds in preventing you from making the remark) is

not an act of coercion. It would be an act of coercion, however, if I prevented you from making the remark by pulling a gun and threatening to shoot you if you insulted my friend; and this is something I would not have a right to do, not only because I do not represent the state but also because your insulting remark (while distasteful and perhaps even immoral) would not be a violation of any law or anyone's right. So my deterrent grimace could not be justified as an act of punishment on Kant's theory, even if it were intended as one. On Kant's theory, then, the function of punishment is, strictly speaking, not to "deter" violations of right but to *prevent* them through *external coercion*. 'Deterrence' seems better suited to express the idea that punishment is intended to impose "costs" on the criminal that will exceed the "benefits" of wrongdoing – a picture that has sometimes been imported into Kant by interpreters, for example, Jeffrie Murphy, *Kant: The Philosophy of Right*, 142ff; Howard Williams, *Kant's Political Philosophy*, pp. 98–102; Aune, *Kant's Theory of Morals*, p. 166; Susan Meld Shell, *The Rights of Reason* (Toronto: University of Toronto Press, 1980), p. 161. But the principle of right, with the claim that it is analytic that an act is right if it coercively prevents wrong, does not justify imposing costs on wrong acts, but only coercively preventing them. So it cannot be assumed that Kant's theory can justify imposing such costs. This is another reason I think there are serious problems with the moral justification of coercion by means of threats.

11.   There is one passage in the Vigilantius lectures, however, where Kant seems to be trying to link the *Ius Talionis* necessarily (or through "universal laws of freedom") with punishment as the coercive protection of right: "In general, all evils that are inflicted on the other under the law of coercion, he inflicts, by a universal law of freedom, on himself; for he can only offend the other to just the extent that the other can compel him to desist from the offense, or not to use his right; but this, by universal laws of freedom, is equal and unconditioned for everyone" (*Metaphysics of Morals Vigilantius* 27:555). This passage illustrates the tension in Kant's views, however, because it is hard to interpret in any way that makes what it says sound even minimally plausible. It hardly seems a necessary truth – indeed, it seems obviously false – that an offense can always be coercively prevented by threatening exactly a penalty "equal" to the offense. For instance, the death penalty is obviously an ineffective deterrent for suicide bombers, and if the only way effectively to deter people from jaywalking were to sentence jaywalkers to a long jail term, that would not make this a just sentence according to the *Ius Talionis*. If the claim is instead that in compelling others we are restricted by right (presumably by the *Ius Talionis*) to employ a form of coercion involving a punishment "equal" to the offense, then Kant's claim merely assumes the *Ius Talionis* rather than arguing for it, and it establishes no necessary link at all between the *Ius Talionis* and the idea of punishment as the coercive protection of right.

12.   Edmund Pincoffs, *The Rationale of Legal Punishment* (New York: Humanities Press, 1966). Cited as "Pincoffs." Samuel Fleischacker, "Kant's Theory of Punishment," *Kant-Studien* 79, no. 4 (1988), pp. 434–49. Cited as "Fleischacker." As Fleischacker notes, this attempt has a long pedigree, including among its precursors Edward Caird, *The Critical Philosophy of Immanuel Kant* (Glasgow: Maclehose, 1909) and Jeffrie G. Murphy, *Kant: The Philosophy of Right*, p. 142. But he rightly rejects these versions of the argument for including in their argument the claim

that the criminal wills his own punishment, because this is a claim Kant expressly and emphatically denies (Fleischacker, p. 438, cf. MS 6:335).

13. Further, in order to use the view expressed in this remark to arrive at the theory that Pincoffs and Fleischacker attribute to him, Kant would have to find some way of redirecting the right claimed in it so that this right belongs to the state rather than to the injured individual and justifies the state in doing to the criminal something "equal" to the crime. However, we never see him explicitly reasoning in any such way. In order to qualify these conclusions, something might be made of the fact that the claim is not that it is morally permissible to do to another what he has done to you, but only that you have a right to do it. I am afraid we cannot absolutely exclude the possibility that Kant might endorse something like the argument Pincoffs and Fleischacker construct for him, because in one quite extraordinary passage (cited by neither Pincoffs nor Fleischacker) Kant does say: "I can never do anything to another without giving him a right to do the same to me under the same conditions" (P 4:358n). However, I cannot bring myself to believe that this could be Kant's considered position. For it would directly license any sort of revenge; two wrongs would always make a right. There would then also be significant classes of exceptions (not otherwise noted by Kant) to *all* his formulations of the moral law. Any maxim that cannot be willed a universal law because you cannot will to be treated in such a way immediately becomes universalizable for you if action on it is directed toward someone who has acted toward you on that same (otherwise nonuniversalizable) maxim. If someone does not treat you as an end in itself, then you have a right not to treat them as an end in itself. If someone refuses to further ends of yours that belong to the realm of ends, then you need no longer further ends of theirs that belong to that realm (or what would come to the same thing, you may regard them and all their ends in general as falling outside the realm of ends). These qualifications would radically revise (or even totally vitiate) all Kant's formulations of the moral law. If they were accepted, there would be nothing at all left of Kantian ethics (nothing worth saving, anyway).

14. *Hegel's Ethical Thought* (New York: Cambridge University Press, 1990), pp. 108–26.

15. Fleischacker notes this kind of problem with the interpretation of Kant offered by Carlos S. Nino, "A Consensual Theory of Punishment," *Philosophy and Public Affairs* 12 (1983) (Fleischacker, p. 440). But he seems not to appreciate the extent to which his own interpretation is vulnerable to the same charge. Of course, because my basic criticism of the Pincoffs–Fleischacker argument is that it provides no clear reason at all why we are justified (even "warranted") in inflicting harm on the criminal following a maxim no one wills or can rationally will, it is always possible that an effective answer to this criticism would explain why we are not only warranted but absolutely obligated to do this. But the closest approximation to a convincing response to this criticism that I can comprehend (namely, that contained in Hegel's argument) does justify at most a warrant or permission, not an obligation.

16. I make this point about Hegel's argument in *Hegel's Ethical Thought*, pp. 116–17. Perhaps the most natural way to arrive at something like Hegel's argument on Kantian premises would be to begin not (as Pincoffs and Fleischacker do) with FUL but rather with FA. Kant holds that all laws of practical reason are

binding on us only because, as rational beings, we legislate for ourselves and all others (G 4:431). Therefore, if the retributivist "law of punishment" is a law of reason, it is so only because the idea of each of us wills it as a universal law. In other words, each of us as a rational being wills the conditional: "If someone commits a crime, then they should be punished." Granted that, if I have committed a crime, then as a rational legislator I have already willed that I should punished. Even if Kant accepted this argument, however, it would provide no justification for his retributivism – for the simple reason that is a *premise* of the argument, not its *conclusion*, that the law of punishment is a law of reason. This argument, therefore, does not support the inference that the law of punishment is binding *because* the criminal wills his own punishment; in fact, it says exactly the opposite. We may even learn something important about FA if we understand why he does. Kant accepts the main premise of the argument: "I subject myself together with everyone else to the laws, which will naturally also be penal laws if there are any criminals among the people" (MS 6:335). But Kant always carefully distinguishes between the rational being as a *legislator* of practical laws and the rational being as *subject* of the same legislation (see G 4:33). Hence immediately after saying that I subject myself to penal laws, he hastens to add: "As a co-legislator in dictating penal law, I cannot possibly be the same person who, as a subject, is punished in accordance with the law; for as one who is punished, namely, as a criminal, I cannot possibly have a voice in legislation (the legislator is holy). Consequently, when I draw up a penal law against myself as a criminal, it is pure reason in me (*homo noumenon*), legislating with regard to rights, which subjects me, as someone capable of crime and so as another person (*homo phaenomenon*) to the penal law, along with all others in the civil union" (MS 6:335). Further, Kant argues that the law of punishment could not possibly rest on the criminal's will because "if the authorization to punish had to be based on . . . his willing to let himself be punished, it would also have to be left to him to find himself punishable and the criminal would be his own judge" (MS 6:335). Kant therefore explicitly rejects *any* claim of the form: "It is right to punish the criminal because the criminal wills his own punishment." He says instead: "No one suffers punishment because he has willed *it*, but because he has willed *a punishable action*" (MS 6:335). On the basis of this remark, I think we should view Kant's rejection of the idea that criminals are punished because they will their own punishment as his endorsement of the directness thesis in a particularly strong form. The performance of a wrongful action necessarily and immediately entails that the wrongdoer should be punished: The entailment is not mediated even by the claim that the wrongdoer wills this punishment. The law of punishment, regarded as an *a priori* law of pure practical reason, may be valid because it is legislated by me (along with all others) as a rational being. But for this very reason it should not be viewed as valid conditionally on some contingent volition of mine, and so particular provisions of rational laws, as they apply to me (such as my being punishable if I commit a crime) are not to be regarded as applying validly to me because of some *argument* that I will them to apply to me. To understand the law of punishment as acquiring its validity in some such way is therefore to misunderstand FA in a fundamental way. I thank Claus Dierksmeyer for pressing me to clarify this point.

17. Notice also that if wicked people were exceptions to the ethical duty to include everyone's happiness (and no one's unhappiness) among your ends, then because Kant thinks that the will of every human being contains a radical propensity to evil and no one a will free from evil, then it would follow that there is no longer any duty at all to make the happiness of others your end. Or if someone wanted to draw the distinction between "good" and "evil" people in some other way than this for the purpose of making exceptions, I think they would find no way of doing so. I have heard people say that the doctrine of radical evil is objectionable because by placing everyone in the evil camp, it destroys the absolute distinction between good and evil. This is an interesting reaction, because it indicates that those who say this do not draw the distinction between good and evil, as Kant does, by distinguishing between a good and an evil will (good and evil maxims or principles, or even good and evil actions) but can conceive of it only as a distinction between good and evil *people* – so that it takes only the single form of love and admiration for the former and enmity or hatred for the latter. But there is a disgraceful human propensity – part of the propensity to radical evil – to want to divide the human race into "good people" and "bad people" – always, of course, counting ourselves among the former. One of the best things about Kantian ethics, and especially Kant's doctrine of the radical evil in human nature, is that it is irreconcilably opposed to this tendency. Many of the wisest sayings of the Christian gospels also support Kant's position here, though the most popular (and politically influential) forms of Christianity nowadays pay at most a hypocritical lip service to them, and their entire world view is based on fundamentally rejecting them in practice.

18. We have seen already that Kant's law of punishment cannot be validly derived from FUL, and that attempts to derive it from something like FA misconceive that formula in a fundamental way. But it is still a possible thought that the retributivist law of punishment might also be derivable from FH, if we regarded punishing a person who did wrong as a way of showing a kind of respect for their rational nature. (This suggestion was urged by both Lorraine Besser-Jones and Rega Wood.) There is perhaps some such thought behind Hegel's remark that when the criminal is punished, he is honored as a rational being (Hegel PR, §100R). Taken in context, however, that remark contrasts honoring the criminal as a rational being by drawing the measure of his punishment from his own act (on retributivist grounds) with treating him as a dangerous animal who must be made harmless. It is plausible, and no doubt something Kant would endorse, that a criminal is honored more by punishing him in the first way than the second. But I find no trace in Kant of the thought that we must punish criminals in order properly to honor them. (The closest passage to this, MS 6:333–4, actually says nothing of the kind, but only that a man of honor would prefer a just punishment – in the case under consideration, death – while only a scoundrel would prefer a lesser one.) It does not follow from the fact that we punish a criminal in part because he has a property (say, personality) that we honor or respect that the criminal is honored by being punished. Honors, properly speaking, are something people are free to accept or refuse, and most criminals, I imagine, would choose to decline the honor, as Sartre honorably chose to do when the Legion of Honor and the Nobel Prize were conferred

upon him. If Kant were to draw such an inference from FH, then because he also draws from this formula the conclusion that we have a duty to include the happiness of others (never their unhappiness) among our ends, he would be drawing from the same formula two mutually contradictory conclusions. In the absence of any explicit attempt to derive the law of punishment from FH, it seems gratuitously uncharitable to suppose that Kant did this.

19. An analogous argument from Kant's ethical theory shows the impermissibility of using punishment to make people feel safer, or satisfying the public's vengeful desires, or expressing its moral disapproval. For it is wrong to *coerce* anyone for any purpose except protecting right. You may not do so in order to make yourself (or others) happier, or to express moral disapproval. It is not only immoral to do this, but contrary to right. On grounds of right, you yourself should be coercively prevented from exercising coercion for any of these purposes. Of course, just punishment might incidentally have certain effects on people's feelings, or they might privately regard it as an expression of their moral attitudes, and that would be permissible. But on Kantian grounds, it would be *wrong* (a violation of duties of justice) for the state to include these ends among the publicly recognized aims of punishment, or in any way to shape its institutions of punishment by any of them. It would be permissible on Kantian grounds for the state to use punishment to alter the behavioral dispositions of the criminal in such a way as to make him less likely to do wrong or violate duties of justice in the future; but it would be positively wrong (unjust) to use *coercion* in an attempt to improve the *moral character* of an adult human being (in accordance with *someone else's ideas of morality*). So it would therefore be wrong (unjust) for the state to use punishment for that end as well. "Moral improvement" theories of punishment, therefore, despite the spirit of charitableness and fatuous good will in which they are usually offered, seem not only un-Kantian, but they would underwrite practices of punishment that would systematically violate fundamental human rights. Perhaps this is just as well, because when you consider the actual effects that existing practices of punishment have on criminals, it would be false to the point of obscenity to suggest that these practices morally improve those who are punished.

20. Cf. *Romans* 12:19, which Kant quotes in this connection, or *Deuteronomy* 32:35, to which Paul is presumably referring. But perhaps the most suitable scripture would be *Genesis* 50:19, in which Joseph wisely leaves to God's justice the brothers who sold him into slavery.

Chapter 13. Sex

1. In the course of trying to explain his doctrine that a just punishment must do "the same thing" to the criminal that the criminal has done, he even suggests quite monstrous punishments for "unnatural" sexual acts: "The punishment for rape and paederasty is castration . . . , that for bestiality, permanent expulsion from civil society" (MS 6:363). This, together with Kant's instance of suicide as an example of the violation of the right of humanity in one's own person (MS 6:422), might lead us to question the whole idea that we could violate a right of humanity in our own person, which might even seem inconsistent with Kant's

endorsement of the principle *volenti non fit iniuria* (no injury can be done to one who wills it) (MS 6:314). But there seems a place for the idea when we consider contracts in which people might sell themselves into slavery or other form of bondage, because it can be argued that their invalidity in principle is based on the idea that it violates the right of humanity in one's own person to make such a contract (MS 6:283).

2. Barbara Herman, "Could It Be Worth Thinking About Kant on Sex and Marriage?" in *A Mind of One's Own*, eds. Louise Antony and Charlotte Witt (Boulder, Colo.: Westview Press, 1993).

3. Andrea Dworkin, *Intercourse* (New York: Free Press, 1987).

4. Sartre, *Being and Nothingness*, tr. Hazel Barnes (New York: Philosophical Library, 1956), Part 3, Chapter 3. Simone de Beauvoir, *The Second Sex*, tr. H. M. Parshley (New York: Knopf, 1952).

5. For obvious reasons, it is difficult to obtain precise and reliable information about this, and estimates vary. One-third is a conservative estimate given the figures produced by most studies. Sigmund Freud noted the high rate at which his female patients reported molestation, especially incest, but he always remained skeptical of these reports and fashioned a complex theory to explain the evidence. More recent studies tend to side with Freud's patients against Freud. See "Freud and Seduction Theory Reconsidered," http://www.geocities.com/skews_me/freud.html. See John N. Briere, *Child Abuse Trauma* (Newbury Park, Calif.: Sage Publications, 1992); Gail Elizabeth Wyatt, "The Sexual Abuse of Afro-American and White Women in Childhood," *Child Abuse and Neglect* 9 (1985): 507–19; Diana E. Russell, *The Secret Trauma: Incest in the Lives of Girls and Women* (New York: Basic Books, 1986). Russell found 38 percent and Wyatt 45 percent of women interviewed reported memories of sexual abuse during their childhood. One in three is a conservative estimate. Only about 25 percent of the molesters are strangers. Most often the molester is the girl's father.

6. Kant's interpretation of the voice of God as that of animal instinct rather than of morality is perhaps unusual but not unprecedented in the interpretation of the *Genesis* story: Compare the commentary of the thirteenth-century commentator Rabbi Moshe ben Nachman (or "Ramban"): "Man's original nature was such that he did whatever was proper to him to do naturally, just as heaven and all their hosts do, faithful workers whose work is truth, and in whose deeds there is no love or hatred. Now it was the fruit of this tree that gave rise to will and desire, that those who ate it should choose a thing or its opposite, for good or evil . . . After he ate of the fruit of the tree of knowledge, he possessed the power of choice; he could now willingly do evil or good to himself or others." *Ramban's Commentary on the Torah (Genesis)*, tr. C. B. Chavel (New York: Shilo, 1971), pp. 72–3.

7. These were *On Marriage* (1774, with subsequent editions in 1775 and 1792), and *On the Civil Improvement of Women* (1792).

8. One recent attempt to give substance to the rumors, contrary to Kant's public position, is Ursula Pia Jauch, *Immanuel Kant zur Gechlechterdifferenz: Aufklärische Vorurteilskritik und bürgerliche Geschlechtsvormundschaft* (Vienna: Passagen, 1980), pp. 203–36.

Chapter 14. Lies

1. It would be similar if we accepted the stipulation that the term "murder" is equivalent to "wrongful homicide" – as Kant himself does when he characterizes murder as *homocidium dolosum* (MS 6:336, 422). Then it would be analytic, hence true without exception, that every act of murder is wrongful. But that would settle nothing about when a homicide is considered wrongful – or even about when an act of killing counts as a homicide. Its being analytic that murder is always wrong would involve neither strict nor lax views about the morality of killing.

2. See *Kant's Ethical Thought* (New York: Cambridge University Press, 1999), pp. 322–3; "The Final Form of Kant's Practical Philosophy," in Mark Timmons (ed.), *Kant's Metaphysics of Morals: Interpretive Essays* (Oxford: Oxford University Press, 2002), pp. 5–10. For a contrasting view, see Paul Guyer, "Kant's Deductions of the Principles of Right," in the same volume, pp. 23–64. However, I do not think the claims I am making here depend on which side of the dispute we take, as long as we are agreed on the undeniable fact that duties of right (*Recht*) and duties of ethics (*Ethik*) belong to two different spheres within Kant's entire theory of morals (*Sitten*).

3. I do not say this is an impossible way of looking at duties of right, and Kant does think we can consider violations of people's rights in this way, at least for the purpose of illustrating the Formula of Humanity (G 4:430). But because it confuses things by considering a duty of right only insofar as it exemplifies an ethical principle, it is not a perspicuous way to present this duty. I think this is why Kant himself, either in the *Metaphysics of Morals* or in his lectures on ethics, or especially in the late essay on the supposed right to lie, never discusses lying as a violation of a duty to others by relating it to the formula of universal law or the formula of humanity.

4. Some people with whom I have discussed this topic find this curious. Why should a confession of religious faith be considered binding, and something on which others might be authorized by right to rely? (Are we not free to change our religious beliefs? Can we be coerced to continue professing a religious faith we have once professed?) My suggestion is that Kant understands professions of religious faith to be among the most solemn avowals people can make. It is perhaps only in an age where religion has ceased to be a serious matter at all among many people that Kant's assumptions here seem questionable. If religious beliefs mean anything, they surely commit those who profess them to certain actions that the faith requires. We may be free to change our religious beliefs, but as long as we continue to profess a certain faith, others may be entitled to rely on us to live up to the beliefs we have solemnly declared ourselves to hold. Suppose, for instance, that it an important beliefs of one religion that other religions should be treated with tolerance. Then someone who has professed that religion has declared that he will deal tolerantly with those who belong to a different religion, and they are warranted in counting on tolerant conduct from him. If he participates in the persecution of other religions, this may be considered a violation of a basic principle of right, much as it would be if someone made a promise and then broke it.

5. However, it should be observed that those who, in philosophical discussions, lightheartedly stipulate that in the example they are considering we can be sure

the lie will never be found out, or that its discovery will have only marginal influence on people's confidence in trials or contracts, usually far underestimate the assurance we could ever have that these stipulated conditions would hold in practice.

6. In particular, it needs no derivation from FUL, or any other formula of the principle of morality. A system of right, once established, might – Kant says – hold even for a "nation of devils" – beings that systematically fail to do their ethical duties but under the system of right can be coerced to respect one another's rights (EF 8:366). It may be that Kant's conception of right is unacceptable to some people for various reasons. They may not value coercively protected external freedom as much as Kant thinks the right of humanity requires us to, or they may not think that our freedom requires protection by a coercive system with such strict laws. Objections of this kind would strike at the fundamentals of Kant's entire conception of right. If someone rejects that conception, there is no mystery about why that person would reject Kant's principle that intentionally untruthful declarations are always lies – that is, are always violations of right. In fact, I think such a person would even be rejecting (or holding inapplicable to human actions) the very concept of a "declaration," because that concept involves the concept of a system of right and of a kind of statement whose truthfulness is demanded by such a system. But of course if we reject the very terms in which the issue is posed, then it is a misunderstanding to think that Kant is taking a position that could be described only in quite different terms, or using the same words but with quite a different meaning. If we accept the Kantian idea of right and the attendant idea of a declaration but are worried that Kant's system of right makes too many statements into "declarations" or is too inflexible in its prohibition on false declarations, then some of those worries will be considered immediately below, in connection with the famous dispute between Kant and Constant. We will see that Kant is far from holding all statements to be declarations, and that he may even allow for untruthful declarations under certain circumstances.

7. Constant, *Des réactions politiques*, sixième cahier no. 1, Écrits et Discours politiques (ed. O. Pozzo di Borgo, Pauvert, 1964), pp. 63–71; Kant VRL 8:429.

8. The chronology here is puzzling. No other passage anywhere in Kant's writings bears any relation to the example of the murderer at the door, and yet Constant could not possibly be referring to it, because Constant's essay (published in May 1796) predates the publication of the Doctrine of Virtue (in August 1797, only a month before the right-to-lie itself). It seems most likely that Constant's information about Kant's views on lying were furnished by K. F. Cramer, who translated Constant's essay into German and was responsible for the publication of Kant's essay in reply. Constant's remark seems to have been based on Cramer's reports of Kant's views rather than on anything Kant had actually said or written. Constant's reference to the example may also have been influenced by his knowledge of J. D. Michaelis, whom Cramer cites as someone who had stated notoriously strict views on lying prior to Kant; but Cramer assures us that it was Kant to whom Constant was referring (VRL 8:425). Kant's apparent willingness to accept the views that Constant attributes to him is therefore also curious, especially because it plays such a large role in the scandalous reputation the right-to-lie essay has enjoyed. It is hard to avoid the impression that Cramer was egging on both sides, so as to make the dispute seem as extreme (and sensational) as possible.

This has often been seen as a sign that Kant is eager to embrace even the most rigid and extreme position on our moral obligations, in total disregard of the consequences or countervailing arguments. But to me it seems more reasonable to understand his position in the essay as a principled but more moderate and sensible response to the issues about right that he took Constant to be raising. I am grateful for discussions on the history of the right-to-lie essay with James Mahon and Jens Timmerman.

9. Constant ignores the fact that Kant discusses the example in the context of an ethical duty, not a duty of right. But Kant is in fact considering the servant's action under the heading of right when he describes it as falling under the heading of "what is mine or yours" (MS 6:431). Though Kant takes the example in the direction of ethical principles and the duty to oneself the servant is violating, he could also have made the point that the servant might be criminally liable (as an accessory) for the crime his master commits. Kant does explicitly make an analogous point about liability for consequences of a lying declaration in the right-to-lie essay (VRL 8:427).

10. The example occurs in a casuistical question not about lying as a violation of right but lying as a violation of a perfect duty to oneself, grounded on self-respect. I suggest that the most pointed issue raised by the example in this regard is whether it violates the servant's self-respect to obey a command to lie to the police, making him complicit in his master's crime. And Kant does explore the question of that complicity – namely, the imputability to the servant of the guilt for the crime – in his discussion of the example. And at the end he returns to the fact that the lie was a "violation of the servant's duty to himself, whose results his conscience imputes to him" (MS 6:431). If that is the issue, then Constant's reworking of the example totally changes the issue that is supposed to be raised by it. Constant ignores too the fact that this example is presented as part of a "casuistical question," where the aim even of what might seem a decisive argument is more to raise moral issues than to settle them, and so nothing Kant says may be taken, without a considerable degree of caution, as expressing his definitive view.

11. That this is Kant's position is further reinforced by his claims regarding the friend's responsibility for the consequences of his lie: If by chance the intended victim has slipped away, and the friend's lie, instead of saving him, causes the murderer to meet and kill him, then the friend is responsible for the death (VRL 8:426–7). This argument, however, depends on Kant's controversial views about responsibility for the consequences of actions, which are independent of the question of whether the lie in this case is justified.

12. Just prior to the passage quoted above, Constant writes: "It is beyond doubt that the abstract principles of morality if they are separated from mediating principles, would create just as much disorder in the social relations among men as abstract principles of politics, separated from their connecting principles would do in civil relations." Constant, *Des réactions politiques*, p. 63. Kant's defense of the view that politicians and statesmen should always be truthful in public declarations is found in his two "principles of publicity," EF 8:370–86.

13. Kant does not always seem happy with the idea of a "necessary lie." In some places he seems to question whether really there is such a thing, or he accepts the

concept of a necessary lie only reluctantly (VP 9:940, VE 29:701). He roundly rejects the idea that we are permitted to deceive another simply because the other has deceived us. On the contrary, in Kant's view the right course of conduct will sometimes leave you open, at least to a limited extent, to the attacks of evil people; this policy of leaving yourself vulnerable is required of you by your respect for the right of humanity: "When one country has broken the peace, the other cannot do so in retaliation, for if that were allowable, no peace would be secure. And thus though [a lie to a deceptive or unjust person] may not infringe [his] particular right, it is still already a lie, and contrary to the right of humanity" (VE 27:447). But as a passage quoted earlier also clearly says, Kant thinks that when you are forced to make a false declaration in order to prevent the truth from being used unjustly, that would normally be considered a mere *falsiloquium* and not a *mendacium*, and it would violate no duty of right.

14. Tamar Schapiro, "Compliance, Complicity, and the Nature of Nonideal Conditions," *The Journal of Philosophy*, 100:7 (July 2003), 329–55.

15. Of course some declarations might be given under conditions of confidentiality, as in the case of a letter of recommendation for someone to a prospective employer. But special cases like this do not seem to constitute counterexamples to the claim Kant is making. For although not everyone is entitled to have access to the content of such declarations, there is no relaxation, as far as I can see, of the requirement that they be truthful. It is not as though the recommender is required to make truthful declarations to the prospective employer but is permitted to make *untruthful declarations* to anyone not entitled to confidential communications.

16. Just about the only discussion that even takes proper account of the fact that the right-to-lie essay is about *right*, not *ethics*, is Hans Wagner, "Kant gegen 'ein vermeintes Recht, aus Menschenliebe zu lügen,'" in G. Geismann and H. Oberer (eds.), *Kant und das Recht der Lüge* (Würzburg: Königshausen & Neumann, 1986), pp. 95–103. Wagner even sees the relevance to the dispute of the point that we would not regard it permissible to testify falsely at a trial in order to achieve what we think is a just result. See also Julius Ebbinghaus, *Briefwechsel mit H. J. Paton*, ibid., pp. 66–8, and the Introduction to the same volume by Hariolf Oberer, pp. 19–20. The Anglophone literature, however, seems virtually oblivious to the fact that the issue is one of right, as well as to the fact that Kant's strict prohibition on lying in this essay apples only to lying *declarations*.

17. Perhaps this is merely one of the pitfalls of an approach to ethics grounded on "intuitions" about examples. According to this approach, if a theory gets the "intuitively wrong answer" about any example, that is a death sentence on the theory and all its principles. Or maybe it is merely one of the pitfalls of the flawed manner in which the dominant kind of ethical theory is applied by people with no good sense of what matters in moral philosophy. Sidgwick and Rawls should not be blamed for the bad philosophy done by the people influenced by them.

18. This example is suggested by some of Kant's own examples in his lectures (VE 27:493, 506, 508), but even more by a remark by Sidgwick. "In speaking truth to a jury, I may possibly foresee that my words, operating along with other statements and indications, will unavoidably lead them to a wrong conclusion as to the guilt

or innocence of the accused, as certainly as I foresee that they will produce a right impression as to the particular matter of fact to which I am testifying" (Sidgwick, p. 97). Sidgwick admits that the morality of common sense would call it truth-speaking to testify truthfully to the particular fact in question. But he appears to conclude – though without quite saying this explicitly – that there is a certain artificiality in the commonsense notion of veracity here, as though a witness who is *really* interested in *the truth* might do better to lie about the particular fact in order to bring it about that the jury draws the *right* conclusion about the guilt or innocence of the accused. That would justify a conclusion directly contrary to the Kantian one about our example. However, it would also be a most remarkable conception of what the oath to tell the truth at trials binds us to do. It would imply that a witness might lie whenever he thought the jury would be misled in its conclusions about the case by truthful testimony and would be more likely to reach the right conclusions about the case by being fed intentionally false testimony. Imagine what would happen if a witness refused to take the oath without adding this qualification: "I will speak the truth, the whole truth, and nothing but the truth, unless I am convinced that lying will result in a more just outcome, in which case I will feel free to lie." If Sidgwick were called as a witness at a trial, and I were in the position of the attorney cross-examining him with the aim of discrediting his testimony, I think all I would need to do is read to the jury this passage from the *Methods of Ethics* and suggest to them the non-quite-stated conclusion that it looks like Sidgwick wants to draw. Unless Sidgwick were prepared to repudiate this interpretation of his meaning and were capable of doing so quite convincingly, I submit that the jury would be quite justified in ignoring everything he says on the stand as totally lacking in credibility.

Or imagine a witness who insisted on modifying the oath to read: "I will tell the truth, the whole truth, and nothing but the truth, unless I think this is a case sufficiently like the 'murderer at the door' example, and in that case I will feel free to lie." Such a witness's testimony would lack the credibility required for declarations to serve their function in a system of right. Such testimony would not be accepted, nor should it be.

19. Of course I would naturally feel deeply conflicted about doing this, but then I think even those who think they should lie in this witness's circumstances ought to feel conflicted about that position too. If they did not, then I would regard them as clearly guilty of a serious moral error even if I did not condemn their choice to lie as clearly wrong. This is another one of those cases that show standard moral theories to place too great a premium on getting the "right answer" to every example (Chapter 3, §2). It may matter here to get your priorities right (which, according to Kantian ethics, means telling the truth), but it matters even more not to omit any of the considerations that make the decision a difficult one, and not to pretend that the moral situation is free of conflict. That Kant himself understood this is indicated by his own discussion of this very kind of example: "When it is thought there is a conflict (collision) of duties, this says no more than that *rationes obligandi* [obligating reasons] are in conflict with an obligation, or among themselves ... The grounds of a dutiful action may be exposed to a contradiction, e.g. a brother as witness; in his case, truth is in collision with kinship" (VE 27:493).

20. Stephen Holmes, *Benjamin Constant and the Making of Modern Liberalism* (New Haven, Conn.: Yale University Press, 1984), pp. 107–10.

21. The issue Kant means to raise here is sometimes misleadingly stated by those arguing on the other side as an issue about whether the standards of "private morality" apply to the "public" realm of politics, statesmanship, war, and the like. For example, Carl Schmitt holds that the political has its "own criteria" that are distinct from those that can be traced back to moral concepts of good and evil. See Carl Schmitt, *The Concept of the Political*, trans. George Schwab (Chicago: University of Chicago Press, 1996), p. 26. When Kant speaks of "morality" in relation to politicians, as he does in *Perpetual Peace*, the standards he is using are never those of private ethics but always of public right. If Schmitt's claim is that politicians or statesmen are bound not by the criteria of private morality but by standards appropriate to the political realm, then Kant agrees. Kant thinks they are bound by the standards appropriate to their position as exercisers of public coercive force, which must be regulated by laws of right. These standards are looser than private ethical standards, because they relate to a system of laws that are in general coercively enforceable – and this is looser than the system of ethical laws according to which each of us should inwardly regulate our private behavior. As I have already mentioned, however, not all standards of right are coercively enforceable, and Kant is famous (or infamous) for holding that subjects have rights against heads of state, and heads of state have duties of right, that no one is in a position to enforce coercively (as by violent revolution, which might be the only conceivable means for enforcing them). So Kant's position, while no doubt different from Schmitt's, is not as different from it (or as vulnerable to criticism) as people like Schmitt often think. The problem is that for many politicians (and the "realist" theorists who enjoy identifying with those who exercise great power over their fellow human beings), any constraint on the use of that power based on mere principle (rather than arising from external constraints or political self-interest) feels like an annoying incursion on their prerogatives according to "inappropriate" standards.

22. Lyndon Johnson obtained the Gulf of Tonkin Resolution from the Senate (with only two dissenting votes) by straightforwardly lying about what had happened there. The Pentagon Papers disclosed a systematic pattern of official lying to the public about the reasons for the Vietnam war, war policies, and the facts on the ground in Vietnam. G. Gordon Liddy – convicted and imprisoned as a Watergate conspirator but now the popular host of a right-wing radio talk show – has repeatedly said that Richard Nixon and his associates were entirely justified in lying under oath to the U.S. Congress during the Watergate cover-up. Oliver North – another popular figure in the far-right media that now enjoy a near monopoly on the dissemination of public information in this country – has insisted it was right for him to lie to the Congress about covert sales of arms to Iran to finance (also covertly and illegally) the *contras* in Nicaragua. Bill Clinton's lies about his personal misconduct, because they involved no wrongful exercise of governmental power in the public realm, were not impeachable offenses, but when made under oath they were clearly wrong.

23. This seems especially true in situations of war, probably because – even if a war under those circumstances might seem necessary and might in theory have met reasonable criteria for being a "just war" – no actual war waged by human beings

seems to limit itself to what justice would require. Therefore, as the saying goes, the truth is the first casualty in any war.

24. The only *argument* Kant ever gives for saying that all intentional falsehood is contrary to a duty to oneself is his claim that falsehood always manifests a lack of respect for oneself. He supports this claim with only one argument, an argument from the natural purposiveness of speech, which is analogous to his argument against suicide in the *Groundwork* (MS 6:429, G 4:422). Both arguments are part of a strategy of showing that we fail to respect ourselves when we fail to respect the natural purposiveness built into our predispositions or faculties. Both arguments assume dubious premises about natural purposiveness and draw conclusions that few enlightened people today would find plausible, at least in the extreme form Kant appears to present them.

25. Sidgwick points out quite correctly that "it is obviously a most effective protection for legitimate secrets that it should be universally understood and expected that those who ask questions which they have no right to ask will have lies told them" (Sidgwick, p. 318). This observation further serves to show why the maxim of telling people falsehoods in response to such questions could certainly be willed as a universal law, satisfying both the Formula of Universal Law and the Formula of the Law of Nature.

26. Two more examples may be drawn from Robert Adams's *Finite and Infinite Goods* (a book that has something true and important to say about most questions in moral philosophy). Sometimes telling an untruth is the only way to protect a secret with which we have been entrusted, hence the only way to avoid seriously betraying a friend. In the course of resisting the Nazis, Dietrich Bonhoeffer was forced to deceive and tell falsehoods of many kinds, including giving the Nazi salute when he did not mean it and deceiving the authorities in order to conceal a plot to kill Hitler. No decent person could blame Bonhoeffer for these deceptions. Robert Adams, *Finite and Infinite Goods* (Oxford: Oxford University Press, 1999), pp. 158–60, 216–17.

27. If one has a taste for malicious irony, it is possible to present this situation in an especially unflattering light if we say that as moralist, Kant permitted himself to make statements (and on the morality of truthfulness, of all subjects!) that were *knowingly false*. This is an indictment that Nietzsche, for example, enjoys bringing against moralists generally. See *Twilight of the Idols*, in Walter Kaufmann (ed.), *The Portable Nietzsche* (New York: Viking Press, 1968), p. 505. But it is a shallow criticism, even a "cheap shot," to treat rhetorical exaggeration as if it were the same as deliberate untruthfulness.

28. "Inner" (in Kant's usage) tends to mean: "in relation to oneself." "Inner sense" (of which time is the *a priori* form) is that in which we are related only to our own subjective states, whereas in "outer sense" (whose *a priori* form is space) we are related to objects distinct from ourselves. A person's "inner" worth is his worth as compared only to his own self-given moral law, not in comparison with others (G 4:426, KpV 5:88, MS 6:387, 391, 435, VE 27:349, 462). Thus it is *not*, for example, the worth of some inner part of oneself as contrasted with the worth of one's outward actions or outward appearance. (Many distorted images of Kant – as a moral introvert or proponent of a one-sided *Gesinnungsethik* – rest at least in part on misunderstandings of this term.) An "inner" lie, accordingly, is simply a lie to oneself rather than a lie to someone else.

29. Consider, for example, the case of religious fundamentalists who clutch at any skeptical argument against evolution while paying little heed to the powerful reasons for doubting the evidential value of the Bible even as history, let alone regarding matters that fall in the province of natural science. In earlier ages, their beliefs about cosmology and the origins of life were merely ignorant conjectures, perhaps assisted by some degree of wishful thinking. But in the face of the systematic refutation of these beliefs by modern cosmology and biology, they can be sustained only through a process of lying most contemptibly to themselves and to one another. Every fundamentalism is a superstition that has lost its innocence. See my book *Unsettling Obligations: Essays on Reason, Reality and the Ethics of Belief* (Stanford: CSLI Publications, 2002), Chapter 2.

30. Religion again provides us with a vivid illustration of this, as when its apologists try to defend beliefs based on wishful thinking through getting us to feel pity (or self-pity) for the human condition and the cruelties and sorrows of life, for which (it is claimed) only religious faith can provide poor suffering humanity with the consolation needed to make its condition bearable. What kind of God could they believe in, if they think he has subjected his noblest creatures to a condition in which they must so degrade themselves merely in order to endure the gift of life he has given them?

Chapter 15. Consequences

1. Sometimes it is argued, on consequentialist grounds, that exceptions should be made to moral rules (against lying, for instance, or taking innocent human life) whenever the consequences of observing the rule will be bad enough (for instance, if many more lives will otherwise be lost). These situations are then depicted as involving a conflict between "deontological" rules and "consequentialist" considerations that may override them. But that is not a good way to look at the situation no matter what sort of ethical theory you have. If the moral rule in question belongs to a practice – presumably, one that can be justified in terms of its consequences – then what determines whether the bad consequences justify overriding the rule is whether they are of a kind that makes the practice lose its point (at least in that situation). For instance, if the only point of a certain rule is to avoid unnecessary loss of life, it should be overridden when more lives will be saved by violating it. Or we might make an exception to one moral rule when it comes into conflict with another that should take precedence (for a consequentialist, these priorities are ultimately to be decided on consequentialist grounds). But beyond the most basic level at which moral rules and practices are justified, this is essentially the same kind of rationale for making exceptions to moral rules that a Kantian can (and should) provide, and it is based not on the naked opposition of consequences to rules but on relationships between moral rules and what we take their point to be. See the reference to Tamar Schapiro's work on this subject in Chapter 14, §2.

2. "While we are sometimes guided by the notion that it would be the best of worlds in which morality were universally respected and all men were of a disposition to affirm it, we have, in fact, deep and persistent reasons to be grateful that that is not the world we have" (Williams, p. 23). But Williams draws exactly the wrong conclusion from this point when he infers that moral obligation must be

"escapable." And it is just as easy for a level-headed consequentialist to correct him on this point as it is for a Kantian to do so.

3. David Cummiskey, *Kantian Consequentialism* (Oxford: Oxford University Press, 1996). Shelley Kagan, "Kantianism for Consequentialists," in A. Wood (ed.), *Kant: Groundwork for the Metaphysics of Morals* (Rethinking the Western Tradition) (New Haven, Conn.: Yale University Press, 2002), pp. 111–56, especially pp. 140–52. See also R. M. Hare, "Could Kant have been a utilitarian?", in *Sorting Out Ethics* (Oxford: Oxford University Press, 1997).

4. Bentham, *The Principles of Morals and Legislation* (New York: Hafner, 1948), pp. 1–7.

5. On this point, see Scanlon, pp. 91–3.

6. One aspect of the "shadow of hedonism" that may be operative here is the assumption that pleasure and pain admit of ordinal measures of "intensity," "duration," and so forth, that Bentham proposed to use in calculating the greatest happiness. But it is far from clear that there is any psychological reality to such assumptions, so that even the assumption of hedonism may not suffice to justify some of the presuppositions ethical theorists make about the measurability of good states of affairs. Mill was right in insisting that pleasures differ in quality as well as quantity, and even Bentham had to admit that pain and pleasure differ in quality. Mill tended to emphasize qualitative differences in pleasures, but he did so largely for the purpose of declaring some pleasures to be of higher quality than others. The same insight might have been used to make quite a different point – namely, that pleasures are valued not solely for their intrinsic felt properties (whether "quantitative" or "qualitative") but for reasons that are altogether independent of hedonic considerations. For example, Mill himself regards pleasures as higher in quality if they exercise our "higher faculties" (Mill, p. 9). This suggests that a significant part – perhaps the most significant part – of the value of pleasures is determined by someone's conception of human functioning, the faculties it involves, and choices about which faculties they want to exercise – in other words, about the kind of life they want to lead. Such a person's standard for ranking pleasures is thus parasitic on their judgment about the value of different kinds of activities, and this judgment might be quite independent of purely hedonic considerations. For instance, a person might value the pleasures of mountain climbing, even though mountain climbing involves fatigue and other painful sensations, more than the pleasures associated with less strenuous activities, because the person thinks that mountain climbing is a more worthwhile activity than the activities whose pleasures are accompanied by fewer painful states. If hedonism is the doctrine that such preferences must be grounded solely on the felt quality of the pleasures associated with the activities, then hedonism seems to be an empirically false psychological doctrine, and some of Mill's own best insights point to this conclusion.

7. *Marx Engels Werke* (Berlin: Dietz Verlag, 1961–1966); Ergänzungsheft 1, p. 459, *Marx Engels Collected Works* (New York: International Publishers, 1975), p. 227.

8. Compare the careful formulation of Philo's purely philosophical concession to Cleanthes' argument for theism at the end of Hume's *Dialogues*: "What can [one] do more than give a plain, philosophical assent to the proposition, as often as it occurs, and believe that the arguments on which it is established exceed the

objections which lie against it?" Hume, D p. 88. Philo does not say that he must *believe* the conclusion of the argument, only that he should assert it because he believes that the arguments for it exceed the objections against it. Hume seems to me here to have formulated admirably the attitude that should be taken toward all theories and theses about philosophical matters that will never be finally settled.

Index

1890747R0023

Printed in Great Britain
by Amazon.co.uk, Ltd.,
Marston Gate.